W. E. Gladstone, Joseph Butler

The Works of Joseph Butler

Divided into sections; with sectional headings, an index to each volume; and some occasional notes, also prefatory matter. Vol. 2

W. E. Gladstone, Joseph Butler

The Works of Joseph Butler
Divided into sections; with sectional headings, an index to each volume; and some occasional notes, also prefatory matter. Vol. 2

ISBN/EAN: 9783337254476

Printed in Europe, USA, Canada, Australia, Japan

Cover: Foto ©Thomas Meinert / pixelio.de

More available books at **www.hansebooks.com**

THE WORKS

OF

JOSEPH BUTLER, D.C.L.

SOMETIME LORD BISHOP OF DURHAM

DIVIDED INTO SECTIONS; WITH SECTIONAL HEADINGS
AN INDEX TO EACH VOLUME; AND SOME OCCASIONAL NOTES
ALSO PREFATORY MATTER

EDITED BY

THE RIGHT HON. W. E. GLADSTONE

Cuius sacra fero ingenti perculsus amore

IN TWO VOLUMES
VOL. II: SERMONS, ETC.

Oxford
AT THE CLARENDON PRESS
1897

Oxford
PRINTED AT THE CLARENDON PRESS
BY HORACE HART, M.A.
PRINTER TO THE UNIVERSITY

SERMONS

BY

JOSEPH BUTLER, D.C.L.

SOMETIME LORD BISHOP OF DURHAM

PREFACE: THREE SERMONS ON HUMAN NATURE
TWELVE FURTHER SERMONS PREACHED AT THE ROLLS
SIX SERMONS PREACHED ON PUBLIC OCCASIONS
CHARGE TO THE CLERGY OF DURHAM
WITH AN APPENDIX

EDITED BY

THE RIGHT HON. W. E. GLADSTONE

Oxford
AT THE CLARENDON PRESS
1897

CONTENTS OF VOL. II

PREFACE . . . . PAGE 1

FIFTEEN SERMONS.

SERMON I, II, III.

UPON HUMAN NATURE, OR MAN CONSIDERED AS A MORAL AGENT.

SERMON I.

UPON THE SOCIAL NATURE OF MAN.

For as we have many members in one body, and all members have not the same office: so we, being many, are one body in Christ, and every one members one of another. *Romans* xii. 4, 5 27

SERMON II, III.

UPON THE NATURAL SUPREMACY OF CONSCIENCE.

For when the Gentiles, which have not the law, do by nature the things contained in the law, these, having not the law, are a law unto themselves. *Romans* ii. 14 . . . 44, 57

SERMON IV.

UPON THE GOVERNMENT OF THE TONGUE.

If any man among you seem to be religious, and bridleth not his tongue, but deceiveth his own heart, this man's religion is vain. *James* i. 26 66

SERMON V, VI.

UPON COMPASSION.

Rejoice with them that do rejoice, and weep with them that weep. *Romans* xii. 15 . . . . 78, 92

SERMON VII.

UPON THE CHARACTER OF BALAAM.

Let me die the death of the righteous, and let my last end be like his. *Numbers* xxiii. 10 103

SERMON VIII, IX.

UPON RESENTMENT, AND FORGIVENESS OF INJURIES.

Ye have heard that it hath been said, Thou shalt love thy neighbour, and hate thine enemy. But I say unto you, Love your enemies, bless them that curse you, do good to them that hate you, and pray for them which despitefully use you, and persecute you. *Matthew* v. 43, 44 . . . 115, 127

SERMON X.

UPON SELF-DECEIT.

And Nathan said to David, Thou art the man. 2 *Samuel* xii. 7 . 142

SERMON XI, XII.

UPON THE LOVE OF OUR NEIGHBOUR.

And if there be any other commandment, it is briefly comprehended in this saying, namely, Thou shalt love thy neighbour as thyself. *Romans* xiii. 9 . . . . . 156, 176

SERMON XIII, XIV.

UPON PIETY, OR THE LOVE OF GOD.

PAGE

Thou shalt love the Lord thy God with all thy heart, and with all thy soul, and with all thy mind. *Matthew* xxii. 37 . 193, 205

SERMON XV.

UPON THE IGNORANCE OF MAN.

When I applied mine heart to know wisdom, and to see the business that is done upon the earth: then I beheld all the work of God, that a man cannot find out the work that is done under the sun: because though a man labour to seek it out, yet he shall not find it; yea further, though a wise man think to know it, yet shall he not be able to find it. *Ecclesiastes* viii. 16, 17 218

SIX SERMONS
PREACHED UPON PUBLIC OCCASIONS.

SERMON I.

PREACHED BEFORE THE SOCIETY FOR PROPAGATING THE GOSPEL.

And this gospel of the kingdom shall be preached in all the world, for a witness unto all nations. *Matthew* xxiv. 14 . 235

SERMON II.

PREACHED BEFORE THE LORD MAYOR, ALDERMEN, AND SHERIFFS, AND THE GOVERNORS OF THE SEVERAL HOSPITALS OF THE CITY OF LONDON.

The rich and poor meet together: the Lord is the maker of them all. *Proverbs* xxii. 2 251

SERMON III.

PREACHED BEFORE THE HOUSE OF LORDS, JAN. 30, 1740-41.

And not using your liberty for a cloke of maliciousness, but as the servants of God. 1 *Peter* ii. 16 268

SERMON IV.

PREACHED AT THE ANNUAL MEETING OF THE CHARITY CHILDREN AT CHRIST CHURCH.

Train up a child in the way he should go: and when he is old, he will not depart from it. *Proverbs* xxii. 6 . . 286

SERMON V.

PREACHED BEFORE THE HOUSE OF LORDS ON THE ANNIVERSARY OF HIS MAJESTY'S ACCESSION TO THE THRONE.

I exhort, that, first of all, supplications, prayers, intercessions, and giving of thanks, be made for all men; for kings, and for all that are in authority; that we may lead a quiet and peaceable life in all godliness and honesty. 1 *Timothy* ii. 1, 2 304

SERMON VI.

PREACHED BEFORE THE GOVERNORS OF THE LONDON INFIRMARY.

And above all things have fervent charity among yourselves: for charity shall cover the multitude of sins. 1 *Peter* iv. 8 . 316

A Charge to the Clergy of the Diocese of Durham . . 334
Appendix 353
Index 377

THE PREFACE

§ 1. *Judgments, such as are usually formed, do not deserve the name.*

THOUGH it is scarce possible to avoid judging, in some way or other, of almost every thing which offers itself to one's thoughts; yet it is certain, that many persons, from different causes, never exercise their judgment, upon what comes before them, in the way of determining whether it be conclusive, and holds. They are perhaps entertained with some things, not so with others; they like, and they dislike: but whether that which is proposed to be made out be really made out or not; whether a matter be stated according to the real truth of the case, seems to the generality of people merely a circumstance of no consideration at all. Arguments are often wanted for some accidental purpose: but proof as such is what they never want for themselves; for their own satisfaction of mind, or conduct in life. Not to mention the multitudes who read merely for the sake of talking, or to qualify themselves for the world, or some such kind of reasons; there are, even of the few who read for their own entertainment, and have a real curiosity to see what is said, several, which is prodigious, who have no sort of curiosity to see what is true: I say, curiosity; because it is too obvious to be mentioned, how much that religious and sacred attention, which is due to truth, and to the important question, What is the rule of life? is lost out of the world.

For the sake of this whole class of readers, for they are of different capacities, different kinds, and get into this way from different occasions, I have often wished, that it had been the custom to lay before people nothing in matters of argument but premises, and leave them to draw conclusions themselves; which, though it could not be done in all cases, might in many.

§ 2. *The number of amusing books favours this evil; and reading is mostly idling.*

The great number of books and papers of amusement, which, of one kind or another, daily come in one's way, have in part occasioned, and most perfectly fall in with and humour, this idle way of reading and considering things. By this means, time even in solitude is happily got rid of, without the pain of attention: neither is any part of it more put to the account of idleness, one can scarce forbear saying, is spent with less thought, than great part of that which is spent in reading.

Thus people habituate themselves to let things pass through their minds, as one may speak, rather than to think of them. Thus by use they become satisfied merely with seeing what is said, without going any further. Review and attention, and even forming a judgment, becomes fatigue; and to lay any thing before them that requires it, is putting them quite out of their way.

There are also persons, and there are at least more of them than have a right to claim such superiority, who take for granted, that they are acquainted with every thing; and that no subject, if treated in the manner it should be, can be treated in any manner but what is familiar and easy to them.

§ 3. *Attention proportioned to each subject is due, and indispensable.*

It is true indeed, that few persons have a right to demand attention; but it is also true, that nothing can be understood without that degree of it, which the very nature of the thing requires. Now morals, considered as a science, concerning which speculative difficulties are daily raised, and treated with regard to those difficulties, plainly require a very peculiar attention. For here ideas never are in themselves determinate, but become so by the train of reasoning and the place they stand in; since it is impossible that words can always stand for the same ideas, even in the same author, much less in different ones[1]. Hence an argument may not readily be apprehended, which is different from its being mistaken; and even caution to avoid being mistaken may, in some cases, render it less readily apprehended. It is very unallowable for a work of imagination or entertainment not to be of easy comprehension, but may be unavoidable in a work of another kind, where a man is not to form or accommodate, but to state things as he finds them.

§ 4. *Admits obscurity in these Discourses; but was it avoidable?*

It must be acknowledged, that some of the following Discourses are very abstruse and difficult; or, if you please, obscure; but I must take leave to add, that those alone are judges, whether or no and how far this is a fault, who are judges, whether or no and how far it might have been avoided; those only, who will be at the trouble to understand what is here said, and to see how far the things here insisted upon, and not other things, might have been put in a plainer manner; which yet I am very far from asserting that they could not.

Thus much however will be allowed, that general criticisms concerning obscurity considered as a distinct thing from confusion and perplexity of thought, as in some cases there may be ground for them; so in others, they may be nothing

---

[1] Compare Aristotle, *Eth. Nic.* I. iii. 4 : πεπαιδευμένου γάρ ἐστιν ἐπὶ τοσοῦτον τἀκριβὲς ἐπιζητεῖν καθ' ἕκαστον γένος, ἐφ' ὅσον ἡ τοῦ πράγματος φύσις ἐπιδέχεται· παραπλήσιον γὰρ φαίνεται μαθηματικοῦ τε πιθανολογοῦντος ἀποδέχεσθαι καὶ ῥητορικὸν ἀποδείξεις ἀπαιτεῖν. And *ibid.* vii. 18 : μεμνῆσθαι δὲ καὶ τῶν προειρημένων χρή, καὶ τὴν ἀκρίβειαν μὴ ὁμοίως ἐν ἅπασιν ἐπιζητεῖν, ἀλλ' ἐν ἑκάστοις κατὰ τὴν ὑποκειμένην ὕλην καὶ ἐπὶ τοσοῦτον ἐφ' ὅσον οἰκεῖον τῇ μεθόδῳ. This repetition, within a short compass, of a very important principle by no means sufficiently recognised, perhaps indicates that he attached to it a high practical value.

more at the bottom than complaints, that every thing is not to be understood with the same ease that some things are. Confusion and perplexity in writing is indeed without excuse, because any one may, if he pleases, know whether he understands and sees through what he is about : and it is unpardonable for a man to lay his thoughts before others, when he is conscious that he himself does not know whereabouts he is, or how the matter before him stands. It is coming abroad in disorder, which he ought to be dissatisfied to find himself in at home.

§ 5. *May be due to inadequate familiarity on the reader's part.*

But even obscurities arising from other causes than the abstruseness of the argument may not be always inexcusable. Thus a subject may be treated in a manner, which all along supposes the reader acquainted with what has been said upon it, both by ancient and modern writers; and with what is the present state of opinion in the world concerning such subject. This will create a difficulty of a very peculiar kind, and even throw an obscurity over the whole before those who are not thus informed ; but those who are will be disposed to excuse such a manner, and other things of the like kind, as a saving of their patience.

§ 6. *In Sermons it is a defect.*

However upon the whole, as the title of Sermons gives some right to expect what is plain and of easy comprehension, and as the best auditories are mixed, I shall not set about to justify the propriety of preaching, or under that title publishing, Discourses so abstruse as some of these are : neither is it worth while to trouble the reader with the account of my doing either. He must not however impute to me, as a repetition of the impropriety, this second edition [a], but to the demand for it.

---

[a] The Preface stands exactly as it did before the second edition of the Sermons.

Whether he will think he has any amends made him by the following illustrations of what seemed most to require them, I myself am by no means a proper judge.

§ 7. *The two methods of handling morals, and their reciprocal service and respective merits.*

There are two ways[1] in which the subject of morals may be treated. One begins from inquiring into the abstract relations of things: the other from a matter of fact, namely, what the particular nature of man is, its several parts, their economy or constitution; from whence it proceeds to determine what course of life it is, which is correspondent to this whole nature. In the former method the conclusion is expressed thus, that vice is contrary to the nature and reason of things: in the latter, that it is a violation or breaking in upon our own nature. Thus they both lead us to the same thing, our obligations to the practice of virtue; and thus they exceedingly strengthen and enforce each other. The first seems the most direct formal proof, and in some respects the least liable to cavil and dispute: the latter is in a peculiar manner adapted to satisfy a fair mind: and is more easily applicable to the several particular relations and circumstances in life.

§ 8. *The Three Sermons touch only the relation of morals to our nature.*

The following Discourses proceed chiefly in this latter method. The three first wholly. They were intended to explain what is meant by the nature of man, when it is said that virtue consists in following, and vice in deviating from it; and by explaining to shew that the assertion is true. That the ancient moralists had some inward feeling or other, which they chose to express in this manner; that man is born to virtue, that it consists in following nature,

---

[1] The first pursued by Clarke, the second by Shaftesbury. These are the two authors whom Butler may be supposed to have had especially in his view.

and that vice[1] is more contrary to this nature than tortures[2] or death[1], their works in our hands are instances.

§ 9. *But this has been so darkened as to require further explication.*

Now a person who found no mystery in this way of speaking of the ancients; who, without being very explicit with himself, kept to his natural feeling, went along with them, and found within himself a full conviction, that what they laid down was just and true; such an one would probably wonder to see a point, in which he never perceived any difficulty, so laboured as this is, in the second and third Sermons; insomuch perhaps as to be at a loss for the occasion, scope, and drift of them. But it need not be thought strange that this manner of expression, though familiar with them, and, if not usually carried so far, yet not uncommon amongst ourselves, should want explaining; since there are several perceptions daily felt and spoken of, which yet it may not be very easy at first view to explicate, to distinguish from all others, and ascertain exactly what the idea or perception is. The many treatises upon the passions are a proof of this; since so many would never have undertaken to unfold their several complications, and trace and resolve them into their principles, if they had thought, what they were endeavouring to show was obvious to every one, who felt and talked of those passions. Thus, though there seems no ground to doubt, but that the generality of mankind have the inward perception expressed so commonly in that manner by the ancient moralists, more than to doubt whether they have those passions; yet it appeared of use to unfold that inward conviction, and lay it open in a more explicit manner, than I had seen done; especially when there were not wanting persons, who mani-

---

[1] Compare Cicero, *De Off*. iii. 5: 'Detrahere aliquid alteri, et hominem hominis incommodo suum augere commodum, magis est contra naturam quam mors, quam paupertas, quam dolor, quam cetera, quae possunt aut corpori accidere aut rebus externis.'

[2] See Serm. iii. 2.

festly mistook the whole thing, and so had great reason to express themselves dissatisfied with it. A late author of great and deserved reputation says, that to place virtue in following nature, is at best a loose way of talk. And he has reason to say this, if what I think he intends to express, though with great decency, be true, that scarce any other sense can be put upon those words, but acting as any of the several parts, without distinction, of a man's nature happened most to incline him [b].

§ 10. *A nature is an integer; its parts having reciprocal relations needful to be known.*

Whoever thinks it worth while to consider this matter thoroughly, should begin with stating to himself exactly the idea of a system, economy, or constitution of any particular nature, or particular any thing: and he will, I suppose, find, that it is an one or a whole, made up of several parts; but yet, that the several parts even considered as a whole do not complete the idea, unless in the notion of a whole you include the relations and respects which those parts have to each other. Every work both of nature and of art is a system: and as every particular thing, both natural and artificial, is for some use or purpose out of and beyond itself, one may add, to what has been already brought into the idea of a system, its conduciveness to this one or more ends.

§ 11. *Illustrated by a watch.*

Let us instance in a watch—Suppose the several parts of it taken to pieces, and placed apart from each other: let a man have ever so exact a notion of these several parts, unless he considers the respects and relations which they have to each other, he will not have any thing like the idea of a watch. Suppose these several parts brought together and any how united: neither will he yet, be the union ever so close, have an idea which will bear any resemblance to

---

[b] Wollaston, *Rel. of Nature delin.*, ed. 1724, pp. 22, 23.

that of a watch. But let him view those several parts put together, or consider them as to be put together in the manner of a watch; let him form a notion of the relations which those several parts have to each other—all conducive in their respective ways to this purpose, showing the hour of the day; and then he has the idea of a watch [1].

§ 12. *In man the principal relation is that of conscience to the rest.*

Thus it is with regard to the inward frame of man. Appetites, passions, affections, and the principle of reflection, considered merely as the several parts of our inward nature, do not at all give us an idea of the system or constitution of this nature; because the constitution is formed by somewhat not yet taken into consideration, namely, by the relations which these several parts have to each other; the chief of which is the authority of reflection or conscience. It is from considering the relations which the several appetites and passions in the inward frame have to each other, and, above all, the supremacy of reflection or conscience, that we get the idea of the system or constitution of human nature.

§ 13. *Thus we find our nature adapted to virtue, as a watch to measuring time.*

And from the idea itself it will as fully appear, that this our nature, i. e. constitution, is adapted to virtue, as from the idea of a watch it appears, that its nature, i. e. constitution or system, is adapted to measure time. What in fact or event commonly happens is nothing to this question [2]. Every work of art is apt to be out of order: but this is so

---

[1] This illustration, so famous since the time of Paley, has probably been taken in its brief form by Butler from Nieuwentyt's *Religious Philosopher*, to whom Paley doubtless owed it, and who has given it in detail. See Lecture on Paley, by Lord Neaves, pp. 24−7, and 32−4 (Blackwood, 1873).

[2] Comp. *Analogy*, I. v. 35; Cic. *Tusc. Disp.* ii. 4, 5.

far from being according to its system, that let the disorder increase, and it will totally destroy it. This is merely by way of explanation, what an economy, system, or constitution is. And thus far the cases are perfectly parallel. If we go further, there is indeed a difference, nothing to the present purpose, but too important an one ever to be omitted. A machine is inanimate and passive: but we are agents. Our constitution is put in our own power. We are charged with it; and therefore are accountable for any disorder or violation of it.

§ 14. *Vice, injustice, misery, all contrary to our nature; variously in mode and degree.*

Thus nothing can possibly be more contrary to nature than vice; meaning by nature not only the *several parts* of our internal frame, but also the *constitution* of it. Poverty and disgrace, tortures and death, are not so contrary to it. Misery and injustice[1] are indeed equally contrary to some different parts of our nature taken singly: but injustice is moreover contrary to the whole constitution of the nature.

If it be asked, whether this constitution be really what those philosophers meant, and whether they would have explained themselves in this manner; the answer is the same, as if it should be asked, whether a person, who had often used the word resentment, and felt the thing, would have explained this passion exactly in the same manner, in which it is done in one of these Discourses. As I have no doubt, but that this is a true account of that passion, which he referred to and intended to express by the word resentment; so I have no doubt, but that this is the true account of the ground of that conviction which they referred to, when they said, vice was contrary to nature. And though it should be thought that they meant no more than that vice

---

[1] Butler does not here take injustice out of the category of vice for his present purpose, but selects it as an instance; since it lies at the root of Vice, and the repugnance of man to injustice is with him an early and favourite topic of proof.

was contrary to the higher and better part of our nature; even this implies such a constitution as I have endeavoured to explain. For the very terms, higher and better, imply a relation or respect of parts to each other; and these relative parts, being in one and the same nature, form a constitution, and are the very idea of it. They had a perception that injustice was contrary to their nature, and that pain was so also. They observed these two perceptions totally different, not in degree, but in kind: and the reflecting upon each of them, as they thus stood in their nature, wrought a full intuitive conviction, that more was due and of right belonged to one of these inward perceptions, than to the other; that it demanded in all cases to govern such a creature as man. So that, upon the whole, this is a fair and true account of what was the ground of their conviction; of what they intended to refer to, when they said, virtue consisted in following nature: a manner of speaking not loose and undeterminate, but clear and distinct, strictly just and true.

§ 15. *Men and brutes compared, as to instincts of action.*

Though I am persuaded the force of this conviction is felt by almost every one; yet since, considered as an argument and put in words, it appears somewhat abstruse, and since the connection of it is broken in the three first Sermons, it may not be amiss to give the reader the whole argument here in one view.

Mankind has various instincts and principles of action, as brute creatures have; some leading most directly and immediately to the good of the community, and some most directly to private good.

Man has several which brutes have not; particularly reflection or conscience, an approbation of some principles or actions, and disapprobation of others.

Brutes obey their instincts or principles of action, according to certain rules; suppose the constitution of their body, and the objects around them.

§ 16. *The generality of men obey these instincts in the mass, both the bad and the good.*

The generality of mankind also obey their instincts and principles, all of them; those propensions we call good, as well as the bad, according to the same rules; namely, the constitution of their body, and the external circumstances which they are in. [Therefore it is not a true representation of mankind to affirm, that they are wholly governed by self-love, the love of power and sensual appetites: since, as on the one hand they are often actuated by these, without any regard to right or wrong; so on the other it is manifest fact, that the same persons, the generality, are frequently influenced by friendship, compassion, gratitude; and even a general abhorrence of what is base, and liking of what is fair and just, takes its turn amongst the other motives of action. This is the partial inadequate notion of human nature treated of in the first Discourse: and it is by this nature, if one may speak so, that the world is in fact influenced, and kept in that tolerable order, in which it is.]

§ 17. *Brutes the like: but their nature has no discords.*

Brutes in acting according to the rules before mentioned, their bodily constitution and circumstances, act suitably to their whole nature. [It is however to be distinctly noted, that the reason why we affirm this is not merely that brutes in fact act so; for this alone, however universal, does not at all determine, whether such course of action be correspondent to their whole nature: but the reason of the assertion is, that as in acting thus they plainly act conformably to somewhat in their nature, so, from all observations we are able to make upon them, there does not appear the least ground to imagine them to have any thing else in their nature, which requires a different rule or course of action.]

Mankind also in acting thus would act suitably to their whole nature, if no more were to be said of man's nature than what has been now said; if that, as it is a true, were also a complete, adequate account of our nature.

§ 18. *But man has a ruling faculty of conscience or reflection.*

But that is not a complete account of man's nature. Somewhat further must be brought in to give us an adequate notion of it; namely, that one of those principles of action, conscience or reflection, compared with the rest as they all stand together in the nature of man, plainly bears upon it marks of authority over all the rest, and claims the absolute direction of them all, to allow or forbid their gratification: a disapprobation of reflection being in itself a principle manifestly superior to a mere propension. And the conclusion is, that to allow no more to this superior principle or part of our nature, than to other parts; to let it govern and guide only occasionally in common with the rest, as its turn happens to come, from the temper and circumstances one happens to be in; this is not to act conformably to the constitution of man: neither can any human creature be said to act conformably to his constitution of nature, unless he allows to that superior principle the absolute authority which is due to it. And this conclusion is abundantly confirmed from hence, that one may determine what course of action the economy of man's nature requires, without so much as knowing in what degrees of *strength* the several principles prevail, or which of them have actually the greatest influence.

§ 19. *Which claims to be his universal governor.*

The practical reason of insisting so much upon this natural authority of the principle of reflection or conscience is, that it seems in great measure overlooked by many, who are by no means the worse sort of men. It is thought sufficient to abstain from gross wickedness, and to be humane and kind to such as happen to come in their way. Whereas in reality the very constitution of our nature requires, that we bring our whole conduct before this superior faculty; wait its determination; enforce upon ourselves its authority, and make it the business of our lives, as it is absolutely the whole business of a moral agent, to conform ourselves to it. This is the true meaning of that ancient precept, *Reverence thyself*.

§ 20. *Lord Shaftesbury's supposed cases without remedy.*

The not taking into consideration this authority, which is implied in the idea of reflex approbation or disapprobation, seems a material deficiency or omission in Lord Shaftesbury's *Inquiry concerning Virtue*. He has shown beyond all contradiction, that virtue is naturally the interest or happiness, and vice the misery, of such a creature as man, placed in the circumstances which we are in this world. But suppose there are particular exceptions; a case which this author was unwilling to put, and yet surely it is to be put: or suppose a case which he has put and determined, that of a sceptic not convinced of this happy tendency of virtue, or being of a contrary opinion. His determination is, that it would be *without remedy*[c]. One may say more explicitly, that leaving out the authority of reflex approbation or disapprobation, such an one would be under an obligation to act viciously; since interest, one's own happiness, is a manifest obligation, and there is not supposed to be any other obligation in the case. 'But does it much mend the matter, to take in that natural authority of reflection ? There indeed would be an obligation to virtue; but would not the obligation from supposed interest on the side of vice remain ?'

§ 21. *Obligation to obey conscience provides one.*

If it should, yet to be under two contrary obligations, i. e. under none at all, would not be exactly the same, as to be under a formal obligation to be vicious, or to be in circumstances in which the constitution of man's nature plainly required that vice should be preferred. But the obligation on the side of interest really does not remain. For the natural authority of the principle of reflection is an obligation the most near and intimate, the most certain and known : whereas the contrary obligation can at the

---

[c] *Characteristics,* vol. ii. p. 69.

utmost appear no more than probable; since no man can be *certain* in any circumstances that vice is his interest in the present world, much less can he be certain against another: and thus the certain obligation would entirely supersede and destroy the uncertain one; which yet would have been of real force without the former.

§ 22. *Our inward approval of goodness imports the nearest and surest obligation.*

In truth, the taking in this consideration totally changes the whole state of the case; and shows, what this author does not seem to have been aware of, that the greatest degree of scepticism which he thought possible will still leave men under the strictest moral obligations[1], whatever their opinion be concerning the happiness of virtue. For that mankind upon reflection felt an approbation of what was good, and disapprobation of the contrary, he thought a plain matter of fact, as it undoubtedly is, which none could deny, but from mere affectation. Take in then that authority and obligation, which is a constituent part of this reflex approbation, and it will undeniably follow, though a man should doubt of every thing else, yet, that he would still remain under the nearest and most certain obligation to the practice of virtue; an obligation implied in the very idea of virtue, in the very idea of reflex approbation.

§ 23. *Self-love should accept a small sacrifice to shun a great one.*

And how little influence soever this obligation alone can be expected to have in fact upon mankind, yet one may appeal even to interest and self-love, and ask, since from man's nature, condition, and the shortness of life, so little, so very little indeed, can possibly in any case be gained by vice[2]; whether it be so prodigious a thing to sacrifice that

---

[1] 'Et virtutis et vitiorum, sine ullâ divinâ ratione, grave ipsius conscientiae pondus est: quâ sublatâ, jacent omnia.' Cic. *De Nat. Deor.* iii. 35.

[2] *Analogy*, I. vii. 12.

little to the most intimate of all obligations; and which a man cannot transgress without being self-condemned, and, unless he has corrupted his nature, without real self-dislike: this question, I say, may be asked, even upon supposition that the prospect of a future life were ever so uncertain.

§ 24. *For man is a law unto himself, and will not be exempted from consequences by disbelieving them.*

The observation that man is thus by his very nature a law to himself, pursued to its just consequences, is of the utmost importance; because from it it will follow, that though men should, through stupidity or speculative scepticism, be ignorant of, or disbelieve, any authority in the universe to punish the violation of this law; yet, if there should be such authority, they would be as really liable to punishment, as though they had been beforehand convinced, that such punishment would follow. For in whatever sense we understand justice, even supposing, what I think would be very presumptuous to assert,-that the end of Divine punishment is no other than that of civil punishment, namely, to prevent future mischief; upon this bold supposition, ignorance or disbelief of the sanction would by no means exempt even from this justice; because it is not foreknowledge of the punishment which renders us obnoxious to it; but merely violating a known obligation.

§ 25. *In contradiction to Shaftesbury, goodness is the just object of fear.*

And here it comes in one's way to take notice of a manifest error or mistake in the author now cited, unless perhaps he has incautiously expressed himself so as to be misunderstood; namely, that *it is malice only, and not goodness, which can make us afraid* [d]. Whereas in reality, goodness is the natural and just object of the greatest fear to an ill man. Malice may be appeased or satiated; humour may change,

---

[d] *Characteristics,* vol. i. p. 39.

but goodness is a fixed, steady, immovable principle of action [1]. If either of the former holds the sword of justice, there is plainly ground for the greatest of crimes to hope for impunity: but if it be goodness, there can be no possible hope, whilst the reasons of things, or the ends of government, call for punishment. Thus every one sees how much greater chance of impunity an ill man has in a partial administration, than in a just and upright one. It is said, that *the interest or good of the whole must be the interest of the universal Being, and that he can have no other.* Be it so. This author has proved, that vice is naturally the misery of mankind in this world. Consequently it was for the good of the whole that it should be so. What shadow of reason then is there to assert, that this may not be the case hereafter? Danger of future punishment (and if there be danger, there is ground of fear) no more supposes malice, than the present feeling of punishment does.

§ 26. *Of falseness and artfulness with ourselves.*
Sermons VII, X.

The Sermon *upon the character of Balaam*, and that *upon Self-Deceit*, both relate to one subject. I am persuaded, that a very great part of the wickedness of the world is, one way or other, owing to the self-partiality, self-flattery, and self-deceit, endeavoured there to be laid open and explained. It is to be observed amongst persons of the lowest rank, in proportion to their compass of thought, as much as amongst men of education and improvement. It seems, that people are capable of being thus artful with themselves, in proportion as they are capable of being so with others. Those who have taken notice that there is really such a thing, namely, plain falseness and insincerity in men with regard to themselves, will readily see the drift and design of these Discourses: and nothing that I can add will explain the design of them to him, who has not beforehand

---

[1] Εἰ δὴ ὁ φόβος τοῦτ' ἐστίν, ἀνάγκη τὰ τοιαῦτα φοβερὰ εἶναι. ... Τοιαῦτα δὲ ἔχθρα τε καὶ ὀργὴ δυναμένων ποιεῖν τι. ... Καὶ ἀρετὴ ὑβριζομένη, δύναμιν ἔχουσα. Aristot. *Rhet.* II. v.

·remarked, at least, somewhat of the character. And yet the admonitions they contain may be as much wanted by such a person, as by others; for it is to be noted, that a man may be entirely possessed by this unfairness of mind, without having the least speculative notion what the thing is.

§ 27. *Of Resentment, and its ground.* Serm. VIII.

The account given of *Resentment* in the eighth Sermon is introductory to the following one *upon Forgiveness of Injuries.* It may possibly have appeared to some, at first sight, a strange assertion, that injury is the only natural object of settled resentment, or that men do not in fact resent deliberately any thing but under this appearance of injury. But I must desire the reader not to take any assertion alone by itself, but to consider the whole of what is said upon it: because this is necessary, not only in order to judge of the truth of it, but often, such is the nature of language, to see the very meaning of the assertion. Particularly as to this, injury and injustice is, in the Sermon itself, explained to mean, not only the more gross and shocking instances of wickedness, but also contempt, scorn, neglect, any sort of disagreeable behaviour towards a person, which he thinks other than what is due to him. And the general notion of injury or wrong plainly comprehends this, though the words are mostly confined to the higher degrees of it.

§ 28. *Of forgiveness of injuries, why so strongly inculcated.* Serm. IX.

Forgiveness of injuries is one of the very few moral obligations which has been disputed. But the proof, that it is really an obligation, what our nature and condition require, seems very obvious, were it only from the consideration, that revenge is doing harm merely for harm's sake[1]. And as to the love of our enemies: resentment cannot supersede the obligation to universal benevolence, unless they are in the nature of the thing inconsistent, which they plainly are not.

---

[1] Serm. ix. 8, 9.

This Divine precept, to forgive injuries and love our enemies, though to be met with in Gentile moralists, yet is in a peculiar sense a precept of Christianity[1]; as our Saviour has insisted more upon it than upon any other single virtue. One reason of this doubtless is, that it so peculiarly becomes an imperfect, faulty creature. But it may be observed also, that a virtuous temper of mind, consciousness of innocence, and good meaning towards every body, and a strong feeling of injustice and injury, may itself, such is the imperfection of our virtue, lead a person to violate this obligation if he be not upon his guard. And it may well be supposed, that this is another reason why it is so much insisted upon by him, who *knew what was in man*.

§ 29. *Confusion which arises from resolving all particular affections into self-love. Serm. XI.*

The chief design of the eleventh Discourse is to state the notion of self-love and disinterestedness, in order to show that benevolence is not more unfriendly to self-love, than any other particular affection whatever. There is a strange affection in many people of explaining away all particular affections, and representing the whole of life as nothing but one continued exercise of self-love[2]. Hence arises that surprising confusion and perplexity in the Epicureans [e] of

---

[e] NOTE. *Instances thereof.* One need only look into Torquatus's account of the Epicurean system, in Cicero's first book *De Finibus*, to see in what a surprising manner this was done by them. Thus the desire of praise, and of being beloved, he explains to be no other than desire of safety: regard to our country, even in the most virtuous character, to be nothing but regard to ourselves. The author of *Reflexions, &c. Morales,* says, Curiosity proceeds from interest or pride; which pride also would doubtless have been

---

[1] Cicero gives it in a limited form and subject to doubt: 'Sunt quaedam officia etiam adversus eos servanda, a quibus iniuriam acceperis; est enim ulciscendi et puniendi modus; atque haud scio an satis sit, eum, qui lacessiverit, iniuriae suae paenitere.' *De Officiis,* i. 11.

[2] Comp. Serm. i. 6 n., and xi. 3, 6, 8 (where see Editor's note).

old, Hobbes, the author of *Reflexions, Sentences, et Maximes Morales*, and this whole set of writers; the confusion of calling actions interested which are done in contradiction to the most manifest known interest, merely for the gratification of a present passion. Now all this confusion might easily be avoided, by stating to ourselves wherein the idea of self-love in general consists, as distinguished from all particular movements towards particular external objects; the appetites of sense, resentment, compassion, curiosity, ambition, and the rest [f]. When this is done, if the words *selfish* and *interested* cannot be parted with, but must be applied to every thing; yet, to avoid such total confusion of all language, let the distinction be made by epithets: and the first may be called cool or settled selfishness, and the other passionate or sensual selfishness. But the most natural way of speaking plainly is, to call the first only, self-love, and the actions proceeding from it, interested: and to say of the latter, that they are not love to ourselves, but movements towards somewhat external: honour, power, the harm or good of another: and that the pursuit of these external objects, so far as it proceeds from these movements, (for it may proceed from self-love [g],) is no otherwise interested, than as every action of every creature must, from the nature of the thing, be; for no one can act but from a desire, or choice, or preference of his own.

§ 30. *Self-love may blend with particular passions, or be set aside thereby.*

Self-love and any particular passion may be joined together; and from this complication, it becomes impossible in numberless instances to determine precisely, how far an action, perhaps even of one's own, has for its principle general self-love, or some particular passion. But this need

---

explained to be self-love. Page 85, ed. 1725. As if there were no such passions in mankind as desire of esteem, or of being beloved, or of knowledge. Hobbes's account of the affections of good-will and pity are instances of the same kind.

[f] Serm. xi. 2, 3.   [g] See the note, Serm. i. 5.

create no confusion in the ideas themselves of self-love and particular passions. We distinctly discern what one is, and what the other are: though we may be uncertain how far one or the other influences us. And though, from this uncertainty, it cannot but be that there will be different opinions concerning mankind, as more or less governed by interest; and some will ascribe actions to self-love, which others will ascribe to particular passions: yet it is absurd to say that mankind are wholly actuated by either; since it is manifest that both have their influence. For as, on the one hand, men form a general notion of interest, some placing it in one thing, and some in another, and have a considerable regard to it throughout the course of their life, which is owing to self-love; so, on the other hand, they are often set on work by the particular passions themselves, and a considerable part of life is spent in the actual gratification of them, i. e. is employed, not by self-love, but by the passions.

§ 31. *Particular affections necessary to interest, and happiness.*

Besides, the very idea of an interested pursuit necessarily presupposes particular passions or appetites; since the very idea of interest or happiness consists in this, that an appetite or affection enjoys its object. It is not because we love ourselves that we find delight in such and such objects, but because we have particular affections towards them. Take away these affections, and you leave self-love absolutely nothing at all to employ itself about[h]; no end or object for it to pursue, excepting only that of avoiding pain. Indeed the Epicureans[1], who maintained that absence of pain was the highest happiness, might, consistently with themselves, deny all affection, and, if they had so pleased, every sensual

---

[h] Serm. xi. 5, 6.

[1] 'Maximam illam voluptatum habemus, quae percipitur omni dolore detracto.' Cic. *De Finibus*, i. 11. 'Dicunt enim voluptatis magnitudinem doloris detractione finiri.' *De Officiis*, iii. 33.

appetite too: but the very idea of interest or happiness other than absence of pain, implies particular appetites or passions; these being necessary to constitute that interest or happiness.

§ 32. *Benevolence in no special degree opposed to self-love.*

The observation, that benevolence is no more disinterested than any of the common particular passions [i], seems in itself worth being taken notice of; but is insisted upon to obviate that scorn, which one sees rising upon the faces of people who are said to know the world, when mention is made of a disinterested, generous, or public-spirited action. The truth of that observation might be made appear in a more formal manner of proof: for whoever will consider all the possible respects and relations which any particular affection can have to self-love and private interest, will, I think, see demonstrably, that benevolence is not in any respect more at variance with self-love, than any other particular affection whatever, but that it is in every respect, at least, as friendly to it.

§ 33. *To be distinguished from self-love, not opposed to it.*

If the observation be true, it follows, that self-love and benevolence, virtue and interest, are not to be opposed, but only to be distinguished from each other; in the same way as virtue and any other particular affection, love of arts, suppose, are to be distinguished. Every thing is what it is, and not another thing. The goodness or badness of actions does not arise from hence, that the epithet, interested or disinterested, may be applied to them, any more than that any other indifferent epithet, suppose inquisitive or jealous, may or may not be applied to them; not from their being attended with present or future pleasure or pain; but from their being what they are; namely, what becomes such creatures as we are, what the state of the case requires, or the contrary.

---

[i] Serm. xi. 19.

§ 34. *Interested or disinterested, not the criterion of good or evil.*

Or in other words, we may judge and determine, that an action is morally good[1] or evil, before we so much as consider, whether it be interested or disinterested. This consideration no more comes in to determine whether an action be virtuous, than to determine whether it be resentful. Self-love in its due degree is as just and morally good, as any affection whatever. Benevolence towards particular persons may be to a degree of weakness, and so be blamable: and disinterestedness is so far from being in itself commendable, that the utmost possible depravity which we can in imagination conceive, is that of disinterested cruelty.

§ 35. *Self-love does not require reduction in quantity.*

Neither does there appear any reason to wish self-love were weaker in the generality of the world than it is. The influence which it has seems plainly owing to its being constant and habitual, which it cannot but be, and not to the degree or strength of it. Every caprice of the imagination, every curiosity of the understanding, every affection of the heart, is perpetually showing its weakness, by prevailing over it[2]. Men daily, hourly sacrifice the greatest known interest, to fancy, inquisitiveness, love, or hatred, any vagrant inclination. The thing to be lamented is, not that men have so great regard to their own good or interest in the present world, for they have not enough[k]; but that they have so little to the good of others. And this seems plainly owing to their being so much engaged in the gratifi-

---

[k] Serm. i. 13–15.

---

[1] Aristot. *Eth. Nic.* IX. viii. 7: τὸν μὲν ἀγαθὸν δεῖ φίλαυτον εἶναι. In this chapter Aristotle expounds with force, fullness, and clearness, the relations of self-love and moral excellences: winding it up with the following words (11): ἐν πᾶσι δὴ τοῖς ἐπαινετοῖς ὁ σπουδαῖος φαίνεται ἑαυτῷ τοῦ καλοῦ πλέον νέμων. οὕτω μὲν οὖν φίλαυτον εἶναι δεῖ, καθάπερ εἴρηται· ὡς δὲ οἱ πολλοί, οὐ χρή.

[2] Comp. *Analogy*, I. v. 243.

cation of particular passions unfriendly to benevolence, and which happen to be most prevalent in them, much more than to self-love. As a proof of this may be observed, that there is no character more void of friendship, gratitude, natural affection, love to their country, common justice, or more equally and uniformly hardhearted, than the *abandoned* in, what is called, the way of pleasure——hardhearted and totally without feeling in behalf of others; except when they cannot escape the sight of distress, and so are interrupted by it in their pleasures. And yet it is ridiculous to call such an abandoned course of pleasure interested, when the person engaged in it knows beforehand, and goes on under the feeling and apprehension, that it will be as ruinous to himself, as to those who depend upon him.

§ 36. *But should be more considerate and with greater insight.*

Upon the whole, if the generality of mankind were to cultivate within themselves the principle of self-love; if they were to accustom themselves often to set down and consider, what was the greatest happiness they were capable of attaining for themselves in this life, and if self-love were so strong and prevalent, as that they would uniformly pursue this their supposed chief temporal good, without being diverted from it by any particular passion; it would manifestly prevent numberless follies and vices. This was in a great measure the Epicurean system of philosophy. It is indeed by no means the religious or even moral institution of life. Yet, with all the mistakes men would fall into about interest, it would be less mischievous than the extravagances of mere appetite, will, and pleasure: for certainly self-love, though confined to the interest of this life, is, of the two, a much better guide than passion [1], which has absolutely no bound nor measure, but what is set to it by this self-love, or moral considerations.

---

[1] Serm. ii. 16.

§ 37. *Every affection has its own proper end; that of virtue most of all.*

From the distinction above made between self-love, and the several particular principles or affections in our nature, we may see how good ground there was for that assertion, maintained by the several ancient schools of philosophy against the Epicureans, namely, that virtue is to be pursued as an end, eligible in and for itself. For, if there be any principles or affections in the mind of man distinct from self-love, that the things those principles tend towards, or that the objects of those affections are, each of them, in themselves eligible, to be pursued upon its own account, and to be rested in as an end, is implied in the very idea of such principle or affection [m]. They indeed asserted much higher things of virtue, and with very good reason; but to say thus much of it, that it is to be pursued for itself, is to say no more of it, than may truly be said of the object of every natural affection whatever.

The question, which was a few years ago disputed in France [1], concerning *the love of God*, which was there called enthusiasm, as it will every where by the generality of the world; this question, I say, answers in religion to that old one in morals now mentioned. And both of them are, I think, fully determined by the same observation, namely, that the very nature of affection, the idea itself, necessarily implies resting in its object as an end [2].

§ 38. *God, apart from reward and punishment, as an object of affection. See Sermons XIII, XIV.*

I shall not here add any thing further to what I have said in the two Discourses upon that most important sub-

---

[m] Serm. xiii. 4.

[1] Between Bossuet and Fénelon. See Macintosh's *Dissertation on the Progress of Ethical Philosophy*, Art. Fénelon-Bossuet (Carmichael).

[2] It is perhaps from a sentiment of reverence that Butler does not describe the love of God as a 'particular affection.' Yet it falls within the definition; and he seems to have the idea in view both in this passage and in § 38.

ject, but only this: that if we are constituted such sort of creatures, as from our very nature to feel certain affections or movements of mind, upon the sight or contemplation of the meanest inanimate part of the creation, for the flowers of the field have their beauty; certainly there must be somewhat due to him himself, who is the Author and Cause of all things; who is more intimately present to us than any thing else can be, and with whom we have a nearer and more constant intercourse, than we can have with any creature: there must be some movements of mind and heart which correspond to his perfections, or of which those perfections are the natural object: and that when we are commanded to *love the Lord our God with all our heart, and with all our mind, and with all our soul;* somewhat more must be meant than merely that we live in hope of rewards or fear of punishments from him; somewhat more than this must be intended: though these regards themselves are most just and reasonable, and absolutely necessary to be often recollected in such a world as this.

§ 39. *Collection of these Discourses, in great part accidental.*

It may be proper just to advertise the reader, that he is not to look for any particular reason for the choice of the greatest part of these Discourses; their being taken from amongst many others, preached in the same place, through a course of eight years, being in great measure accidental. Neither is he to expect to find any other connection between them, than that uniformity of thought and design, which will always be found in the writings of the same person, when he writes with simplicity and in earnest.

STANHOPE,
Sept. 16, 1729.

SERMON I

UPON HUMAN NATURE

For as we have many members in one body, and all members have not the same office: so we, being many, are one body in Christ, and every one members one of another.—ROMANS xii. 4, 5.

§ 1. *The primitive sense of the Christian incorporation; why so direct and lively.*

THE Epistles in the New Testament have all of them a particular reference to the condition and usages of the Christian world at the time they were written. Therefore as they cannot be thoroughly understood, unless that condition and those usages are known and attended to: so further, though they be known, yet if they be discontinued or changed; exhortations, precepts, and illustrations of things, which refer to such circumstances now ceased or altered, cannot at this time be urged in that manner, and with that force which they were to the primitive Christians. Thus the text now before us, in its first intent and design, relates to the decent management of those extraordinary gifts which were then in the church[a], but which are now totally ceased[1]. And even as to the allusion that *we are one*

---

[a] 1 Cor. xii.

---

[1] How far are we to consider Butler's great authority as staked on this broad assertion? But slightly, as I think. A writer

body in Christ; though what the apostle here intends is equally true of Christians in all circumstances; and the consideration of it is plainly still an additional motive, over and above moral considerations, to the discharge of the several duties and offices of a Christian: yet it is manifest this allusion must have appeared with much greater force to those, who, by the many difficulties they went through for the sake of their religion [1], were led to keep always in view the relation they stood in to their Saviour, who had undergone the same; to those, who, from the idolatries of all around them, and their ill treatment, were taught to consider themselves as not of the world in which they lived, but as a distinct society of themselves; with laws and ends, and principles of life and action, quite contrary to those which the world professed themselves at that time influenced by. Hence the relation of a Christian was by them considered as nearer than that of affinity and blood; and they almost literally esteemed themselves as members one of another [2].

---

absorbed in a great subject can hardly address his faculties with equal force to outlying matters touched collaterally, and with no special reason to require exactitude, in the course of his argument. It perhaps was not material to Butler's purpose that the extraordinary gifts should have ceased totally: but only that they should have ceased to enter into the daily food and life of the Church. May not this then be considered as what, in dealing with the utterances of Judges in the Law Courts, is called an *obiter dictum*? Perhaps here is an assumption of the common opinion, rather than a well-digested and separately tested conclusion.

[1] It would in truth require almost a Treatise to bring out fully the causes which bound so closely together Christians of the Apostolic age. Probably the most prominent among them is the sharpness of the separation between the Church and the world lying in wickedness around it. The spirits of the two are still in conflict as much as ever; but the innumerable victories, externally achieved by the Christian tradition, have clouded the atmosphere and coated over the field in which the struggle is carried on. It seems beyond our power, even after the greatest effort has been used, fully to recall and bring before the mind the position of the first Christians, and their relation to the business of life and their companions in it, after their conversion.

[2] Butler speaks figuratively; but the figure seems appropriate, especially when we bear in mind the vast alteration in the laws of life and action which, after conversion, became applicable to Christians, as beings compounded of body, soul, and spirit,

§ 2. *Though our nature supplies religion with a claim anterior to the Gospel.*

It cannot indeed possibly be denied, that our being God's creatures, and virtue being the natural law we are born under, and the whole constitution of man being plainly adapted to it, are prior obligations to piety and virtue, than the consideration that God sent his Son into the world to save it, and the motives which arise from the peculiar relation of Christians, as members one of another under Christ our head. However, though all this be allowed, as it expressly is by the inspired writers; yet it is manifest that Christians at the time of the revelation, and immediately after, could not but insist mostly upon considerations of this latter kind.

These observations show the original particular reference of the text; and the peculiar force with which the thing intended by the allusion in it, must have been felt by the primitive Christian world. They likewise afford a reason for treating it at this time in a more general way.

§ 3. *Our nature shows we are made for both a personal and a common end*[1].

The relation which the several parts or members of the natural body have to each other and to the whole body, is here compared to the relation which each particular person in society has to other particular persons and to the whole society; and the latter is intended to be illustrated by the former[2]. And if there be a likeness between these two

---

[1] Our nature as a whole proves that as each part of a body has a function for itself and has also an office to discharge on behalf of the body to which it belongs, so every member of a society or incorporation has to discharge in it duties to himself and other duties to the association.

[2] The common life of man is strongly dwelt upon by the ancients: ἐπειδὴ φύσει πολιτικὸν ὁ ἄνθρωπος, says Aristotle, *Eth. Nic.* I. vii. 6. Cicero, in the *De Officiis*, i. 3, referring to the material supplied by the Stoic school, has

relations, the consequence is obvious: that the latter shows us we were intended to do good to others, as the former shows us that the several members of the natural body were intended to be instruments of good to each other and to the whole body. But as there is scarce any ground for a comparison between society and the mere material body, this without the mind being a dead unactive thing; much less can the comparison be carried to any length. And since the apostle speaks of the several members as having distinct offices, which implies the mind; it cannot be thought an unallowable liberty; instead of the *body* and *its members*, to substitute the *whole nature of man*, and *all the variety of internal principles which belong to it*. And then the comparison will be between the nature of man as respecting self, and tending to private good, his own preservation and happiness; and the nature of man as having respect to society, and tending to promote public good, the happiness of that society. These ends do indeed perfectly coincide; and to aim at public and private good are so far from being inconsistent, that they mutually promote each other: yet in the following discourse they must be considered as entirely distinct; otherwise the nature of man as tending to one, or as tending to the other, cannot be compared. There can no comparison be made, without considering the things compared as distinct and different.

From this review and comparison of the nature of man as respecting self, and as respecting society, it will plainly appear, that *there are as real and the same kind of indications in human nature, that we were made for society and to do good to our fellow-creatures; as that we were intended to take care of our own life and health and private good: and that the same objections lie against one of these assertions, as against the other.* For,

---

this passage: 'Quorum autem officiorum praecepta traduntur, ea, quamquam pertinent ad finem bonorum, tamen id minus apparet, quia magis ad institutionem vitae communis spectare videntur: de quibus est nobis his libris explicandum.'

§ 4. *Benevolence has, in the social, the place of self-love in our personal, nature.*

First, There is a natural principle of *benevolence*[b] in man; which is in some degree to *society*, what *self-love* is to the *individual*. And if there be in mankind any disposition to

---

[b] NOTE. Suppose a man of learning to be writing a grave book upon *human nature*, and to show in several parts of it that he had an insight into the subject he was considering; amongst other things, the following one would require to be accounted for; the appearance of benevolence or good-will in men towards each other in the instances of natural relation, and in others*. Cautious of being deceived with outward show, he retires within himself to see exactly, what that is in the mind of man from whence this appearance proceeds; and, upon deep reflection, asserts the principle in the mind to be only the love of power, and delight in the exercise of it. Would not every body think here was a mistake of one word for another? that the philosopher was contemplating and accounting for some other *human actions*, some other behaviour of man to man? And could any one be thoroughly satisfied, that what is commonly called benevolence or good-will was really the affection meant, but only by being made to understand that this learned person had a general hypothesis, to which the appearance of good-will could no otherwise be reconciled?

1. *Dogma of Hobbes: benevolence is love of power.*

That what has this appearance is often nothing but ambition; that delight in superiority often (suppose always) mixes itself with benevolence, only makes it more specious to call it ambition than hunger, of the two: but in reality that passion does no more account for the whole appearances of good-will, than this appetite does. Is there not often the appearance of one man's wishing that good to another, which he knows himself unable to procure him; and rejoicing in it, though bestowed by a third person? And can love of power any way possibly come in to account for this desire or delight[1]? Is there not often the appearance of men's distinguishing between two or more persons, preferring one before another, to do good to, in cases where

2. *Cases where this cannot possibly be.*

* Hobbes, *On Human Nature*, c. ix. § 7.

---

[1] The theory of which Butler has here supplied such a masterly confutation is found in the following words of Hobbes, *On Human Nature*, c. ix. § 17: 'There is yet another passion, sometimes called love, but more properly good-will or charity. There can be no greater argument to a man of his own power than to find himself able not only to accomplish his own desires, but to assist other men in theirs. And this is that conception, wherein consisteth charity.'

friendship; if there be any such thing as compassion, for compassion is momentary love; if there be any such thing

---

love of power cannot in the least account for the distinction and preference? For this principle can no otherwise distinguish between objects, than as it is a greater instance and exertion of power to do good to one rather than to another.

Again, suppose good-will in the mind of man to be nothing but delight in the exercise of power: men might indeed be restrained by distant and accidental considerations; but these restraints being removed, they would have a disposition to, and delight in mischief as an exercise and proof of power: and this disposition and delight would arise from, or be the same principle in the mind, as a disposition to, and delight in charity. Thus cruelty, as distinct from envy and resentment, would be exactly the same in the mind of man as good-will: that one tends to the happiness, the other to the misery of our fellow-creatures, is, it seems, merely an accidental circumstance, which the mind has not the least regard to. These are the absurdities which even men of capacity run into, when they have occasion to belie their nature, and will perversely disclaim that image of God which was originally stamped upon it, the traces of which, however faint, are plainly discernible upon the mind of man.

3. If true, benevolence agrees in essence with cruelty.

If any person can in earnest doubt, whether there be such a thing as good-will in one man towards another; (for the question is not concerning either the degree or extensiveness of it, but concerning the affection itself:) let it be observed, that *whether man be thus, or otherwise constituted, what is the inward frame in this particular*, is a mere question of fact or natural history, not provable immediately by reason. It is therefore to be judged of and determined in the same way other facts or matters of natural history are: by appealing to the external senses, or inward perceptions, respectively, as the matter under consideration is cognizable by one or the other: by arguing from acknowledged facts and actions; for a great number of actions in the same kind, in different circumstances, and respecting different objects, will prove, to a certainty, what principles they do not, and, to the greatest probability, what principles they do proceed from: and lastly, by the testimony of mankind. Now that there is some degree of benevolence amongst men, may be as strongly and plainly proved in all these ways, as it could possibly be proved, supposing there was this affection in our nature. And should any one think fit to assert, that resentment in the mind of man was absolutely nothing but reasonable concern for our own safety, the falsity of this, and what is the real nature of that passion, could be shown in no other ways than those in which it may be shown, that

4. Reality of good-will or benevolence a question of fact: provable like others.

as the paternal or filial affections; if there be any affection in human nature, the object and end of which is the good of another; this is itself benevolence, or the love of another. Be it ever so short, be it in ever so low a degree, or ever so unhappily confined; it proves the assertion, and points out what we were designed for, as really as though it were in a higher degree and more extensive.

§ 5. *Benevolence and self-love greatly coincide.*

I must however remind you that though benevolence and self-love are different; though the former tends most directly to public good, and the latter to private: yet they are so perfectly coincident, that the greatest satisfactions to ourselves depend upon our having benevolence in a due degree; and that self-love is one chief security of our right behaviour towards society. It may be added, that their mutual coinciding, so that we can scarce promote one without the other, is equally a proof that we were made for both.

§ 6. *The other affections lead to both private and public good; sometimes promoted without intention.*

Secondly, This will further appear, from observing that the *several passions* and *affections*, which are distinct [c] both

---

there is such a thing in *some degree* as *real* good-will in man towards man. It is sufficient that the seeds of it be implanted in our nature by God.

There is, it is owned, much left for us to do upon our own heart and temper; to cultivate, to improve, to call it forth, to exercise it in a steady, uniform manner. This is our work: this is virtue and religion [1].

5. *Much remains to be done.*

[c] NOTE. Every body makes a distinction between self-love, and the several particular passions, appetites, and affections; and yet they are often confounded again. That they are totally different, will be seen by any one who will distinguish between the passions and appetites *themselves*, and *endeavouring* after the means of their gratification. Consider the appetite of hunger, and the desire of esteem: these being the occasion both of

1. *Self-love is separate from particular appetites and passions.*

---

[1] Οὔτ' ἄρα φύσει οὔτε παρὰ φύσιν ἐγγίνονται αἱ ἀρεταί, ἀλλὰ πεφυκόσι μὲν ἡμῖν δέξασθαι αὐτάς, τελειουμένοις δὲ διὰ τοῦ ἔθους. Aristot. *Eth. Nic.* II. i. 3.

from benevolence and self-love[1], do in general contribute and lead us to *public* good as really as to *private*. It might be thought too minute and particular, and would carry us too great a length, to distinguish between and compare together the several passions or appetites distinct from benevolence, whose primary use and intention is the security and good of society; and the passions distinct from self-love, whose primary intention and design is the security and good of the individual[d]. It is enough to the present argument, that

pleasure and pain, the coolest *self-love*, as well as the appetites and passions themselves, may put us upon making use of the *proper methods of obtaining* that pleasure, and avoiding that pain; but the *feelings themselves*, the pain of hunger and shame, and the delight from esteem, are no more self-love than they are any thing in the world. Though a man hated himself, he would as much feel the pain of hunger as he would that of the gout: and it is plainly supposable there may be creatures with self-love in them to the highest degree, who may be quite insensible and indifferent (as men in some cases are) to the contempt and esteem of those, upon whom their happiness does not in some further respects depend. And as self-love and the several particular passions and appetites are in themselves totally different; so, that some actions proceed from one, and some from the other, will be manifest to any who will observe the two following very supposable cases. One man rushes upon certain ruin for the gratification of a present desire: nobody will call the principle of this action self-love. Suppose another man to go through some laborious work upon promise of a great reward, without any distinct knowledge what the reward will be: this course of action cannot be ascribed to any particular passion.

2. *Though sometimes blended.*

The former of these actions is plainly to be imputed to some particular passion or affection, the latter as plainly to the general affection or principle of self-love. That there are some particular pursuits or actions concerning which we cannot determine how far they are owing to one, and how far to the other, proceeds from this, that the two principles are frequently mixed together, and run up into each other. This distinction is further explained in the eleventh sermon.

Illustration from hunger, and love of esteem.

[d] NOTE. If any desire to see this distinction and comparison made in a particular instance, the appetite and passion now mentioned may serve for one. Hunger is to be considered as a private appetite; because the end for which it was given us is the preservation of the individual. Desire of esteem is a public passion; because the

---

[1] See Editor's note on Serm. xi. 3.

desire of esteem from others, contempt and esteem of them, love of society as distinct from affection to the good of it, indignation against successful vice, that these are public affections or passions; have an immediate respect to others, naturally lead us to regulate our behaviour in such a manner as will be of service to our fellow-creatures. If any or all of these may be considered likewise as private affections, as tending to private good; this does not hinder them from being public affections too, or destroy the good influence of them upon society, and their tendency to public good. It may be added, that as persons without any conviction from reason of the desirableness of life, would yet of course preserve it merely from the appetite of hunger; so by acting merely from regard (suppose) to reputation, without any consideration of the good of others, men often contribute to public good. In both these instances they are plainly instruments in the hands of another, in the hands of Providence, to carry on ends, the preservation of the individual and good of society, which they themselves have not in their view or intention. The sum is, men have various appetites, passions, and particular affections, quite distinct both from self-love and from benevolence: all of these have a tendency to promote both public and private good, and may be considered as respecting others and ourselves equally and in common: but some of them seem most immediately to respect others, or tend to public good; others of them most immediately to respect self, or tend to private good: as the former are not benevolence, so the latter are not self-love: neither sort are instances of our love either to ourselves or others; but only instances of our Maker's care and love both of the individual and the species, and proofs that

---

end for which it was given us is to regulate our behaviour towards society. The respect which this has to private good is as remote as the respect that has to public good: and the appetite is no more self-love, than the passion is benevolence. The object and end of the former is merely food; the object and end of the latter is merely esteem: but the latter can no more be gratified, without contributing to the good of society; than the former can be gratified, without contributing to the preservation of the individual.

he intended we should be instruments of good to each other, as well as that we should be so to ourselves.

§ 7. *We have a reflecting principle, which awards to actions their moral need.*

Thirdly, There is a principle of reflection in men, by which they distinguish between, approve and disapprove their own actions. We are plainly constituted such sort of creatures as to reflect upon our own nature. The mind can take a view of what passes within itself, its propensions, aversions, passions, affections, as respecting such objects, and in such degrees; and of the several actions consequent thereupon. In this survey it approves of one, disapproves of another, and towards a third is affected in neither of these ways, but is quite indifferent.

§ 8. *This is conscience; it works for good;*

This principle in man, by which he approves or disapproves his heart, temper, and actions, is conscience; for this is the strict sense of the word, though sometimes it is used so as to take in more. And that this faculty tends to restrain men from doing mischief to each other, and leads them to do good, is too manifest to need being insisted upon. Thus a parent has the affection of love to his children: this leads him to take care of, to educate, to make due provision for them; the natural affection leads to this: but the reflection that it is his proper business, what belongs to him, that it is right and commendable so to do; this added to the affection becomes a much more settled principle, and carries him on through more labour and difficulties for the sake of his children, than he would undergo from that affection alone, if he thought it, and the course of action it led to, either indifferent or criminal. This indeed is impossible, to do that which is good, and not to approve of it; for which reason they are frequently not considered as distinct, though they really are: for men often approve of the actions of others, which they will not imitate, and likewise do that which they approve not. It cannot possibly be denied, that there is this principle of reflection or conscience¹ in human nature. Suppose a man to relieve an innocent person in great distress; suppose the same man afterwards, in the fury of anger, to do the greatest mischief to a person who had given no just cause of offence; to aggravate the injury, add the circumstances of former friendship, and obligation from the injured person; let the man who is supposed to have done these two different actions, <u>coolly</u> reflect upon them afterwards, without regard to their consequences to himself: to assert that any common man would be affected in the same way towards these different actions, that he would make no distinction between them, but approve or disapprove them equally, is too glaring a falsity to need being confuted. There is therefore this principle of reflection or conscience in mankind.

§ 9. *For good, public and private: so that our being has a social end.*

It is needless to compare the respect it has to private good, with the respect it has to public; since it plainly tends as much to the latter as to the former, and is commonly thought to tend chiefly to the latter². This faculty is now mentioned merely as another part in the inward frame of man, pointing out to us in some degree what we

---

¹ In Butler's treatment of moral actions these two words are very commonly combined. But they are by no means synonymous. Speaking generally they unite to make up the provision furnished by our nature for the great business of moral judgment. Reflection, however, by itself, institutes as it were the process, but does not carry it through. It marks a certain stage of intellectual faculty, but is not essentially moral. On the other hand conscience, exercised habitually, tends to act instinctively, and without recognition of any reflective operation. The distinction of the two is recognised in Serm. ii. 5. Moreover we should observe that there is a right and a wrong beyond the sphere of moral action, and that the approving and disapproving faculty extends beyond that sphere. But this portion of its office does not fall within Butler's design.

² The special office here seems to be the detection and prevention of wrong. For in the pursuit of substantive good, each man is of necessity (unless in public function) occupied mainly with himself.

are intended for, and as what will naturally and of course have some influence. The particular place assigned to it by nature, what authority it has, and how great influence it ought to have, shall be hereafter considered.

From this comparison of benevolence and self-love, of our public and private affections, of the courses of life they lead to, and of the principle of reflection or conscience as respecting each of them, it is as manifest, that *we were made for society, and to promote the happiness of it ; as that we were intended to take care of our own life, and health, and private good.*

§ 10. *Other multifarious bonds of sentiment and action between man and man.*

And from this whole review must be given a different draught of human nature from what we are often presented with. Mankind are by nature so closely united, there is such a correspondence between the inward sensations of one man and those of another, that disgrace is as much avoided as bodily pain, and to be the object of esteem and love as much desired as any external goods: and in many particular cases, persons are carried on to do good to others, as the end their affection tends to and rests in ; and manifest that they find real satisfaction and enjoyment in this course of behaviour. There is such a natural principle of attraction in man towards man, that having trod the same tract of land, having breathed in the same climate, barely having been born in the same artificial district or division, becomes the occasion of contracting acquaintances and familiarities many years after : for any thing may serve the purpose. Thus relations merely nominal are sought and invented, not by governors, but by the lowest of the people ; which are found sufficient to hold mankind together in little fraternities and copartnerships : weak ties indeed, and what may afford fund enough for ridicule, if they are absurdly considered as the real principles of that union : but they are in truth merely the occasions, as any thing may be of any thing, upon which our nature carries us on according to its own previous bent and bias[1]; which occasions therefore would be nothing at all, were there not this prior disposition and bias of nature. Men are so much one body, that in a peculiar manner they feel for each other, shame, sudden danger, resentment, honour, prosperity, distress; one or another, or all of these, from the social nature in general, from benevolence, upon the occasion of natural relation, acquaintance, protection, dependence; each of these being distinct cements of society. And therefore to have no restraint from, no regard to others in our behaviour, is the speculative absurdity of considering ourselves as single and independent, as having nothing in our nature which has respect to our fellow-creatures, reduced to action and practice. And this is the same absurdity, as to suppose a hand, or any part to have no natural respect to any other, or to the whole body.

§ 11. *Malevolence is contrary to nature, like self-hatred.*

But allowing all this, it may be asked, 'Has not man dispositions and principles within, which lead him to do evil to others, as well as to do good? Whence come the many miseries else, which men are the authors and instruments of to each other?' These questions, so far as they relate to the foregoing discourse, may be answered by asking, Has not man also dispositions and principles within, which lead him to do evil to himself, as well as good? Whence come the many miseries else, sickness, pain, and death, which men are the instruments and authors of to themselves?

It may be thought more easy to answer one of these questions than the other, but the answer to both is really the same; that mankind have ungoverned passions which they will gratify at any rate, as well to the injury of others, as in contradiction to known private interests: but that as

---

[1] 'Ut apium examina non fingendorum favorum causà congregantur, sed, cum congregabilia natura sint, fingunt favos; sic homines, et multo etiam magis, natura congregati, adhibent agendi cogitandique solertiam.' Cic. *De Officiis*, i. 44.

there is no such thing as self-hatred, so neither is there any such thing as ill-will[1] in one man towards another, emulation and resentment being away; whereas there is plainly benevolence or good-will: there is no such thing as love of injustice, oppression, treachery, ingratitude; but only eager desires after such and such external goods; which, according to a very ancient observation, the most abandoned would choose to obtain by innocent means, if they were as easy, and as effectual to their end: that even emulation and resentment, by any one who will consider what these passions really are in nature[e], will be found nothing to the purpose of this objection.

---

[e] NOTE. *Difference between emulation and envy.* Emulation is merely the desire and hope of equality with, or superiority over others, with whom we compare ourselves. There does not appear to be any *other grief* in the natural passion, but only *that want* which is implied in desire. However this may be so strong as to be the occasion of great *grief*. To desire the attainment of this equality or superiority by the *particular means* of others being brought down to our own level, or below it, is, I think, the distinct notion of envy. From whence it is easy to see, that the real end, which the natural passion, emulation, and which the unlawful one, envy, aims at, is exactly the same[2]; namely, that equality or superiority: and consequently, that to do mischief is not the end of envy, but merely the means it makes use of to attain this end. As to resentment, see the eighth sermon.

---

[1] Comp. Analogy, I. iii. 19. See Milton, *Par. Lost*, i. 490-2:

'Belial came last, than whom a spirit more lewd
Fell not from heaven, or more gross to love
Vice for itself.'

Comp. Serm. ix. 18. The state is one to which the spirit at length approximates in extreme cases under judicial blindness.

[2] May not this be doubted? Emulation grudges nothing, only desires: is as much gratified in taking a class by the side of another, as in gaining, and so taking away from him, a prize. But envy, the basest perhaps among the passions, desires another to be deprived of something, and that not exclusively or always in order that we may obtain it. It is λύπη τις ἐπὶ εὐπραγίᾳ φαινομένῃ τῶν εἰρημένων ἀγαθῶν, περὶ τοὺς ὁμοίους, μὴ ἵνα τι αὐτῷ, ἀλλὰ δι' ἐκείνους. Aristot. *Rhet.* II. x. 1. And further: ἐπιεικές ἐστιν ὁ ζῆλος, καὶ ἐπιεικῶν· τὸ δὲ φθονεῖν φαῦλον καὶ φαύλων· ὁ μὲν γὰρ αὑτὸν παρασκευάζει διὰ τὸν ζῆλον τυγχάνειν τῶν ἀγαθῶν, ὁ δέ, τὸν πλησίον μὴ

§ 12. *We have powers, besides self-love and benevolence, which primarily tend to good.*

And that the principles and passions in the mind of man, which are distinct both from self-love and benevolence[1], primarily and most directly lead to right behaviour with regard to others as well as himself, and only secondarily and accidentally to what is evil. Thus, though men, to avoid the shame of one villainy, are sometimes guilty of a greater, yet it is easy to see, that the original tendency of shame is to prevent the doing of shameful actions; and its leading men to conceal such actions when done, is only in consequence of their being done; i.e. of the passion's not having answered its first end.

§ 13. *Natural affection may indeed fail, as towards others or ourselves.*

If it be said, that there are persons in the world, who are in great measure without the natural affections towards their fellow-creatures: there are likewise instances of persons without the common natural affections to themselves: but the nature of man is not to be judged of by either of these, but by what appears in the common world, in the bulk of mankind.

§ 14. *We offend as much against self as against society.*

I am afraid it would be thought very strange, if to confirm the truth of this account of human nature, and make out the justness of the foregoing comparison, it should be added, that, from what appears, men in fact as much and as often contradict that *part* of their nature which respects *self*, and which leads them to their *own private* good and happiness; as they contradict that *part* of it which respects

---

ἔχειν διὰ τὸν φθόνον. *Ibid.* xi. 1. To bring envy within Butler's account, it seems necessary to suppose that the envious man covets for himself all possible good: but then he should covet it at all times, and not merely when his neighbour is getting something.

[1] For example: good husbandry, the love of order, liberality.

society, and tends to *public* good : that there are as few persons, who attain the greatest satisfaction and enjoyment which they might attain in the present world, as who do the greatest good to others which they might do : nay, that there are as few who can be said really and in earnest to aim at one, as at the other.

§ 15. *But for religion, men in general would pursue objects known to be disappointing.*

Take a survey of mankind : the world in general, the good and bad, almost without exception, equally are agreed, that were religion out of the case, the happiness of the present life would consist in a manner wholly in riches, honours, sensual gratifications; insomuch that one scarce hears a reflection made upon prudence, life, conduct, but upon this supposition. Yet on the contrary, that persons in the greatest affluence of fortune are no happier than such as have only a competency; that the cares and disappointments of ambition for the most part far exceed the satisfactions of it; as also the miserable intervals of intemperance and excess, and the many untimely deaths occasioned by a dissolute course of life : these things are all seen, acknowledged, by every one acknowledged ; but are thought no objections against, though they expressly contradict, this universal principle, that the happiness of the present life consists in one or other of them. Whence is all this absurdity and contradiction ? Is not the middle way obvious ? Can any thing be more manifest, than that the happiness of life consists in these possessed and enjoyed only to a certain degree [1]; that to pursue them beyond this degree, is always attended with more inconvenience than advantage to a man's self, and often with extreme misery and unhappiness. Whence then, I say, is all this absurdity and contradiction ? Is it really the result of consideration in mankind, how they may become most easy to them-

---

[1] Τί οὖν κωλύει λέγειν εὐδαίμονα τὸν κατ' ἀρετὴν τελείαν ἐνεργοῦντα, καὶ τοῖς ἐκτὸς ἀγαθοῖς ἱκανῶς κεχορηγημένον, μὴ τὸν τυχόντα χρόνον, ἀλλὰ τέλειον βίον ; Aristot. *Eth. Nic.* I. x. 15.

selves, most free from care, and enjoy the chief happiness attainable in this world? Or is it not manifestly owing either to this, that they have not cool and reasonable concern enough for themselves to consider wherein their chief happiness in the present life consists; or else, if they do consider it, that they will not act conformably to what is the result of that consideration: i. e. reasonable concern for themselves, or cool self-love is prevailed over by passion and appetite. So that from what appears, there is no ground to assert that those principles in the nature of man, which most directly lead to promote the good of our fellow-creatures, are more generally or in a greater degree violated, than those, which most directly lead us to promote our own private good and happiness.

§ 16. *We violate our nature as to self, no less than as to others.*

The sum of the whole is plainly this. The nature of man considered in his single capacity, and with respect only to the present world, is adapted and leads him to attain the greatest happiness he can for himself in the present world. The nature of man considered in his public or social capacity leads him to a right behaviour in society, to that course of life which we call virtue. Men follow or obey their nature in both these capacities and respects to a certain degree, but not entirely: their actions do not come up to the whole of what their nature leads them to in either of these capacities or respects: and they often violate their nature in both, i. e. as they neglect the duties they owe to their fellow-creatures, to which their nature leads them; and are injurious, to which their nature is abhorrent: so there is a manifest negligence in men of their real happiness or interest in the present world, when that interest is inconsistent with a present gratification; for the sake of which they negligently, nay, even knowingly, are the authors and instruments of their own misery and ruin. Thus they are as often unjust to themselves as to others, and for the most part are equally so to both by the same actions.

SERMON II, III

UPON HUMAN NATURE

—◆◆—

For when the Gentiles, which have not the law, do by nature the things contained in the law, these, having not the law, are a law unto themselves.—ROMANS ii. 14.

—◆◆—

SERMON II

§ 1. *Adaptations of nature indicate the Maker's purpose.*

AS speculative truth admits of different kinds of proof, so likewise moral obligations may be shown by different methods. If the real nature of any creature leads him and is adapted to such and such purposes only, or more than to any other; this is a reason to believe the Author of that nature intended it for those purposes. Thus there is no doubt the eye was intended for us to see with. And the more complex any constitution is, and the greater variety of parts there are which thus tend to some one end, the stronger is the proof that such end was designed.

§ 2. *Double caution:* (a) *not to take the abnormal as the normal;* (b) *not to dethrone conscience.*

However, when the inward frame of man is considered as any guide in morals, the utmost caution must be used that none make peculiarities in their own temper, or any thing which is the effect of particular customs, though observable in several, the standard of what is common to the species;

and above all, that the highest principle be not forgot or excluded, that to which belongs the adjustment and correction of all other inward movements and affections: which principle will of course have some influence, but which being in nature supreme, as shall now be shown, ought to preside over and govern all the rest. The difficulty of rightly observing the two former cautions; the appearance there is of some small diversity amongst mankind with respect to this faculty, with respect to their natural sense of moral good and evil; and the attention necessary to survey with any exactness what passes within, have occasioned that it is not so much agreed what is the standard of the internal nature of man, as of his external form. Neither is this last exactly settled[1]. Yet we understand one another when we speak of the shape of a human body: so likewise we do when we speak of the heart and inward principles, how far soever the standard is from being exact or precisely fixed. There is therefore ground for an attempt of showing men to themselves, of showing them what course of life and behaviour their real nature points out and would lead them to.

§ 3. *The purpose, e. g., of shame is as plain as the purpose of the eye.*

Now obligations of virtue shown, and motives to the practice of it enforced, from a review of the nature of man, are to be considered as an appeal to each particular person's heart and natural conscience: as the external senses are appealed to for the proof of things cognizable by them. Since then our inward feelings, and the perceptions we receive from our external senses, are equally real; to argue

---

[1] Does he refer to the opinions of those who hold that beauty is a floating opinion and rests on no foundation of principle? In our age Butler would have seen the works of Hay, Story, and others, who seek to establish relations between beauty and rules of line and form: perhaps not without hope as to the ultimate result. For his own belief in a substantive idea of beauty, see Serm. xi. 21. The strange power called fashion founds itself upon the negation of all principles of beauty. Fashion seems to be a modern invention: either it did not exist or it was far less traceable among the Greeks.

from the former to life and conduct is as little liable to exception, as to argue from the latter to absolute speculative truth. A man can as little doubt whether his eyes were given him to see with, as he can doubt of the truth of the science of *optics*, deduced from ocular experiments. And allowing the inward feeling, shame; a man can as little doubt whether it was given him to prevent his doing shameful actions, as he can doubt whether his eyes were given him to guide his steps. And as to these inward feelings themselves; that they are real, that man has in his nature passions and affections, can no more be questioned, than that he has external senses. Neither can the former be wholly mistaken; though to a certain degree liable to greater mistakes than the latter [1].

§ 4. *We have no propension to evil corresponding with that to social good.*

There can be no doubt but that several propensions or instincts, several principles in the heart of man, carry him to society, and to contribute to the happiness of it, in a sense and a manner in which no inward principle leads him to evil. These principles, propensions, or instincts which lead him to do good, are approved of by a certain faculty within, quite distinct from these propensions themselves. All this hath been fully made out in the foregoing discourse.

§ 5. *A cavil.* '*These follow nature indifferently, be it passion or be it conscience.*'

But it may be said, 'What is all this, though true, to the purpose of virtue and religion? these require, not only that we do good to others, when we are led this way, by benevolence or reflection, happening to be stronger than other

---

[1] 'We can see the wisest and best reasons why this is permitted to be so. The correction of mistakes in the former case may be more safely left to time and experience, and in fact such correction forms and strengthens the character; whereas mistakes in the latter would be more immediately attended with danger, or perhaps destruction, to the individual.' Carmichael.

principles, passions, or appetites; but likewise that the *whole* character be formed upon thought and reflection; that *every* action be directed by some determinate rule, some other rule than the strength and prevalency of any principle or passion. What sign is there in our nature (for the inquiry is only about what is to be collected from thence) that this was intended by its Author? Or how does so various and fickle a temper as that of man appear adapted thereto? It may indeed be absurd and unnatural for men to act without any reflection; nay, without regard to that particular kind of reflection which you call conscience; because this does belong to our nature. For as there never was a man but who approved one place, prospect, building, before another: so it does not appear that there ever was a man who would not have approved an action of humanity rather than of cruelty; interest and passion being quite out of the case. But interest and passion do come in, and are often too strong for and prevail over reflection and conscience. Now as brutes have various instincts, by which they are carried on to the end the Author of their nature intended them for: is not man in the same condition; with this difference only, that to his instincts (i.e. appetites and passions) is added the principle of reflection or conscience? And as brutes act agreeably to their nature, in following that principle or particular instinct which for the present is strongest in them: does not man likewise act agreeably to his nature, or obey the law of his creation, by following that principle, be it passion or conscience, which for the present happens to be strongest in him[1]? Thus

---

[1] Carmichael quotes the following passage from Wollaston's *Religion of Nature delineated*: 'They who place all in following nature, if they mean by that phrase acting according to the natures of things (that is, treating things as being what they in nature are, or according to truth), say what is right. But this does not seem to be their meaning. And if it is only that a man must follow his own nature, since his nature is not purely rational, but there is a part of him which he has in common with brutes, they appoint him a guide which, I fear, will mislead him, this being commonly more likely to prevail than the rational part. At best this talk is loose.'

Publishing before Butler, Wollaston in this passage does not aim his criticism at Butler's statement of the case.

different men are by their particular nature hurried on to pursue honour, or riches, or pleasure: there are also persons whose temper leads them in an uncommon degree to kindness, compassion, doing good to their fellow-creatures: as there are others who are given to suspend their judgment, to weigh and consider things, and to act upon thought and reflection. Let every one then quietly follow his nature; as passion, reflection, appetite, the several parts of it, happen to be strongest: but let not the man of virtue take upon him to blame the ambitious, the covetous, the dissolute; since these equally with him obey and follow their nature. Thus, as in some cases we follow our nature in doing the works *contained in the law*, so in other cases we follow nature in doing contrary.'

§ 6. '*Nature*' *is construed in diverse senses.*

Now all this licentious talk entirely goes upon a supposition, that men follow their nature in the same sense, in violating the known rules of justice and honesty for the sake of a present gratification, as they do in following those rules when they have no temptation to the contrary. And if this were true, that could not be so which St. Paul asserts, that men are *by nature a law to themselves*. If by following nature were meant only acting as we please, it would indeed be ridiculous to speak of nature as any guide in morals: nay the very mention of deviating from nature would be absurd; and the mention of following it, when spoken by way of distinction, would absolutely have no meaning. For did ever any one act otherwise than as he pleased? And yet the ancients speak of deviating from nature as vice; and of following nature so much as a distinction, that according to them the perfection of virtue consists therein. So that language itself should teach people another sense to the words *following nature*, than barely acting as we please. Let it however be observed, that though the words *human nature* are to be explained, yet the real question of this discourse is not concerning the meaning of words, any otherwise than as the explanation of them may be needful to make out and explain the assertion, that *every man is naturally a law to himself,* that *every one may find within himself the rule of right, and obligations to follow it.* This St. Paul affirms in the words of the text, and this the foregoing objection really denies by seeming to allow it. And the objection will be fully answered, and the text before us explained, by observing that *nature* is considered in different views, and the word used in different senses; and by showing in what view it is considered, and in what sense the word is used, when intended to express and signify that which is the guide of life, that by which men are a law to themselves. I say, the explanation of the term will be sufficient, because from thence it will appear, that in some senses of the word *nature* cannot be, but that in another sense it manifestly is, a law to us.

§ 7. *With conflicting feelings, we may at once follow and contradict*

[I.] By nature is often meant no more than some principle in man, without regard either to the kind or degree of it. Thus the passion of anger, and the affection of parents to their children, would be called equally *natural.* And as the same person hath often contrary principles, which at the same time draw contrary ways, he may by the same action both follow and contradict his nature in this sense of the word; he may follow one passion and contradict another.

§ 8. *Or may simply follow the strongest impulse,*

[II.] *Nature* is frequently spoken of as consisting in those passions which are strongest, and most influence the actions; which being vicious ones, mankind is in this sense naturally vicious, or vicious by nature. Thus St. Paul says of the Gentiles, *who were dead in trespasses and sins, and walked according to the spirit of disobedience, that they were by nature the children of wrath*[a]. They could be no otherwise *children of wrath* by nature, than they were vicious by nature.

---

[a] Ephes. ii. 3.

§ 9. *But also there is a righteous law written in our nature.*

Here then are two different senses of the word *nature*, in neither of which men can at all be said to be a law to themselves. They are mentioned only to be excluded; to prevent their being confounded, as the latter is in the objection, with another sense of it, which is now to be inquired after and explained.

[III.] The apostle asserts, that the Gentiles *do by NATURE the things contained in the law.* Nature is indeed here put by way of distinction from revelation, but yet it is not a mere negative. He intends to express more than that by which they *did not,* that by which they *did* the works of the law; namely, by *nature.* It is plain the meaning of the word is not the same in this passage as in the former, where it is spoken of as evil; for in this latter it is spoken of as good; as that by which they acted, or might have acted virtuously. What that is in man by which he is *naturally a law to himself,* is explained in the following words: *which show the work of the law written in their hearts, their consciences also bearing witness, and their thoughts the meanwhile accusing or else excusing one another.* If there be a distinction to be made between the *works written in their hearts,* and the *witness of conscience;* by the former must be meant the natural disposition to kindness and compassion, to do what is of good report, to which this apostle often refers: that part of the nature of man, treated of in the foregoing discourse, which with very little reflection and of course leads him to society, and by means of which he naturally acts a just and good part in it, unless other passions or interest lead him astray.

§ 10. *To decide the true sense, conscience magisterially intervenes.*

Yet since other passions, and regards to private interest, which lead us (though indirectly, yet they lead us) astray, are themselves in a degree equally natural, and often most prevalent; and since we have no method of seeing the particular degrees in which one or the other is placed in us by nature; it is plain the former, considered merely as natural, good and right as they are, can no more be a law to us than the latter. But there is a superior principle of reflection or conscience in every man, which distinguishes between the internal principles of his heart, as well as his external actions: which passes judgment upon himself and them; pronounces determinately some actions to be in themselves just, right, good; others to be in themselves evil, wrong, unjust: which, without being consulted, without being advised with, magisterially exerts itself, and approves or condemns him the doer of them accordingly: and which, if not forcibly stopped, naturally and always of course goes on to anticipate a higher and more effectual sentence, which shall hereafter second and affirm its own. But this part of the office of conscience is beyond my present design explicitly to consider.

§ 11. *This supreme faculty makes us moral agents;*

It is by this faculty, natural to man, that he is a moral agent, that he is a law to himself: by this faculty, I say, not to be considered merely as a principle in his heart, which is to have some influence as well as others; but considered as a faculty in kind and in nature supreme over all others, and which bears its own authority of being so.

§ 12. *And our acts natural or unnatural.*

This *prerogative*, this *natural supremacy*, of the faculty which surveys, approves or disapproves the several affections of our mind and actions of our lives, being that by which men *are a law to themselves*, their conformity or disobedience to which law of our nature renders their actions, in the highest and most proper sense, natural or unnatural; it is fit it be further explained to you: and I hope it will be so, if you will attend to the following reflections.

§ 13. *Brute, allured into a snare, contrasted with a man in like case.*

Man may act according to that principle or inclination which for the present happens to be strongest, and yet act in a way disproportionate to, and violate, his real proper nature. Suppose a brute creature by any bait to be allured into a snare, by which he is destroyed. He plainly followed the bent of his nature, leading him to gratify his appetite: there is an entire correspondence between his whole nature and such an action: such action therefore is natural. But suppose a man, foreseeing the same danger of certain ruin, should rush into it for the sake of a present gratification; he in this instance would follow his strongest desire, as did the brute creature: but there would be as manifest a disproportion, between the nature of a man and such an action, as between the meanest work of art and the skill of the greatest master in that art.

§ 14. *The contrast is established by comparing the act with the agent.*

Which disproportion arises, not from considering the action singly in *itself*, or in its *consequences;* but from *comparison* of it with the nature of the agent[1]. And since such an action is utterly disproportionate to the nature of man, it is in the strictest and most proper sense unnatural; this word expressing that disproportion. Therefore instead of the words *disproportionate to his nature*, the word *unnatural* may now be put; this being more familiar to us: but let it be observed, that it stands for the same thing precisely.

§ 15. *He contradicts not merely a part of his nature;*

Now what is it which renders such a rash action unnatural? Is it that he went against the principle of reasonable and cool self-love, considered *merely* as a part of his nature[2]? No: for if he had acted the contrary way,

---

[1] So Serm. iii. 13. Comp. Diss. ii., on Virtue, § 7.

[2] In this section, Butler speaks of self-love sometimes simply and without epithet, sometimes with: and this, too, diversely; we have

he would equally have gone against a principle, or part of his nature, namely, passion or appetite. But to deny a present appetite, from foresight that the gratification of it would end in immediate ruin or extreme misery, is by no means an unnatural action : whereas to contradict or go against cool self-love for the sake of such gratification, is so in the instance before us. Such an action then being unnatural ; and its being so not arising from a man's going against a principle or desire barely, nor in going against that principle or desire which happens for the present to be strongest ; it necessarily follows, that there must be some other difference or distinction to be made between these two principles, passion and cool self-love, than what I have yet taken notice of.

§ 16. *But prefers passion to self-love, which is superior in kind.*

And this difference, not being a difference in strength or degree, I call a difference in *nature* and in *kind*. And since, in the instance still before us, if passion[1] prevails over self-love, the consequent action is unnatural ; but if self-love prevails over passion, the action is natural : it is manifest that self-love is in human nature a superior principle to passion. This may be contradicted without violating that nature ; but the former cannot. So that, if we will act conformably to the economy of man's nature, reasonable self-love must govern. Thus, without particular consideration of conscience, we may have a clear conception of the *superior nature* of one inward principle to another ;

---

in different passages 'reasonable and cool,' 'cool' alone, and 'reasonable' alone. It seems plain (a) that all these are intended to be equivalent, and (b) that where 'self-love' stands alone, we are to consider the epithet as implied. He tells us in the *Analogy* (I. v. 38) that self-love is apt to diverge from the will of God, and that it stands in need of a corrective. This corrective is supplied by 'cool,' implying that it is reflective, not merely impulsive ; and 'reasonable,' conforming to the law of fitness, not of mere desire.

[1] The word 'passion' seems to imply in itself some degree of excess, and a loss, in a greater or less degree, of equilibrium ; and herein it differs from affection.

and see that there really is this natural superiority, quite distinct from degrees of strength and prevalency.

§ 17. *Between conscience, and passions, it is not a mere question of strength.*

Let us now take a view of the nature of man, as consisting partly of various appetites, passions, affections, and partly of the principle of reflection or conscience; leaving quite out all consideration of the different degrees of strength, in which either of them prevail, and it will further appear that there is this natural superiority of one inward principle to another, and that it is even part of the idea of reflection or conscience.

Passion or appetite implies a direct simple tendency towards such and such objects, without distinction of the means by which they are to be obtained. Consequently it will often happen there will be a desire of particular objects, in cases where they cannot be obtained without manifest injury to others. Reflection or conscience comes in, and disapproves the pursuit of them in these circumstances; but the desire remains. Which is to be obeyed, appetite or reflection? Cannot this question be answered, from the economy and constitution of human nature merely, without saying which is strongest? Or need this at all come into consideration?

§ 18. *If passion prevail, it is mere usurpation.*

Would not the question be *intelligibly* and fully answered by saying that, the principle of reflection or conscience being compared with the various appetites, passions, and affections in men, the former is manifestly superior and chief, without regard to strength? And how often soever the latter happens to prevail, it is mere *usurpation*: the former remains in nature and in kind its superior; and every instance of such prevalence of the latter is an instance of breaking in upon and violation of the constitution of man.

§ 19. *Conscience de jure claims universal rule, if we follow the law of our nature.*

All this is no more than the distinction, which every body is acquainted with, between mere power and authority[1]: only instead of being intended to express the difference between what is possible, and what is lawful in civil government; here it has been shown applicable to the several principles in the mind of man. Thus that principle, by which we survey, and either approve or disapprove our own heart, temper, and actions, is not only to be considered as what is in its turn to have some influence; which may be said of every passion, of the lowest appetites: but likewise as being superior; as from its very nature manifestly claiming superiority over all others: insomuch that you cannot form a notion of this faculty, conscience, without taking in judgment, direction, superintendency. This is a constituent part of the idea, that is, of the faculty itself: and, to preside and govern, from the very economy and constitution of man, belongs to it. Had it strength, as it has right; had it power, as it has manifest authority; it would absolutely govern the world[2].

This gives us a further view of the nature of man; shows us what course of life we were made for: not only that our real nature leads us to be influenced in some degree by reflection and conscience; but likewise in what degree we are to be influenced by it, if we will fall in with, and act agreeably to the constitution of our nature: that this faculty was placed within to be our proper governor; to direct and regulate all under principles, passions, and motives of action. This is its right and office: thus sacred is its authority. And how often soever men violate and rebelliously refuse to submit to it, for supposed interest which they cannot otherwise obtain, or for the sake of passion

---

[1] Comp. Plato, *Minos*, ii. 8 : τὸ μὲν ὀρθὸν νόμος ἐστὶ βασιλικός. Also Diss. ii. 1-3 on the nature of Virtue.

[2] With this passage we may compare the case of the ideal State supposed in the *Analogy* I. iii. 30, and its inevitable acquisition of power.

which they cannot otherwise gratify; this makes no alteration as to the *natural right* and *office* of conscience.

§ 20. *Consequence of accepting degrees of strength as the criterion of just action;*

Let us now turn this whole matter another way, and suppose there was no such thing at all as this natural supremacy of conscience; that there was no distinction to be made between one inward principle and another, but only that of strength; and see what would be the consequence.

§ 21. *As regards God,*

Consider then what is the latitude and compass of the actions of man with regard to himself, his fellow-creatures, and the Supreme Being? What are their bounds, besides that of our natural power? With respect to the two first, they are plainly no other than these: no man seeks misery as such for himself; and no one unprovoked does mischief to another for its own sake. For in every degree within these bounds, mankind knowingly from passion or wantonness bring ruin and misery upon themselves and others. And impiety and profaneness, I mean, what every one would call so who believes the being of God, have absolutely no bounds at all. Men blaspheme the Author of nature, formally and in words renounce their allegiance to their Creator. Put an instance then with respect to any one of these three. Though we should suppose profane swearing, and in general that kind of impiety now mentioned, to mean nothing, yet it implies wanton disregard and irreverence towards an infinite Being, our Creator; and is this as suitable to the nature of man, as reverence and dutiful submission of heart towards that Almighty Being?

§ 22. *As regards our neighbour.*

Or suppose a man guilty of parricide, with all the circumstances of cruelty which such an action can admit of. This action is done in consequence of its principle being for the present strongest: and if there be no difference between inward principles, but only that of strength; the strength being given, you have the whole nature of the man given, so far as it relates to this matter. The action plainly corresponds to the principle, the principle being in that degree of strength it was: it therefore corresponds to the whole nature of the man. Upon comparing the action and the whole nature, there arises no disproportion, there appears no unsuitableness between them. Thus the *murder of a father* and the *nature of man* correspond to each other, as the same nature and an act of filial duty. If there be no difference between inward principles, but only that of strength; we can make no distinction between these two actions, considered as the actions of such a creature; but in our coolest hours must approve or disapprove them equally: than which nothing can be reduced to a greater absurdity.

SERMON III

§ 1. *Human nature means a group of attributes, under one which is supreme.*

THE natural supremacy of reflection or conscience being thus established; we may from it form a distinct notion of what is meant by *human nature*, when virtue is said to consist in following it, and vice in deviating from it.

As the idea of a civil constitution implies in it united strength, various subordinations, under one direction, that of the supreme authority; the different strength of each particular member of the society not coming into the idea; whereas, if you leave out the subordination, the union, and the one direction, you destroy and lose it: so reason, several appetites, passions, and affections, prevailing in different degrees of strength, is not *that* idea or notion of *human nature*; but *that nature* consists in these several principles considered as having a natural respect to each other, in the several passions being naturally subordinate to the one superior principle of reflection or conscience[1]. Every bias, instinct, propension within, is a real part of our nature, but not the whole: add to these the superior faculty, whose office it is to adjust, manage, and preside over them, and take in this its natural superiority, and you complete the idea of human nature. And as in civil government the constitution is broken in upon, and violated by power and strength prevailing over authority; so the constitution of man is broken in upon and violated by the lower faculties or principles within prevailing over that which is in its nature supreme over them all.

§ 2. *Injustice, how more contrary to it than torture and death.*

Thus, when it is said by ancient writers, that tortures and death are not so contrary to human nature as injustice; by this to be sure is not meant, that the aversion to the former in mankind is less strong and prevalent than their aversion to the latter: but that the former is only contrary to our nature considered in a partial view, and which takes in only the lowest part of it, that which we have in common with the brutes; whereas the latter is contrary to our nature, considered in a higher sense, as a system and constitution contrary to the whole economy of man [b].

---

[b] NOTE. Every man in his physical nature is one individual single agent. He has likewise properties and principles, each of which may be considered separately, and without regard to the respects which they have to each other. Neither of these are the nature we are taking a view of. But it is the inward frame of man considered as a *system* or *constitution:* whose several parts are united, not by a physical principle of individuation, but by the respects they

The requisites are two: (a) *Entire subjection of the appetites to conscience:* (b) *Their just proportion to each other.*

---

[1] In Plato's Dialogue on the Republic, as in Butler's Sermons, the human soul is represented as a system, a constitution, an organised whole, in which the different elements have not merely their places side by side, but their places above and below each other, with their appointed offices; and virtue, or moral rightness, consists in the due operation of this constitution, the actual realisation of this organised subordination. Whewell.

§ 3. *Man hath the law of right within: contrasted with brutes.*

And from all these things put together, nothing can be more evident, than that, exclusive of revelation, man cannot be considered as a creature left by his Maker to act at random, and live at large up to the extent of his natural power, as passion, humour, wilfulness, happen to carry him; which is the condition brute creatures are in: but that *from his make, constitution, or nature, he is in the strictest and most proper sense a law to himself.* He hath the rule of right within: what is wanting is only that he honestly attend to it.

---

have to each other; the chief of which is the subjection which the appetites, passions, and particular affections have to the one supreme principle of reflection or conscience. The system or constitution is formed by and consists in these respects and this subjection. Thus the body is a *system* or *constitution:* so is a tree: so is every machine. Consider all the several parts of a tree without the natural respects they have to each other, and you have not at all the idea of a tree; but add these respects, and this gives you the idea. The body may be inpaired by sickness, a tree may decay, a machine be out of order, and yet the system and constitution of them not totally dissolved. There is plainly somewhat which answers to all this in the moral constitution of man. Whoever will consider his own nature, will see that the several appetites, passions, and particular affections, have different respects amongst themselves. They are restraints upon, and are in a proportion to each other. This proportion is just and perfect, when all those under principles are perfectly coincident with conscience, so far as their nature permits, and in all cases under its absolute and entire direction. The least excess or defect, the least alteration of the due proportions amongst themselves, or of their coincidence with conscience, though not proceeding into action, is some degree of disorder in the moral constitution. But perfection, though plainly intelligible and supposable, was never attained by any man. If the higher principle of reflection maintains its place, and as much as it can corrects that disorder, and hinders it from breaking out into action, this is all that can be expected in such a creature as man. And though the appetites and passions have not their exact due proportion to each other; though they often strive for mastery with judgment or reflection: yet, since the superiority of this principle to all others is the chief respect which forms the constitution, so far as this superiority is maintained, the character, the man, is good, worthy, virtuous.

§ 4. *The rule of right not hard for fair minds to distinguish.*

The inquiries which have been made by men of leisure, after some general rule, the conformity to, or disagreement from which, should denominate our actions good or evil, are in many respects of great service. Yet let any plain honest man, before he engages in any course of action, ask himself, Is this I am going about right, or is it wrong? Is it good, or is it evil? I do not in the least doubt, but that this question would be answered agreeably to truth and virtue, by almost any fair man in almost any circumstance.

§ 5. *Case of superstition partly excepted.*

Neither do there appear any cases which look like exceptions to this; but those of superstition, and of partiality to ourselves. Superstition may perhaps be somewhat of an exception: but partiality to ourselves is not; this being itself dishonesty. For a man to judge that to be the equitable, the moderate, the right part for him to act, which he would see to be hard, unjust, oppressive in another; this is plain vice, and can proceed only from great unfairness of mind.

§ 6. *Apart from reward and punishment, the voice of conscience obliges us to obey.*

But allowing that mankind hath the rule of right within himself, yet it may be asked, 'What obligations are we under to attend to and follow it?' I answer: it has been proved that man by his nature is a law to himself, without the particular distinct consideration of the positive sanctions of that law; the rewards and punishments which we feel, and those which from the light of reason we have ground to believe are annexed to it. The question then carries its own answer along with it. Your obligation to obey this law, is its being the law of your nature. That your conscience approves of and attests to such a course of action, is itself alone an obligation. Conscience does not only offer itself to show us the way we should walk in, but it likewise carries its own authority with it, that it is our natural guide; the guide assigned us by the Author of our nature: it therefore belongs to our condition of being, it is our duty to walk in that path, and follow this guide, without looking about to see whether we may not possibly forsake them with impunity.

§ 7. *Cavil: why not dismiss regard to others?*

However, let us hear what is to be said against obeying this law of our nature. And the sum is no more than this: 'Why should we be concerned about any thing out of and beyond ourselves? If we do find within ourselves regards to others, and restraints of we know not how many different kinds; yet these being embarrassments, and hindering us from going the nearest way to our own good, why should we not endeavour to suppress and get over them?'

§ 8. *Enjoyment cannot be had in mere self-regard.*

Thus people go on with words, which, when applied to human nature, and the condition in which it is placed in this world, have really no meaning. For does not all this kind of talk go upon supposition, that our happiness in this world consists in somewhat quite distinct from regards to others; and that it is the privilege of vice to be without restraint or confinement? Whereas, on the contrary, the enjoyments, in a manner all the common enjoyments of life, even the pleasures of vice, depend upon these regards of one kind or another to our fellow-creatures. Throw off all regards to others, and we should be quite indifferent to infamy and to honour; there could be no such thing at all as ambition; and scarce any such thing as covetousness; for we should likewise be equally indifferent to the disgrace of poverty, the several neglects and kinds of contempt which accompany this state; and to the reputation of riches, the regard and respect they usually procure[1]. Neither is restraint by any means peculiar to one course

---

[1] Yet perhaps not so absolutely to the pinch of poverty, and to the enjoyments procured by riches.

of life: but our very nature, exclusive of conscience and our condition, lays us under an absolute necessity of it. We cannot gain any end whatever without being confined to the proper means, which is often the most painful and uneasy confinement. And in numberless instances a present appetite cannot be gratified without such apparent and immediate ruin and misery, that the most dissolute man in the world chooses to forego the pleasure, rather than endure the pain.

§ 9. *Cavil, as amended, yields the main ground.*

Is the meaning then, to indulge those regards to our fellow-creatures, and submit to those restraints, which upon the whole are attended with more satisfaction than uneasiness, and get over only those which bring more uneasiness and inconvenience than satisfaction? 'Doubtless this was our meaning.' You have changed sides then. Keep to this; be consistent with yourselves; and you and the men of virtue are *in general* perfectly agreed.

§ 10. *Virtues that give more satisfaction than vices: and have regard to others.*

But let us take care and avoid mistakes. Let it not be taken for granted that the temper of envy, rage, resentment, yields greater delight than meekness, forgiveness, compassion, and good-will[1]: especially when it is acknowledged that rage, envy, resentment, are in themselves mere misery; and the satisfaction arising from the indulgence of them is little more than relief from that misery; whereas the temper of compassion and benevolence is itself delightful; and the indulgence of it, by doing good, affords new positive delight and enjoyment. Let it not be taken for granted, that the satisfaction arising from the reputation of riches and power, however obtained, and from the respect paid to them, is greater than the satisfaction arising from the reputation of justice, honesty, charity, and the esteem

---

[1] On the smallness of the satisfactions derivable from vice, see *Analogy*, I. iii. 7, vii. 12.

which is universally acknowledged to be their due. And if it be doubtful which of these satisfactions is the greatest, as there are persons who think neither of them very considerable, yet there can be no doubt concerning ambition and covetousness, virtue and a good mind, considered in themselves, and as leading to different courses of life; there can, I say, be no doubt, which temper and which course is attended with most peace and tranquillity of mind, which with most perplexity, vexation, and inconvenience. And both the virtues and vices which have been now mentioned, do in a manner equally imply in them regards of one kind or another to our fellow-creatures.

§ 11. *Other pains of vice.*

And with respect to restraint and confinement: whoever will consider the restraints from fear and shame, the dissimulation, mean arts of concealment, servile compliances, one or other of which belong to almost every course of vice, will soon be convinced that the man of virtue is by no means upon a disadvantage in this respect. How many instances are there in which men feel and own and cry aloud under the chains of vice with which they are enthralled, and which yet they will not shake off? How many instances, in which persons manifestly go through more pains and self-denial to gratify a vicious passion, than would have been necessary to the conquest of it? To this is to be added, that when virtue is become habitual, when the temper of it is acquired, what was before confinement ceases to be so, by becoming choice and delight. Whatever restraint and guard upon ourselves may be needful to unlearn any unnatural distortion or odd gesture; yet, in all propriety of speech, natural behaviour must be the most easy and unrestrained[1]. It is manifest that, in the common course of life, there is seldom any inconsistency between our duty and what is *called* interest: it is much seldomer

---

[1] Quintil. *Inst. Orat.* xii. 11: 'Nam, ut aqua piscibus, ut sicca terrenis, circumfusus nobis volucribus spiritus, convenit; ita certè facilius esse oportebat, secundum naturam, quam contra eam vivere.'

that there is an inconsistency between duty and what is really our present interest; meaning by interest, happiness and satisfaction.

§ 12. *Self-love coincides with virtue: exceptions only partial and temporary.*

Self-love then, though confined to the interest of the present world, does in general perfectly coincide with virtue; and leads us to one and the same course of life. But, whatever exceptions there are to this, which are much fewer than they are commonly thought, all shall be set right at the final distribution of things. It is a manifest absurdity to suppose evil prevailing finally over good, under the conduct and administration of a perfect Mind.

§ 13. *Summary of the argument of Sermon III.*

The whole argument, which I have been now insisting upon, may be thus summed up, and given you in one view. The nature of man is adapted to some course of action or other. Upon comparing some actions with this nature, they appear suitable and correspondent to it: from comparison of other actions with the same nature, there arises to our view some unsuitableness or disproportion. The correspondence of actions to the nature of the agent renders them natural: their disproportion to it, unnatural. That an action is correspondent to the nature of the agent, does not arise from its being agreeable to the principle which happens to be the strongest: for it may be so, and yet be quite disproportionate to the nature of the agent. The correspondence therefore, or disproportion, arises from somewhat else. This can be nothing but a difference in nature and kind, altogether distinct from strength, between the inward principles. Some then are in nature and kind superior to others. And the correspondence arises from the action being conformable to the higher principle; and the unsuitableness from its being contrary to it. Reasonable self-love and conscience are the chief or superior principles in the nature of man: because an action may be suitable to this nature, though all other principles be violated; but becomes unsuitable, if either of those are[1]. Conscience and self-love, if we understand our true happiness, always lead us the same way. Duty and interest are perfectly coincident; for the most part in this world, but entirely and in every instance if we take in the future, and the whole; this being implied in the notion of a good and perfect administration of things. Thus they who have been so wise in their generation as to regard only their own supposed interest, at the expense and to the injury of others, shall at last find, that he who has given up all the advantages of the present world, rather than violate his conscience and the relations of life, has infinitely better provided for himself, and secured his own interest and happiness.

---

[1] As, in the system of Butler, reasonable self-love is held to be of the nature of virtue, and duty to coincide with interest, there is no direct disparagement to conscience in assigning to it a place by the side of conscience, in respect of superiority to passions and affections. But Butler could hardly mean to predicate of self-love that it was, like conscience, a judicial faculty; or was invested with a like sovereignty.

SERMON IV

UPON THE GOVERNMENT OF THE TONGUE

—•—

If any man among you seem to be religious, and bridleth not his tongue, but deceiveth his own heart, this man's religion is vain.— JAMES i. 26.

—••—

§ 1. *Semblance of Religion, without rule over the tongue, is vain.*

THE translation of this text would be more determinate by being more literal, thus: *If any man among you seemeth to be religious, not bridling his tongue, but deceiving his own heart, this man's religion is vain.* This determines that the words, *but deceiveth his own heart,* are not put in opposition to, *seemeth to be religious,* but to, *bridleth not his tongue.* The certain determinate meaning of the text then being, that he who seemeth to be religious, and bridleth not his tongue, but in that particular deceiveth his own heart, this man's religion is vain; we may observe somewhat very forcible and expressive in these words of St. James. As if the apostle had said, No man surely can make any pretences to religion, who does not at least believe that he bridleth his tongue: if he puts on any appearance or face of religion, and yet does not govern his tongue, he must surely deceive himself in that particular, and think he does: and whoever is so unhappy as to deceive himself in this, to imagine he keeps that unruly faculty in due subjection, when indeed he does not, whatever the other part of his life be, his religion is vain; the government of the tongue being a most material restraint which virtue lays us under: without it no man can be truly religious.

In treating upon this subject, I will consider;—

§ 2. *Partition.*

First, What is the general vice or fault here referred to: or what disposition in men is supposed in moral reflections and precepts concerning *bridling the tongue.*

Secondly, When it may be said of any one, that he has a due government over himself in this respect.

§ 3. *The evil struck at is talkativeness.*

[I.] Now the fault referred to, and the disposition supposed, in precepts and reflections concerning the government of the tongue, is not evil-speaking from malice, nor lying or bearing false witness from indirect selfish designs. The disposition to these, and the actual vices themselves, all come under other subjects. The tongue may be employed about, and made to serve all the purposes of vice, in tempting and deceiving, in perjury and injustice. But the thing here supposed and referred to, is talkativeness: a disposition to be talking, abstracted from the consideration of what is to be said; with very little or no regard to, or thought of doing, either good or harm. And let not any imagine this to be a slight matter, and that it deserves not to have so great weight laid upon it; till he has considered, what evil is implied in it, and the bad effects which follow from it. It is perhaps true, that they who are addicted to this folly would choose to confine themselves to trifles and indifferent subjects, and so intend only to be guilty of being impertinent: but as they cannot go on for ever talking of nothing, as common matters will not afford a sufficient fund for perpetual continued discourse;

§ 4. *Which introduces defamation, scandal, figments.*

when subjects of this kind are exhausted, they will go on to defamation, scandal, divulging of secrets, their own secrets as well as those of others, any thing rather than be silent. They are plainly hurried on in the heat of their talk to say quite different things from what they first intended, and which they afterwards wish unsaid : or improper things, which they had no other end in saying, but only to afford employment to their tongue. And if these people expect to be heard and regarded, for there are some content merely with talking, they will invent, to engage your attention : and, when they have heard the least imperfect hint of an affair, they will out of their own head add the circumstances of time and place, and other matters to make out their story, and give the appearance of probability to it : not that they have any concern about being believed, otherwise than as a means of being heard. The thing is, to engage your attention ; to take you up wholly for the present time : what reflections will be made afterwards, is in truth the least of their thoughts. And further, when persons, who indulge themselves in these liberties of the tongue, are in any degree offended with another, as little disgusts and misunderstandings will be, they allow themselves to defame and revile such an one without any moderation or bounds ; though the offence is so very slight, that they themselves would not do, nor perhaps wish him an injury in any other way. And in this case the scandal and revilings are chiefly owing to talkativeness, and not bridling their tongue ; and so come under our present subject. The least occasion in the world will make the humour break out in this particular way, or in another. It is like a torrent, which must and will flow ; but the least thing imaginable will first of all give it either this or another direction, turn it into this or that channel : or like a fire ; the nature of which, when in a heap of combustible matter, is to spread and lay waste all around ; but any one of a thousand little accidents will occasion it to break out first either in this or another particular part.

§ 5. *Not by premeditation ; but the fruit of talking for talking's sake :*

The subject then before us, though it does run up into, and can scarce be treated as entirely distinct from all others; yet it needs not be so much mixed or blended with them as it often is. Every faculty and power may be used as the instrument of premeditated vice and wickedness, merely as the most proper and effectual means of executing such designs. But if a man, from deep malice and desire of revenge, should meditate a falsehood with a settled design to ruin his neighbour's reputation, and should with great coolness and deliberation spread it; nobody would choose to say of such an one, that he had no government of his tongue. A man may use the faculty of speech as an instrument of false witness, who yet has so entire a command over that faculty, as never to speak but from forethought and cool design. Here the crime is injustice and perjury: and, strictly speaking, no more belongs to the present subject, than perjury and injustice in any other way. But there is such a thing as a disposition to be talking for its own sake; from which persons often say any thing, good or bad, of others, merely as a subject of discourse, according to the particular temper they themselves happen to be in, and to pass away the present time.

§ 6. *And of eager thirst for attention.*

There is likewise to be observed in persons such a strong and eager desire of engaging attention to what they say, that they will speak good or evil, truth or otherwise, merely as one or the other seems to be most hearkened to: and this, though it is sometimes joined, is not the same with the desire of being thought important and men of consequence. There is in some such a disposition to be talking, that an offence of the slightest kind, and such as would not raise any other resentment, yet raises, if I may so speak, the resentment of the tongue, put it into a flame, into the most ungovernable motions. This outrage, when the person it respects is present, we distinguish in the lower rank of people by a peculiar term: and let it be observed, that though the decencies of behaviour are a little kept, the same outrage and virulence, indulged when he is absent, is an offence of the same kind. But not to distinguish any further in this manner: men run into faults and follies, which cannot so properly be referred to any one general head as this, that they have not a due government over their tongue.

§ 7. *Not praising and blaming according to desert, it perverts equity.*

And this unrestrained volubility and wantonness of speech is the occasion of numberless evils and vexations in life. It begets resentment in him who is the subject of it; sows the seeds of strife and dissension amongst others; and inflames little disgusts and offences, which if let alone would wear away of themselves: it is often of as bad effect upon the good name of others, as deep envy or malice: and, to say the least of it in this respect, it destroys and perverts a certain equity of the utmost importance to society to be observed; namely, that praise and dispraise, a good or bad character, should always be bestowed according to desert. The tongue used in such a licentious manner is like a sword in the hand of a madman; it is employed at random, it can scarce possibly do any good, and for the most part does a world of mischief; and implies not only great folly and a trifling spirit, but great viciousness of mind, great indifference to truth and falsity, and to the reputation, welfare, and good of others. So much reason is there for what St. James says of the tongue, "*It is a fire, a world of iniquity, it defileth the whole body, setteth on fire the course of nature, and is itself set on fire of hell.* This is the faculty or disposition which we are required to keep a guard upon: these are the vices and follies it runs into, when not kept under due restraint.

§ 8. *The tongue given us for pleasure as well as necessary use.*

[II.] Wherein the due government of the tongue consists, or when it may be said of any one in a moral and religious sense that he *bridleth his tongue*, I come now to consider.

---

[a] Chap. iii. ver. 6.

The due and proper use of any natural faculty or power, is to be judged of by the end and design for which it was given us. The chief purpose, for which the faculty of speech was given to man, is plainly that we might communicate our thoughts to each other, in order to carry on the affairs of the world; for business, and for our improvement in knowledge and learning. But the good Author of our nature designed us not only necessaries, but likewise enjoyment and satisfaction, in that being he hath graciously given, and in that condition of life he hath placed us in. There are secondary uses of our faculties: they administer to delight, as well as to necessity: and as they are equally adapted to both, there is no doubt but he intended them for our gratification, as well as for the support and continuance of our being. The secondary use of speech is to please and be entertaining to each other in conversation. This is in every respect allowable and right: it unites men closer in alliances and friendships; gives us a fellow-feeling of the prosperity and unhappiness of each other; and is in several respects serviceable to virtue, and to promote good behaviour in the world. And provided there be not too much time spent in it, if it were considered only in the way of gratification and delight, men must have strange notions of God and of religion, to think that he can be offended with it, or that it is any way inconsistent with the strictest virtue. But the truth is, such sort of conversation, though it has no particular good tendency, yet it has a general good one: it is social and friendly, and tends to promote humanity, good-nature, and civility.

§ 9. *Fraught with peril: but this is avoidable;*

As the end and use, so likewise the abuse of speech, relates to the one or other of these; either to business, or to conversation. As to the former; deceit in the management of business and affairs does not properly belong to the subject now before us: though one may just mention that multitude, that endless number of words, with which business is perplexed; when a much fewer would, as it

should seem, better serve the purpose: but this must be
left to those who understand the matter. The government
of the tongue, considered as a subject of itself, relates
chiefly to conversation; to that kind of discourse which
usually fills up the time spent in friendly meetings, and
visits of civility. And the danger is, lest persons entertain
themselves and others at the expense of their wisdom and
their virtue, and to the injury or offence of their neighbour.
If they will observe and keep clear of these, they may be as
free, and easy, and unreserved, as they can desire.

§ 10. *As is the instinct of mere excess in talk.*

The cautions to be given for avoiding these dangers, and
to render conversation innocent and agreeable, fall under
the following particulars: silence; talking of indifferent
things; and, which makes up too great a part of conversation, giving of characters, speaking well or evil of others.

The Wise Man observes, that *there is a time to speak, and
a time to keep silence.* One meets with people in the world,
who seem never to have made the last of these observations.
And yet these great talkers do not at all speak from their
having any thing to say, as every sentence shows, but only
from their inclination to be talking. Their conversation is
merely an exercise of the tongue: no other human faculty
has any share in it. It is strange these persons can help
reflecting, that unless they have in truth a superior capacity,
and are in an extraordinary manner furnished for conversation; if they are entertaining, it is at their own
expense. Is it possible, that it should never come into
people's thoughts to suspect, whether or no it be to their
advantage to show so very much of themselves? *O that you
would altogether hold your peace, and it should be your
wisdom* [b]. Remember likewise there are persons who love
fewer words, an inoffensive sort of people, and who deserve
some regard, though of too still and composed tempers for
you. Of this number was the Son of Sirach: for he plainly
speaks from experience, when he says, *As hills of sand are to*

---

[b] Job xiii.

the steps of the aged, so is one of many words to a quiet man. But one would think it should be obvious to every one, that when they are in company with their superiors of any kind, in years, knowledge, and experience; when proper and useful subjects are discoursed of, which they cannot bear a part in; that these are times for silence: when they should learn to hear, and be attentive; at least in their turn. It is indeed a very unhappy way these people are in: they in a manner cut themselves out from all advantage of conversation, except that of being entertained with their own talk: their business in coming into company not being at all to be informed, to hear, to learn; but to display themselves; or rather to exert their faculty, and talk without any design at all.

§ 11. *Recreative conversation should be mutual.*

And if we consider conversation as an entertainment, as somewhat to unbend the mind; as a diversion from the cares, the business, and the sorrows of life; it is of the very nature of it, that the discourse be mutual. This, I say, is implied in the very notion of what we distinguish by conversation, or being in company. Attention to the continued discourse of one alone grows more painful often, than the cares and business we come to be diverted from. He therefore who imposes this upon us is guilty of a double offence; arbitrarily enjoining silence upon all the rest, and likewise obliging them to this painful attention.

§ 12. *The evil not to be passed by as trivial.*

I am sensible these things are apt to be passed over, as too little to come into a serious discourse: but in reality men are obliged, even in point of morality and virtue, to observe all the decencies of behaviour. The greatest evils in life have had their rise from somewhat, which was thought of too little importance to be attended to. And as to the matter we are now upon, it is absolutely necessary to be considered. For if people will not maintain a due government over themselves, in regarding proper times and seasons for silence, but *will* be talking; they certainly, whether they design it or not at first, will go on to scandal and evil-speaking, and divulging secrets.

§ 13. *How loquacity brings men to insignificance.*

If it were needful to say any thing further, to persuade men to learn this lesson of silence; one might put them in mind, how insignificant they render themselves by this excessive talkativeness: insomuch that, if they do chance to say any thing which deserves to be attended to and regarded, it is lost in the variety and abundance which they utter of another sort.

§ 14. *Of special occasions for silence.*

The occasions of silence then are obvious, and one would think should be easily distinguished by every body: namely, when a man has nothing to say; or nothing, but what is better unsaid: better, either in regard to the particular persons he is present with; or from its being an interruption to conversation itself; or to conversation of a more agreeable kind; or better, lastly, with regard to himself. I will end this particular with two reflections of the Wise Man: one of which, in the strongest manner, exposes the ridiculous part of this licentiousness of the tongue; and the other, the great danger and viciousness of it. *When he that is a fool walketh by the way side, his wisdom faileth him, and he saith to every one that he is a fool* [c]. The other is, *In the multitude of words there wanteth not sin* [d].

§ 15. *Beware of treating as indifferent things not so.*

As to the government of the tongue in respect to talking upon indifferent subjects: after what has been said concerning the due government of it in respect to the occasions and times for silence, there is little more necessary, than only to caution men to be fully satisfied, that the subjects are indeed of an indifferent nature; and not to spend too much

---

[c] Eccles. x. 3.   [d] Prov. x. 19.

time in conversation of this kind. But persons must be sure to take heed, that the subject of their discourse be at least of an indifferent nature: that it be no way offensive to virtue, religion, or good manners; that it be not of a licentious dissolute sort, this leaving always ill impressions upon the mind; that it be no way injurious or vexatious to others; and that too much time be not spent this way, to the neglect of those duties and offices of life which belong to their station and condition in the world. However, though there is not any necessity that men should aim at being important and weighty in every sentence they speak: yet since useful subjects, at least of some kinds, are as entertaining as others; a wise man, even when he desires to unbend his mind from business, would choose that the conversation might turn upon somewhat instructive.

§ 16. *Be slow to handle the character and concerns of others;*

The last thing is, the government of the tongue as relating to discourse of the affairs of others, and giving of characters. These are in a manner the same: and one can scarce call it an indifferent subject, because discourse upon it almost perpetually runs into somewhat criminal.

And first of all, it were very much to be wished that this did not take up so great a part of conversation; because it is indeed a subject of a dangerous nature. Let any one consider the various interests, competitions, and little misunderstandings which arise amongst men; and he will soon see, that he is not unprejudiced and impartial; that he is not, as I may speak, neutral enough, to trust himself with talking of the character and concerns of his neighbour, in a free, careless, and unreserved manner. There is perpetually, and often it is not attended to, a rivalship amongst people of one kind or another, in respect to wit, beauty, learning, fortune, and that one thing will insensibly influence them to speak to the disadvantage of others, even where there is no formed malice or ill design. Since therefore it is so hard to enter into this subject without offending, the first thing to be observed is, that people should learn to decline it; to get over that strong inclination most have to be talking of the concerns and behaviour of their neighbour.

§ 17. *And, in handling them, religiously scrupulous.*

But since it is impossible that this subject should be wholly excluded conversation; and since it is necessary that the characters of men should be known: the next thing is, that it is a matter of importance what is said; and therefore, that we should be religiously scrupulous and exact to say nothing, either good or bad, but what is true. I put it thus, because it is in reality of as great importance to the good of society, that the characters of bad men should be known, as that the characters of good men should. People, who are given to scandal and detraction, may indeed make an ill use of this observation; but truths, which are of service towards regulating our conduct, are not to be disowned, or even concealed, because a bad use may be made of them. This however would be effectually prevented, if these two things were attended to. First, That, though it is equally of bad consequence to society, that men should have either good or ill characters which they do not deserve; yet, when you say somewhat good of a man which he does not deserve, there is no wrong done him in particular; whereas, when you say evil of a man which he does not deserve, here is a direct formal injury, a real piece of injustice done him. This therefore makes a wide difference; and gives us, in point of virtue, much greater latitude in speaking well than ill of others.

§ 18. *Mere truth does not warrant reporting evil: much caution required.*

Secondly, A good man is friendly to his fellow-creatures, and a lover of mankind; and so will, upon every occasion, and often without any, say all the good he can of every body: but, so far as he is a good man, will never be disposed to speak evil of any, unless there be some other reason for it, besides barely that it is true. If he be charged with having given an ill character, he will scarce think it a sufficient justification of himself to say it was a true one, unless he can also give some farther account how he came to do so: a just indignation against particular instances of villainy, where they are great and scandalous; or to prevent an innocent man from being deceived and betrayed, when he has great trust and confidence in one who does not deserve it. Justice must be done to every part of a subject when we are considering it. If there be a man, who bears a fair character in the world, whom yet we know to be without faith or honesty, to be really an ill man; it must be allowed in general, that we shall do a piece of service to society, by letting such an one's true character be known. This is no more than what we have an instance of in our Saviour himself[c]; though he was mild and gentle beyond example. However, no words can express too strongly the caution which should be used in such a case as this.

§ 19. *In sum;* (a) *esteem silence,* (b) *eschew talebearing,* (c) *court not attention.*

Upon the whole matter: If people would observe the obvious occasions of silence, if they would subdue the inclination to talebearing, and that eager desire to engage attention, which is an original disease in some minds; they would be in little danger of offending with their tongue; and would, in a moral and religious sense, have due government over it.

I will conclude with some precepts and reflections of the Son of Sirach upon this subject. *Be swift to hear; and, if thou hast understanding, answer thy neighbour; if not, lay thy hand upon thy mouth. Honour and shame is in talk. A man of an ill tongue is dangerous in his city, and he that is rash in his talk shall be hated. A wise man will hold his tongue till he see opportunity; but a babbler and a fool will regard no time. He that useth many words shall be abhorred; and he that taketh to himself authority therein, shall be hated. A backbiting tongue hath disquieted many; strong cities hath it pulled down, and overthrown the houses of great men. The tongue of a man is his fall; but if thou love to hear, thou shalt receive understanding.*

---

[c] Mark xii. 38, 40.

SERMON V

UPON COMPASSION

Rejoice with them that do rejoice, and weep with them that weep.—ROMANS xii. 15.

§ 1. *We have a duty* (a) *to ourselves.* (b) *to our fellow-creatures.*

EVERY man is to be considered in two capacities, the private and public; as designed to pursue his own interest, and likewise to contribute to the good of others[1]. Whoever will consider, may see, that in general there is no contrariety between these; but that from the original constitution of man, and the circumstances he is placed in, they perfectly coincide, and mutually carry on each other. But, amongst the great variety of affections or principles of action in our nature, some in their primary intention and design seem to belong to the single or private, others to the public or social capacity. The affections required in the text are of the latter sort. When we rejoice in the prosperity of others, and compassionate their distresses, we, as it were, substitute them for ourselves, their interest for our own; and have the same kind of pleasure in their prosperity, and sorrow in their distress, as we have from reflection upon our own. Now there is nothing strange or unaccountable in our being thus carried out, and affected

---

[1] The classification would be complete as follows: Duty of man, (a) To himself; (b) To others: and this last (a) to his fellows individually; (β) (the same) collectively.

towards the interests of others. For, if there be any appetite, or any inward principle besides self-love; why may there not be an affection to the good of our fellow-creatures, and delight from that affection's being gratified, and uneasiness from things going contrary to it ª?

ª NOTE. There being manifestly this appearance of men's substituting others for themselves, and being carried out and affected towards them as towards themselves; some persons, who have a system which excludes every affection of this sort, have taken a pleasant method to solve it; and tell you it is *not another* you are at all concerned about, but your *self only*, when you feel the affection called compassion; i.e. Here is a plain matter of fact, which men cannot reconcile with the general account they think fit to give of things: they therefore, instead of *that* manifest fact, substitute *another*, which is reconcilable to their own scheme. For does not every body by compassion mean an affection, the object of which is another in distress? Instead of this, but designing to have it mistaken for this, they speak of an affection or passion, the object of which is ourselves, or danger to ourselves. Hobbes defines *pity, imagination, or fiction of future calamity to ourselves, proceeding from the sense* (he means sight or knowledge) *of another man's calamity*[1]. Thus fear and compassion

1. *False contention, that pity is self-regard, confuted.*

[1] 'Pity is imagination or fiction of future calamity to ourselves, proceeding from the sense of another man's calamity. But when it lighteth on such as we think have not deserved the same, the comparison is greater, because then there appeareth more probability that the same may happen to us; for the evil, that happeneth to an innocent man, may happen to every man. But when we see a man suffer for great crimes, which we cannot easily think will fall upon ourselves, the pity is the less. And therefore men are apt to pity those whom they love; for, whom they love, they think worthy of good, and therefore not worthy of calamity.' *On Human Nature*, c. ix.

Carmichael charges the responsibility for this doctrine upon Aristotle, who (*Rhet.* II. viii. 2) defines pity thus: ἔστω δὴ ἔλεος λύπη τις ἐπὶ φαινομένῳ κακῷ φθαρτικῷ καὶ λυπηρῷ τοῦ ἀναξίου τυγχάνειν, ὃ κἂν αὐτὸς προσδοκήσειεν ἂν παθεῖν, ἢ τῶν αὐτοῦ τινά· καὶ τοῦτο ὅταν πλησίον φαίνηται.

Aristotle's definition differs from that of Hobbes in his limitation of pity absolutely to those who have not deserved to suffer: and in his specifying that the danger to the person who pities must be proximate. Also, on the other side, in his allowing that it may be enough to stir pity if the risk be not to ourselves but to our friends. He is therefore both better and worse than Hobbes.

But pity is a Christian virtue, and to ask a perfect definition of it from Aristotle is like asking him to conceive and define humility.

The word ἔλεος occurs but once

§ 2. (a) *Compassion is more common than* (b) συγχαίρειν.

Of these two, delight in the prosperity of others, and compassion for their distresses, the last is felt much more generally than the former. Though men do not universally

---

would be the same idea, and a fearful and a compassionate man the same character, which every one immediately sees are totally different. Further, to those who give any scope to their affections, there is no perception or inward feeling more universal than this: that one who has been merciful and compassionate throughout the course of his behaviour, should himself be treated with kindness, if he happens to fall into circumstances of distress. Is fear, then, or cowardice, so great a recommendation to the favour of the bulk of mankind? Or is it not plain, that mere fearlessness (and therefore not the contrary) is one of the most popular qualifications? This shows that mankind are not affected towards compassion as fear, but as somewhat totally different.

Nothing would more expose such accounts as these of the affections which are favourable and friendly to our fellow-creatures, than to substitute the definitions, which this author, and others who follow his steps, give of such affections, instead of the words by which they are commonly expressed. Hobbes, after having laid down, that pity or compassion is only fear for ourselves, goes on to explain the reason why we pity our friends in distress more than others. Now substitute the *definition* instead of the word *pity* in this place, and the inquiry will be, why we fear our friends, &c. which words (since he really does not mean why we are afraid of them) make no question or sentence at all[1]. So that common language, the words *to compassionate, to pity,* cannot be accommodated to his account of compassion. The

---

in Homer, *Il.* xxiv. 44, where Apollo, pleading before the gods for Hector, says that Achilles has cast aside pity. But this pity seems to mean moderation in the infliction of suffering or dishonour. On the other hand, there is a situation in the *Iliad* which appears vividly to show that pity was so to speak a blank in the Achaian mind. On the death of Patroclos, Briseis keenly laments the loss she has thereby sustained. The attendant women groan in concert, ostensibly about Patroclos, but really each for her own personal sorrows.

ἐπὶ δὲ στενάχοντο γυναῖκες, Πάτροκλον πρόφασιν, σφῶν δ' αὐτῶν κήδε' ἑκάστη. *Il.* xix. 301.

Carmichael refers for other views of pity to *Tusc. Disp.* iii. 13 (Epicurus), and to Adam Smith, *The Moral Sentiments*, c. i.

[1] This passage is parenthetical, and not connected with the main argument. It is also open to exception from the side of Hobbes, who has said nothing to warrant the demand it contains: for his 'fear' is not the active verb as in 'fear our friends,' but the neuter as in his own defining phrase, 'fear for ourselves.'

rejoice with all whom they see rejoice, yet, accidental obstacles removed, they naturally compassionate all, in some degree, whom they see in distress: so far as they have any

---

very joining of the words to *pity our friends*, is a direct contradiction to his definition of pity: because those words, so joined, necessarily express that our friends are the objects of the passion: whereas his definition of it asserts, that ourselves (or danger to ourselves) are the only objects of it. He might indeed have avoided this absurdity, by plainly saying what he is going to account for; namely, why the sight of the innocent, or of our friends in distress, raises greater fear for ourselves than the sight of other persons in distress. But had he put the thing thus plainly, the fact itself would have been doubted; that *the sight of our friends in distress raises in us greater fear for ourselves, than the sight of others in distress*. And in the next place it would immediately have occurred to every one, that the fact now mentioned, which at least is *doubtful*, whether true or false, was not the same with this fact, which nobody ever doubted, that *the sight of our friends in distress raises in us greater compassion than the sight of others in distress*: every one, I say, would have seen that these are not the *same*, but *two different* inquiries; and consequently, that fear and compassion are not the same. Suppose a person to be in real danger, and by some means or other to have forgot it; any trifling accident, any sound might alarm him, recall the danger to his remembrance, and renew his fear: but it is almost too grossly ridiculous (though it is to show an absurdity) to speak of that sound or accident as an object of compassion; and yet, according to Mr. Hobbes, our greatest friend in distress is no more to us, no more the object of compassion, or of any affection in our heart: neither the one nor the other raises any emotion in our mind, but only the thoughts of our liableness to calamity, and the fear of it; and both equally do this. It is fit such sort of accounts of human nature should be shown to be what they really are, because there is raised upon them a general scheme, which undermines the whole foundation of common justice and honesty. See Hobbes, *On Human Nature*, c. ix. § 10.

There are often three distinct perceptions or inward feelings upon sight of persons in distress: real sorrow and concern for the misery of our fellow-creatures; some degree of satisfaction from a consciousness of our freedom from that misery; and as the mind passes on from one thing to another, it is not unnatural from such an occasion to reflect upon our own liableness to the same or other calamities. The two last frequently accompany the first, but it is the first *only* which is properly compassion, of which the distressed are the objects, and which directly carries us with calmness and thought to their assistance. Any one of these, from various and complicated

2. *The alleged fear is at most only a part of pity.*

real perception or sense of that distress: insomuch that words expressing this latter, pity, compassion, frequently occur; whereas we have scarce any single one, by which the former is distinctly expressed. Congratulation indeed answers condolence: but both these words are intended to signify certain forms of civility, rather than any inward sensation or feeling. This difference or inequality is so remarkable, that we plainly consider compassion as itself an original, distinct, particular affection in human nature; whereas to rejoice in the good of others, is only a consequence of the general affection of love and good-will to them.

§ 3. *For in* (a) *an active faculty of aid is needed.*

The reason and account of which matter is this: when a man has obtained any particular advantage or felicity, his end is gained; and he does not in that particular want the assistance of another: there was therefore no need of a distinct affection towards that felicity of another already obtained; neither would such affection directly carry him on to do good to that person: whereas men in distress want assistance; and compassion leads us directly to assist them. The object of the former is the present felicity of

---

reasons, may in particular cases prevail over the other two; and there are, I suppose, instances, where the bare *sight* of distress, without our feeling any compassion for it, may be the occasion of either or both of the two latter perceptions. One might add, that if there be really any such thing as the fiction or imagination of danger to ourselves from sight of the miseries of others, which Hobbes speaks of, and which he has absurdly mistaken for the whole of compassion; if there be any thing of this sort common to mankind, distinct from the reflection of reason, it would be a most remarkable instance of what was furthest from his thoughts, namely, of a mutual sympathy between each particular of the species, a fellow-feeling common to mankind. It would not indeed be an example of our substituting others for ourselves, but it would be an example of our substituting ourselves for others. And as it would not be an instance of benevolence, so neither would it be any instance of self-love: for this phantom of danger to ourselves, naturally rising to view upon sight of the distresses of others, would be no more an instance of love to ourselves, than the pain of hunger is.

another; the object of the latter is the present misery of another. It is easy to see that the latter wants a particular affection for its relief, and that the former does not want one, because it does not want assistance. And upon supposition of a distinct affection in both cases, the one must rest in the exercise of itself, having nothing further to gain; the other does not rest in itself, but carries us on to assist the distressed.

§ 4. *A cavil: that affection interferes with judgment.*

But, supposing these affections natural to the mind, particularly the last; 'Has not each man troubles enough of his own? must he indulge an affection which appropriates to himself those of others? which leads him to contract the least desirable of all friendships, friendships with the unfortunate? Must we invert the known rule of prudence, and choose to associate ourselves with the distressed? or, allowing that we ought, so far as it is in our power to relieve them, yet is it not better to do this from reason and duty[1]? Does not passion and affection of every kind perpetually mislead us? Nay, is not passion and affection itself a weakness, and what a perfect being must be entirely free from?' Perhaps so: but it is mankind I am speaking of; imperfect creatures, and who naturally and, from the condition we are placed in, necessarily depend upon each other. With respect to such creatures, it would be found of as bad consequence to eradicate all natural affections, as to be entirely governed by them. This would almost sink us to the condition of brutes; and that would leave us without a sufficient principle of action. Reason alone, whatever any one may wish, is not in reality a sufficient motive of virtue in such a creature as man; but this reason joined with those affections which God has impressed upon his heart: and when these are allowed scope to exercise themselves, but under strict government and direction of reason; then it is we act suitably to our nature, and to the circumstances God has placed us in. Neither is affection itself at all a weakness; nor does it argue defect, any

[1] Cic. *Tusc. Disp.* iv. 26.

otherwise than as our senses and appetites do; they belong to our condition of nature, and are what we cannot be without.

§ 5. *Case of the Divine nature: affords no parallel.*

God Almighty is, to be sure, unmoved by passion or appetite, unchanged by affection: but then it is to be added, that he neither sees, nor hears, nor perceives things by any senses like ours; but in a manner infinitely more perfect. Now, as it is an absurdity almost too gross to be mentioned, for a man to endeavour to get rid of his senses, because the Supreme Being discerns things more perfectly without them; it is as real, though not so obvious an absurdity, to endeavour to eradicate the passions he has given us, because he is without them. For, since our passions are as really a part of our constitution as our senses; since the former as really belong to our condition of nature as the latter; to get rid of either is equally a violation of and breaking in upon that nature and constitution he has given us. Both our senses and our passions are a supply to the imperfection of our nature: thus they show that we are such sort of creatures, as to stand in need of those helps which higher orders of creatures do not. But it is not the supply, but the deficiency; as it is not a remedy, but a disease, which is the imperfection.

§ 6. *Affections which are part of our nature, not a defect in it.*

However, our appetites, passions, senses, no way imply disease: nor indeed do they imply deficiency or imperfection of any sort; but only this, that the constitution of nature, according to which God has made us, is such as to require them. And it is so far from being true, that a wise man must entirely suppress compassion, and all fellow-feeling for others, as a weakness; and trust to reason alone to teach and enforce upon him the practice of the several charities we owe to our kind; that, on the contrary, even the bare exercise of such affections would itself be for the good and happiness of the world; and the imperfection of the higher principles of reason and religion in man, the little influence they have upon our practice, and the strength and prevalency of contrary ones, plainly require these affections to be a restraint upon these latter, and a supply to the deficiencies of the former.

§ 7. *How, on a balance, life would be bettered by freer scope for the affections (proper).*

First, The very exercise itself of these affections in a just and reasonable manner and degree, would upon the whole increase the satisfactions, and lessen the miseries of life.

It is the tendency and business of virtue and religion to procure, as much as may be, universal good-will, trust, and friendship amongst mankind. If this could be brought to obtain; and each man enjoyed the happiness of others, as every one does that of a friend; and looked upon the success and prosperity of his neighbour, as every one does upon that of his children and family; it is too manifest to be insisted upon, how much the enjoyments of life would be increased. There would be so much happiness introduced into the world, without any deduction or inconvenience from it, in proportion as the precept of *rejoicing with those who rejoice* was universally obeyed. Our Saviour has owned this good affection as belonging to our nature, in the parable of the *lost sheep*[1]; and does not think it to the disadvantage of a perfect state, to represent its happiness as capable of increase, from reflection upon that of others.

But since in such a creature as man, compassion or sorrow for the distress of others seems so far necessarily connected with joy in their prosperity, as that whoever rejoices in one must unavoidably compassionate the other; there cannot be that delight or satisfaction, which appears to be so considerable, without the inconveniences, whatever they are, of compassion[2].

---

[1] Luke xv. 4–7.
[2] It seems that we have here an example of the rare fairness of Butler's mind. He appears for himself to give little or no weight to the pain more or less attending upon compassion as a real inconvenience: but as the opponent has alleged it, and it cannot be absolutely denied, he deals with it and inquires on which side lies the balance of advantage.

§ 8. *Compassion itself gives a clear balance of satisfactions.*

However, without considering this connection, there is no doubt but that more good than evil, more delight than sorrow, arises from compassion itself; there being so many things which balance the sorrow of it. There is first the relief which the distressed feel from this affection in others towards them. There is likewise the additional misery which they would feel from the reflection, that no one commiserated their case[1]. It is indeed true, that any disposition[2], prevailing beyond a certain degree, becomes somewhat wrong; and we have ways of speaking, which, though they do not directly express that excess, yet, always lead our thoughts to it, and give us the notion of it. Thus, when mention is made of delight in being pitied, this always conveys to our mind the notion of somewhat which is really a weakness: the manner of speaking, I say, implies a certain weakness and feebleness of mind, which is and ought to be disapproved. But men of the greatest fortitude would in distress feel uneasiness, from knowing that no person in the world had any sort of compassion or real concern for them; and in some cases, especially when the temper is enfeebled by sickness, or any long and great distress, doubtless, would feel a kind of relief even from the helpless good-will and ineffectual assistances of those about them. Over against the sorrow of compassion is likewise to be set a peculiar calm kind of satisfaction, which accompanies it, unless in cases where the distress of another is by some means so brought home to ourselves, as to become in a manner our own; or when from weakness of mind the affection rises too high, which ought to be corrected. This tranquillity or calm satisfaction proceeds partly from consciousness of a right affection and temper of mind, and partly from a sense of our own freedom from the misery we compassionate. This last

---

[1] κουφίζονται γὰρ οἱ λυπούμενοι συναλγούντων τῶν φίλων. Arist. *Eth. Nic.* IX. xi. 2.

[2] *Disposition* seems here to be the equivalent of *affection*.

may possibly appear to some at first sight faulty; but it really is not so. It is the same with that positive enjoyment, which sudden ease from pain for the present affords, arising from a real sense of misery, joined with a sense of our freedom from it [1]; which in all cases must afford some degree of satisfaction.

§ 9. *Loss attaching to callousness.*

To these things must be added the observation, which respects both the affections we are considering; that they who have got over all fellow-feeling for others, have withal contracted a certain callousness of heart, which renders them insensible to most other satisfactions, but those of the grossest kind.

§ 10. *How all conduct requires the stimulus or the restraint of affection.*

Secondly, Without the exercise of these affections men would certainly be much more wanting in the offices of charity they owe to each other, and likewise more cruel and injurious, than they are at present.

The private interest of the individual would not be sufficiently provided for by reasonable and cool self-love alone; therefore the appetites and passions are placed within as a guard and further security, without which it would not be taken due care of. It is manifest our life would be neglected, were it not for the calls of hunger, and thirst, and weariness; notwithstanding that without them reason would assure us, that the recruits of food and sleep are the necessary means of our preservation. It is therefore absurd to imagine, that, without affection, the same reason alone would be more effectual to engage us to perform the duties we owe to our fellow-creatures. One of this make would be as defective, as much wanting, considered with respect to society, as one of the former make would be defective, or wanting, considered as an individual, or in his private capacity. Is it possible any

---

[1] Sometimes latent, and not rising into consciousness.

can in earnest think, that a public spirit, i. e. a settled reasonable principle of benevolence to mankind, is so prevalent and strong in the species, as that we may venture to throw off the under affections, which are its assistants, carry it forward and mark out particular courses for it; family, friends, neighbourhood, the distressed, our country? The common joys and the common sorrows, which belong to these relations and circumstances, are as plainly useful to society, as the pain and pleasure belonging to hunger, thirst, and weariness, are of service to the individual. In defect of that higher principle of reason, compassion is often the only way by which the indigent can have access to us: and therefore, to eradicate this, though it is not indeed formally to deny them that assistance which is their due; yet it is to cut them off from that which is too frequently their only way of obtaining it.

§ 11. *Men without right affection have to reckon with its effects through others.*

And as for those who have shut up this door against the complaints of the miserable, and conquered this affection in themselves; even these persons will be under great restraints from the same affection in others. Thus a man who has himself no sense of injustice, cruelty, oppression, will be kept from running the utmost lengths of wickedness, by fear of that detestation, and even resentment of inhumanity, in many particular instances of it, which compassion for the object towards whom such inhumanity is exercised, excites in the bulk of mankind. And this is frequently the chief danger, and the chief restraint, which tyrants and the great oppressors of the world feel.

§ 12. *Want of affection is like want of appetite; the obstinacy of bad affections.*

In general, experience will show, that as want of natural appetite to food supposes and proceeds from some bodily disease; so the apathy the Stoics talk of, as much supposes, or is accompanied with, somewhat amiss in the moral character, in that which is the health of the mind. Those who formerly aimed at this upon the foot of philosophy, appear to have had better success in eradicating the affections of tenderness and compassion, than they had with the passions of envy, pride, and resentment: these latter, at best, were but concealed, and that imperfectly too. How far this observation may be extended to such as endeavour to suppress the natural impulses of their affections, in order to form themselves for business and the world, I shall not determine. But there does not appear any capacity or relation to be named, in which men ought to be entirely deaf to the calls of affection, unless the judicial one is to be excepted.

§ 13. *Men of pleasure: motive of their opinion: their losses.*

And as to those who are commonly called the men of pleasure, it is manifest, that the reason they set up for hardness of heart, is to avoid being interrupted in their course, by the ruin and misery they are the authors of: neither are persons of this character always the most free from the impotencies of envy and resentment. What may men at last bring themselves to, by suppressing their passions and affections of one kind, and leaving those of the other in their full strength? but surely it might be expected that persons who make pleasure their study and their business, if they understood what they profess, would reflect, how many of the entertainments of life, how many of those kind of amusements which seem peculiarly to belong to men of leisure and education, they become insensible to by this acquired hardness of heart.

§ 14. *The compassion of Christ.*

I shall close these reflections with barely mentioning the behaviour of that divine Person, who was the example of all perfection in human nature, as represented in the Gospels mourning, and even, in a literal sense, weeping over the distresses of his creatures.

The observation already made, that, of the two affections mentioned in the text, the latter exerts itself much more than the former; that, from the original constitution of human nature, we much more generally and sensibly compassionate the distressed, than rejoice with the prosperous, requires to be particularly considered. This observation, therefore, with the reflections which arise out of it, and which it leads our thoughts to, shall be the subject of another discourse.

§ 15. *Morality and religion are not abstruse.*

For the conclusion of this, let me just take notice of the danger of over-great refinements; of going beside or beyond the plain, obvious, first appearances of things, upon the subject of morals and religion. The least observation will show, how little the generality of men are capable of speculations. Therefore morality and religion must be somewhat plain and easy to be understood: it must appeal to what we call plain common sense, as distinguished from superior capacity and improvement; because it appeals to mankind.

§ 16. *Persons of capacity, without common sense, fall into gross error.*

Persons of superior capacity and improvement have often fallen into errors, which no one of mere common understanding could. Is it possible that one of this latter character could ever of himself have thought, that there was absolutely no such thing in mankind as affection to the good of others? suppose of parents to their children; or that what he felt upon seeing a friend in distress was only fear for himself; or, upon supposition of the affections of kindness and compassion, that it was the business of wisdom and virtue to set him about extirpating them as fast as he could? And yet each of these manifest contradictions to nature has been laid down by men of speculation, as a discovery in moral philosophy; which they, it seems, have found out through all the specious appearances to the contrary [1]. This reflection may be extended further. The extravagancies of enthusiasm and superstition do not at all lie in the road of common sense; and therefore, so far as they are *original*

---

[1] The reference appears to be to Hobbes.

mistakes, must be owing to going beside or beyond it. Now, since inquiry and examination can relate only to things so obscure and uncertain as to stand in need of it, and to persons who are capable of it; the proper advice to be given to plain honest men, to secure them from the extremes both of superstition and irreligion, is that of the Son of Sirach: *In every good work trust thy own soul, for this is the keeping of the commandment* [b].

---

[b] Ecclus. xxxii. 23.

SERMON VI

UPON COMPASSION

PREACHED THE FIRST SUNDAY IN LENT.

—••—

Rejoice with them that do rejoice, and weep with them that weep.— ROMANS xii. 15.

—••—

§ 1. *Final causes exhibited in the adaptation of man's nature to his environment.*

THERE is a much more exact correspondence between the natural and moral world, than we are apt to take notice of. The inward frame of man does in a peculiar manner answer to the external condition and circumstances of life, in which he is placed. This is a particular instance of that general observation of the Son of Sirach: *All things are double one against another, and God hath made nothing imperfect* [a]. The several passions and affections in the heart of man, compared with the circumstances of life in which he is placed, afford, to such as will attend to them, as certain instances of final causes, as any whatever, which are more commonly alleged for such: since those affections lead him to a certain determinate course of action suitable to those circumstances; as (for instance) compassion, to relieve the distressed [1]. And as all observations of final

---

[a] Ecclus. xlii. 24.

[1] Whewell (Preface to Six Sermons, p. ix) points out that our duty is taught us by special commands, and that it also may be

causes, drawn from the principles of action in the heart of man, compared with the condition he is placed in, serve all the good uses which instances of final causes in the material world about us do; and both these are equally proofs of wisdom and design in the Author of nature: so the former serve to further good purposes; they show us what course of life we are made for, what is our duty, and in a peculiar manner enforce upon us the practice of it.

§ 2. *We can do more for and against misery, than joy. Hence the special need for compassion.*

Suppose we are capable of happiness and of misery in degrees equally intense and extreme, yet, we are capable of the latter for a much longer time, beyond all comparison. We see men in the tortures of pain for hours, days, and, excepting the short suspensions of sleep, for months together, without intermission; to which no enjoyments of life do, in degree and continuance, bear any sort of proportion. And such is our make and that of the world about us, that any thing may become the instrument of pain and sorrow to us. Thus almost any one man is capable of doing mischief to any other, though he may not be capable of doing him good: and if he be capable of doing him some good, he is capable of doing him more evil. And it is, in numberless cases, much more in our power to lessen the miseries of others, than to promote their positive happiness, any otherwise than as the former often includes the latter; ease from misery occasioning for some time the greatest positive enjoyment. This constitution of nature, namely, that it is so much more in our power to occasion

---

inferred from the constitution of our nature: and adds, 'To many minds the consideration of God's workmanship, as shown in our souls no less than in our bodies, adds impressiveness to all other reasons for controuling perverted and extravagant affections.'

It is a method of regarding duty which enhances its dignity by exhibiting it in immediate conjunction with its lofty parentage. It seems to be adapted to the higher class of minds. It is, at least, as old as Dante:

'Considerate la vostra semenza:
Fatti non foste a viver come bruti,
Ma per seguir virtute e conoscenza.'

Inferno, xxvi. 118.

and likewise to lessen misery, than to promote positive happiness, plainly required a particular affection, to hinder us from abusing, and to incline us to make a right use of the former powers, i. e. the powers both to occasion and to lessen misery; over and above what was necessary to induce us to make a right use of the latter power, that of promoting positive happiness. The power we have over the misery of our fellow-creatures, to occasion or lessen it, being a more important trust than the power we have of promoting their positive happiness; the former requires and has a further, an additional security and guard against its being violated, beyond and over and above what the latter has. The social nature of man, and general good-will to his species, equally prevent him from doing evil, incline him to relieve the distressed, and to promote the positive happiness of his fellow-creatures: but compassion only restrains from the first, and carries him to the second; it hath nothing to do with the third.

§ 3. *Its double office:* (a) *to prevent,* (b) *to relieve.*

The final causes then of compassion are to prevent and to relieve misery.

As to the former: this affection may plainly be a restraint upon resentment, envy, unreasonable self-love; that is, upon all the principles from which men do evil to one another. Let us instance only in resentment. It seldom happens, in regulated societies, that men have an enemy so entirely in their power, as to be able to satiate their resentment with safety. But if we were to put this case, it is plainly supposable, that a person might bring his enemy into such a condition, as from being the object of anger and rage, to become an object of compassion, even to himself, though the most malicious man in the world: and in this case compassion would stop him, if he could stop with safety, from pursuing his revenge any farther. But since nature has placed within us more powerful restraints to prevent mischief, and since the final cause of compassion is much more to relieve misery, let us go on to the consideration of it in this view.

§ 4. *There is a law of mitigation and relief for sorrow.*

As this world was not intended to be a state of any great satisfaction or high enjoyment; so neither was it intended to be a mere scene of unhappiness and sorrow. Mitigations and reliefs are provided by the merciful Author of nature, for most of the afflictions in human life. There is kind provision made even against our frailties; as we are so constituted, that time abundantly abates our sorrows, and begets in us that resignment of temper, which ought to have been produced by a better cause; a due sense of the authority of God, and our state of dependence[1]. This holds in respect to far the greatest part of the evils of life; I suppose, in some degree, as to pain and sickness. Now this part of the constitution or make of man, considered as some relief to misery, and not as provision for positive happiness, is, if I may so speak, an instance of nature's compassion for us; and every natural remedy or relief to misery may be considered in the same view.

§ 5. *Chiefly* (b). *Here is an advocate to procure consideration for any case.*

But since in many cases it is very much in our power to alleviate the miseries of each other; and benevolence, though natural in man to man, yet is in a very low degree kept down by interest and competitions[2]; and men, for the most part, are so engaged in the business and pleasures of the world, as to overlook and turn away from objects of misery; which are plainly considered as interruptions to

---

[1] Carmichael quotes the explanation given by Locke as to the mode in which the mitigation is brought about:

'The death of a child that was the daily delight of its mother's eyes, and joy of her soul, rends from her heart the whole comfort of her life, and gives her all the torment imaginable: use the consolations of reason in this case, and you were as good preach ease to one on the rack, and hope to allay, by rational discourses, the pain of his joints tearing asunder. Till time has by disuse separated the sense of that enjoyment and its loss, from the idea of the child returning to her memory, all representations, though ever so reasonable, are in vain.' *On the Understanding,* ii. 33. § 13.

[2] That is to say, is thus affected when only existing in a very low degree.

them in their way, as intruders upon their business, their gaiety and mirth: compassion is an advocate within us in their behalf, to gain the unhappy admittance and access, to make their case attended to. If it sometimes serves a contrary purpose, and makes men industriously turn away from the miserable, these are only instances of abuse and perversion: for the end, for which the affection was given us, most certainly is not to make us avoid, but to make us attend to, the objects of it. And if men would only resolve to allow thus much to it; let it bring before their view, the view of their mind, the miseries of their fellow-creatures; let it gain for them that their case be considered; I am persuaded it would not fail of gaining more, and that very few real objects of charity would pass unrelieved. Pain and sorrow and misery have a right to our assistance: compassion puts us in mind of the debt, and that we owe it to ourselves as well as to the distressed.

§ 6. *May be got rid of: but compare the case of hunger.*

For, to endeavour to get rid of the sorrow of compassion by turning from the wretched, when yet it is in our power to relieve them, is as unnatural, as to endeavour to get rid of the pain of hunger by keeping from the sight of food. That we can do one with greater success than we can the other, is no proof that one is less a violation of nature than the other. Compassion is a call, a demand of nature, to relieve the unhappy; as hunger is a natural call for food. This affection plainly gives the objects of it an additional claim to relief and mercy, over and above what our fellow-creatures in common have to our good-will.

§ 7. *How distinguished from mercy.*

Liberality and bounty are exceedingly commendable; and a particular distinction in such a world as this, where men set themselves to contract their heart, and close it to all interests but their own. It is by no means to be opposed to mercy, but always accompanies it: the distinction between them is only, that the former leads our thoughts to a more promiscuous and undistinguished distribution of favours; to those who are not, as well as those who are necessitous; whereas the object of compassion is misery. But in the comparison, and where there is not a possibility of both, mercy is to have the preference: the affection of compassion manifestly leads us to this preference[1]. Thus, to relieve the indigent and distressed, to single out the unhappy, from whom can be expected no returns either of present entertainment or future service, for the objects of our favours; to esteem a man's being friendless as a recommendation; dejection, and incapacity of struggling through the world, as a motive for assisting him; in a word, to consider these circumstances of disadvantage, which are usually thought a sufficient reason for neglect and overlooking a person, as a motive for helping him forward: this is the course of benevolence which compassion marks out and directs us to: this is that humanity, which is so peculiarly becoming our nature and circumstances in this world.

§ 8. *It regards the indigent; prefers* (b) *to* (a): *for more good is thus done.*

To these considerations, drawn from the nature of man, must be added the reason of the thing itself we are recommending, which accords to and shows the same. For since it is so much more in our power to lessen the misery of our fellow-creatures, than to promote their positive happiness; in cases where there is an inconsistency, we shall be likely to do much more good by setting ourselves to mitigate the former, than by endeavouring to promote the latter. Let the competition be between the poor and the rich. It is easy, you will say, to see which will have the preference. True: but the question is, which ought to have the preference? What proportion is there between the happiness produced by doing a favour to the indigent, and that produced by doing the same favour to one in easy

---

[1] It does not appear that the two are in competition, so much as that their provinces are partially distinct. Mercy is lenient and tender dealing. All compassion is mercy: but all mercy is not compassion. Mercy looks more at the case; compassion more at the person.

circumstances? It is manifest, that the addition of a very large estate to one who before had an affluence, will in many instances yield him less new enjoyment or satisfaction, than an ordinary charity would yield to a necessitous person. So that it is not only true, that our nature, i. e. the voice of God within us, carries us to the exercise of charity and benevolence in the way of compassion or mercy, preferably to any other way; but we also manifestly discern much more good done by the former; or, if you will allow me the expressions, more misery annihilated, and happiness created. If charity and benevolence, and endeavouring to do good to our fellow-creatures, be any thing, this observation deserves to be most seriously considered by all who have to bestow. And it holds with great exactness, when applied to the several degrees of greater and less indigency throughout the various ranks in human life: the happiness or good produced not being in proportion to what is bestowed, but in proportion to this joined with the need there was of it.

§ 9. *Encourage affection favourable to our fellow-men.*

It may perhaps be expected, that upon this subject notice should be taken of occasions, circumstances, and characters, which seem at once to call forth affections of different sorts. Thus vice may be thought the object both of pity and indignation: folly, of pity and of laughter. How far this is strictly true, I shall not inquire; but only observe upon the appearance, how much more humane it is to yield and give scope to affections, which are more directly in favour of, and friendly towards, our fellow-creatures; and that there is plainly much less danger of being led wrong by these, than by the other.

§ 10. *It is capable of excess; but the prevailing excess is that of the world set against it.*

But, notwithstanding all that has been said in recommendation of compassion, that it is most amiable, most becoming human nature, and most useful to the world; yet it must be owned, that every affection, as distinct from a principle of reason, may rise too high, and be beyond its just proportion. And by means of this one carried too far, a man throughout his life is subject to much more uneasiness than belongs to his share : and in particular instances, it may be in such a degree, as to incapacitate him from assisting the very person who is the object of it. But as there are some who upon principle set up for suppressing this affection itself as weakness, there is also I know not what of fashion on this side ; and, by some means or other, the whole world almost is run into the extremes of insensibility towards the distresses of their fellow-creatures : so that general rules and exhortations must always be on the other side.

§ 11. *Increase of enjoyment less an object than avoidance of misery.*

And now to go on to the uses we should make of the foregoing reflections, the further ones they lead to, and the general temper they have a tendency to beget in us. There being that distinct affection implanted in the nature of man, tending to lessen the miseries of life, that particular provision made for abating its sorrows, more than for increasing its positive happiness, as before explained ; this may suggest to us what should be our general aim respecting ourselves, in our passage through this world : namely, to endeavour chiefly to escape misery, keep free from uneasiness, pain, and sorrow, or to get relief and mitigation of them ; to propose to ourselves peace and tranquillity of mind, rather than pursue after high enjoyments[1]. This is what the constitution of nature before explained marks out as the course we should follow, and the end we should aim at. To make pleasure and mirth and jollity our business, and be constantly hurrying about after some gay amusement, some new gratification of sense or appetite, to those who

---

[1] Butler here applies to our own case a rule brought home to him by the general nature of compassion : and seems to say 'as compassion aims more at diminishing misery than increasing enjoyment, so, for each man, to ward off suffering is more reasonable than to study the pursuit of pleasure.'

will consider the nature of man and our condition in this world, will appear the most romantic scheme of life that ever entered into thought. And yet how many are there who go on in this course, without learning better from the daily, the hourly disappointments, listlessness, and satiety, which accompany this fashionable method of wasting away their days!

§ 12. *Compassion begets a sober and discerning view of our human state;*

The subject we have been insisting upon would lead us into the same kind of reflections, by a different connection. The miseries of life brought home to ourselves by compassion, viewed through this affection considered as the sense by which they are perceived, would beget in us that moderation, humility, and soberness of mind, which has been now recommended; and which peculiarly belongs to a season of recollection, the only purpose of which is to bring us to a just sense of things, to recover us out of that forgetfulness of ourselves, and our true state, which it is manifest far the greatest part of men pass their whole life in. Upon this account Solomon says, that *it is better to go to the house of mourning, than to go to the house of feasting;* i. e. it is more to a man's advantage to turn his eyes towards objects of distress, to recall sometimes to his remembrance the occasions of sorrow, than to pass all his days in thoughtless mirth and gaiety. And he represents the wise as choosing to frequent the former of these places; to be sure not for its own sake, but because *by the sadness of the countenance the heart is made better.* Every one observes how temperate and reasonable men are when humbled and brought low by afflictions, in comparison of what they are in high prosperity. By this voluntary resort to the house of mourning, which is here recommended, we might learn all those useful instructions which calamities teach, without undergoing them ourselves; and grow wiser and better at a more easy rate than men commonly do. The objects themselves, which in that place of sorrow lie before our view, naturally give us a seriousness and attention, check that wantonness which is the growth of prosperity and ease, and lead us to reflect upon the deficiencies of human life itself; that *every man, at his best estate, is altogether vanity.* This would correct the florid and gaudy prospects and expectations which we are too apt to indulge, teach us to lower our notions of happiness and enjoyment, bring them down to the reality of things, to what is attainable, to what the frailty of our condition will admit of, which, for any continuance, is only tranquillity, ease, and moderate satisfactions. Thus we might at once become proof against the temptations with which the whole world almost is carried away; since it is plain, that not only what is called a life of pleasure, but also vicious pursuits in general, aim at somewhat besides and beyond these moderate satisfactions.

§ 13. *And docility of mind and heart;*

And as to that obstinacy and wilfulness, which renders men so insensible to the motives of religion; this right sense of ourselves and of the world about us would bend the stubborn mind, soften the heart, and make it more apt to receive impression: and this is the proper temper in which to call our ways to remembrance, to review and set home upon ourselves the miscarriages of our past life. In such a compliant state of mind, reason and conscience will have a fair hearing; which is the preparation for, or rather the beginning of, that repentance, the outward show of which we all put on at this season [1].

§ 14. *And a sense that we are but travellers in a foreign country.*

Lastly, The various miseries of life which lie before us wherever we turn our eyes, the frailty of this mortal state we are passing through, may put us in mind that the present world is not our home; that we are merely strangers and travellers in it, as all our fathers were. It is therefore to be

---

[1] Here is a weighty though accidental testimony to the effect that there was still in Butler's day a general outward compliance with the ancient prescriptions touching Lent.

considered as a foreign country; in which our poverty and wants, and the insufficient supplies of them, were designed to turn our views to that higher and better state we are heirs to: a state where will be no follies to be overlooked, no miseries to be pitied, no wants to be relieved; where the affection we have been now treating of will happily be lost, as there will be no objects to exercise it upon: for *God shall wipe away all tears from their eyes, and there shall be no more death, neither sorrow, nor crying; neither shall there be any more pain; for the former things are passed away.*

SERMON VII

UPON THE CHARACTER OF BALAAM

Preached the Second Sunday after Easter.

———

Let me die the death of the righteous, and let my last end be like his.—NUMBERS xxiii. 10.

———

§ 1. *Consider here (a) life as well as death, (b) the speaker as well as the thing spoken.*

THESE words, taken alone, and without respect to him who spoke them, lead our thoughts immediately to the different ends of good and bad men. For though the comparison is not expressed, yet it is manifestly implied; as is also the preference of one of these characters to the other in that last circumstance, death. And, since dying the death of the righteous or of the wicked necessarily implies men's being righteous or wicked, i. e. having lived righteously or wickedly; a comparison of them in their lives also might come into consideration, from such a single view of the words themselves. But my present design is to consider them with a particular reference or respect to him who spoke them; which reference, if you please to attend, you will see. And if what shall be offered to your consideration at this time be thought a discourse upon the whole history of this man, rather than upon the particular words I have read, this is of no consequence: it is sufficient, if it afford reflection of use and service to ourselves.

But, in order to avoid cavils respecting this remarkable

relation in scripture, either that part of it which you have heard in the first lesson for the day, or any other; let me just observe, that as this is not a place for answering them, so they no way affect the following discourse; since the character there given is plainly a real one in life, and such as there are parallels to.

§ 2. *After sacrifice, Balaam retires to receive the inspired word.*

The occasion of Balaam's coming out of his own country into the land of Moab, where he pronounced this solemn prayer or wish, he himself relates in the first parable or prophetic speech, of which it is the conclusion. In which is a custom referred to, proper to be taken notice of: that of devoting enemies to destruction, before the entrance upon a war with them. This custom appears to have prevailed over a great part of the world; for we find it amongst the most distant nations. The Romans had public officers, to whom it belonged as a stated part of their office. But there was somewhat more particular in the case now before us; Balaam being looked upon as an extraordinary person, whose blessing or curse was thought to be always effectual.

In order to engage the reader's attention to this passage, the sacred historian has enumerated the preparatory circumstances, which are these. Balaam requires the king of Moab to build him seven altars, and to prepare him the same number of oxen and of rams. The sacrifice being over, he retires alone to a solitude sacred to these occasions, there to wait the divine inspiration or answer, for which the foregoing rites were the preparation. *And God met Balaam, and put a word in his mouth* [a]; upon receiving which, he returns back to the altars, where was the king, who had all this while attended the sacrifice, as appointed; he and all the princes of Moab standing, big with expectation of the Prophet's reply. *And he took up his parable, and said, Balak the king of Moab hath brought me from Aram, out of the mountains of the east, saying, Come, curse me Jacob, and come, defy Israel. How*

---

[a] Ver. 4, 5.

shall I curse, whom God hath not cursed? Or how shall I defy, whom the Lord hath not defied? For from the top of the rocks I see him, and from the hills I behold him: lo, the people shall dwell alone, and shall not be reckoned among the nations. Who can count the dust of Jacob, and the number of the fourth part of Israel? Let me die the death of the righteous, and let my last end be like his [b]*!*

§ 3. '*The righteous*' *is explained by Micah, ch.* vi.

It is necessary, as you will see in the progress of this discourse, particularly to observe what he understood by *righteous*. And he himself is introduced in the book of Micah [c] explaining it; if by *righteous* is meant *good*, as to be sure it is. *O my people, remember now what Balak king of Moab consulted, and what Balaam the son of Beor answered him from Shittim unto Gilgal.* From the mention of Shittim it is manifest, that it is this very story which is here referred to, though another part of it, the account of which is not now extant; as there are many quotations in scripture out of books which are not come down to us. *Remember what Balaam answered, that ye may know the righteousness of the Lord;* i.e. the righteousness which God will accept. Balak demands, *Wherewith shall I come before the Lord, and bow myself before the high God? Shall I come before him with burnt-offerings, with calves of a year old? Will the Lord be pleased with thousands of rams, or with ten thousands of rivers of oil? Shall I give my first-born for my transgression, the fruit of my body for the sin of my soul?* Balaam answers him, *He hath showed thee, O man, what is good: and what doth the Lord require of thee, but to do justly, and to love mercy, and to walk humbly with thy God?* Here is a good man expressly characterized, as distinct from a dishonest and a superstitious man. No words can more strongly exclude dishonesty and falseness of heart, than *doing justice,* and *loving mercy:* and both these, as well as *walking humbly with God,* are put in opposition to those ceremonial methods of recommendation, which Balak hoped might have served the

---

[b] Ver. 7-10. [c] Micah vi.

turn. From hence appears what he meant by the *righteous*, whose *death* he desires to die.

§ 4. *Balaam refuses to accompany the first embassy.*

Whether it was his own character shall now be inquired : and in order to determine it, we must take a view of his whole behaviour upon this occasion. When the elders of Moab came to him, though he appears to have been much allured with the rewards offered, yet he had such regard to the authority of God, as to keep the messengers in suspense until he had consulted his will. *And God said to him, Thou shalt not go with them, thou shalt not curse the people, for they are blessed*[d]. Upon this he dismisses the ambassadors, with an absolute refusal of accompanying them back to their king. Thus far his regards to his duty prevailed, neither does there any thing appear as yet amiss in his conduct.

§ 5. *Yields to the increased inducements of the second, conditionally on obtaining permission.*

His answer being reported to the king of Moab, a more honourable embassy is immediately despatched, and greater rewards proposed. Then the iniquity of his heart began to disclose itself. A thorough honest man would without hesitation have repeated his former answer, that he could not be guilty of so infamous a prostitution of the sacred character with which he was invested, as in the name of a prophet to curse those whom he knew to be blessed. But instead of this, which was the only honest part in these circumstances that lay before him, he desires the princes of Moab to tarry that night with him also ; and for the sake of the reward deliberates, whether by some means or other he might not be able to obtain leave to curse Israel ; to do that, which had been before revealed to him to be contrary to the will of God, which yet he resolves not to do without that permission [1].

---

[d] Numbers xxii. 12.

---

[1] Comp. *Macbeth*, Act i. sc. 5.
' What thou wouldst highly,
That wouldst thou holily : wouldst not play false,
And yet wouldst wrongly win.

§ 6. *The permission given.*

Upon which, as when this nation afterwards rejected God from reigning over them, he gave them a king in his anger; in the same way, as appears from other parts of the narration, he gives Balaam the permission he desired: for this is the most natural sense of the words. Arriving in the territories of Moab, and being received with particular distinction by the king, and he repeating in person the promise of the rewards he had before made to him by his ambassadors: he seeks, the text says, by *sacrifices* and *enchantments*, (what these were is not to our purpose,) to obtain leave of God to curse the people; keeping still his resolution, not to do it without that permission: which not being able to obtain, he had such regard to the command of God, as to keep this resolution to the last. The supposition of his being under a supernatural restraint is a mere fiction of Philo[1]: he is plainly represented to be under no other force or restraint, than the fear of God. However, he goes on persevering in that endeavour, after he had declared, that *God had not beheld iniquity in Jacob, neither had he seen perverseness in Israel*[c]; i. e. they were a people of virtue and piety, so far as not to have drawn down, by their iniquity, that curse which he was soliciting leave to pronounce upon them. So that the state of Balaam's mind was this: he wanted to do what he knew to be very wicked, and contrary to the express command of God; he had inward checks and restraints, which he could not entirely get over; he therefore casts about for ways to reconcile this wickedness with his duty. How great a paradox soever this may appear, as it is indeed a contradiction in terms, it is the very account which the scripture gives us of him.

§ 7. *Balaam's evil counsel to the Israelites.*

But there is a more surprising piece of iniquity yet behind. Not daring in his religious character, as a prophet, to assist

---

[c] Ver. 21.

[1] *On the Confusion of Languages*, c. xx.

the king of Moab, he considers whether there might not be found some other means of assisting him against that very people, whom he himself by the fear of God was restrained from cursing in words. One would not think it possible, that the weakness, even of religious self-deceit in its utmost excess, could have so poor a distinction, so fond an evasion, to serve itself of. But so it was: and he could think of no other method, than to betray the children of Israel to provoke his wrath, who was their only strength and defence. The temptation which he pitched upon, was that concerning which Solomon afterwards observed, that it had *cast down many wounded; yea, many strong men had been slain by it:* and of which he himself was a sad example, when *his wives turned away his heart after other gods.* This succeeded: the people sin against God; and thus the Prophet's counsel brought on that destruction, which he could by no means be prevailed upon to assist with the religious ceremony of execration, which the king of Moab thought would itself have effected it. Their crime and punishment are related in Deuteronomy [f], and Numbers [g]. And from the relation repeated in Numbers [h], it appears, that Balaam was the contriver of the whole matter [1]. It is also ascribed to him in the Revelation [i], where he is said to have *taught Balak to cast a stumblingblock before the children of Israel.*

This was the man, this Balaam, I say, was the man who desired to *die the death of the righteous*, and that his *last end might be like his:* and this was the state of his mind, when he pronounced these words.

[f] Chap. iv.   [g] Chap. xxv.   [h] Chap. xxxi.   [i] Chap. ii.

---

[1] There is no such recital in the principal narrative of Balak and Balaam (Numbers xxiii-iv), nor in Deuteronomy. In Numbers xxxi. 16 we have, not 'repeated' but for the first time introduced, the following notice: 'Behold, these caused the children of Israel, through the counsel of Balaam, to commit trespass against the Lord in the matter of Peor, and there was a plague among the congregation of the Lord.' This trespass is related, without any mention of Balaam or of the relations with Balak, in Numbers xxv. 1-9. A more detailed consideration of the case of Balaam will be found in a remarkable sermon of Newman's, Vol. iv. Serm. ii.

§ 8. *Violent contrasts in the character of Balaam.*

So that the object we have now before us is the most astonishing in the world : a very wicked man, under a deep sense of God and religion, persisting still in his wickedness, and preferring the wages of unrighteousness, even when he had before him a lively view of death, and that approaching period of his days, which should deprive him of all those advantages for which he was prostituting himself; and likewise a prospect, whether certain or uncertain, of a future state of retribution : all this joined with an explicit ardent wish, that, when he was to leave this world, he might be in the condition of a righteous man. Good God, what inconsistency, what perplexity is here! With what different views of things, with what contradictory principles of action, must such a mind be torn and distracted! It was not unthinking carelessness, by which he run on headlong in vice and folly, without ever making a stand to ask himself what he was doing: no; he acted upon the cool motives of interest and advantage. Neither was he totally hard and callous to impressions of religion, what we call abandoned ; for he absolutely denied to curse Israel. When reason assumes her place, when convinced of his duty, when he owns and feels, and is actually under the influence of the divine authority ; whilst he is carrying on his views to the grave, the end of all temporal greatness ; under this sense of things, with the better character and more desirable state present—full before him—in his thoughts, in his wishes, voluntarily to choose the worse—what fatality is here! Or how otherwise can such a character be explained?

§ 9. *His case not uncommon now.*

And yet, strange as it may appear, it is not altogether an uncommon one : nay, with some small alterations, and put a little lower, it is applicable to a very considerable part of the world. For if the reasonable choice be seen and acknowledged, and yet men make the unreasonable one, is not this the same contradiction ; that very inconsistency, which appeared so unaccountable?

§ 10. *Since reason will not sustain the bad man,
he takes to subterfuge.*

To give some little opening to such characters and behaviour, it is to be observed in general, that there is no account to be given in the way of reason, of men's so strong attachments to the present world: our hopes and fears and pursuits are in degrees beyond all proportion to the known value of the things they respect. This may be said without taking into consideration religion and a future state; and when these are considered, the disproportion is infinitely heightened. Now when men go against their reason, and contradict a more important interest at a distance, for one nearer, though of less consideration; if this be the whole of the case, all that can be said is, that strong passions, some kind of brute force within, prevails over the principle of rationality. However, if this be with a clear, full, and distinct view of the truth of things, then it is doing the utmost violence to themselves, acting in the most palpable contradiction to their very nature. But if there be any such thing in mankind as putting half-deceits upon themselves; which there plainly is, either by avoiding reflection, or (if they do reflect) by religious equivocation, subterfuges, and palliating matters to themselves; by these means conscience may be laid asleep, and they may go on in a course of wickedness with less disturbance. All the various turns, doubles, and intricacies in a dishonest heart, cannot be unfolded or laid open; but that there is somewhat of that kind is manifest, be it to be called self-deceit, or by any other name. Balaam had before his eyes the authority of God, absolutely forbidding him what he, for the sake of a reward, had the strongest inclination to: he was likewise in a state of mind sober enough to consider death and his last end: by these considerations he was restrained, first from going to the king of Moab; and after he did go, from cursing Israel. But notwithstanding this, there was great wickedness in his heart. He could not forego the rewards of unrighteousness: he therefore first seeks for indulgences; and when these could not be obtained, he sins against the whole meaning, end, and design of the prohibition, which no consideration in the world could prevail with him to go against the letter of. And surely that impious counsel he gave to Balak against the children of Israel, was, considered in itself, a greater piece of wickedness, than if he had cursed them in words.

§ 11. *He abandons high hope: yet not all hope.*

If it be inquired what his situation, his hopes and fears were, in respect to this his wish; the answer must be, that consciousness of the wickedness of his heart must necessarily have destroyed all settled hopes of dying the death of the righteous: he could have no calm satisfaction in this view of his last end: yet, on the other hand, it is possible that those partial regards to his duty, now mentioned, might keep him from perfect despair.

§ 12. *He combined sound belief with wicked conduct.*

Upon the whole, it is manifest, that Balaam had the most just and true notions of God and religion; as appears, partly from the original story itself, and more plainly from the passage in Micah; where he explains religion to consist in real virtue and real piety, expressly distinguished from superstition, and in terms which most strongly exclude dishonesty and falseness of heart. Yet you see his behaviour: he seeks indulgences for plain wickedness; which not being able to obtain, he glosses over that same wickedness, dresses it up in a new form, in order to make it pass off more easily with himself. That is, he deliberately contrives to deceive and impose upon himself, in a matter which he knew to be of the utmost importance.

§ 13. *The endeavour is, to make a composition with God.*

To bring these observations home to ourselves: it is too evident, that many persons allow themselves in very unjustifiable courses, who yet make great pretences to religion; not to deceive the world, none can be so weak as to think this will pass in our age; but from principles, hopes, and fears, respecting God and a future state; and go on thus with a sort of tranquillity and quiet of mind. This cannot be upon a thorough consideration, and full resolution, that the pleasures and advantages they propose are to be pursued at all hazards, against reason, against the law of God, and though everlasting destruction is to be the consequence. This would be doing too great violence upon themselves. No, they are for making a composition with the Almighty. These of his commands they will obey: but as to others—why they will make all the atonements in their power; the ambitious, the covetous, the dissolute man, each in a way which shall not contradict his respective pursuit. Indulgences before, which was Balaam's first attempt, though he was not so successful in it as to deceive himself, or atonements afterwards, are all the same. And here perhaps come in faint hopes that they may, and half-resolves that they will, one time or other, make a change.

§ 14. *Considering our duty often means explaining it away.*

Besides these, there are also persons, who, from a more just way of considering things, see the infinite absurdity of this, of substituting sacrifice instead of obedience; there are persons far enough from superstition, and not without some real sense of God and religion upon their minds; who yet are guilty of most unjustifiable practices, and go on with great coolness and command over themselves. The same dishonesty and unsoundness of heart discovers itself in these another way. In all common ordinary cases we see intuitively at first view what is our duty, what is the honest part. This is the ground of the observation, that the first thought is often the best. In these cases doubt and deliberation is itself dishonesty; as it was in Balaam upon the second message. That which is called considering what is our duty in a particular case, is very often nothing but endeavouring to explain it away. Thus those courses, which, if men would fairly attend to the dictates of their own consciences, they would see to be corruption, excess, oppression, uncharitableness; these are refined upon— things were so and so circumstantiated—great difficulties are raised about fixing bounds and degrees: and thus every moral obligation whatever may be evaded. Here is scope, I say, for an unfair mind to explain away every moral obligation to itself. Whether men reflect again upon this internal management and artifice, and how explicit they are with themselves, is another question. There are many operations of the mind, many things pass within, which we never reflect upon again; which a bystander, from having frequent opportunities of observing us and our conduct, may make shrewd guesses at.

§ 15. *For all self-deceit the remedy lies in becoming 'little children.'*

That great numbers are in this way of deceiving themselves is certain. There is scarce a man in the world, who has entirely got over all regards, hopes, and fears, concerning God and a future state; and these apprehensions in the generality, bad as we are, prevail in considerable degrees: yet men will and can be wicked, with calmness and thought; we see they are. There must therefore be some method of making it sit a little easy upon their minds; which, in the superstitious, is those indulgences and atonements before mentioned, and this self-deceit of another kind in persons of another character. And both these proceed from a certain unfairness of mind, a peculiar inward dishonesty; the direct contrary to that simplicity which our Saviour recommends, under the notion of *becoming little children*, as a necessary qualification for our entering into the kingdom of heaven.

§ 16. *As all wish 'the death of the righteous,' only plain dealing with ourselves is needed.*

But to conclude: How much soever men differ in the course of life they prefer, and in their ways of palliating and excusing their vices to themselves; yet all agree in the one thing, desiring to *die the death of the righteous*. This is surely remarkable. The observation may be extended further, and put thus: Even without determining what that is which we call guilt or innocence, there is no man but would choose, after having had the pleasure or advantage of a vicious action, to be free of the guilt of it, to be in the state of an innocent man. This shows at least the disturbance and implicit dissatisfaction in vice. If we inquire into the grounds of it, we shall find it proceeds partly from an immediate sense of having done evil, and partly from an apprehension, that this inward sense shall one time or another be seconded by an higher judgment, upon which our whole being depends. Now to suspend and drown this sense, and these apprehensions, be it by the hurry of business or of pleasure, or by superstition, or moral equivocations, this is in a manner one and the same, and makes no alteration at all in the nature of our case. Things and actions are what they are, and the consequences of them will be what they will be: why then should we desire to be deceived? As we are reasonable creatures, and have any regard to ourselves, we ought to lay these things plainly and honestly before our mind, and upon this, act as you please, as you think most fit; make that choice, and prefer that course of life, which you can justify to yourselves, and which sits most easy upon your own mind. It will immediately appear, that vice cannot be the happiness, but must upon the whole be the misery, of such a creature as man; a moral, an accountable agent. Superstitious observances, self-deceit though of a more refined sort, will not in reality at all mend matters with us. And the result of the whole can be nothing else, but that with simplicity and fairness we *keep innocency, and take heed unto the thing that is right; for this alone shall bring a man peace at the last.*

SERMON VIII

UPON RESENTMENT

Ye have heard that it hath been said, Thou shalt love thy neighbour, and hate thine enemy. But I say unto you, Love your enemies, bless them that curse you, do good to them that hate you, and pray for them which despitefully use you, and persecute you.—MATTHEW V. 43, 44.

§ 1. *To inquire why we are not otherwise placed and constituted, worse than frivolous.*

SINCE perfect goodness in the Deity is the principle from whence the universe was brought into being, and by which it is preserved; and since general benevolence is the great law of the whole moral creation: it is a question which immediately occurs, *Why had man implanted in him a principle, which appears the direct contrary to benevolence?* Now the foot upon which inquiries of this kind should be treated is this: to take human nature as it is, and the circumstances in which it is placed as they are; and then consider the correspondence between that nature and those circumstances, or what course of action and behaviour, respecting those circumstances, any particular affection or passion leads us to. This I mention to distinguish the matter now before us from disquisitions of quite another kind; namely, *Why we are not made more perfect creatures, or placed in better circumstances?* these being questions which we have not, that I know of, any thing at all to do with. God Almighty undoubtedly foresaw the disorders, both natural and moral, which would happen in this state of things. If upon this we set ourselves to search and examine why he did not prevent them; we shall, I am afraid, be in danger of running into somewhat worse than impertinent curiosity.

§ 2. *But useful to scan the relation of our nature to its environment.*

But upon this to examine how far the nature which he hath given us hath a respect to those circumstances, such as they are; how far it leads us to act a proper part in them; plainly belongs to us: and such inquiries are in many ways of excellent use. Thus the thing to be considered is, not, *Why we were not made of such a nature, and placed in such circumstances, as to have no need of so harsh and turbulent a passion as resentment:* but, taking our nature and condition as being what they are, *Why or for what end such a passion was given us:* and this chiefly in order to show what are the abuses of it.

§ 3. Lex talionis *is simple but unsatisfactory.*

The persons who laid down for a rule, *Thou shalt love thy neighbour, and hate thine enemy,* made short work with this matter. They did not, it seems, perceive any thing to be disapproved in hatred, more than in good-will: and, according to their system of morals, our enemy was the proper natural object of one of these passions, as our neighbour was of the other of them [1].

This was all they had to say, and all they thought needful to be said, upon the subject. But this cannot be satisfactory; because hatred, malice, and revenge, are directly contrary to the religion we profess, and to the nature and reason of the thing itself.

§ 4. *God's purpose in enduing us with resentment.*

Therefore, since no passion God hath endued us with can be in itself evil; and yet since men frequently indulge

---

[1] Arist. *Eth. Nic.* V. v. 1 : Δοκεῖ δέ τισι καὶ τὸ ἀντιπεπονθὸς εἶναι ἁπλῶς δίκαιον, ὥσπερ οἱ Πυθαγόρειοι ἔφασαν· ὡρίζοντο γὰρ ἁπλῶς τὸ δίκαιον τὸ ἀντιπεπονθὸς ἄλλῳ.

a passion in such ways and degrees that at length it becomes quite another thing from what it was originally in our nature; and those vices of malice and revenge in particular take their occasion from the natural passion of resentment: it will be needful to trace this up to its original, that we may see, *what it is in itself, as placed in our nature by its Author;* from which it will plainly appear, *for what ends it was placed there.* And when we know what the passion is in itself, and the ends of it, we shall easily see, *what are the abuses of it, in which malice and revenge consist;* and which are so strongly forbidden in the text, by the direct contrary being commanded.

§ 5. *St. Paul's distinction between anger and sin.*

Resentment is of two kinds: *hasty and sudden,* or *settled and deliberate.* The former is called anger, and often *passion;* which, though a general word, is frequently appropriated and confined to the particular feeling, sudden anger, as distinct from deliberate resentment, malice, and revenge. In all these words is usually implied somewhat vicious; somewhat unreasonable as to the occasion of the passion, or immoderate as to the degree or duration of it. But that the natural passion itself is indifferent, St. Paul has asserted in that precept, *Be ye angry, and sin not*[a]: which though it is by no means to be understood as an encouragement to indulge ourselves in anger, the sense being certainly this, *Though ye be angry, sin not;* yet here is evidently a distinction made between anger and sin; between the natural passion, and sinful anger.

§ 6. *Sudden anger is often instinctive, and without injury received.*

Sudden anger, upon certain occasions, is mere instinct: as merely so, as the disposition to close our eyes upon the apprehension of somewhat falling into them; and no more

---

[a] Ephes. iv. 26.

necessarily implies any degree of reason. I say, *necessarily*: for to be sure *hasty*, as well as *deliberate*, anger may be occasioned by injury or contempt; in which cases reason suggests to our thoughts that injury and contempt, which is the occasion of the passion: but I am speaking of the former only so far as it is to be distinguished from the latter. The only way in which our reason and understanding can raise anger, is by representing to our mind injustice or injury of some kind or other. Now momentary anger is frequently raised, not only without any real, but without any apparent reason; that is, without any appearance of injury, as distinct from hurt or pain. It cannot, I suppose, be thought, that this passion, in infants; in the lower species of animals; and, which is often seen, in men towards them; it cannot, I say, be imagined, that these instances of this passion are the effect of reason: no, they are occasioned by mere sensation and feeling. It is opposition, sudden hurt, violence, which naturally excites the passion; and the real demerit or fault of him who offers that violence, or is the cause of that opposition or hurt, does not, in many cases, so much as come into thought.

§ 7. *But often the only defence against destruction.*

The reason and end, for which man was made thus liable to this passion, is, that he might be better qualified to prevent, and likewise (or perhaps chiefly) to resist and defeat, sudden force, violence, and opposition, considered merely as such, and without regard to the fault or demerit of him who is the author of them. Yet, since violence may be considered in this other and further view, as implying fault; and since injury, as distinct from harm, may raise sudden anger; sudden anger may likewise accidentally serve to prevent, or remedy, such fault and injury. But, considered as distinct from settled anger, it stands in our nature for self-defence, and not for the administration of justice. There are plainly cases, and in the uncultivated parts of the world, and where regular governments are not formed, they frequently happen, in which there is no time for consideration, and yet to be passive is certain destruction; in which, sudden resistance is the only security.

§ 8. *Settled anger is properly a resentment against injury and wickedness:*

But from *this, deliberate anger or resentment* is essentially distinguished, as the latter is not naturally excited by, or intended to prevent mere harm without appearance of wrong or injustice. Now, in order to see, as exactly as we can, what is the natural object and occasion of such resentment; let us reflect upon the manner in which we are touched with reading, suppose, a feigned story of baseness and villany, properly worked up to move our passions. This immediately raises indignation, somewhat of a desire that it should be punished. And though the designed injury be prevented, yet that it was designed is sufficient to raise this inward feeling. Suppose the story true, this inward feeling would be as natural and as just: and one may venture to affirm, that there is scarce a man in the world, but would have it upon some occasions. It seems *in us* plainly connected with a sense of virtue and vice, of moral good and evil. Suppose further, we knew both the person who did and who suffered the injury: neither would this make any alteration, only that it would probably affect us more. The indignation raised by cruelty and injustice, and the desire of having it punished, which persons unconcerned would feel, is by no means malice. No, it is resentment against vice and wickedness: it is one of the common bonds, by which society is held together; a fellow-feeling, which each individual has in behalf of the whole species, as well as of himself. And it does not appear that this, generally speaking, is at all too high amongst mankind. Suppose now the injury I have been speaking of to be done against ourselves; or those whom we consider as ourselves. It is plain, the way in which we should be affected would be exactly the same in kind: but it would certainly be in a higher degree, and less transient; because a sense of our own happiness and misery is most intimately and always present to us; and from the very constitution of our nature, we cannot but have a greater sensibility to, and be more deeply interested in, what concerns ourselves [1].

§ 9. *Heightened when these are against ourselves;*

And this seems to be the whole of this passion, which is, properly speaking, natural to mankind: namely, a resentment against injury and wickedness in general; and in a higher degree when towards ourselves, in proportion to the greater regard which men naturally have for themselves, than for others. From hence it appears, that it is not natural, but moral evil; it is not suffering, but injury, which raises that anger or resentment, which is of any continuance. The natural object of it is not one, who appears to the suffering person to have been only the innocent occasion of his pain or loss; but one, who has been in a moral sense injurious either to ourselves or others. This is abundantly confirmed by observing what it is which heightens or lessens resentment; namely, the same which aggravates or lessens the fault: friendship, and former obligations, on one hand; or inadvertency, strong temptations, and mistake, on the other. All this is so much understood by mankind, how little soever it be reflected upon, that a person would be reckoned quite distracted, who should coolly resent an harm, which had not to himself the appearance of injury or wrong. Men do indeed resent what is occasioned through carelessness: but then they expect observance as their due, and so that carelessness is considered as faulty.

§ 10. *And it is against injury done, as compared with injury planned.*

It is likewise true, that they resent more strongly an injury done, than one which, though designed, was prevented, in cases where the guilt is perhaps the same: the

---

[1] That is to say, habitually and in the generality of men; but in men of special characters, and in many men on special occasions, it may be otherwise.

reason however is, not that bare pain or loss raises resentment, but, that it gives a new, and, as I may speak, additional sense of the injury or injustice. According to the natural course of the passions, the degrees of resentment are in proportion, not only to the degree of design and deliberation in the injurious person; but in proportion to this, joined with the degree of the evil designed or premeditated; since this likewise comes in to make the injustice greater or less. And the evil or harm will appear greater when they feel it, than when they only reflect upon it: so therefore will the injury: and consequently the resentment will be greater.

§ 11. *Prevention of injury and its results the final cause of settled anger.*

The natural object or occasion of settled resentment then being injury, as distinct from pain or loss; it is easy to see, that to prevent and to remedy such injury, and the miseries arising from it, is the end for which this passion was implanted in man. It is to be considered as a weapon, put into our hands by nature, against injury, injustice, and cruelty: how it may be innocently employed and made use of, shall presently be mentioned.

§ 12. *Possible coincidence of the two kinds: and essential distinction.*

The account which has been now given of this passion is, in brief, that sudden anger is raised by, and was chiefly intended to prevent or remedy, mere harm distinct from injury: but that it *may* be raised by injury, and *may* serve to prevent or to remedy it; and then the occasions and effects of it are the same with the occasions and effects of deliberate anger. But they are essentially distinguished in this, that the latter is never occasioned by harm, distinct from injury; and its natural proper end is to remedy or prevent only that harm, which implies, or is supposed to imply, injury or moral wrong. Every one sees that these observations do not relate to those, who have habitually suppressed the course of their passions and affections, out of regard either to interest or virtue; or who, from habits of vice and folly, have changed their nature. But, I suppose, there can be no doubt but this, now described, is the general course of resentment, considered as a natural passion, neither increased by indulgence, nor corrected by virtue, nor prevailed over by other passions, or particular habits of life.

§ 13. *Abuses of anger:* (a) *passion:* (b) *in feebler natures, peevishness;*

As to the abuses of anger, which it is to be observed may be in all different degrees, the first which occurs is what is commonly called *passion;* to which some men are liable, in the same way as others are to the *epilepsy,* or any sudden particular disorder. This distemper of the mind seizes them upon the least occasion in the world, and perpetually without any real reason at all: and by means of it they are plainly, every day, every waking hour of their lives, liable and in danger of running into the most extravagant outrages. Of a less boisterous, but not of a less innocent[1] kind, is *peevishness;* which I mention with pity, with real pity to the unhappy creatures, who, from their inferior station, or other circumstances and relations, are obliged to be in the way of, and to serve for a supply to it. Both these, for ought that I can see, are one and the same principle: but, as it takes root in minds of different makes, it appears differently, and so is come to be distinguished by different names. That which in a more feeble temper is peevishness, and languidly discharges itself upon every thing which comes in its way; the same principle, in a temper of greater force and stronger passions, becomes rage and fury. In one, the humour discharges itself at once; in the other, it is continually discharging. This is the account of *passion* and *peevishness,* as distinct from each other, and appearing in different persons. It is no objection against the truth of it, that

---

[1] So in all the editions: but the meaning seems to be less nocent.

they are both to be seen sometimes in one and the same person.

§ 14. *Or: injury (a) imagined; (b) exaggerated; (c) done by another; (d) disproportionate: or, seeking only to gratify resentment;*

With respect to deliberate resentment, the chief instances of abuse are: when, from partiality to ourselves, we imagine an injury done us, when there is none: when this partiality represents it to us greater than it really is: when we fall into that extravagant and monstrous kind of resentment, towards one who has innocently been the occasion of evil to us; that is, resentment upon account of pain or inconvenience, without injury; which is the same absurdity, as settled anger at a thing that is inanimate: when the indignation against injury and injustice rises too high, and is beyond proportion to the particular ill action it is exercised upon: or, lastly, when pain or harm of any kind is inflicted merely in consequence of, and to gratify, that resentment, though naturally raised.

§ 15. *Or: deafness to reasonable justification.*

It would be endless to descend into and explain all the peculiarities of perverseness and wayward humour which might be traced up to this passion. But there is one thing, which so generally belongs to and accompanies all excess and abuse of it, as to require being mentioned: a certain determination, and resolute bent of mind, not to be convinced or set right; though it be ever so plain, that there is no reason for the displeasure, that it was raised merely by error or misunderstanding. In this there is doubtless a great mixture of pride; but there is somewhat more, which I cannot otherwise express, than, that resentment has taken possession of the temper and of the mind, and will not quit its hold. It would be too minute to inquire whether this be any thing more than bare obstinacy: it is sufficient to observe, that it, in a very particular manner and degree, belongs to the abuses of this passion.

§ 16. *Yet needed* (a) *to balance pity,* (b) *to assist just severity.*

But, notwithstanding all these abuses, 'Is not just indignation against cruelty and wrong one of the *instruments of death*, which the Author of our nature hath provided? Are not cruelty, injustice, and wrong, the natural objects of that indignation? Surely then it may one way or other be innocently employed against them.' True. Since therefore it is necessary for the very subsistence of the world, that injury, injustice, and cruelty should be punished; and since compassion, which is so natural to mankind, would render that execution of justice exceedingly difficult and uneasy; indignation against vice and wickedness is, and may be allowed to be, a balance to that weakness of pity, and also to any thing else which would prevent the necessary methods of severity. Those who have never thought upon these subjects, may perhaps not see the weight of this: but let us suppose a person guilty of murder, or any other action of cruelty, and that mankind had naturally no indignation against such wickedness and the authors of it; but that every body was affected towards such a criminal in the same way as towards an innocent man: compassion, amongst other things, would render the execution of justice exceedingly painful and difficult, and would often quite prevent it[1]. And notwithstanding that the principle of benevolence is denied by some, and is really in a very low degree, [2]that men are in great measure insensible to the happiness of their fellow-creatures; yet they are not insensible to their misery, but are very strongly moved with it: insomuch that there plainly is occasion for that feeling, which is raised

---

[1] Our own time has witnessed cases notable for the growth of this morbid sympathy. Suppose a murderess imprisoned for life. The guilt is perhaps long past: the suffering present, and ever pleading its accumulation. The past becomes weak as it recedes into the distance; and the present steadily gains upon it.

This applies especially to the case of murder, though extreme: because it is silently suggested that there is no one before us entitled to claim reparation, and to dwell upon the fact that it is being rendered by public justice.

[2] Query insert 'and.'

by guilt and demerit, as a balance to that of compassion. Thus much may, I think, justly be allowed to resentment, in the strictest way of moral consideration.

§ 17. *Its good influence; though inferior to pure reason.*

The good influence which this passion has in fact upon the affairs of the world, is obvious to every one's notice. Men are plainly restrained from injuring their fellow-creatures by fear of their resentment ; and it is very happy that they are so, when they would not be restrained by a principle of virtue. And after an injury is done, and there is a necessity that the offender should be brought to justice ; the cool consideration of reason, that the security and peace of society requires examples of justice should be made, might indeed be sufficient to procure laws to be enacted, and sentence passed : but is it that cool reflection in the injured person, which, for the most part, brings the offender to justice ? Or is it not resentment and indignation against the injury and the author of it ? I am afraid there is no doubt, which is commonly the case. This however is to be considered as a good effect, notwithstanding it were much to be wished that men would act from a better principle, reason and cool reflection.

§ 18. *It is an inward witness on behalf of virtue;*

The account now given of the passion of resentment, as distinct from all the abuses of it, may suggest to our thoughts the following reflections :

First, That vice is indeed of ill desert, and must finally be punished. Why should men dispute concerning the reality of virtue, and whether it be founded in the nature of things, which yet surely is not matter of question ; but why should this, I say, be disputed, when every man carries about him this passion, which affords him demonstration, that the rules of justice and equity are to be the guide of his actions ? For every man naturally feels an indignation upon seeing instances of villainy and baseness, and therefore cannot commit the same without being self-condemned.

§ 19. *And against the only object of a just abhorrence.*

Secondly, That we should learn to be cautious, lest we *charge God foolishly,* by ascribing that to him, or the nature he has given us, which is owing wholly to our own abuse of it. Men may speak of the degeneracy and corruption of the world, according to the experience they have had of it; but human nature, considered as the divine workmanship, should methinks be treated as sacred: for *in the image of God made he man.* That passion, from whence men take occasion to run into the dreadful vices of malice and revenge; even that passion, as implanted in our nature by God, is not only innocent, but a generous movement of mind. It is in itself, and in its original, no more than indignation against injury and wickedness: that which is the only deformity in the creation, and the only reasonable object of abhorrence and dislike. How manifold evidence have we of the divine wisdom and goodness, when even pain in the natural world, and the passion we have been now considering in the moral, come out instances of it!

SERMON IX

UPON FORGIVENESS OF INJURIES

—♦♦—

Ye have heard that it hath been said, Thou shalt love thy neighbour, and hate thine enemy. But I say unto you, Love your enemies, bless them that curse you, do good to them that hate you, and pray for them which despitefully use you, and persecute you.—MATTHEW v. 43, 44.

—♦♦—

§ 1. *On provisions useful for our present state, but of a mixed nature.*

AS God Almighty foresaw the irregularities and disorders, both natural and moral, which would happen in this state of things; he hath graciously made some provision against them, by giving us several passions and affections, which arise from, or whose objects are, those disorders. Of this sort are fear, resentment, compassion, and others; of which there could be no occasion or use in a perfect state: but in the present we should be exposed to greater inconveniences without them; though there are very considerable ones, which they themselves are the occasions of. They are encumbrances indeed, but such as we are obliged to carry about with us, through this various journey of life: some of them as a guard against the violent assaults of others, and in our own defence; some in behalf of others; and all of them to put us upon, and help to carry us through a course of behaviour suitable to our condition, in default of that perfection of wisdom and virtue, which would be in all respects our better security.

§ 2. *Not resentment, but only its excess, forbidden against wrong done to ourselves.*

The passion of anger or resentment hath already been largely treated of [1]. It hath been shown, that mankind naturally feel some emotion of mind against injury and injustice, whoever are the sufferers by it; and even though the injurious design be prevented from taking effect. Let this be called anger, indignation, resentment, or by whatever name any one shall choose; the thing itself is understood, and is plainly natural. It has likewise been observed, that this natural indignation is generally moderate and low enough in mankind, in each particular man, when the injury which excites it doth not affect himself, or one whom he considers as himself. Therefore the precepts to *forgive*, and to *love our enemies*, do not relate to that general indignation against injury and the authors of it, but to this feeling, or resentment when raised by private or personal injury. But no man could be thought in earnest, who should assert, that, though indignation against injury, when others are the sufferers, is innocent and just; yet the same indignation against it, when we ourselves are the sufferers, becomes faulty and blameable. These precepts therefore cannot be understood to forbid this in the latter case, more than in the former. Nay they cannot be understood to forbid this feeling in the latter case, though raised to a higher degree than in the former: because, as was also observed further, from the very constitution of our nature, we cannot but have a greater sensibility to what concerns ourselves. Therefore the precepts in the text, and others of the like import with them, must be understood to forbid only the excess and abuse of this natural feeling, in cases of personal and private injury: the chief instances of which excess and abuse have likewise been already remarked; and

---

[1] As the object of Serm. viii was to point out the use and abuse of resentment, so the object of the present Discourse is to indicate the limits by which the legitimate exercise of this principle is regulated, and to establish the general obligation of the forgiveness of injuries. Carmichael.

all of them, excepting that of retaliation, do so plainly in the very terms express somewhat unreasonable, disproportionate, and absurd, as to admit of no pretence or shadow of justification.

§ 3. *Revenge is forbidden; love of enemies obligatory.*

But since custom and false honour are on the side of retaliation and revenge, when the resentment is natural and just; and reasons are sometimes offered in justification of revenge in these cases; and since love of our enemies is thought *too hard a saying* to be obeyed: I will show *the absolute unlawfulness of the former; the obligations we are under to the latter;* and then proceed to *some reflections, which may have a more direct and immediate tendency to beget in us a right temper of mind towards those who have offended us.*

In showing the unlawfulness of revenge, it is not my present design to examine what is alleged in favour of it, from the tyranny of custom and false honour, but only to consider the nature and reason of the thing itself; which ought to have prevented, and ought now to extirpate, every thing of that kind.

§ 4. *Revenge (or retaliation) engenders counter-revenge;*

First, Let us begin with the supposition of that being innocent, which is pleaded for, and which shall be shown to be altogether vicious, the supposition that we were allowed to *render evil for evil,* and see what would be the consequence. Malice or resentment towards any man hath plainly a tendency to beget the same passion in him who is the object of it; and this again increases it in the other. It is of the very nature of this vice to propagate itself, not only by way of example, which it does in common with other vices, but in a peculiar way of its own; for resentment itself, as well as what is done in consequence of it, is the object of resentment: hence it comes to pass, that the first offence, even when so slight as presently to be dropped and forgotten, becomes the occasion of entering into a long intercourse of ill offices: neither is it at all uncommon to see persons, in this progress of strife and variance, change parts; and him, who was at first the injured person, become more injurious and blameable than the aggressor. Put the case then, that the law of retaliation was universally received, and allowed, as an innocent rule of life, by all; and the observance of it thought by many (and then it would soon come to be thought by all) a point of honour: this supposes every man in private cases to pass sentence in his own cause; and likewise, that anger or resentment is to be the judge.

§ 5. *Especially in connection with the almost certain excess.*

Thus, from the numberless partialities which we all have for ourselves, every one would often think himself injured when he was not: and in most cases would represent an injury as much greater than it really is; the imagined dignity of the person offended would scarce ever fail to magnify the offence. And, if bare retaliation, or returning just the mischief received, always begets resentment in the person upon whom we retaliate, what would that excess do? Add to this, that he likewise has his partialities—there is no going on to represent this scene of rage and madness: it is manifest there would be no bounds, nor any end. *If the beginning of strife is as when one letteth out water*, what would it come to when allowed this free and unrestrained course? *As coals are to burning coals, or wood to fire;* so would these *contentious men be to kindle strife.* And, since the indulgence of revenge hath manifestly this tendency, and does actually produce these effects in proportion as it is allowed; a passion of so dangerous a nature ought not to be indulged, were there no other reason against it.

§ 6. *Just resentment is bound to intend the production of some greater good.*

Secondly, It hath been shown that the passion of resentment was placed in man, upon supposition of, and as a prevention or remedy to, irregularity and disorder. Now whether it be allowed or not, that the passion itself and the gratification of it, joined together, are painful to the malicious person; it must however be so with respect to the person towards whom it is exercised, and upon whom the revenge is taken. Now, if we consider mankind, according to that fine allusion of St. Paul[1], as *one body, and every one members one of another;* it must be allowed that resentment is, with respect to society, a painful remedy. Thus then the very notion or idea of this passion, as a remedy or prevention of evil, and as in itself a painful means, plainly shows that it ought never to be made use of, but only in order to produce some greater good.

§ 7. *As resentment, a secondary passion, aims at the prevention of greater evil.*

It is to be observed, that this argument is not founded upon an allusion or simile; but that it is drawn from the very nature of the passion itself, and the end for which it was given us. We are obliged to make use of words taken from sensible things, to explain what is the most remote from them: and every one sees from whence the words Prevention and Remedy are taken. But, if you please, let these words be dropped: the thing itself, I suppose, may be expressed without them.

That mankind is a community, that we all stand in a relation to each other, that there is a public end and interest of society which each particular is obliged to promote, is the sum of morals[2]. Consider then the passion of resentment, as given to this one body, as given to society. Nothing can be more manifest, than that resentment is to be considered as a secondary passion, placed in us upon supposition, upon account of, and with regard to, injury; not, to be sure, to promote and further it, but to render it,

---

[1] 1 Cor. xii. 14; Rom. xii. 5.
[2] I. e. of morals in that department of the science which contemplates the public good, or relative right and duty. The language of this section seems to be, at one or two points, less exactly measured, than is usual with Butler.

and the inconveniences and miseries arising from it, less and fewer than they would be without this passion. It is as manifest, that the indulgence of it is, with regard to society, a painful means of obtaining these ends. Considered in itself, it is very undesirable, and what society must very much wish to be without. It is in every instance absolutely an evil in itself[1], because it implies producing misery: and consequently must never be indulged or gratified for itself, by any one who considers mankind as a community or family, and himself as a member of it.

§ 8. *Unlike other affections, is tied down to subserving its chief end.*

Let us now take this in another view. Every natural appetite, passion, and affection, may be gratified in particular instances, without being subservient to the particular chief end, for which these several principles were respectively implanted in our nature. And, if neither this end, nor any other moral obligation, be contradicted, such gratification is innocent. Thus, I suppose, there are cases in which each of these principles, this one of resentment excepted, may innocently be gratified, without being subservient to what is the main end of it: that is, though it does not conduce to, yet it may be gratified without contradicting, that end, or any other obligation[2]. But the gratification of resentment, if it be not conducive to the end for which it was given us, must necessarily contradict, not only the general obligation to benevolence, but likewise that particular end itself. The end, for which it was given, is to prevent or remedy injury; i. e. the misery occasioned by

---

[1] For it is administered through pain, which Butler is regarding as evil in a secondary sense: born of evil, incidental and ministering to evil in this connection. Compare the corresponding use of the word 'good' in the preceding section: and 'mischief' in the following one.

[2] See § 6 *sub initio*, and Serm. viii. 8, where it is shown that resentment was given us to be a foe to moral evil. As to some of our particular affections, e. g. love of reputation, it may seem doubtful whether they also are not properly subjected to the condition of subserving their main end in order to their lawful exercise.

injury; i.e. misery itself: and the gratification of it consists in producing misery; i. e. in contradicting the end for which it was implanted in our nature.

This whole reasoning is built upon the difference there is between this passion and all others. No other principle, or passion, hath for its end the misery of our fellow-creatures. But malice and revenge meditates evil itself; and to do mischief, to be the author of misery, is the very thing which gratifies the passion: this is what it directly tends towards, as its proper design. Other vices eventually do mischief: this alone aims at it as an end [1].

Nothing can with reason be urged in justification of revenge [2], from the good effects which the indulgence of it was before mentioned [a] to have upon the affairs of the world; because, though it be a remarkable instance of the wisdom of Providence to bring good out of evil, yet vice is vice to him who is guilty of it. 'But suppose these good effects are foreseen:' that is, suppose reason in a particular case leads a man the same way as passion? Why then, to be sure, he should follow his reason, in this as well as in all other cases. So that, turn the matter which way ever you will, no more can be allowed to this passion, than that hath been already [3].

§ 9. *Love to enemies is the natural action of benevolence, on removal of the bar.*

As to that love of our enemies, which is commanded; this supposes the general obligation to benevolence or good-will towards mankind: and this being supposed, that precept is no more than to forgive injuries; that is, to keep clear of those abuses before mentioned: because that we have the habitual temper of benevolence is taken for granted.

---

[a] Serm. viii. 15.

[1] Observe that with revenge Butler here combines malice, which is gratuitous, while revenge is provoked.

[2] That is to say, in so far as it goes beyond resentment: which may degenerate into it, but need not. And 'misery' as used above seems to be simply the equivalent of pain.

[3] See Serm. viii. 15: where the concession made is made only to resentment, not revenge.

§ 10. *Incompatible with revenge; not with resentment.*

Resentment is not inconsistent with good-will; for we often see both together in very high degrees; not only in parents towards their children, but in cases of friendship and dependence, where there is no natural relation. These contrary passions, though they may lessen, do not necessarily destroy each other. We may therefore love our enemy, and yet have resentment against him for his injurious behaviour towards us. But when this resentment entirely destroys our natural benevolence towards him, it is excessive, and becomes malice or revenge. The command to prevent its having this effect, i. e. to forgive injuries, is the same as to love our enemies; because that love is always supposed, unless destroyed by resentment.

'But though mankind is the natural object of benevolence, yet may it not be lessened upon vice, i. e. injury?' Allowed: but if every degree of vice or injury must destroy that benevolence, then no man is the object of our love; for no man is without faults.

§ 11. *Is not to be cancelled by guilt.*

'But if lower instances of injury may lessen our benevolence, why may not higher, or the highest, destroy it?' The answer is obvious. It is not man's being a social creature, much less his being a moral agent, from whence *alone* our obligations to good-will towards him arise. There is an obligation to it prior to either of these, arising from his being a sensible creature; that is, capable of happiness or misery. Now this obligation cannot be superseded by his moral character. What justifies public executions is, not that the guilt or demerit of the criminal dispenses with the obligation of good-will, neither would this justify any severity; but, that his life is inconsistent with the quiet and happiness of the world: that is, a general and more enlarged obligation necessarily destroys a particular and more confined one of the same kind, inconsistent with it. Guilt or injury then does not dispense with or supersede the duty of love and good-will.

§ 12. *Natural self-regard does not dispense with it.*

Neither does that peculiar regard to ourselves, which was before allowed to be natural [b] to mankind, dispense with it: because that can no way innocently heighten our resentment against those who have been injurious to ourselves in particular, any otherwise than as it heightens our sense of the injury or guilt; and guilt, though in the highest degree, does not, as hath been shown, dispense with or supersede the duty of love and good-will.

If all this be true, what can a man say, who will dispute the reasonableness, or the possibility, of obeying the Divine precept we are now considering? Let him speak out, and it must be thus he will speak. 'Mankind, i.e. a creature defective and faulty, is the proper object of good-will, whatever his faults are, when they respect others; but not when they respect me myself.' That men should be *affected* in this manner, and *act* accordingly, is to be accounted for like other vices; but to *assert* that it *ought*, and *must* be thus, is self-partiality possessed of the very understanding.

Thus love to our enemies, and those who have been injurious to us, is so far from being a *rant*, as it has been profanely called, that it is in truth the law of our nature, and what every one must see and own, who is not quite blinded with self-love.

§ 13. *The injured man should have the same feeling as a good man not injured.*

From hence it is easy to see, what is the degree in which we are commanded to love our enemies, or those who have been injurious to us. It were well if it could as easily be reduced to practice. It cannot be imagined, that we are required to love them with any peculiar kind of affection [1].

---

[b] Serm. viii. 9.

---

[1] This seems undeniable as a rule: yet not always true. For the injurer becomes an object of special attention to the injured. Particular circumstances, or qualities about the injury, are disclosed, which appeal to him. Or a keen desire to make amends

But suppose the person injured to have a due natural sense of the injury, and no more; he ought to be affected towards the injurious person in the same way any good men, uninterested in the case, would be; if they had the same just sense, which we have supposed the injured person to have, of the fault: after which there will yet remain real good-will towards the offender.

§ 14. *This is reasonable; and surely not impracticable.*

Now what is there in all this, which should be thought impracticable? I am sure there is nothing in it unreasonable. It is indeed no more than that we should not indulge a passion, which, if generally indulged, would propagate itself so as almost to lay waste the world: that we should suppress that partial, that false self-love, which is the weakness of our nature: that uneasiness and misery should not be produced, without any good purpose to be served by it: and that we should not be affected towards persons differently from what their nature and character require.

But since to be convinced that any temper of mind, and course of behaviour, is our duty, and the contrary vicious, hath but a distant influence upon our temper and actions; let me add some few reflections, which may have a more direct tendency to subdue those vices in the heart, to beget in us this right temper, and lead us to a right behaviour towards those who have offended us: which reflections however shall be such as will further show the obligations we are under to it.

§ 15. *How hard it is, in these cases, to obtain a proper point of view.*

No one, I suppose, would choose to have an indignity put upon him, or to be injuriously treated. If then there be any probability of a misunderstanding in the case, either

---

is exhibited. In these and other ways it will happen that injury done becomes, in the mind of a good man, the occasion of special kindly sentiments towards the injurer.

from our imagining we are injured when we are not, or representing the injury to ourselves as greater than it really is; one would hope an intimation of this sort might be kindly received, and that people would be glad to find the injury not so great as they imagined. Therefore, without knowing particulars, I take upon me to assure all persons who think they have received indignities or injurious treatment, that they may depend upon it, as in a manner certain, that the offence is not so great as they themselves imagine. We are in such a peculiar situation, with respect to injuries done to ourselves, that we can scarce any more see them as they really are, than our eye can see itself. If we could place ourselves at a due distance, i.e. be really unprejudiced, we should frequently discern that to be in reality inadvertence and mistake in our enemy, which we now fancy we see to be malice or scorn. From this proper point of view, we should likewise in all probability see something of these latter in ourselves, and most certainly a great deal of the former. Thus the indignity or injury would almost infinitely lessen, and perhaps at last come out to be nothing at all. Self-love is a medium of a peculiar kind: in these cases it magnifies every thing which is amiss in others, at the same time that it lessens every thing amiss in ourselves.

§ 16. *Anger and hatred interpose a falsifying medium.*

Anger also or hatred may be considered as another false medium of viewing things, which always represents characters and actions much worse than they really are. Ill-will not only never speaks, but never thinks well, of the person towards whom it is exercised. Thus in cases of offence and enmity, the whole character and behaviour is considered with an eye to that particular part which has offended us, and the whole man appears monstrous, without any thing right or human in him: whereas the resentment should surely at least be confined to that particular part of the behaviour which gave offence: since the other parts of a man's life and character stand just the same as they did before.

§ 17. *Observe, we only ask men to look at things as they are.*

In general, there are very few instances of enmity carried to any length, but inadvertency, misunderstanding, some real mistake of the case, on one side however, if not on both, has a great share in it.

If these things were attended to, these ill-humours could not be carried to any length amongst good men, and they would be exceedingly abated amongst all. And one would hope they might be attended to: for all that these cautions come to is really no more than desiring, that things may be considered and judged of as they are in themselves, that we should have an eye to, and beware of, what would otherwise lead us into mistakes. So that to make allowances for inadvertence, misunderstanding, for the partialities of self-love, and the false light which anger sets things in; I say, to make allowances for these, is not to be spoken of as an instance of humbleness of mind, or meekness and moderation of temper; but as what common sense should suggest, to avoid judging wrong of a matter before us, though virtue and morals were out of the case. And therefore it as much belongs to ill men, who will indulge the vice I have been arguing against, as to good men, who endeavour to subdue it in themselves. In a word, all these cautions, concerning anger and self-love, are no more than desiring a man, who was looking through a glass, which either magnified or lessened, to take notice, that the objects are not in themselves what they appear through that medium.

§ 18. *Injuries do not spring from pure ill-will.*

To all these things one might add, that, resentment being out of the case, there is not, properly speaking, any such thing as direct ill-will in one man towards another[1]: therefore the first indignity or injury, if it be not owing to

---

[1] Though Butler rarely optimises in his dealings with human nature, yet this seems rather a bold assertion in its favour, when we consider the force of habit, and the wild extremes towards which a man is brought by perseverance in ill doing. Compare Serm. i. 11.

inadvertence or misunderstanding, may however be resolved into other particular passions or self-love: principles quite distinct from ill-will, and which we ought all to be disposed to excuse in others, from experiencing so much of them in ourselves. A great man of antiquity is reported to have said, that as he never was indulgent to any one fault in himself, he could not excuse those of others. This sentence could scarce with decency come out of the mouth of any human creature. But if we invert the former part, and put it thus: that he was indulgent to many faults in himself, as it is to be feared the best of us are, and yet was implacable; how monstrous would such an assertion appear! And this is the case in respect to every human creature, in proportion as he is without the forgiving spirit I have been recommending.

§ 19. *The injurer (a) is to be pitied, (b) most injures himself.*

Further, though injury, injustice, oppression, the baseness of ingratitude, are the natural objects of indignation, or if you please of resentment, as before explained; yet they are likewise the objects of compassion, as they are their own punishment, and without repentance will for ever be so. No one ever did a designed injury to another, but at the same time he did a much greater to himself. If therefore we would consider things justly, such an one is, according to the natural course of our affections, an object of compassion, as well as of displeasure: and to be affected really in this manner, I say really, in opposition to show and pretence, argues the true greatness of mind. We have an example of forgiveness in this way in its utmost perfection, and which indeed includes in it all that is good, in that prayer of our blessed Saviour on the cross: *Father, forgive them; for they know not what they do.*

§ 20. *Implacability, in union with sinfulness, terrible to reflect on.*

But lastly, The offences which we are all guilty of against God, and the injuries which men do to each other, are often mentioned together: and, making allowances for the infinite distance between the Majesty of heaven, and a frail mortal, and likewise for this, that he cannot possibly be affected or moved as we are; offences committed by others against ourselves, and the manner in which we are apt to be affected with them, give a real occasion for calling to mind our own sins against God. Now there is an apprehension and presentiment, natural to mankind, that we ourselves shall one time or other be dealt with as we deal with others; and a peculiar acquiescence in, and feeling of, the equity and justice of this equal distribution. This natural notion of equity the Son of Sirach has put in the strongest way. *He that revengeth shall find vengeance from the Lord, and he will surely keep his sins in remembrance. Forgive thy neighbour the hurt that he hath done unto thee, so shall thy sins also be forgiven when thou prayest. One man beareth hatred against another; and doth he seek pardon from the Lord? He showeth no mercy to a man, which is like himself; and doth he ask forgiveness of his own sins*[c]? Let any one read our Saviour's parable of *the king who took account of his servants*[d]; and the equity and rightness of the sentence which was passed upon him who was unmerciful to his fellow-servant, will be felt. There is somewhat in human nature, which accords to and falls in with that method of determination. Let us then place before our eyes the time which is represented in the parable; that of our own death, or the final judgment. Suppose yourselves under the apprehensions of approaching death; that you were just going to appear naked and without disguise before the Judge of all the earth, to give an account of your behaviour towards your fellow-creatures: could any thing raise more dreadful apprehensions of that judgment, than the reflection that you had been implacable, and without mercy towards those who had offended you: without that forgiving spirit towards others, which that it may now be exercised towards yourselves, is your only hope? And these natural apprehensions are authorized by our Saviour's application of the parable: *So likewise shall my heavenly*

---

[c] Ecclus. xxviii. 1-4.   [d] Matt. xviii.

Father do also unto you, if ye from your hearts forgive not every one his brother their trespasses.

§ 21. *But the placable have encouragement from our Lord.*

On the other hand, suppose a good man in the same circumstance, in the last part and close of life; conscious of many frailties, as the best are, but conscious too that he had been meek, forgiving, and merciful; that he had in simplicity of heart been ready to pass over offences against himself: the having felt this good spirit will give him, not only a full view of the amiableness of it, but the surest hope that he shall meet with it in his Judge. This likewise is confirmed by his own declaration: *If ye forgive men their trespasses, your heavenly Father will likewise forgive you.* And that we might have a constant sense of it upon our mind, the condition is expressed in our daily prayer. A forgiving spirit is therefore absolutely necessary, as ever we hope for pardon of our own sins, as ever we hope for peace of mind in our dying moments, or for the divine mercy at that day when we shall most stand in need of it.

SERMON X

UPON SELF-DECEIT

And Nathan said to David, Thou art the man.—2 SAMUEL xii. 7.

§ 1. *Nathan charges the self-complacent David.*

THESE words are the application of Nathan's parable to David, upon occasion of his adultery with Bathsheba, and the murder of Uriah her husband. The parable, which is related in the most beautiful simplicity, is this:[a] *There were two men in one city; the one rich, and the other poor. The rich man had exceeding many flocks and herds: but the poor man had nothing, save one little ewe lamb, which he had bought and nourished up: and it grew up together with him, and with his children: it did eat of his own meat, and drank of his own cup, and lay in his bosom, and was unto him as a daughter. And there came a traveller unto the rich man, and he spared to take of his own flock and of his own herd, to dress for the wayfaring man that was come unto him; but took the poor man's lamb, and dressed it for the man that was come to him. And David's anger was greatly kindled against the man; and he said to Nathan, As the Lord liveth, the man that hath done this thing shall surely die: and he shall restore the lamb fourfold, because he did this thing, and because he had no pity.* David passes sentence, not only that there should be a fourfold restitution made; but he proceeds to the rigour of justice, *the man that hath done this thing shall die:* and this judgment

---

[a] Ver. 1.

is pronounced with the utmost indignation against such an act of inhumanity; *As the Lord liveth, he shall surely die: and his anger was greatly kindled against the man.* And the Prophet answered, *Thou art the man.* He had been guilty of much greater inhumanity, with the utmost deliberation, thought, and contrivance. Near a year must have passed, between the time of the commission of his crimes, and the time of the Prophet's coming to him; and it does not appear from the story, that he had in all this while the least remorse or contrition.

§ 2. *Nothing is more strange than our self-partiality.*

There is not any thing, relating to men and characters, more surprising and unaccountable, than this partiality to themselves, which is observable in many; as there is nothing of more melancholy reflection, respecting morality, virtue, and religion. Hence it is that many men seem perfect strangers to their own characters. They think, and reason, and judge quite differently upon any matter relating to themselves, from what they do in cases of others where they are not interested. Hence it is one hears people exposing follies, which they themselves are eminent for; and talking with great severity against particular vices, which, if all the world be not mistaken, they themselves are notoriously guilty of. This self-ignorance and self-partiality may be in all different degrees. It is a lower degree of it which David himself refers to in these words, *Who can tell how oft he offendeth? O cleanse thou me from my secret faults.* This is the ground of that advice of Elihu to Job: *Surely it is meet to be said unto God,—That which I see not, teach thou me; if I have done iniquity, I will do no more.* And Solomon saw this thing in a very strong light, when he said, *He that trusteth his own heart is a fool.*

§ 3. *Hence the 'Know thyself' of the ancients.*

This likewise was the reason why that precept, *Know thyself,* was so frequently inculcated by the philosophers of old. For if it were not for that partial and fond regard to ourselves, it would certainly be no great difficulty to know our own character, what passes within, the bent and bias of our mind; much less would there be any difficulty in judging rightly of our own actions. But from this partiality it frequently comes to pass, that the observation of many men's being themselves last of all acquainted with what falls out in their own families, may be applied to a nearer home, to what passes within their own breasts.

§ 4. *Usual temper: (a) absence of mistrust: (b) assumption that all is right: (c) disregard of precept, when against ourselves.*

There is plainly, in the generality of mankind, an absence of doubt or distrust, in a very great measure, as to their moral character and behaviour; and likewise a disposition to take for granted, that all is right and well with them in these respects. The former is owing to their not reflecting, not exercising their judgment upon themselves; the latter, to self-love. I am not speaking of that extravagance, which is sometimes to be met with; instances of persons declaring in words at length, that they never were in the wrong, nor had ever any diffidence to the justness of their conduct, in their whole lives. No, these people are too far gone to have any thing said to them. The thing before us is indeed of this kind, but in a lower degree, and confined to the moral character; somewhat of which we almost all of us have, without reflecting upon it. Now consider how long, and how grossly, a person of the best understanding might be imposed upon by one of whom he had not any suspicion, and in whom he placed an entire confidence; especially if there were friendship and real kindness in the case: surely this holds even stronger with respect to that self we are all so fond of. Hence arises in men a disregard of reproof and instruction, rules of conduct and moral discipline, which occasionally come in their way: a disregard, I say, of these; not in every respect, but in this single one, namely, as what may be of service to them in particular towards mending their own hearts and tempers, and making them better men. It never in earnest comes into their thoughts, whether such admonitions may not relate, and be of service to themselves; and this quite distinct from a positive persuasion to the contrary, a persuasion from reflection that they are innocent and blameless in those respects. Thus we may invert the observation which is somewhere made upon Brutus, that he never read, but in order to make himself a better man. It scarce comes into the thoughts of the generality of mankind, that this use is to be made of moral reflections which they meet with; that this use, I say, is to be made of them by themselves, for every body observes and wonders that it is not done by others.

§ 5. *Also exclusive self-interest.*

Further, there are instances of persons having so fixed and steady an eye upon their own interest, whatever they place it in, and the interest of those whom they consider as themselves, as in a manner to regard nothing else; their views are almost confined to this alone. Now we cannot be acquainted with, or in any propriety of speech be said to know any thing, but what we attend to. If therefore they attend only to one side, they really will not, cannot see or know what is to be alleged on the other. Though a man hath the best eyes in the world, he cannot see any way but that which he turns them. Thus these persons, without passing over the least, the most minute thing, which can possibly be urged in favour of themselves, shall overlook entirely the plainest and most obvious things on the other side.

§ 6. *They inquire only to justify.*

And whilst they are under the power of this temper, thought and consideration upon the matter before them has scarce any tendency to set them right: because they are engaged; and their deliberation concerning an action to be done, or reflection upon it afterwards, is not to see whether it be right, but to find out reasons to justify or palliate it; palliate it, not to others, but to themselves.

§ 7. *With self-ignorance, perhaps, only in the favourite propensity.*

In some there is to be observed a general ignorance of themselves, and wrong way of thinking and judging in every thing relating to themselves; their fortune, reputation, every thing in which self can come in: and this perhaps attended with the rightest judgment in all other matters. In others this partiality is not so general, has not taken hold of the whole man, but is confined to some particular favourite passion, interest, or pursuit; suppose ambition, covetousness, or any other. And these persons may probably judge and determine what is perfectly just and proper, even in things in which they themselves are concerned, if these things have no relation to their particular favourite passion or pursuit. Hence arises that amazing incongruity, and seeming inconsistency of character, from whence slight observers take it for granted, that the whole is hypocritical and false; not being able otherwise to reconcile the several parts: whereas in truth there is real honesty, so far as it goes. There is such a thing as men's being honest to such a degree, and in such respects, but no further. And this, as it is true, so it is absolutely necessary to be taken notice of, and allowed them; such general and undistinguishing censure of their whole character, as designing and false, being one main thing which confirms them in their self-deceit. They know that the whole censure is not true; and so take for granted that no part of it is.

§ 8. *The judgment is perverted through the passions.*

But to go on with the explanation of the thing itself: Vice in general consists in having an unreasonable and too great regard to ourselves, in comparison of others. Robbery and murder is never from the love of injustice or cruelty, but to gratify some other passion, to gain some supposed advantage: and it is false selfishness alone, whether cool or passionate, which makes a man resolutely pursue that end, be it ever so much to the injury of another. But whereas, in common and ordinary wickedness, this unreasonableness, this partiality and selfishness, relates only, or chiefly, to the temper and passions, in the characters we are now considering, it reaches to the understanding, and influences the very judgment [b]. And, besides that general want of distrust and diffidence concerning our own character, there are, you see, two things, which may thus prejudice and darken the understanding itself: that overfondness for ourselves, which we are all so liable to; and also being under the power of any particular passion or appetite, or engaged in any particular pursuit. And these, especially the last of the two, may be in so great a degree, as to influence our judgment, even of other persons and their behaviour. Thus a man, whose temper is formed to ambition or covetousness, shall even approve of them sometimes in others.

§ 9. *Great part of wrong-doing is from this source. Its extreme consequences.*

This seems to be in a good measure the account of self-partiality and self-deceit, when traced up to its original.

---

[b] NOTE. That peculiar regard for ourselves which frequently produces this partiality of judgment in our own favour, may have a quite contrary effect, and occasion the utmost diffidence and distrust of ourselves; were it only, as it may set us upon a more frequent and strict survey and review of our own character and behaviour. This search or recollection itself implies somewhat of diffidence; and the discoveries we make, what is brought to our view, may possibly increase it. Good-will to another may either blind our judgment, so as to make us overlook his faults; or it may put us upon exercising that judgment with greater strictness, to see whether he is so faultless and perfect as we wish him. If that peculiar regard to ourselves leads us to examine our own character with this greater severity, in order really to improve and grow better, it is the most commendable turn of mind possible, and can scarce be to excess. But if, as every thing hath its counterfeit, we are so much employed about ourselves in order to disguise what is amiss, and to make a better appearance; or if our attention to ourselves has chiefly this effect; it is liable to run up into the greatest weakness and excess, and is like all other excesses its own disappointment: for scarce any show themselves to advantage, who are over solicitous of doing so.

There may be a morbid excess in self-inspection.

Whether it be or be not thought satisfactory, that there is such a thing is manifest; and that it is the occasion of great part of the unreasonable behaviour of men towards each other: that by means of it they palliate their vices and follies to themselves: and that it prevents their applying to themselves those reproofs and instructions, which they meet with either in scripture or in moral and religious discourses, though exactly suitable to the state of their own mind, and the course of their behaviour. There is one thing further to be added here, that the temper we distinguish by hardness of heart with respect to others, joined with this self-partiality, will carry a man almost any lengths of wickedness, in the way of oppression, hard usage of others, and even to plain injustice; without his having, from what appears, any real sense at all of it. This indeed was not the general character of David: for he plainly gave scope to the affections of compassion and good-will, as well as to his passions of another kind.

But as some occasions and circumstances lie more open to this self-deceit, and give it greater scope and opportunities than others, these require to be particularly mentioned.

§ 10. *Frequent difficulty of defining: enhanced by vice.*

It is to be observed then, that as there are express determinate acts of wickedness, such as murder, adultery, theft: so, on the other hand, there are numberless cases in which the vice and wickedness cannot be exactly defined; but consists in a certain general temper and course of action, or in the neglect of some duty, suppose charity or any other, whose bounds and degrees are not fixed. This is the very province of self-deceit and self-partiality: here it governs without check or control. 'For what commandment is there broken? Is there a transgression where there is no law? a vice which cannot be defined?'

Whoever will consider the whole commerce of human life, will see that a great part, perhaps the greatest part, of the intercourse amongst mankind, cannot be reduced to fixed determinate rules. Yet in these cases there is a right and a wrong: a merciful, a liberal, a kind and compassionate behaviour, which surely is our duty; and an unmerciful contracted spirit, an hard and oppressive course of behaviour, which is most certainly immoral and vicious. But who can define precisely, wherein that contracted spirit and hard usage of others consist, as murder and theft may be defined? there is not a word in our language, which expresses more detestable wickedness than *oppression*: yet the nature of this vice cannot be so exactly stated, nor the bounds of it so determinately marked, as that we shall be able to say in all instances, where rigid right and justice ends, and oppression begins. In these cases there is great latitude left, for every one to determine for, and consequently to deceive himself. It is chiefly in these cases that self-deceit comes in; as every one must see that there is much larger scope for it here, than in express, single, determinate acts of wickedness. However, it comes in with respect to the *circumstances* attending the most gross and determinate acts of wickedness.

§ 11. *David a prodigious instance of self-deceit: how, we know not.*

Of this, the story of David, now before us, affords the most astonishing instance. It is really prodigious, to see a man, before so remarkable for virtue and piety, going on deliberately from adultery to murder, with the same cool contrivance, and, from what appears, with as little disturbance, as a man would endeavour to prevent the ill consequences of a mistake he had made in any common matter. That total insensibility of mind with respect to those horrid crimes, after the commission of them, manifestly shows that he did some way or other delude himself: and this could not be with respect to the crimes themselves, they were so manifestly of the grossest kind. What the particular circumstances were, with which he extenuated them, and quieted and deceived himself, is not related.

§ 12. *It is in itself extreme guilt; the blinding of the inward eye.*

Having thus explained the nature of internal hypocrisy and self-deceit, and remarked the occasions upon which it exerts itself; there are several things further to be observed concerning it: that all of the sources, to which it was traced up, are sometimes observable together in one and the same person: but that one of them is more remarkable, and to a higher degree, in some, and others of them are so in others: that in general it is a complicated thing; and may be in all different degrees and kinds: that the temper itself is essentially in its own nature vicious and immoral. It is unfairness; it is dishonesty; it is falseness of heart: and is therefore so far from extenuating guilt, that it is itself the greatest of all guilt in proportion to the degree it prevails; for it is a corruption of the whole moral character in its principle. Our understanding, and sense of good and evil, is the light and guide of life: *If therefore this light that is in thee be darkness, how great is that darkness*[c]*!* For this reason our Saviour puts an *evil eye* as the direct opposite to a *single eye;* the absence of that simplicity, which these last words imply, being itself evil and vicious. And whilst men are under the power of this temper, in proportion still to the degree they are so, they are fortified on every side against conviction: and when they hear the vice and folly of what is in truth their own course of life, exposed in the justest and strongest manner, they will often assent to it, and even carry the matter further; persuading themselves, one does not know how, but some way or other persuading themselves, that they are out of the case, and that it hath no relation to them.

§ 13. *Often or always attended with some implicit suspicion.*

Yet, notwithstanding this, there *frequently appears* a suspicion, that all is not right, or as it should be; and perhaps there *is always* at bottom somewhat of this sort. There are

---

[c] Matt. vi. 23.

doubtless many instances of the ambitious, the revengeful, the covetous, and those whom with too great indulgence we only call the men of pleasure, who will not allow themselves to think how guilty they are, who explain and argue away their guilt to themselves: and though they do really impose upon themselves in some measure, yet there are none of them but have, if not a proper knowledge, yet at least an implicit suspicion, where the weakness lies, and what part of their behaviour they have reason to wish unknown or forgotten for ever. Truth, and real good sense, and thorough integrity, carry along with them a peculiar consciousness of their own genuineness: there is a feeling belonging to them, which does not accompany their counterfeits, error, folly, half-honesty, partial and slight regards to virtue and right, so far only as they are consistent with that course of gratification which men happen to be set upon. And, if this be the case, it is much the same as if we should suppose a man to have had a general view of some scene, enough to satisfy him that it was very disagreeable, and then to shut his eyes, that he might not have a particular or distinct view of its several deformities. It is as easy to close the eyes of the mind, as those of the body: and the former is more frequently done with wilfulness, and yet not attended to, than the latter; the actions of the mind being more quick and transient, than those of the senses.

§ 14. *Comparison with those who avoid looking into the state of their affairs.*

This may be further illustrated by another thing observable in ordinary life. It is not uncommon for persons, who run out their fortunes, entirely to neglect looking into the state of their affairs, and this from a general knowledge, that the condition of them is bad. These extravagant people are perpetually ruined before they themselves expected it: and they tell you for an excuse, and tell you truly, that they did not think they were so much in debt, or that their expenses so far exceeded their income.

And yet no one will take this for an excuse, who is sensible that their ignorance of their particular circumstances was owing to their general knowledge of them; that is, their general knowledge, that matters were not well with them, prevented their looking into particulars. There is somewhat of the like kind with this in respect to morals, virtue, and religion. Men find that the survey of themselves, their own heart and temper, their own life and behaviour, doth not afford them satisfaction: things are not as they should be: therefore they turn away, will not go over particulars, or look deeper, lest they should find more amiss. For who would choose to be put out of humour with himself? No one, surely, if it were not in order to mend, and to be more thoroughly and better pleased with himself for the future.

If this sincere self-enjoyment and home satisfaction be thought desirable, and worth some pains and diligence: the following reflections will, I suppose, deserve your attention; as what may be of service and assistance to all who are in any measure honestly disposed, for avoiding that fatal self-deceit, and towards getting acquainted with themselves.

§ 15. *Each owns self-deception to be in all except himself.*

The first is, that those who have never had any suspicion of, who have never made allowances for, this weakness in themselves, who have never (if I may be allowed such a manner of speaking) caught themselves in it, may almost take for granted that they have been very much misled by it. For consider: nothing is more manifest, than that affection and passion of all kinds influence the judgment. Now as we have naturally a greater regard to ourselves than to others, as the private affection is more prevalent than the public; the former will have proportionally a greater influence upon the judgment, upon our way of considering things. People are not backward in owning this partiality of judgment, in cases of friendship and natural relation. The reason is obvious, why it is not so readily acknowledged, when the interest which misleads us is more confined, confined to ourselves: but we all take notice of it in each other in these cases. There is not any observation more common, than that there is no judging of a matter from hearing only one side. This is not founded upon supposition, at least it is not always, of a formed design in the relater to deceive: for it holds in cases, where he expects that the whole will be told over again by the other side. But the supposition, which this observation is founded upon, is the very thing now before us; namely, that men are exceedingly prone to deceive themselves, and judge too favourably in every respect, where themselves and their own interest are concerned. Thus, though we have not the least reason to suspect that such an interested person hath any intention to deceive us, yet we of course make great allowances for his having deceived himself.

§ 16. *But ought to take it for granted that he has it largely.*

If this be general, almost universal, it is prodigious that every man can think himself an exception, and that he is free from this self-partiality. The direct contrary is the truth. Every man may take for granted that he has a great deal of it, till, from the strictest observation upon himself, he finds particular reason to think otherwise.

§ 17. *As a partial test: 'what would your enemy first charge upon you?'*

Secondly, There is one easy and almost sure way to avoid being misled by this self-partiality, and to get acquainted with our real character: to have regard to the suspicious part of it, and keep a steady eye over ourselves in that respect. Suppose then a man fully satisfied with himself, and his own behaviour; such an one, if you please, as the Pharisee in the Gospel, or a better man.—Well; but allowing this good opinion you have of yourself to be true, yet every one is liable to be misrepresented. Suppose then an enemy were to set about defaming you, what part of your character would he single out? What particular scandal, think you, would he be most likely to fix upon you? And what would the world be most ready to believe? There is scarce a man living but could, from the most transient superficial view of himself, answer this question. What is that ill thing, that faulty behaviour, which I am apprehensive an enemy, who was thoroughly acquainted with me, would be most likely to lay to my charge, and which the world would be most apt to believe? It is indeed possible that a man may not be guilty in that respect. All that I say is, let him in plainness and honesty fix upon that part of his character for a particular survey and reflection; and by this he will come to be acquainted, whether he be guilty or innocent in that respect, and how far he is one or the other.

§ 18. *The double substitution enjoined by our Lord.*

Thirdly, It would very much prevent our being misled by this self-partiality, to reduce that practical rule of our Saviour, *Whatsoever ye would that men should do to you, even so do unto them*, to our judgment and way of thinking. This rule, you see, consists of two parts. One is, to substitute another for yourself, when you take a survey of any part of your behaviour, or consider what is proper and fit and reasonable for you to do upon any occasion: the other part is, that you substitute yourself in the room of another; consider yourself as the person affected by such a behaviour, or towards whom such an action is done: and then you would not only see, but likewise feel, the reasonableness or unreasonableness of such an action or behaviour. But, alas! the rule itself may be dishonestly applied: there are persons who have not impartiality enough with respect to themselves, nor regard enough for others, to be able to make a just application of it. This just application, if men would honestly make it, is in effect all that I have been recommending; it is the whole thing, the direct contrary to that inward dishonesty as respecting our intercourse with our fellow-creatures. And even the bearing this rule in their thoughts may be of some service; the attempt thus to apply it, is an attempt towards being fair and impartial, and may chance unawares to show them to themselves, to show them the truth of the case they are considering.

§ 19. *It is safer to be wicked in the ordinary way, than from this corruption lying at the root.*

Upon the whole it is manifest, that there is such a thing as this self-partiality and self-deceit: that in some persons it is to a degree which would be thought incredible, were not the instances before our eyes; of which the behaviour of David is perhaps the highest possible one, in a single particular case; for there is not the least appearance, that it reached his general character: that we are almost all of us influenced by it in some degree, and in some respects: that therefore every one ought to have an eye to and beware of it. And all that I have further to add upon this subject is, that either there is a difference between right and wrong, or there is not: religion is true, or it is not. If it be not, there is no reason for any concern about it: but if it be true, it requires real fairness of mind and honesty of heart. And, if people will be wicked, they had better of the two be so from the common vicious passions without such refinements, than from this deep and calm source of delusion; which undermines the whole principle of good; darkens that light, that *candle of the Lord within*, which is to direct our steps; and corrupts conscience, which is the guide of life.

SERMON XI

UPON THE LOVE OF OUR NEIGHBOUR

Preached on Advent Sunday.

And if there be any other commandment, it is briefly comprehended in this saying, namely, Thou shalt love thy neighbour as thyself.—Romans xiii. 9.

§ 1. *Enhanced profession of self-interest a note of the age.*

IT is commonly observed, that there is a disposition in men to complain of the viciousness and corruption of the age in which they live, as greater than that of former ones; which is usually followed with this further observation, that mankind has been in that respect much the same in all times. Now, not to determine whether this last be not contradicted by the accounts of history; thus much can scarce be doubted, that vice and folly takes different turns, and some particular kinds of it are more open and avowed in some ages than in others: and, I suppose, it may be spoken of as very much the distinction of the present to profess a contracted spirit, and greater regards to self-interest, than appears to have been done formerly. Upon this account it seems worth while to inquire, whether private interest is likely to be promoted in proportion to the degree in which self-love engrosses us, and prevails over all other principles; *or whether the contracted affection may not possibly be so prevalent as to disappoint itself, and even contradict its own end, private good.*

§ 2. *Benevolence and self-love are not in conflict.*

And since, further, there is generally thought to be some peculiar kind of contrariety between self-love and the love of our neighbour, between the pursuit of public and of private good; insomuch that when you are recommending one of these, you are supposed to be speaking against the other; and from hence arises a secret prejudice against, and frequently open scorn of all talk of public spirit, and real good-will to our fellow-creatures; it will be necessary to *inquire what respect benevolence hath to self-love, and the pursuit of private interest to the pursuit of public:* or whether there be any thing of that peculiar inconsistence and contrariety between them, over and above what there is between self-love and other passions and particular affections, and their respective pursuits.

These inquiries, it is hoped, may be favourably attended to: for there shall be all possible concessions made to the favourite passion, which hath so much allowed to it, and whose cause is so universally pleaded: it shall be treated with the utmost tenderness and concern for its interests.

In order to this, as well as to determine the fore-mentioned questions, it will be necessary to *consider the nature, the object, and end of that self-love, as distinguished from other principles or affections in the mind, and their respective objects.*

§ 3. *Self-love seeks happiness at large; of particular affections, each rests upon its own object.*

Every man hath a general desire of his own happiness; and likewise a variety of particular affections, passions, and appetites to particular external objects. The former proceeds from, or is self-love; and seems inseparable from all sensible creatures, who can reflect upon themselves and their own interest or happiness, so as to have that interest an object to their minds: what is to be said of the latter is, that they proceed from, or together make up that particular nature, according to which man is made. The object the former pursues is somewhat internal, our own happiness, enjoyment, satisfaction; whether we have, or have not, a distinct particular perception what it is, or wherein it consists: the objects of the latter are this or that particular external thing, which the affections tend towards, and of which it hath always a particular idea or perception. The principle we call self-love never seeks any thing external for the sake of the thing, but only as a means of happiness or good: particular affections rest in the external things themselves. One belongs to man as a reasonable creature reflecting upon his own interest or happiness. The other, though quite distinct from reason, are as much a part of human nature.

That all particular appetites and passions are towards *external things themselves,* distinct from the *pleasure arising from them,* is manifested from hence; that there could not be this pleasure, were it not for that prior suitableness between the object and the passion: there could be no enjoyment or delight from one thing more than another, from eating food more than from swallowing a stone, if there were not an affection or appetite to one thing more than another.

§ 4. *Such affections are not to be resolved into self-love.*

Every particular affection, even the love of our neighbour, is as really our own affection, as self-love; and the pleasure arising from its gratification is as much my own pleasure, as the pleasure self-love would have, from knowing I myself should be happy some time hence, would be my own pleasure. And if, because every particular affection is a man's own, and the pleasure arising from its gratification his own pleasure, or pleasure to himself, such particular affection must be called self-love; according to this way of speaking, no creature whatever can possibly act but merely from self-love; and every action and every affection whatever is to be resolved up into this one principle. But then this is not the language of mankind: or if it were, we should want words to express the difference, between the principle of an action, proceeding from cool consideration that it will be to my own advantage; and an action, suppose of revenge, or of friendship, by which a man runs upon certain ruin, to do evil or good to another. It is manifest the principles of these actions are totally different, and so want different words to be distinguished by : all that they agree in is, that they both proceed from, and are done to gratify an inclination in a man's self. But the principle or inclination in one case is self-love ; in the other, hatred or love of another. There is then a distinction between the cool principle of self-love, or general desire of our own happiness, as one part of our nature, and one principle of action ; and the particular affections towards particular external objects, as another part of our nature, and another principle of action. How much soever therefore is to be allowed for self-love, yet it cannot be allowed to be the whole of our inward constitution ; because, you see, there are other parts or principles which come into it.

§ 5. *Their acts are named according to their objects : acts of self-love are called interested.*

Further, private happiness or good is all which self-love can make us desire, or be concerned about : in having this consists its gratification : it is an affection to ourselves ; a regard to our own interest, happiness, and private good : and in the proportion a man hath this, he is interested, or a lover of himself. Let this be kept in mind ; because there is commonly, as I shall presently have occasion to observe, another sense put upon these words. On the other hand, particular affections tend towards particular external things : these are their objects ; having these is their end : in this consists their gratification : no matter whether it be, or be not, upon the whole, our interest or happiness. An action done from the former of these principles is called an interested action. An action proceeding from any of the latter has its denomination of passionate, ambitious, friendly, revengeful, or any other, from the particular appetite or affection from which it proceeds. Thus self-love as one part of human nature, and the several particular principles as the other part, are, themselves, their objects and ends, stated and shown.

§ 6. *Happiness lies not in self-love; but in the enjoyment of objects suited to our nature.*

From hence it will be easy to see, how far, and in what ways, each of these can contribute and be subservient to the private good of the individual. Happiness does not consist in self-love. The desire of happiness is no more the thing itself, than the desire of riches is the possession or enjoyment of them. People may love themselves with the most entire and unbounded affection, and yet be extremely miserable. Neither can self-love any way help them out, but by setting them on work to get rid of the causes of their misery, to gain or make use of those objects which are by nature adapted to afford satisfaction. Happiness or satisfaction consists only in the enjoyment of those objects, which are by nature suited to our several particular appetites, passions, and affections[1]. So that if self-love wholly engrosses us, and leaves no room for any other principle, there can be absolutely no such thing at all as happiness, or enjoyment of any kind whatever; since happiness consists in the gratification of particular passions, which supposes the having of them. Self-love then does not constitute *this* or *that* to be our interest or good; but, our interest or good being constituted by nature and supposed, self-love only puts us upon obtaining and securing it.

§ 7. *A contracted self-love may work against our happiness; and how.*

Therefore, if it be possible, that self-love may prevail and exert itself in a degree or manner which is not subservient to this end; then it will not follow, that our interest will be promoted in proportion to the degree in which that principle engrosses us, and prevails over others. Nay further, the private and contracted affection, when it is not subservient to this end, private good, may, for any thing that appears, have a direct contrary tendency and effect. And if we will consider the matter, we shall see that it often

---

[1] Compare *inf.* §§ 13, 14, 16.

really has. *Disengagement* is absolutely necessary to enjoyment: and a person may have so steady and fixed an eye upon his own interest, whatever he places it in, as may hinder him from *attending* to many gratifications within his reach, which others have their minds *free* and *open* to. Overfondness for a child is not generally thought to be for its advantage: and, if there be any guess to be made from appearances, surely that character we call selfish is not the most promising for happiness. Such a temper may plainly be, and exert itself in a degree and manner which may give unnecessary and useless solicitude and anxiety, in a degree and manner which may prevent obtaining the means and materials of enjoyment, as well as the making use of them. Immoderate self-love does very ill consult its own interest: and, how much soever a paradox it may appear, it is certainly true, that even from self-love we should endeavour to get over all inordinate regard to, and consideration of ourselves. Every one of our passions and affections hath its natural stint and bound, which may easily be exceeded; whereas our enjoyments can possibly be but in a determinate measure and degree. Therefore such excess of the affection, since it cannot procure any enjoyment, must in all cases be useless; but is generally attended with inconveniences, and often is downright pain and misery. This holds as much with regard to self-love as to all other affections. The natural degree of it, so far as it sets us on work to gain and make use of the materials of satisfaction, may be to our real advantage; but beyond or besides this, it is in several respects an inconvenience and disadvantage. Thus it appears, that private interest is so far from being likely to be promoted in proportion to the degree in which self-love engrosses us, and prevails over all other principles; that *the contracted affection may be so prevalent as to disappoint itself, and even contradict its own end, private good.*

§ 8. *Counter-plea: 'self-love delights in the particular affections, competes with the love of our neighbour.'*

'But who, except the most sordidly covetous, ever thought there was any rivalship between the love of greatness, honour, power, or between sensual appetites, and self-love? No, there is a perfect harmony between them. It is by means of these particular appetites and affections that self-love is gratified in enjoyment, happiness, and satisfaction. The competition and rivalship is between self-love and the love of our neighbour: that affection which leads us out of ourselves, makes us regardless of our own interest, and substitute that of another in its stead[1].' Whether then there

---

[1] Butler sets up a rather sharp distinction between self-love and particular affections or propensions. See his note on Serm. i. 6.

The particular affection is with him an ὄρεξις, appetence, or active desire, for some particular object, which terminates upon that object.

Of these he enumerates many, in different connections. Among them are love of money, reputation, power, sensual pleasures, pride, revenge, resentment, love of arts.

Whereas these affections in the main contemplate single objects, self-love is inclusive (in its various forms, good or bad) of them all: employing them, with good judgment or bad, as means to an ulterior end, which is our own happiness. And, in this Sermon, he defines or describes happiness repeatedly, and well.

The objector causes him to consider fully the question how far and how self-love competes with benevolence. And here it appears that he regards benevolence itself mainly from a point of view which gives it the form of one of these particular affections.

There is another view of it, under which, instead of standing apart from self-love as a particular affection, it stands by the side of it. In this view, while self-love is a comprehensive affection which uses all appropriate objects as instruments for our own happiness, so benevolence is an affection of the like kind, which uses them for the happiness of our neighbour.

Butler appears distinctly to take this view where (*inf.* § 16) he says, 'love of our neighbour,' 'as a *virtuous principle*, is gratified by a consciousness of *endeavouring* to promote the good of others.'

In this view he seems plainly to associate benevolence with self-love, and to take it out of the category of 'particular affections.' In the narrower view he places it there: as is expressly declared *inf.* §§ 13, 16.

This duality of treatment is probably to be explained by the fact that with mankind in general self-love is wakeful and in continuous action, overlapping our entire existence, in search of means to promote its purpose, whereas benevolence is intermittent, and only stirred into activity by appropriate occasion. It may also be said that, when benevolence is in action, there is a self-love behind it; but there is no benevolence behind self-love.

It seems also to be laid down (*inf.* § 17) that when what would otherwise be a particular affection contemplates its immediate object only as a means to some end or purpose lying beyond it, it ceases to be a particular affection, and becomes a form or phase of self-love.

Whewell (Preface to Six Sermons, p. vii) justly observes that

be any peculiar competition and contrariety in this case, shall now be considered.

§ 9. *No: self-love, not including, does not exclude, benevolence.*

Self-love and interestedness was stated to consist in or be an affection to ourselves, a regard to our own private good: it is therefore distinct from benevolence, which is an affection to the good of our fellow-creatures. But that benevolence is distinct from, that is, not the same thing with self-love, is no reason for its being looked upon with any peculiar suspicion; because every principle whatever, by means of which self-love is gratified, is distinct from it: and all things which are distinct from each other are equally so. A man has an affection or aversion to another: that one of these tends to, and is gratified by doing good, that the other tends to, and is gratified by doing harm, does not in the least alter the respect which either one or the other of these inward feelings has to self-love. We use the word *property* so as to exclude any other persons having an interest in that of which we say a particular man has the property. And we often use the word *selfish* so as to exclude in the same manner all regards to the good of others. But the cases are not parallel: for though that exclusion is really part of the idea of property; yet such positive exclusion, or bringing this peculiar disregard to the good of others into the idea of self-love, is in reality adding to the idea, or changing it from what it was before stated to consist in, namely, in an affection to ourselves[a]. This being the whole idea of self-love, it can no otherwise exclude good-will or love of others, than merely by not including it, no otherwise, than it excludes love of arts or reputation, or of any thing else. Neither

---

[a] *Sup.* § 4.

'the abstract and general desire not only includes the particular desire, but may come to replace it.' When self-love impels us towards some aim which is also the object of a particular desire (and this is the usual form of its activity) the two are for the time amalgamated, and either of them may be said to be absorbed in the other.

on the other hand does benevolence, any more than love of arts or of reputation, exclude self-love. Love of our neighbour then has just the same respect to, is no more distant from, self-love, than hatred of our neighbour, or than love or hatred of any thing else.

§ 10. *All particular affections, including virtue, are equally interested or the reverse.*

Thus the principles, from which men rush upon certain ruin for the destruction of an enemy, and for the preservation of a friend, have the same respect to the private affection, and are equally interested, or equally disinterested: and it is of no avail, whether they are said to be one or the other [1]. Therefore to those who are shocked to hear virtue spoken of as disinterested, it may be allowed that it is indeed absurd to speak thus of it; unless hatred, several particular instances of vice, and all the common affections and aversions in mankind, are acknowledged to be disinterested too. Is there any less inconsistence, between the love of inanimate things, or of creatures merely sensitive, and self-love; than between self-love and the love of our neighbour? Is desire of and delight in the happiness of another any more a diminution of self-love, than desire of and delight in the esteem of another? They are both

---

[1] There seems to be something of paradox in saying that the love of virtue and the love of revenge are equally interested or disinterested.

The meaning appears to be that in the contemplation of each of these there is included a regard to our own interest as estimated at the moment of action.

But virtue is loved for its own sake by a noble impulse: and revenge is loved, whether for its own sake or not, by an impulse essentially ignoble.

So that if we admit the idea of interest to be common to the two cases, the idea or conception of interest is radically and essentially different.

Whewell (Six Sermons, p. viii) cites this section on virtue, hatred, revenge, and adds: 'if when we entertain those feelings, we suppose that we also perform a reflex act of thought, by which we imagine ourselves as persons who have a pleasure, and therefore an interest, in the gratification of this hatred or revenge, it would seem, on Butler's own view, that then the actions, by which we gratify those affections, are interested actions.' The same remark however applies to virtue.

equally desire of and delight in somewhat external to ourselves: either both or neither are so. The object of self-love is expressed in the term *self*: and every appetite of sense, and every particular affection of the heart, are equally interested or disinterested, because the objects of them all are equally self or somewhat else. Whatever ridicule therefore the mention of a disinterested principle or action may be supposed to lie open to, must, upon the matter being thus stated, relate to ambition, and every appetite and particular affection, as much as to benevolence. And indeed all the ridicule, and all the grave perplexity, of which this subject hath had its full share, is merely from words. The most intelligible way of speaking of it seems to be this: that self-love and the actions done in consequence of it (for these will presently appear to be the same as to this question) are interested; that particular affections towards external objects, and the actions done in consequence of those affections, are not so. But every one is at liberty to use words as he pleases. All that is here insisted upon is, that ambition, revenge, benevolence, all particular passions whatever, and the actions they produce, are equally interested or disinterested [1].

§ 11. *Self-love and benevolence are not in special competition.*

Thus it appears that there is no peculiar contrariety between self-love and benevolence; no greater competition between these, than between any other particular affections and self-love. This relates to the affections themselves. Let us now see whether there be any peculiar contrariety between the respective courses of life which these affections lead to; whether there be any greater competition between the pursuit of private and of public good, than between any other particular pursuits and that of private good.

---

[1] For example: Revenge; interested, because done for gratification of self: disinterested, because not for welfare of self. Benevolence; interested, because for the welfare of self: disinterested, because moved by the welfare of others.

§ 12. *Affection need not, because altruistic, abate the resulting enjoyment: rather the reverse.*

There seems no other reason to suspect that there is any such peculiar contrariety, but only that the course of action which benevolence leads to, has a more direct tendency to promote the good of others, than that course of action which love of reputation, suppose, or any other particular affection leads to. But that any affection tends to the happiness of another, does not hinder its tending to one's own happiness too. That others enjoy the benefit of the air and the light of the sun, does not hinder but that these are as much one's own private advantage now, as they would be if we had the property of them exclusive of all others. So a pursuit which tends to promote the good of another, yet may have as great tendency to promote private interest, as a pursuit which does not tend to the good of another at all, or which is mischievous to him. All particular affections whatever, resentment, benevolence, love of arts, equally lead to a course of action for their own gratification, i. e. the gratification of ourselves; and the gratification of each gives delight: so far then it is manifest they have all the same respect to private interest. Now take into consideration further, concerning these three pursuits, that the end of the first is the harm, of the second, the good of another, of the last, somewhat indifferent; and is there any necessity, that these additional considerations should alter the respect, which we before saw these three pursuits had to private interest; or render any one of them less conducive to it, than any other? Thus one man's affection is to honour as his end; in order to obtain which he thinks no pains too great. Suppose another, with such a singularity of mind, as to have the same affection to public good as his end, which he endeavours with the same labour to obtain. In case of success, surely the man of benevolence hath as great enjoyment as the man of ambition: they both equally having the end their affections, in the same degree, tended to: but in case of disappointment, the benevolent man has clearly the advantage; since endeavouring to do good considered as a virtuous pursuit, is gratified by its own consciousness, i. e. is in a degree its own reward.

§ 13. *Advantages of benevolence as compared, e. g. with ambition.*

And as to these two, or benevolence and any other particular passions whatever, considered in a further view, as forming a general temper, which more or less disposes us for enjoyment of all the common blessings of life, distinct from their own gratification: is benevolence less the temper of tranquillity and freedom than ambition or covetousness? Does the benevolent man appear less easy with himself, from his love to his neighbour? Does he less relish his being? Is there any peculiar gloom seated on his face? Is his mind less open to entertainment, to any particular gratification? Nothing is more manifest, than that being in good humour, which is benevolence whilst it lasts[1], is itself the temper of satisfaction and enjoyment.

Suppose then a man sitting down to consider how he might become most easy to himself, and attain the greatest pleasure he could; all that which is his real natural happiness. This can only consist in the enjoyment of those objects, which are by nature adapted to our several faculties. These particular enjoyments make up the sum total of our happiness: and they are supposed to arise from riches, honours, and the gratification of sensual appetites: be it so: yet none profess themselves so completely happy in these enjoyments, but that there is room left in the mind for others, if they were presented to them: nay, these, as much as they engage us, are not thought so high, but that human nature is capable even of greater.

§ 14. *The good man 'finds his account' in goodness, and a fuller satisfaction.*

Now there have been persons in all ages, who have professed that they found satisfaction in the exercise of charity,

---

[1] Because contact with others is presumed in the phrase.

in the love of their neighbour, in endeavouring to promote the happiness of all they had to do with, and in the pursuit of what is just, and right, and good, as the general bent of their mind, and end of their life; and that doing an action of baseness or cruelty, would be as great violence to *their* self, as much breaking in upon their nature, as any external force. Persons of this character would add, if they might be heard, that they consider themselves as acting in the view of an infinite Being, who is in a much higher sense the object of reverence and of love, than all the world besides; and therefore they could have no more enjoyment from a wicked action done under his eye, than the persons to whom they are making their apology could, if all mankind were the spectators of it; and that the satisfaction of approving themselves to his unerring judgment, to whom they thus refer all their actions, is a more continued settled satisfaction than any this world can afford; as also that they have, no less than others, a mind free and open to all the common innocent gratifications of it, such as they are. And if we go no further, does there appear any absurdity in this? Will any one take upon him to say, that a man cannot find his account in this general course of life, as much as in the most unbounded ambition, and the excesses of pleasure? Or that such a person has not consulted so well for himself, for the satisfaction and peace of his own mind, as the ambitious or dissolute man?

§ 15. *Even apart from the divine approval, these pretensions have been tested by experience.*

And though the consideration, that God himself will in the end justify their taste, and support their cause, is not formally to be insisted upon here; yet thus much comes in, that all enjoyments whatever are much more clear and unmixed from the assurance that they will end well[1]. Is it

---

[1] In a note on § 14 of this Sermon, Carmichael describes Cicero as appealing to 'the voice of all antiquity' as testifying to the immortality of the soul (*Tusc. Disp.* i. 12, 14). Butler nowhere makes this appeal, probably thinking that it cannot be sus-

certain then that there is nothing in these pretensions to happiness? especially when there are not wanting persons, who have supported themselves with satisfactions of this kind in sickness, poverty, disgrace, and in the very pangs of death; whereas it is manifest all other enjoyments fail in these circumstances. This surely looks suspicious of having somewhat in it. Self-love methinks should be alarmed. May she not possibly pass over greater pleasures, than those she is so wholly taken up with?

§ 16. *Benevolence and public good do not specially traverse self-love and private good.*

The short of the matter is no more than this. Happiness consists in the gratification of certain affections, appetites, passions, with objects which are by nature adapted to them. Self-love may indeed set us on work to gratify these: but happiness or enjoyment has no immediate connection with self-love, but arises from such gratification alone. Love of our neighbour is one of those affections. This, considered as a *virtuous principle,* is gratified by a consciousness of endeavouring to promote the good of others; but considered as a natural affection, its gratification consists in the actual accomplishment of this endeavour. Now indulgence or gratification of this affection, whether in that consciousness,

---

tained. I have myself endeavoured to show (*Nineteenth Century,* Oct. 1891) that the belief in immortality, apart from the Gospel, was become with the lapse of time on the whole a fading belief. In the mind of Cicero it was far from being a firm conviction. In the *De Senectute,* c. 23, towards the close, he speaks of it as an opinion from which, and the expectation of reunion it affords, he derives comfort and delight. But he does not exclude the opposite doctrine. If he errs, he errs with satisfaction, and will not readily part from his error. And he proceeds: 'Quod si non sumus immortales futuri, tamen extingui homini suo tempore optabile est. Nam habet natura, ut aliarum omnium rerum, sic et vivendi, modum.' Outside the philosophic circle, the literary and educated mind of the day was probably best represented by Horace:

'Nos, ubi decidimus
Quò pius Aeneas, quo dives Tullus et Ancus,
   Pulvis et umbra sumus.'
      Od. IV. vii. 14.

or this accomplishment, has the same respect to interest, as indulgence of any other affection; they equally proceed from or do not proceed from self-love, they equally include or equally exclude this principle. Thus it appears, that *benevolence and the pursuit of public good*[1] *hath at least as great respect to self-love and the pursuit of private good, as any other particular passions, and their respective pursuits.*

§ 17. *To covet wealth for an end is a phase of self-love.*

Neither is covetousness, whether as a temper or pursuit, any exception to this. For if by covetousness is meant the desire and pursuit of riches for their own sake, without any regard to, or consideration of, the uses of them; this hath as little to do with self-love, as benevolence hath. But by this word is usually meant, not such madness and total distraction of mind, but immoderate affection to and pursuit of riches as possessions in order to some further end; namely, satisfaction, interest, or good. This therefore is not a particular affection, or particular pursuit, but it is the general principle of self-love, and the general pursuit of our own interest; for which reason, the word *selfish* is by every one appropriated to this temper and pursuit. Now as it is ridiculous to assert, that self-love and the love of our neighbour are the same; so neither is it asserted, that following these different affections hath the same tendency and respect to our own interest. The comparison is not between self-love and the love of our neighbour; between pursuit of our own interest, and the interest of others: but between the several particular affections in human nature towards external objects, as one part of the comparison; and the one particular affection to the good of our neighbour, as the other part of it: and it has been shown, that all these have the same respect to self-love and private interest.

---

[1] See *sup.* note on § 1; and the pointedly sarcastic observation, evidently having reference to Butler's estimate of the public life of his own day, in § 12.

§ 18. *Self-love clashes oftener with other particular affections than with benevolence.*

There is indeed frequently an inconsistence or interfering between self-love or private interest, and the several particular appetites, passions, affections, or the pursuits they lead to. But this competition or interfering is merely accidental; and happens much oftener between pride, revenge, sensual gratifications, and private interest, than between private interest and benevolence. For nothing is more common, than to see men give themselves up to a passion or an affection to their known prejudice and ruin, and in direct contradiction to manifest and real interest, and the loudest calls of self-love: whereas the seeming competitions and interfering, between benevolence and private interest, relate much more to the materials or means of enjoyment, than to enjoyment itself. There is often an interfering in the former, when there is none in the latter. Thus as to riches: so much money as a man gives away, so much less will remain in his possession. Here is a real interfering. But though a man cannot possibly give without lessening his fortune, yet there are multitudes might give without lessening their own enjoyment; because they may have more than they can turn to any real use or advantage to themselves. Thus, the more thought and time any one employs about the interests and good of others, he must necessarily have less to attend his own; but he may have so ready and large a supply of his own wants, that such thought might be really useless to himself, though of great service and assistance to others.

§ 19. *The false idea of opposition of benevolence to self-love probably due to the idea of property: and how.*

The general mistake, that there is some greater inconsistence between endeavouring to promote the good of another and self-interest, than between self-interest and pursuing any thing else, seems, as hath already been hinted, to arise from our notions of property; and to be carried on by this property's being supposed to be itself our happiness or good[1]. People are so very much taken up with this one subject, that they seem from it to have formed a general way of thinking, which they apply to other things that they have nothing to do with. Hence, in a confused and slight way, it might well be taken for granted, that another's having no interest in an affection, (i. e. his good not being the object of it,) renders, as one may speak, the proprietor's interest in it greater; and that if another had an interest in it, this would render his less, or occasion that such affection could not be so friendly to self-love, or conducive to private good, as an affection or pursuit which has not a regard to the good of another.

§ 20. *From particular affections, with their extraneous objects, we derive enjoyment; but specially from benevolence.*

This, I say, might be taken for granted, whilst it was not attended to, that the object of every particular affection is equally somewhat external to ourselves; and whether it be the good of another person, or whether it be any other external thing, makes no alteration with regard to its being one's own affection, and the gratification of it one's own private enjoyment. And so far as it is taken for granted, that barely having the means and materials of enjoyment is what constitutes interest and happiness; that our interest or good consists in possessions themselves, in having the property of riches, houses, lands, gardens, not in the enjoyment of them; so far it will even more strongly be taken for granted, in the way already explained, that an affection's conducing to the good of another, must even necessarily occasion it to conduce less to private good, if not to be positively detrimental to it. For, if property and happiness are one and the same thing, as by increasing the property of

---

[1] For the idea of property (1) is exclusive; (2) has a peculiar tendency to beget an affection to simple possession, as distinct from enjoyment; which is an idea radically spurious. The exclusiveness of property (where giving to one is taking from another) stands in contrast with the catholicity (so to call it) of affection, which loses nothing by diffusion, like flame passing from torch to torch.

another, you lessen your own property, so by promoting the happiness of another, you must lessen your own happiness. But whatever occasioned the mistake, I hope it has been fully proved to be one ; as it has been proved, that there is no peculiar rivalship or competition between self-love and benevolence : that as there may be a competition between these two, so there may also between any particular affection whatever and self-love ; that every particular affection, benevolence among the rest, is subservient to self-love by being the instrument of private enjoyment ; and that in one respect benevolence contributes more to private interest, i. e. enjoyment or satisfaction, than any other of the particular common affections, as it is in a degree its own gratification.

§ 21. *Religion does not disown self-love, but appeals to it.*

And to all these things may be added, that religion, from whence arises our strongest obligation to benevolence, is so far from disowning the principle of self-love, that it often addresses itself to that very principle, and always to the mind in that state when reason presides ; and there can no access be had to the understanding, but by convincing men, that the course of life we would persuade them to is not contrary to their interest. It may be allowed, without any prejudice to the cause of virtue and religion, that our ideas of happiness and misery are of all our ideas the nearest and most important to us ; that they will, nay, if you please, that they ought to prevail over those of order, and beauty, and harmony, and proportion, if there should ever be, as it is impossible there ever should be, any inconsistence between them : though these last too, as expressing the fitness of actions, are real as truth itself. Let it be allowed, though virtue or moral rectitude does indeed consist in affection to and pursuit of what is right and good, as such ; yet, that when we sit down in a cool hour, we can neither justify to ourselves this or any other pursuit, till we are convinced that it will be for our happiness, or at least not contrary to it [1].

---

[1] Doubtless this is true, when once we have been challenged and put upon our defence. But it need not be held to imply that the

§ 22. *It is requisite to reconcile virtue with self-love.*

Common reason and humanity will have some influence upon mankind, whatever becomes of speculations: but, so far as the interests of virtue depend upon the theory of it being secured from open scorn, so far its very being in the world depends upon its appearing to have no contrariety to private interest and self-love. The foregoing observations, therefore, it is hoped, may have gained a little ground in favour of the precept before us; the particular explanation of which shall be the subject of the next discourse.

§ 23. *Our Saviour's love in the Incarnation enhances duty.*

I will conclude at present, with observing the peculiar obligation which we are under to virtue and religion, as enforced in the verses following the text, in the epistle for the day, from our Saviour's coming into the world. *The night is far spent, the day is at hand; let us therefore cast off the works of darkness, and let us put on the armour of light,* &c. The meaning and force of which exhortation is, that Christianity lays us under new obligations to a good life, as by it the will of God is more clearly revealed, and as it affords additional motives to the practice of it, over and above those which arise out of the nature of virtue and vice; I might add, as our Saviour has set us a perfect example of goodness in our own nature. Now love and charity is plainly the thing in which he hath placed his religion; in which therefore, as we have any pretence to the name of Christians, we must place ours. He hath at once enjoined it upon us by way of command with peculiar force; and by his example, as having undertaken the work of our salvation out of pure love and good-will to mankind. The endeavour to set home this example upon our minds is a very proper employment

---

pursuit of 'right and good,' of the noble and the true, requires to be waited upon, and as it were certified, by the continual presence and active consciousness of the idea that it will conduce to our personal happiness: which would indeed tend to bring down the pursuit itself from a higher to a lower plane.

of this season, which is bringing on the festival of his birth : which as it may teach us many excellent lessons of humility, resignation, and obedience to the will of God ; so there is none it recommends with greater authority, force, and advantage, than this of love and charity; since it was *for us men, and for our salvation,* that *he came down from heaven, and was incarnate, and was made man;* that he might teach us our duty, and more especially that he might enforce the practice of it, reform mankind, and finally bring us to that *eternal salvation,* of which *he is the Author to all those that obey him.*

SERMON XII

UPON THE LOVE OF OUR NEIGHBOUR

—••—

And if there be any other commandment, it is briefly comprehended in this saying, namely, Thou shalt love thy neighbour as thyself.—ROMANS xiii. 9.

—••—

§ 1. *Threefold partition of the subject.*

HAVING already removed the prejudices against public spirit, or the love of our neighbour, on the side of private interest and self-love; I proceed to the particular explanation of the precept before us, by showing, *Who is our neighbour: In what sense we are required to love him as ourselves: The influence such love would have upon our behaviour in life:* and lastly, *How this commandment comprehends in it all others.*

§ 2. *Our neighbour defined as 'that part of our country which comes under our immediate notice.'*

[I.] The objects and due extent of this affection will be understood by attending to the nature of it, and to the nature and circumstances of mankind in this world. The love of our neighbour is the same with charity, benevolence, or good-will: it is an affection to the good and happiness of our fellow-creatures. This implies in it a disposition to produce happiness: and this is the simple notion of goodness, which appears so amiable wherever we meet with it. From hence it is easy to see, that the perfection of goodness consists in love to the whole universe. This is the perfection of Almighty God.

But as man is so much limited in his capacity, as so small a part of the creation comes under his notice and influence, and as we are not used to consider things in so general a way; it is not to be thought of, that the universe should be the object of benevolence to such creatures as we are. Thus in that precept of our Saviour, *Be ye perfect, even as your Father, which is in heaven, is perfect* [a], the perfection of the divine goodness is proposed to our imitation as it is promiscuous, and extends to the evil as well as the good; not as it is absolutely universal, imitation of it in this respect being plainly beyond us. The object is too vast. For this reason moral writers also have substituted a less general object for our benevolence, mankind. But this likewise is an object too general, and very much out of our view. Therefore persons more practical have, instead of mankind, put our country; and made the principle of virtue, of human virtue, to consist in the entire uniform love of our country: and this is what we call a public spirit; which in men of public stations is the character of a patriot. But this is speaking to the upper part of the world. Kingdoms and governments are large; and the sphere of action of far the greatest part of mankind is much narrower than the government they live under: or however, common men do not consider their actions as affecting the whole community of which they are members. There plainly is wanting a less general and nearer object of benevolence for the bulk of men, than that of their country. Therefore the scripture, not being a book of theory and speculation, but a plain rule of life for mankind, has with the utmost possible propriety put the principle of virtue upon the love of our neighbour; which is that part of the universe, that part of mankind, that part of our country, which comes under our immediate notice, acquaintance, and influence, and with which we have to do.

This is plainly the true account or reason, why our Saviour places the principle of virtue in the love of our *neighbour;* and the account itself shows who are comprehended under that relation.

---

[a] Matt. v. 48.

§ 3. *We are to love him, not as God, but as ourselves.*

[II.] Let us now consider in what sense we are commanded to love our neighbour *as ourselves*.

This precept, in its first delivery by our Saviour, is thus introduced: *Thou shalt love the Lord thy God with all thine heart, with all thy soul, and with all thy strength; and thy neighbour as thyself.* These very different manners of expression do not lead our thoughts to the same measure or degree of love, common to both objects; but to one, peculiar to each. Supposing then, which is to be supposed, a distinct meaning and propriety in the words, *as thyself;* the precept we are considering will admit of any of these senses: that we bear the *same kind* of affection to our neighbour, as we do to ourselves: or, that the love we bear to our neighbour should have *some certain proportion or other* to self-love: or, lastly, that it should bear the particular proportion of *equality*, that *it be in the same degree*.

§ 4. *Viewed* (a) *as in the same kind: with the same sensibility in his behalf as our own.*

First, The precept may be understood as requiring only, that we have the *same kind* of affection to our fellow-creatures, as to ourselves: that, as every man has the principle of self-love, which disposes him to avoid misery, and consult his own happiness; so we should cultivate the affection of good-will to our neighbour, and that it should influence us to have the same kind of regard to him. This at least must be commanded: and this will not only prevent our being injurious to him, but will also put us upon promoting his good. There are blessings in life, which we share in common with others; peace, plenty, freedom, healthful seasons. But real benevolence to our fellow-creatures would give us the notion of a common interest in a stricter sense: for in the degree we love another, his interest, his joys and sorrows, are our own. It is from self-love that we form the notion of private good, and consider it as our own: love of our neighbour would teach us thus to appropriate to ourselves his good and welfare; to consider ourselves as having a real share in his happiness. Thus the principle of benevolence would be an advocate within our own breasts, to take care of the interests of our fellow-creatures in all the interfering and competitions which cannot but be, from the imperfection of our nature, and the state we are in. It would likewise, in some measure, lessen that interfering; and hinder men from forming so strong a notion of private good, exclusive of the good of others, as we commonly do. Thus, as the private affection makes us in a peculiar manner sensible of humanity, justice, or injustice, when exercised towards ourselves; love of our neighbour would give us the same kind of sensibility in his behalf. This would be the greatest security of our uniform obedience to that most equitable rule; *Whatsoever ye would that men should do to you, do ye even so to them.*

§ 5. (b) *Force of the phrase 'as thyself.'*

All this is indeed no more than that we should have a real love to our neighbour: but then, which is to be observed, the words, *as thyself*, express this in the most distinct manner, and determine the precept to relate to the affection itself. The advantage, which this principle of benevolence has over other remote considerations, is that it is itself the temper of virtue; and likewise, that it is the chief, nay, the only effectual security of our performing the several offices of kindness we owe to our fellow creatures. When from distant considerations men resolve upon any thing to which they have no liking, or perhaps an averseness, they are perpetually finding out evasions and excuses; which need never be wanting, if people look for them: and they equivocate with themselves in the plainest cases in the world. This may be in respect to single determinate acts of virtue; but it comes in much more, where the obligation is to a general course of behaviour; and most of all, if it be such as cannot be reduced to fixed determinate rules. This observation may account for the diversity of the expression, in that known passage of the prophet Micah: *to do justly, and to love mercy.* A man's heart must be formed to humanity and benevolence, he must *love mercy*, otherwise he will not act mercifully in any settled course of behaviour. As consideration of the future sanctions of religion is our only security of persevering in our duty, in cases of great temptations: so to get our heart and temper formed to a love and liking of what is good, is absolutely necessary in order to our behaving rightly in the familiar and daily intercourses amongst mankind.

§ 6. *I. e. in proportion as we love ourselves.*

Secondly, The precept before us may be understood to require, that we love our neighbour in some certain *proportion* or other, *according as* we love ourselves. And indeed a man's character cannot be determined by the love he bears to his neighbour, considered absolutely: but the proportion which this bears to self-love, whether it be attended to or not, is the chief thing which forms the character, and influences the actions. For, as the form of the body is a composition of various parts; so likewise our inward structure is not simple or uniform, but a composition of various passions, appetites, affections, together with rationality; including in this last both the discernment of what is right, and a disposition to regulate ourselves by it[1]. There is greater variety of parts in what we call a character, than there are features in a face: and the morality of that is no more determined by one part, than the beauty or deformity of this is by one single feature: each is to be judged of by all the parts or features, not taken singly, but together. In the inward frame the various passions, appetites, affections, stand in different respects to each other. The principles in our mind may be contradictory, or checks and allays only, or incentives and assistants to each other. And principles, which in their nature have no kind of contrariety or affinity, may yet accidentally be each other's allays or incentives.

---

[1] Comp. Diss. on Virtue, 2.

§ 7. *Varieties of forces in the balance of faculties.*

From hence it comes to pass, that though we were able to look into the inward contexture of the heart, and see with the greatest exactness in what degree any one principle is in a particular man; we could not from thence determine, how far that principle would go towards forming the character, or what influence it would have upon the actions, unless we could likewise discern what other principles prevailed in him, and see the proportion which that one bears to the others. Thus, though two men should have the affection of compassion in the same degree exactly; yet one may have the principle of resentment, or of ambition so strong in him, as to prevail over that of compassion, and prevent its having any influence upon his actions; so that he may deserve the character of an hard or cruel man: whereas the other, having compassion in just the same degree only, yet having resentment or ambition in a lower degree, his compassion may prevail over them, so as to influence his actions, and to denominate his temper compassionate. So that, how strange soever it may appear to people who do not attend to the thing, yet it is quite manifest, that, when we say one man is more resenting or compassionate than another, this does not necessarily imply that one has the principle of resentment or of compassion stronger than the other. For if the proportion, which resentment or compassion bears to other inward principles, is greater in one than in the other; this is itself sufficient to denominate one more resenting or compassionate than the other.

§ 8. *Conduct will be determined by the balance between benevolence and self-love or other principles.*

Further, the whole system, as I may speak, of affections, (including rationality,) which constitute the heart, as this word is used in scripture and on moral subjects, are each and all of them stronger in some than in others. Now the proportion which the two general affections, benevolence and self-love, bear to each other, according to this interpretation of the text, denominates men's character as to virtue.

Suppose then one man to have the principle of benevolence in an higher degree than another: it will not follow from hence, that his general temper, or character, or actions will be more benevolent than the other's. For he may have self-love in such a degree as quite to prevail over benevolence; so that it may have no influence at all upon his actions; whereas benevolence in the other person, though in a lower degree, may yet be the strongest principle in his heart; and strong enough to be the guide of his actions, so as to denominate him a good and virtuous man. The case is here as in scales: it is not one weight, considered in itself, which determines whether the scale shall ascend or descend; but this depends upon the proportion which that one weight hath to the other.

It being thus manifest that the influence which benevolence has upon our actions, and how far it goes towards forming our character, is not determined by the degree itself of this principle in our mind; but by the proportion it has to self-love and other principles: a comparison also being made in the text between self-love and the love of our neighbour; these joint considerations afforded sufficient occasion for treating here of that proportion: it plainly is implied in the precept, though it should be questioned whether it be the exact meaning of the words, *as thyself.*

§ 9. *Virtue lies in a due proportion; which each must fix for himself.*

Love of our neighbour then must bear some proportion to self-love, and virtue to be sure consists in the due proportion. What this due proportion is, whether as a principle in the mind, or as exerted in actions, can be judged of only from our nature and condition in this world. Of the degree in which affections and the principles of action, considered in themselves, prevail, we have no measure: let us then proceed to the course of behaviour, the actions they produce.

Both our nature and condition require, that each particular man should make particular provision for himself: and the inquiry, what proportion benevolence should have to self-love, when brought down to practice, will be, what is a competent care and provision for ourselves. And how certain soever it be, that each man must determine this for himself; and how ridiculous soever it would be, for any to attempt to determine it for another: yet it is to be observed, that the proportion is real; and that a competent provision has a bound; and that it cannot be all which we can possibly get and keep within our grasp, without legal injustice. Mankind almost universally bring in vanity, supplies for what is called a life of pleasure, covetousness, or imaginary notions of superiority over others, to determine this question: but every one who desires to act a proper part in society, would do well to consider, how far any of them come in to determine it, in the way of moral consideration. All that can be said is, supposing, what, as the world goes, is so much to be supposed that it is scarce to be mentioned, that persons do not neglect what they really owe to themselves; the more of their care and thought, and of their fortune, they employ in doing good to their fellow-creatures, the nearer they come up to the law of perfection, *Thou shalt love thy neighbour as thyself.*

§ 10. *We may interpret it as 'equally with'; but we must needs be mainly busied on ourselves.*

Thirdly, If the words, *as thyself*, were to be understood of an equality of affection; it would not be attended with those consequences, which perhaps may be thought to follow from it. Suppose a person to have the same settled regard to others, as to himself; that in every deliberate scheme or pursuit he took their interest into the account in the same degree as his own, so far as an equality of affection would produce this: yet he would in fact, and ought to be, much more taken up and employed about himself, and his own concerns, than about others, and their interests. For, besides the one common affection toward himself and his neighbour, he would have several other particular affections, passions, appetites, which he could not possibly feel in common both for himself and others; now these sensations themselves very much employ us; and have perhaps as great influence as self-love. So far indeed as self-love, and cool reflection upon what is for our interest, would set us on work to gain a supply of our own several wants; so far the love of our neighbour would make us do the same for him: but the degree in which we are put upon seeking and making use of the means of gratification, by the feeling of those affections, appetites, and passions, must necessarily be peculiar to ourselves.

That there are particular passions, (suppose shame, resentment,) which men seem to have, and feel in common, both for themselves and others, makes no alteration in respect to those passions and appetites which cannot possibly be thus felt in common. From hence (and perhaps more things of the like kind might be mentioned) it follows, that though there were an equality of affection to both, yet regards to ourselves would be more prevalent than attention to the concerns of others.

§ 11. *Each man is specially intrusted with himself.*

And from moral considerations it ought to be so, supposing still the equality of affection commanded: because we are in a peculiar manner, as I may speak, intrusted with ourselves; and therefore care of our own interests, as well as of our conduct, particularly belongs to us.

§ 12. *And there is a limit in natural possibilities.*

To these things must be added, that moral obligations can extend no further than to natural possibilities. Now we have a perception of our own interests, like consciousness of our own existence, which we always carry about with us; and which, in its continuation, kind, and degree, seems impossible to be felt in respect to the interests of others.

From all these things it fully appears, that though we were to love our neighbour in the same degree as we love ourselves, so far as this is possible; yet the care of ourselves, of the individual, would not be neglected; the apprehended danger of which seems to be the only objection against understanding the precept in this strict sense.

§ 13. *The resulting temper is that set forth in* 1 *Cor.* xiii.

[III.] The general temper of mind which the due love of our neighbour would form us to, and the influence it would have upon our behaviour in life, is now to be considered.

The temper and behaviour of charity is explained at large, in that known passage of St. Paul[b]: *Charity suffereth long, and is kind; charity envieth not, doth not behave itself unseemly, seeketh not her own, thinketh no evil, beareth all things, believeth all things, hopeth all things.* As to the meaning of the expressions, *seeketh not her own, thinketh no evil, believeth all things;* however those expressions may be explained away, this meekness, and in some degree easiness of temper, readiness to forego our right for the sake of peace as well as in the way of compassion, freedom from mistrust, and disposition to believe well of our neighbour, this general temper, I say, accompanies, and is plainly the effect of love and good-will. And, though such is the world in which we live, that experience and knowledge of it not only may, but must beget in us greater regard to ourselves, and doubtfulness of the characters of others, than is natural to mankind; yet these ought not to be carried further than the nature and course of things make necessary. It is still true, even in the present state of things, bad as it is, that a real good man had rather be deceived, than be suspicious; had rather forego his known right, than run the venture of doing even a hard thing. This is the general temper of that charity, of which the apostle asserts, that if he had it not, giving his *body to be burned would avail him nothing;* and which he says *shall never fail.*

§ 14. *Which overspreads the entire life.*

The happy influence of this temper extends to every different relation and circumstance in human life. It

---

[b] 1 Cor. xiii.

plainly renders a man better, more to be desired, as to all the respects and relations we can stand in to each other. The benevolent man is disposed to make use of all external advantages in such a manner as shall contribute to the good of others, as well as to his own satisfaction. His own satisfaction consists in this. He will be easy and kind to his dependants, compassionate to the poor and distressed, friendly to all with whom he has to do. This includes the good neighbour, parent, master, magistrate: and such a behaviour would plainly make dependence, inferiority, and even servitude, easy.

§ 15. *The good man a social blessing to his neighbours.*

So that a good or charitable man of superior rank in wisdom, fortune, authority, is a common blessing to the place he lives in: happiness grows under his influence. This good principle in inferiors would discover itself in paying respect, gratitude, obedience, as due. It were therefore methinks one just way of trying one's own character, to ask ourselves, Am I in reality a better master or servant, a better friend, a better neighbour, than such and such persons; whom, perhaps, I may think not to deserve the character of virtue and religion so much as myself?

§ 16. *Such a temper restrains the 'wretched spirit' of party.*

And as to the spirit of party, which unhappily prevails amongst mankind, whatever are the distinctions which serve for a supply to it, some or other of which have obtained in all ages and countries: one who is thus friendly to his kind will immediately make due allowances for it, as what cannot but be amongst such creatures as men, in such a world as this. And as wrath and fury and overbearing upon these occasions proceed, as I may speak, from men's feeling only on their own side: so a common feeling, for others as well as for ourselves, would render us sensible to this truth, which it is strange can have so little influence; that we ourselves differ from others, just as much as they do from us. I put the matter in this way, because it can scarce be expected that the generality of men should see, that those things which are made the occasions of dissension and fomenting the party-spirit, are really nothing at all: but it may be expected from all people, how much soever they are in earnest about their respective peculiarities, that humanity, and common good-will to their fellow-creatures, should moderate and restrain that wretched spirit.

§ 17. *And strife from other sources.*

This good temper of charity likewise would prevent strife and enmity arising from other occasions: it would prevent our giving just cause of offence, and our taking it without cause. And in cases of real injury, a good man will make all the allowances which are to be made; and, without any attempts of retaliation, he will only consult his own and other men's security for the future, against injustice and wrong.

§ 18. *Of benevolence, as including all virtue*[1].

[IV.] I proceed to consider lastly, what is affirmed of the precept now explained, that it comprehends in it all others; i. e. that to love our neighbour as ourselves includes in it all virtues.

Now the way in which every maxim of conduct, or general speculative assertion, when it is to be explained at large, should be treated, is, to show what are the particular truths which were designed to be comprehended under such a general observation, how far it is strictly true; and then the limitations, restrictions, and exceptions, if there be exceptions, with which it is to be understood. But it is only the former of these; namely, how far the assertion in the text holds, and the ground of the preeminence assigned

---

[1] On benevolence, from another point of view, see *Anal.* I. iii. 3, and Diss. ii. 12, 13, 15.

The assertion that benevolence includes all virtue is not made in the text, nor in 1 Cor. xiii. It may be held to be included, as to all relative virtues, in our Lord's declaration, Matt. xxii. 39, 40.

to the precept of it, which in strictness comes into our present consideration.

§ 19. *To general propositions, reasonable reserves commonly attach.*

However, in almost every thing that is said, there is somewhat to be understood beyond what is explicitly laid down, and which we of course supply; somewhat, I mean, which would not be commonly called a restriction, or limitation. Thus, when benevolence is said to be the sum of virtue, it is not spoken of as a blind propension, but as a principle in reasonable creatures, and so to be directed by their reason: for reason and reflection comes into our notion of a moral agent. And that will lead us to consider distant consequences, as well as the immediate tendency of an action: it will teach us, that the care of some persons, suppose children and families, is particularly committed to our charge by Nature and Providence; as also that there are other circumstances, suppose friendship or former obligations, which require that we do good to some, preferably to others. Reason, considered merely as subservient to benevolence, as assisting to produce the greatest good, will teach us to have particular regard to these relations and circumstances; because it is plainly for the good of the world that they should be regarded. And as there are numberless cases, in which, notwithstanding appearances, we are not competent judges, whether a particular action will upon the whole do good or harm; reason in the same way will teach us to be cautious how we act in these cases of uncertainty. It will suggest to our consideration, which is the safer side; how liable we are to be led wrong by passion and private interest; and what regard is due to laws, and the judgment of mankind. All these things must come into consideration, were it only in order to determine which way of acting is likely to produce the greatest good. Thus, upon supposition that it were in the strictest sense true, without limitation, that benevolence includes in it all virtues; yet reason must come in as its guide and director, in order to attain its own end, the end of benevolence, the greatest public good. Reason then being thus included, let us now consider the truth of the assertion itself.

§ 20. (a) *Our neighbour's due is, his happiness. By aiding this, we do our part.*

First, It is manifest that nothing can be of consequence to mankind or any creature, but happiness. This then is all which any person can, in strictness of speaking, be said to have a right to. We can therefore *owe no man any thing*, but only to further and promote his happiness, according to our abilities. And therefore a disposition and endeavour to do good to all with whom we have to do, in the degree and manner which the different relations we stand in to them require, is a discharge of all the obligations we are under to them.

As human nature is not one simple uniform thing, but a composition of various parts; body, spirit, appetites, particular passions and affections; for each of which reasonable self-love would lead men to have due regard, and make suitable provision: so society consists of various parts, to which we stand in different respects and relations; and just benevolence would as surely lead us to have due regard to each of these, and behave as the respective relations require. Reasonable good-will, and right behaviour towards our fellow-creatures, are in a manner the same: only that the former expresseth the principle as it is in the mind; the latter, the principle as it were become external, i. e. exerted in actions.

§ 21. (b) *Hence a fresh spur to personal virtue.*

And so far as temperance, sobriety, and moderation in sensual pleasures, and the contrary vices, have any respect to our fellow-creatures, any influence upon their quiet, welfare, and happiness; as they always have a real, and often a near influence upon it; so far it is manifest those virtues may be produced by the love of our neighbour, and that the contrary vices would be prevented by it. Indeed, if men's regard to themselves will not restrain them from excess; it may be thought little probable, that their love to others will be sufficient: but the reason is, that their love to others is not, any more than their regard to themselves, just, and in its due degree. There are however manifest instances of persons kept sober and temperate from regard to their affairs, and the welfare of those who depend upon them. And it is obvious to every one, that habitual excess, a dissolute course of life, implies a general neglect of the duties we owe towards our friends, our families, and our country.

§ 22. *The common virtues may thus be traced up to benevolence as its source: thus supporting the text.*

From hence it is manifest that the common virtues, and the common vices of mankind, may be traced up to benevolence, or the want of it. And this entitles the precept, *Thou shalt love thy neighbour as thyself*, to the preeminence given to it; and is a justification of the apostle's assertion, that all other commandments are comprehended in it; whatever cautions and restrictions c there are, which might

---

Conduciveness to happiness and misery apparently not appointed as our sole standard of judgment.

c NOTE. For instance: As we are not competent judges, what is upon the whole for the good of the world, there may be other immediate ends appointed us to pursue, besides that one of doing good, or producing happiness. Though the good of the creation be the only end of the Author of it, yet he may have laid us under particular obligations, which we may discern and feel ourselves under, quite distinct from a perception, that the observance or violation of them is for the happiness or misery of our fellow-creatures. And this is in fact the case. For there are certain dispositions of mind, and certain actions, which are in themselves approved or disapproved by mankind, abstracted from the consideration of their tendency to the happiness or misery of the world; approved or disapproved by reflection, by that principle within, which is the guide of life, the judge of right and wrong. Numberless instances of this kind might be mentioned. There are pieces of treachery, which in themselves appear base and detestable to every one. There are actions, which perhaps can scarce have any other general name given them than indecencies, which yet are odious and shocking to human nature. There is such a thing as

require to be considered, if we were to state particularly and at length, what is virtue and right behaviour in mankind. But,

Secondly, It might be added, that in a higher and more general way of consideration, leaving out the particular nature of creatures, and the particular circumstances in which they are placed, benevolence seems in the strictest sense to include in it all that is good and worthy; all that is good, which we have any distinct particular notion of. We have no clear conception of any positive moral attribute in the supreme Being, but what may be resolved up into goodness. And, if we consider a reasonable creature or moral agent, without regard to the particular relations and circumstances in which he is placed; we cannot conceive any thing else to come in towards determining whether he is to be ranked in an higher or lower class of virtuous beings, but the higher or lower degree in which that principle, and what is manifestly connected with it, prevail in him.

§ 23. *Relation of benevolence to piety arises through God's being perfectly good.*

That which we more strictly call piety, or the love of God, and which is an essential part of a right temper, some may perhaps imagine no way connected with benevolence:

---

meanness, a little mind; which, as it is quite distinct from incapacity, so it raises a dislike and disapprobation quite different from that contempt, which men are too apt to have, of mere folly. On the other hand; what we call greatness of mind is the object of another sort of approbation, than superior understanding. Fidelity, honour, strict justice, are themselves approved in the highest degree, abstracted from consideration of their tendency. Now, whether it be thought that each of these are connected with benevolence in our nature, and so may be considered as the same thing with it; or whether some of them be thought an inferior kind of virtues and vices, somewhat like natural beauties and deformities; or lastly, plain exceptions to the general rule; thus much however is certain, that the things now instanced in, and numberless others, are approved or disapproved by mankind in general, in quite another view than as conducive to the happiness or misery of the world.

yet surely they must be connected, if there be indeed in being an object infinitely good. Human nature is so constituted, that every good affection implies the love of itself; i. e. becomes the object of a new affection in the same person. Thus, to be righteous, implies in it the love of righteousness; to be benevolent, the love of benevolence; to be good, the love of goodness; whether this righteousness, benevolence, or goodness, be viewed as in our own mind, or in another's: and the love of God as a being perfectly good, is the love of perfect goodness contemplated in a being or person. Thus morality and religion, virtue and piety, will at last necessarily coincide, run up into one and the same point, and *love* will be in all senses *the end of the commandment.*

§ 24. *Concluding prayer.*

O Almighty God, inspire us with this divine principle; kill in us all the seeds of envy and ill-will; and help us, by cultivating within ourselves the love of our neighbour, to improve in the love of thee. Thou hast placed us in various kindreds, friendships, and relations, as the school of discipline for our affections: help us, by the due exercise of them, to improve to perfection; till all partial affection be lost in that entire universal one, and thou, O God, shalt be all in all [1].

---

[1] It is to be presumed that this prayer constituted in fact the termination of the Sermon: the Sermon passed into the prayer; died, as may be said, in the prayer. See Six Sermons, iv. 25. I have seen this method practised abroad, and with admirable effect.

SERMON XIII, XIV

UPON THE LOVE OF GOD

———◆———

Thou shalt love the Lord thy God with all thy heart, and with all thy soul, and with all thy mind.—MATTHEW xxii. 37.

———◆———

SERMON XIII

§ 1. *Interaction of extremes in religion.*

EVERY body knows, you therefore need only just be put in mind, that there is such a thing, as having so great horror of one extreme, as to run insensibly and of course into the contrary; and that a doctrine's having been a shelter for enthusiasm, or made to serve the purposes of superstition, is no proof of the falsity of it: truth or right being somewhat real in itself, and so not to be judged of by its liableness to abuse, or by its supposed distance from or nearness to error. It may be sufficient to have mentioned this in general, without taking notice of the particular extravagancies[1], which have been vented under the pretence or endeavour of explaining the love of God; or how manifestly we are got into the contrary extreme, under the notion of a reasonable religion; so very reasonable, as to have

---

[1] The reference seems to be to the opinions of Molinos and Madame Guyon, and to the controversy between Bossuet and Fénélon; also to imply a leaning to the side of Bossuet. See Carmichael's reference to the sketch given by Macintosh, in his *Dissertation*, p. 169.

nothing to do with the heart and affections, if these words signify any thing but the faculty by which we discern speculative truth.

§ 2. *Following the text, he includes in love all affections and regards rightly due to God.*

By the love of God, I would understand all those regards, all those affections of mind which are due immediately to him from such a creature as man, and which rest in him as their end. As this does not include servile fear; so neither will any other regards, how reasonable soever, which respect any thing out of or besides the perfection of the divine nature, come into consideration here. But all fear is not excluded, because his displeasure is itself the natural proper object of fear. Reverence, ambition of his love and approbation, delight in the hope or consciousness of it, come likewise into this definition of the love of God; because he is the natural object of all those affections or movements of mind, as really as he is the object of the affection, which is in the strictest sense called love; and all of them equally rest in him, as their end. And they may all be understood to be implied in these words of our Saviour, without putting any force upon them: for he is speaking of the love of God and our neighbour, as containing the whole of piety and virtue.

§ 3. *And resting on him as their end. Of these, some are more especially due in the present life.*

It is plain that the nature of man is so constituted, as to feel certain affections upon the sight or contemplation of certain objects. Now the very notion of affection implies resting in its object as an end. And the particular affection to good characters, reverence and moral love of them, is natural to all those who have any degree of real goodness in themselves. This will be illustrated by the description of a perfect character in a creature; and by considering the manner, in which a good man in his presence would be affected towards such a character. He would of course feel the affections of love, reverence, desire of his approbation, delight in the hope or consciousness of it. And surely all this is applicable, and may be brought up to that Being, who is infinitely more than an adequate object of all those affections; whom we are commanded to love *with all our heart, with all our soul, and with all our mind*. And of these regards towards Almighty God, some are more particularly suitable to and becoming so imperfect a creature as man, in this mortal state we are passing through; and some of them, and perhaps other exercises of the mind, will be the employment and happiness of good men in a state of perfection[1].

This is a general view of what the following discourse will contain. And it is manifest the subject is a real one: there is nothing in it enthusiastical or unreasonable. And if it be indeed at all a subject, it is one of the utmost importance.

§ 4. *Every genuine affection rests upon its object as an end: like reason resting upon truth.*

As mankind have a faculty by which they discern speculative truth; so we have various affections towards external objects. Understanding and temper, reason and affection, are as distinct ideas, as reason and hunger; and one would think could no more be confounded. It is by reason that we get the ideas of several objects of our affections: but in these cases reason and affection are no more the same, than sight of a particular object, and the pleasure or uneasiness consequent thereupon, are the same. Now, as reason tends to and rests in the discernment of truth, the object of it; so the very nature of affection consists in tending towards, and resting in, its objects as an end. We do indeed often in common language say, that things are loved, desired, esteemed, not for themselves, but for somewhat further, somewhat out of and beyond them: yet, in these cases, whoever will attend, will see, that these things are not in reality the objects of the affections, i. e. are not loved, desired, esteemed, but the somewhat further and beyond them. If we have no affections which rest in what are called their objects, then what is called affection, love, desire, hope, in human nature,

---

[1] See *inf.* § 17.

is only an uneasiness in being at rest; an unquiet disposition to action, progress, pursuit, without end or meaning. But if there be any such thing as delight in the company of one person, rather than of another; whether in the way of friendship, or mirth and entertainment, it is all one, if it be without respect to fortune, honour, or increasing our stores of knowledge, or any thing beyond the present time; here is an instance of an affection absolutely resting in its object as its end, and being gratified, in the same way as the appetite of hunger is satisfied with food. Yet nothing is more common than to hear it asked, What advantage a man hath in such a course, suppose of study, particular friendships, or in any other; nothing, I say, is more common than to hear such a question put in a way which supposes no gain, advantage, or interest, but as a means to somewhat further: and if so, then there is no such thing at all as real interest, gain, or advantage. This is the same absurdity with respect to life, as an infinite series of effects without a cause is in speculation. The gain, advantage, or interest, consists in the delight itself, arising from such a faculty's having its object: neither is there any such thing as happiness or enjoyment, but what arises from hence. The pleasures of hope and of reflection are not exceptions: the former being only this happiness anticipated; the latter, the same happiness enjoyed over again after its time. And even the general expectation of future happiness can afford satisfaction, only as it is a present object to the principle of self-love.

§ 5. *Regard to an ulterior aim may belong to the present state rather than the future.*

It was doubtless intended, that life should be very much a pursuit to the gross of mankind[1]. But this is carried so much further than is reasonable, that what gives immediate satisfaction, i. e. our present interest, is scarce considered as our interest at all. It is inventions which have only a re-

---

[1] Apparently meaning that, for the mass of men, not the objects with which they are immediately conversant or occupied, should be the proper objects of their affection, but somewhat ulterior.

mote tendency towards enjoyment, perhaps but a remote tendency towards gaining the means only of enjoyment, which are chiefly spoken of as useful to the world. And though this way of thinking were just with respect to the imperfect state we are now in, where we know so little of satisfaction without satiety; yet it must be guarded against, when we are considering the happiness of a state of perfection; which happiness being enjoyment and not hope, must necessarily consist in this, that our affections have their objects, and rest in those objects as an end, i. e. be satisfied with them. This will further appear in the sequel of this discourse.

§ 6. *Affection for good objects is itself good and loveable.*

Of the several affections, or inward sensations, which particular objects excite in man, there are some, the having of which implies the love of them, when they are reflected upon[a]. This cannot be said of all our affections, principles, and motives of action. It were ridiculous to assert, that a man upon reflection hath the same kind of approbation of the appetite of hunger, or the passion of fear, as he hath of goodwill to his fellow-creatures. To be a just, a good, a righteous man, plainly carries with it a peculiar affection to or love of justice, goodness, righteousness, when these principles are the objects of contemplation. Now if a man approves of, or hath an affection to, any principle in and for itself; incidental things allowed for, it will be the same whether he views it in his own mind, or in another; in himself, or in his neighbour. This is the account of our approbation of, our moral love and affection to good characters; which cannot but be in those who have any degrees of real goodness in themselves, and who discern and take notice of the same principle in others.

---

[a] St. Austin observes, Amor ipse ordinate amandus est, quo bene amatur quod amandum est, ut sit in nobis virtus, qua vivitur bene. i.e. *The affection which we rightly have for what is lovely, must ordinate justly*; (must) *in due manner and proportion, become the object of a new affection, or be itself beloved, in order to our being endued with that virtue which is the principle of a good life.* De Civ. Dei, l. xv. c. 22.

§ 7. *May extend to a continuous goodness, the perfection of our nature.*

From observation of what passes within ourselves, our own actions, and the behaviour of others, the mind may carry on its reflections as far as it pleases; much beyond what we experience in ourselves, or discern in our fellow-creatures. It may go on, and consider goodness as become an uniform continued principle of action, as conducted by reason, and forming a temper and character absolutely good and perfect, which is in a higher sense excellent, and proportionably the object of love and approbation.

§ 8. *Such a being, in the highest human order, working for the general happiness, must beget love and other affections.*

Let us then suppose a creature perfect according to his created nature: let his form be human, and his capacities no more than equal to those of the chief of men: goodness shall be his proper character; with wisdom to direct it, and power within some certain determined sphere of action to exert it: but goodness must be the simple actuating principle within him; this being the moral quality which is amiable, or the immediate object of love as distinct from other affections of approbation. Here then is a finite object for our mind to tend towards, to exercise itself upon: a creature, perfect according to his capacity, fixed, steady, equally unmoved by weak pity or more weak fury and resentment; forming the justest scheme of conduct; going on undisturbed in the execution of it, through the several methods of severity and reward, towards his end, namely, the general happiness of all with whom he hath to do, as in itself right and valuable. This character, though uniform in itself, in its principle, yet exerting itself in different ways, or considered in different views, may by its appearing variety move different affections. Thus, the severity of justice would not affect us in the same way as an act of mercy: the adventitious qualities of wisdom and power may be considered in themselves: and even the strength of mind, which this immovable goodness supposes, may likewise be viewed as an object of contemplation, distinct from the goodness itself. Superior excellence of any kind, as well as superior wisdom and power, is the object of awe and reverence to all creatures, whatever their moral character be: but so far as creatures of the lowest rank were good, so far the view of this character, as simply good, must appear amiable to them, be the object of, or beget love.

§ 9. *If he have special care for us, we shall be reciprocally moved in proportion.*

Further, suppose we were conscious, that this superior person so far approved of us, that we had nothing servilely to fear from him; that he was really our friend, and kind and good to us in particular, as he had occasionally intercourse with us: we must be other creatures than we are, or we could not but feel the same kind of satisfaction and enjoyment (whatever would be the degree of it) from this higher acquaintance and friendship, as we feel from common ones; the intercourse being real, and the persons equally present, in both cases. We should have a more ardent desire to be approved by his better judgment, and a satisfaction in that approbation of the same sort with what would be felt in respect to common persons, or be wrought in us by their presence.

§ 10. *If he be our ruler and guardian, it will be our main duty to obey, our chief delight to contemplate him.*

Let us now raise the character, and suppose this creature, for we are still going on with the supposition of a creature, our proper guardian and governor; that we were in a progress of being towards somewhat further; and that his scheme of government was too vast for our capacities to comprehend: remembering still that he is perfectly good, and our friend as well as our governor. Wisdom, power, goodness, accidentally viewed any where, would inspire reverence, awe, love: and as these affections would be raised in higher or lower degrees, in proportion as we had occasionally more or less intercourse with the creature endued with those qualities; so this further consideration and knowledge, that he was our proper guardian and governor, would much more bring these objects and qualities home to ourselves; teach us they had a greater respect to us in particular, that we had an higher interest in that wisdom and power and goodness. We should, with joy, gratitude, reverence, love, trust, and dependence, appropriate the character, as what we had a right in; and make our boast in such our relation to it. And the conclusion of the whole would be, that we should refer ourselves implicitly to him, and cast ourselves entirely upon him. As the whole attention of life should be to obey his commands; so the highest enjoyment of it must arise from the contemplation of this character, and our relation to it, from a consciousness of his favour and approbation, and from the exercise of those affections towards him which could not but be raised from his presence. A Being who hath these attributes, who stands in this relation, and is thus sensibly present to the mind, must necessarily be the object of these affections: there is as real a correspondence between them, as between the lowest appetite of sense and its object.

§ 11. *The infinity of his attributes should raise our affections to their highest.*

That this Being is not a creature, but the Almighty God; that he is of infinite power and wisdom and goodness, does not render him less the object of reverence and love, than he would be if he had those attributes only in a limited degree. The Being who made us, and upon whom we entirely depend, is the object of some regards. He hath given us certain affections of mind, which correspond to wisdom, power, goodness; i. e. which are raised upon view of those qualities. If then he be really wise, powerful, good; he is the natural object of those affections, which he hath endued us with, and which correspond to those attributes. That he is infinite in power, perfect in wisdom and goodness, makes no alteration, but only that he is the object of those affections raised to the highest pitch.

§ 12. *His presence is not less intimate, because insensible.*

He is not indeed to be discerned by any of our senses. *I go forward, but he is not there; and backward, but I cannot perceive him: on the left hand, where he doth work, but I cannot behold him: he hideth himself on the right hand, that I cannot see him. O that I knew where I might find him! that I might come even to his seat* [b]! But is he then afar off? does he not fill heaven and earth with his presence? The presence of our fellow-creatures affects our senses, and our senses give us the knowledge of their presence; which hath different kinds of influence upon us; love, joy, sorrow, restraint, encouragement, reverence. However, this influence is not immediately from our senses, but from that knowledge. Thus suppose a person neither to see not hear another, not to know by any of his senses, but yet certainly to know, that another was with him; this knowledge might, and in many cases would, have one or more of the effects before mentioned. It is therefore not only reasonable, but also natural, to be affected with a presence, though it be not the object of our senses: whether it be, or be not, is merely an accidental circumstance, which needs not come into consideration: it is the certainty that he is with us, and we with him, which hath the influence. We consider persons then as present, not only when they are within reach of our senses, but also when we are assured by any other means [1] that they are within such a nearness; nay, if they are not, we can recall them to our mind, and be moved towards them as present: and must he, who is so much more intimately with us, that *in him we live and move and have our being*, be thought too distant to be the object of our affections?

§ 13. *Apply then to the Creator our rule for the creature.*

We own and feel the force of amiable and worthy qualities in our fellow-creatures: and can we be insensible

---

[b] Job xxiii.

---

[1] Say reflection, acting independently of sense; or written record; such a nearness, i. e. as amounts to mental presence.

to the contemplation of perfect goodness? Do we reverence the shadows of greatness here below, are we solicitous about honour and esteem and the opinion of the world: and shall we not feel the same with respect to him, whose are wisdom and power in their original, who *is the God of judgment by whom actions are weighed?* Thus love, reverence, desire of esteem, every faculty, every affection, tends towards, and is employed about its respective object in common cases: and must the exercise of them be suspended with regard to him alone, who is an object, an infinitely more than adequate object, to our most exalted faculties; him, *of whom, and through whom, and to whom are all things?*

§ 14. *Who is alone the adequate object of our affections, and unerring judge of the manner of their exercise.*

As we cannot remove from this earth, or change our general business on it, so neither can we alter our real nature. Therefore no exercise of the mind can be recommended, but only the exercise of those faculties you are conscious of. Religion does not demand new affections, but only claims the direction of those you already have, those affections you daily feel; though unhappily confined to objects, not altogether unsuitable, but altogether unequal to them. We only represent to you the higher, the adequate objects of those very faculties and affections. Let the man of ambition go on still to consider disgrace as the greatest evil; honour, as his chief good. But disgrace, in whose estimation? Honour, in whose judgment? This is the only question. If shame, and delight in esteem, be spoken of as real, as any settled ground of pain or pleasure; both these must be in proportion to the supposed wisdom and worth of him, by whom we are contemned or esteemed. Must it then be thought enthusiastical to speak of a sensibility of this sort, which shall have respect to an unerring judgment, to infinite wisdom; when we are assured this unerring judgment, this infinite wisdom, does observe upon our actions?

§ 15. *This is not to abandon our interest, but to pursue it.*

It is the same with respect to the love of God in the strictest and most confined sense. We only offer and represent the highest object of an affection, supposed already in your mind. Some degree of goodness must be previously supposed: this always implies the love of itself, an affection to goodness: the highest, the adequate object of this affection, is perfect goodness: which therefore we are to *love with all our heart, with all our soul, and with all our strength.* 'Must we then, forgetting our own interest, as it were go out of ourselves, and love God for his own sake?' No more forget your own interest, no more go out of yourselves, than when you prefer one place, one prospect, the conversation of one man to that of another. Does not every affection necessarily imply, that the object of it be itself loved? If it be not, it is not the object of the affection. You may and ought if you can, but it is a great mistake[1] to think you can, love or fear or hate any thing, from consideration that such love or fear or hatred may be a means of obtaining good or avoiding evil.

§ 16. *We are the more stirred, because it is to us that he does good.*

But the question, whether we ought to love God for his sake or for our own, being a mere mistake in language[2]; the real question, which this is mistaken for, will, I suppose, be answered by observing, that the goodness of God already exercised towards us, our present dependence upon him, and our expectation of future benefits, ought, and have

---

[1] Because the affection terminates upon its object, and not upon anything beyond it. But he seems to speak rather of the ordinary course of mental processes, than of what is abstractedly possible.

[2] The suggested antithesis sets up a false issue. God's goodness, exercised towards ourselves, by the law of our nature stirs up affection more strongly than if it were towards others: without raising in us any further question whether that surplus of affection (so to speak is for His sake or for our own.

a natural tendency, to beget in us the affection of gratitude, and greater love towards him, than the same goodness exercised towards others: were it only for this reason, that every affection is moved in proportion to the sense we have of the object of it; and we cannot but have a more lively sense of goodness, when exercised towards ourselves, than when exercised towards others. I added expectation of future benefits, because the ground of that expectation is present goodness.

§ 17. *Further developments of affection possible in a state of perfection.*

Thus Almighty God is the natural object of the several affections, love, reverence, fear, desire of approbation. For though he is simply one, yet we cannot but consider him in partial and different views. He is in himself one uniform Being, and for ever the same without *variableness or shadow of turning:* but his infinite greatness, his goodness, his wisdom, are different objects to our mind. To which is to be added, that from the changes in our own characters, together with his unchangeableness, we cannot but consider ourselves as more or less the objects of his approbation, and really be so. For if he approves what is good, he cannot, merely from the unchangeableness of his nature, approve what is evil. Hence must arise more various movements of mind, more different kinds of affections. And this greater variety also is just and reasonable in such creatures as we are, though it respects a Being simply one, good and perfect. As some of these affections[1] are most particularly suitable to so imperfect a creature as man, in this mortal state we are passing through; so there may be other exercises of mind, or some of these in higher degrees, our employment and happiness in a state of perfection.

---

[1] See *sup.* § 3.

SERMON XIV

§ 1. *Retrospect.*

CONSIDER then our ignorance, the imperfection of our nature, our virtue and our condition in this world, with respect to an infinitely good and just Being, our Creator and Governor; and you will see what religious affections of mind are most particularly suitable to this mortal state we are passing through.

§ 2. *If perfection of love be scarce attainable, yet we may get beyond servile fear to resignation.*

Though we are not affected with any thing so strongly, as what we discern with our senses; and though our nature and condition require, that we be much taken up about sensible things; yet our reason convinces us that God is present with us, and we see and feel the effects of his goodness: he is therefore the object of some regards. The imperfection of our virtue, joined with the consideration of his absolute rectitude or holiness, will scarce permit that perfection of love, which entirely casts out all fear: yet goodness is the object of love to all creatures who have any degree of it themselves; and consciousness of a real endeavour to approve ourselves to him, joined with the consideration of his goodness, as it quite excludes servile dread and horror, so it is plainly a reasonable ground for hope of his favour. Neither fear, nor hope, nor love then are excluded: and one or another of these will prevail, according to the different views we have of God; and ought to prevail, according to the changes we find in our own character. There is a temper of mind made up of, or which follows from all three, fear, hope, love; namely, resignation to the divine will, which is the general temper belonging to this state; which ought to be the habitual frame of our mind and heart, and to be exercised at proper seasons more distinctly, in acts of devotion.

§ 3. *Resignation, what.*

Resignation to the will of God is the whole of piety: it includes in it all that is good, and is a source of the most settled quiet and composure of mind[1]. There is the general principle of submission in our nature.

§ 4. *Of the renunciation of unsuitable advantages.*

Man is not so constituted as to desire things, and be uneasy in the want of them, in proportion to their known value: many other considerations come in to determine the degrees of desire; particularly whether the advantage we take a view of be within the sphere of our rank. Who ever felt uneasiness, upon observing any of the advantages brute creatures have over us? And yet it is plain they have several. It is the same with respect to advantages belonging to creatures of a superior order. Thus, though we see a thing to be highly valuable, yet that it does not belong to our condition of being, is sufficient to suspend our desires after it, to make us rest satisfied without such advantage. Now there is just the same reason for quiet resignation in the want of every thing equally unattainable, and out of our reach in particular, though others of our species be possessed of it. All this may be applied to the whole of life; to positive inconveniences as well as wants; not indeed to the sensations of pain and sorrow, but to all the uneasinesses of reflection, murmuring, and discontent. Thus is human nature formed to compliance, yielding, submission of temper. We find the principles of it within us; and every one exercises it towards some objects or other; i. e. feels it with regard to some persons, and some circumstances.

---

[1] It is evident that we are not to regard this resignation to the will of God as a state of pure passivity: but that, in Butler's view, it implies active concurrence with the will of God, especially as regards ourselves; and an indisposition to have anything ordered otherwise than as God shall order it. See *Analogy*, I. v. 39. This is made quite clear in §§ 5 and 6, by the account given of 'perfect' resignation and on the nature and office of resignation proper, *ibid.* 36, 38.

§ 5. *How resignation rids us of cares and discomfort.*

Now this is an excellent foundation of a reasonable and religious resignation. Nature teaches and inclines us to take up with our lot: the consideration, that the course of things is unalterable, hath a tendency to quiet the mind under it, to beget a submission of temper to it. But when we can add, that this unalterable course is appointed and continued by infinite wisdom and goodness; how absolute should be our submission, how entire our trust and dependence!

This would reconcile us to our condition; prevent all the supernumerary troubles arising from imagination, distant fears, impatience; all uneasiness, except that which necessarily arises from the calamities themselves we may be under. How many of our cares should we by this means be disburdened of! Cares not properly our own, how apt soever they may be to intrude upon us, and we to admit them; the anxieties of expectation, solicitude about success and disappointment, which in truth are none of our concern. How open to every gratification would that mind be, which was clear of these encumbrances!

§ 6. *Of perfect resignation: which the just working of faith, honesty, and fairness ought to produce.*

Our resignation to the will of God may be said to be perfect, when our will is lost and resolved up into his; when we rest in his will as our end, as being itself most just, and right, and good. And where is the impossibility of such an affection to what is just, and right, and good, such a loyalty of heart to the Governor of the universe, as shall prevail over all sinister indirect desires of our own? Neither is this at bottom any thing more than faith, and honesty, and fairness of mind; in a more enlarged sense indeed, than those words are commonly used. And as, in common cases, fear and hope and other passions are raised in us by their respective objects: so this submission of heart and soul and mind, this religious resignation, would be as naturally produced by our having just conceptions of Almighty God, and a real sense of his presence with us. In how low a degree soever this temper usually prevails amongst men, yet it is a temper right in itself: it is what we owe to our Creator: it is particularly suitable to our mortal condition, and what we should endeavour after for our own sakes in our passage through such a world as this; where is nothing upon which we can rest or depend; nothing but what we are liable to be deceived and disappointed in. Thus we might *acquaint ourselves with God, and be at peace.*

§ 7. *This would be to 'walk with God.'*

This is piety and religion in the strictest sense, considered as an habit of mind: an habitual sense of God's presence with us; being affected towards him, as present, in the manner his superior nature requires from such a creature as man: this is to *walk with God*.

§ 8. *Devotion is this temper put in act.*

Little more need be said of devotion or religious worship, than that it is this temper exerted into act. The nature of it consists in the actual exercise of those affections towards God, which are supposed habitual in good men. He is always equally present with us: but we are so much taken up with sensible things, that *Lo, he goeth by us, and we see him not: he passeth on also, but we perceive him not*[a]. Devotion is retirement, from the world he has made, to him alone: it is to withdraw from the avocations of sense, to employ our attention wholly upon him as upon an object actually present, to yield ourselves up to the influence of the divine presence, and to give full scope to the affections of gratitude, love, reverence, trust, and dependence; of which infinite power, wisdom, and goodness, is the natural and only adequate object.

§ 9. *Our most raised affections will still fall short.*

We may apply to the whole of devotion those words of the Son of Sirach, *When you glorify the Lord, exalt him as*

---

[a] Job ix. 11.

much as you can; for even yet will he far exceed: and when you exalt him, put forth all your strength, and be not weary; for you can never go far enough [b]. Our most raised affections of every kind cannot but fall short and be disproportionate, when an infinite Being is the object of them. This is the highest exercise and employment of mind that a creature is capable of. As this divine service and worship is itself absolutely due to God, so also is it necessary in order to a further end, to keep alive upon our minds a sense of his authority, a sense that in our ordinary behaviour amongst men we act under him as our governor and judge.

§ 10. *How far more blessed, when we see face to face.*

Thus you see the temper of mind respecting God, which is particularly suitable to a state of imperfection; to creatures in a progress of being towards somewhat further.

Suppose now this something further attained; that we were arrived at it: what a perception will it be, to see and know and feel that our trust was not vain, our dependence not groundless? that the issue, event, and consummation came out such as fully to justify and answer that resignation? If the obscure view of the divine perfection, which we have in this world, ought in just consequence to beget an entire resignation; what will this resignation be exalted into, when *we shall see face to face, and know as we are known?* If we cannot form any distinct notion of that perfection of the love of God, which *casts out all fear;* of that enjoyment of him, which will be the happiness of good men hereafter; the consideration of our wants and capacities of happiness, and that he will be an adequate supply to them, must serve us instead of such distinct conception of the particular happiness itself.

§ 11. *All earthly objects leave a void in us.*

Let us then suppose a man entirely disengaged from business and pleasure, sitting down alone and at leisure,

---

[b] Ecclus. xliii. 30.

to reflect upon himself and his own condition of being. He would immediately feel that he was by no means complete of himself, but totally insufficient for his own happiness. One may venture to affirm that every man hath felt this, whether he hath again reflected upon it or not. It is feeling this deficiency, that they are unsatisfied with themselves, which makes men look out for assistance from abroad; and which has given rise to various kinds of amusements, altogether needless any otherwise than as they serve to fill up the blank spaces of time, and so hinder their feeling this deficiency, and being uneasy with themselves. Now, if these external things we take up with were really an adequate supply to this deficiency of human nature, if by their means our capacities and desires were all satisfied and filled up; then it might be truly said, that we had found out the proper happiness of man; and so might sit down satisfied, and be at rest in the enjoyment of it. But if it appears, that the amusements, which men usually pass their time in, are so far from coming up to or answering our notions and desires of happiness, or good, that they are really no more than what they are commonly called, somewhat to pass away the time; i. e. somewhat which serves to turn us aside from, and prevent our attending to, this our internal poverty and want; if they serve only, or chiefly, to suspend, instead of satisfying our conceptions and desires of happiness; if the want remains, and we have found out little more than barely the means of making it less sensible, then are we still to seek for somewhat to be an adequate supply to it. It is plain that there is a capacity in the nature of man, which neither riches, nor honours, nor sensual gratifications, nor any thing in this world can perfectly fill up, or satisfy: there is a deeper and more essential want, than any of these things can be the supply of.

§ 12. *Which only God can adequately supply.*

Yet surely there is a possibility of somewhat, which may fill up all our capacities of happiness; somewhat, in which our souls may find rest; somewhat, which may be to us that satisfactory good we are inquiring after. But it cannot be any thing which is valuable only as it tends to some further end. Those therefore who have got this world so much into their hearts, as not to be able to consider happiness as consisting in any thing but property and possessions, which are only valuable as the means to somewhat else, cannot have the least glimpse of the subject before us; which is the end, not the means; the thing itself, not somewhat in order to it. But if you can lay aside that general, confused, undeterminate notion of happiness, as consisting in such possessions; and fix in your thoughts, that it really can consist in nothing but in a faculty's having its proper object; you will clearly see, that in the coolest way of consideration, without either the heat of fanciful enthusiasm, or the warmth of real devotion, nothing is more certain, than that an infinite Being may himself be, if he pleases, the supply to all the capacities of our nature. All the common enjoyments of life are from the faculties he hath endued us with, and the objects he hath made suitable to them. He may himself be to us infinitely more than all these: he may be to us all that we want. As our understanding can contemplate itself, and our affections be exercised upon themselves by reflection, so may each be employed in the same manner upon any other mind: and since the supreme Mind, the Author and Cause of all things, is the highest possible object to himself, he may be an adequate supply to all the faculties of our souls; a subject[1] to our understanding, and an object[1] to our affections.

§ 13. *As the same beings, only in a new scene, what new ideas may come before us.*

Consider then: when we shall have put off this mortal body, when we shall be divested of sensual appetites, and those possessions which are now the means of gratification shall be of no avail; when this restless scene of business

---

[1] The two words seem here to be used in the same sense.

and vain pleasures, which now diverts us from ourselves, shall be all over; we, our proper self, shall still remain: we shall still continue the same creatures we are, with wants to be supplied, and capacities of happiness. We must have faculties of perception, though not sensitive ones[1]; and pleasure or uneasiness from our perceptions, as now we have.

§ 14. *God combines all grace and beauty, all excellence of all kinds, which can beget legitimate delight.*

There are certain ideas, which we express by the words, *order, harmony, proportion, beauty,* the furthest removed from any thing sensual. Now what is there in those intellectual images, forms, or ideas, which begets that approbation, love, delight, and even rapture, which is seen in some persons' faces upon having those objects present to their minds?—'Mere enthusiasm!'—Be it what it will: there are objects, works of nature and of art, which all mankind have delight from, quite distinct from their affording gratification to sensual appetites; and from quite another view of them, than as being for their interest and further advantage. The faculties from which we are capable of these pleasures, and the pleasures themselves, are as natural, and as much to be accounted for, as any sensual appetite whatever, and the pleasure from its gratification. Words to be sure are wanting upon this subject: to say, that every thing of grace and beauty throughout the whole of nature, every thing excellent and amiable shared in differently lower degrees by the whole creation, meet in the Author and Cause of all things; this is an inadequate, and perhaps improper way of speaking of the divine nature:

---

[1] 'We can scarcely, perhaps, in conformity with the great Christian doctrine of the resurrection of the body, say with strict psychological exactness, that in the future state we shall not have sensitive faculties.' Carmichael. Perhaps there is a little verbal ambiguity in the text: and 'though not' may mean 'even though not' or 'though not necessarily,' and rather signify the opening of other channels, than the closing of those now open. Carmichael refers us to *Tusc. Disp.* i. 19.

but it is manifest that absolute rectitude[1], the perfection of being, must be in all senses, and in every respect, the highest object to the mind.

§ 15. *In whatever modes God and his counsels may be presented to us*

In this world it is only the effects[2] of wisdom, and power, and greatness, which we discern: it is not impossible, that hereafter the qualities themselves in the supreme Being may be the immediate object of contemplation. What amazing wonders are opened to view by late improvements! What an object is the universe to a creature, if there be a creature who can comprehend its system! But it must be an infinitely higher exercise of the understanding, to view the scheme of it in that Mind, which projected it, before its foundations were laid. And surely we have meaning to the words, when we speak of going further; and viewing, not only this system in his mind, but the wisdom and intelligence itself from whence it proceeded. The same may be said of power. But since wisdom and power are not God, he is a wise, a powerful Being; the divine nature may therefore be a further object to the understanding. It is nothing to observe that our senses give us but an imperfect knowledge of things: effects themselves, if we knew them thoroughly, would give us but imperfect notions of wisdom and power; much less of his Being, in whom they reside. I am not speaking of any fanciful notion of seeing all things in God[3]; but only representing to you, how much an higher object to the understanding an infinite Being himself is, than the things which he has made: and this is no more than saying, that the Creator is superior to the works of his hands.

---

[1] Carmichael quotes St. Augustine: 'religionis summa est imitari quem colis.'
[2] See Serm. xv. 3.
[3] So Malebranche, quoted by Carmichael from Reid: 'The Deity, being always present to our minds in a more intimate manner than any other being, may, upon occasion of the impressions made on our bodies, discover to us, as far as he thinks proper, and according to fixed laws, his own ideas of the object; and thus we see all things in God, or in the divine idea.'

§ 16. *The vision of faculty is beyond that of effect;*

This may be illustrated by a low example. Suppose a machine, the sight of which would raise, and discoveries in its contrivance gratify, our curiosity: the real delight, in this case, would arise from its being the effect of skill and contrivance. This skill in the mind of the artificer would be an higher object, if we had any senses or ways to discern it. For, observe, the contemplation of that principle, faculty, or power which produced any effect, must be an higher exercise of the understanding, than the contemplation of the effect itself. The cause must be an higher object to the mind than the effect.

§ 17. *And of goodness, (the true end,) beyond that of knowledge.*

But whoever considers distinctly what the delight of knowledge is, will see reason to be satisfied that it cannot be the chief good of man: all this, as it is applicable, so it was mentioned with regard to the attribute of goodness. I say, goodness. Our being and all our enjoyments are the effects of it: just men bear its resemblance: but how little do we know of the original, of what it is in itself? Recall what was before observed concerning the affection to moral characters; which, in how low a degree soever, yet is plainly natural to man, and the most excellent part of his nature: suppose this improved, as it may be improved to any degree whatever, in the *spirits of just men made perfect;* and then suppose that they had a real view of that *righteousness, which is an everlasting righteousness;* of the conformity of the divine will to the *law of truth,* in which the moral attributes of God consist; of that goodness in the sovereign Mind, which gave birth to the universe: add, what will be true of all good men hereafter, a consciousness of having an interest in what they are contemplating; suppose them able to say, *This God is our God for ever and ever:* would they be any longer to seek for what was their chief happiness, their final good? Could the utmost stretch of their capacities look further? Would not infinite perfect goodness be their very end, the last end and object of their affections; beyond which they could neither have, nor desire; beyond which they could not form a wish or thought?

§ 18. *From the effect of human presences, judge what will be the divine.*

Consider wherein that presence of a friend consists, which has often so strong an effect, as wholly to possess the mind, and entirely suspend all other affections and regards; and which itself affords the highest satisfaction and enjoyment. He is within reach of the senses. Now, as our capacities of perception improve, we shall have, perhaps by some faculty entirely new, a perception of God's presence with us in a nearer and stricter way; since it is certain he is more intimately present with us than any thing else can be. Proof of the existence and presence of any being is quite different from the immediate perception, the consciousness of it. What then will be the joy of heart, which his presence, and *the light of his countenance,* who is the life of the universe, will inspire good men with, when they shall have a sensation, that he is the sustainer of their being, that they exist in him; when they shall feel his influence to cheer and enliven and support their frame, in a manner of which we have now no conception? He will be in a literal sense *their strength and their portion for ever.*

§ 19. *The Bible words rise so high as to imply a kind of vision here unknown.*

When we speak of things so much above our comprehension, as the employment and happiness of a future state, doubtless it behoves us to speak with all modesty and distrust of ourselves. But the scripture represents the happiness of that state under the notions of *seeing God, seeing him as he is, knowing as we are known, and seeing face to face.* These words are not general or undetermined, but express a particular determinate happiness. And I will be bold to say, that nothing can account for, or come up to these expressions, but only this, that God himself will be an object to our faculties, that he himself will be our happiness; as distinguished from the enjoyments of the present state, which seem to arise, not immediately from him, but from the objects he has adapted to give us delight.

§ 20. *Copiously shown from the language of the Psalms.*

To conclude: Let us suppose a person tired with care and sorrow and the repetition of vain delights which fill up the round of life; sensible that every thing here below in its best estate is altogether vanity. Suppose him to feel that deficiency of human nature, before taken notice of; and to be convinced that God alone was the adequate supply to it. What could be more applicable to a good man in this state of mind; or better express his present wants and distant hopes, his passage through this world as a progress towards a state of perfection, than the following passages in the devotions of the royal prophet? They are plainly in an higher and more proper sense applicable to this, than they could be to any thing else. *I have seen an end of all perfection. Whom have I in heaven but thee? and there is none upon earth that I desire in comparison of thee. My flesh and my heart faileth: but God is the strength of my heart, and my portion for ever. Like as the hart desireth the water-brooks, so longeth my soul after thee, O God. My soul is athirst for God, yea, even for the living God: when shall I come to appear before him? How excellent is thy lovingkindness, O God! and the children of men shall put their trust under the shadow of thy wings. They shall be satisfied with the plenteousness of thy house: and thou shalt give them drink of thy pleasures, as out of the river. For with thee is the well of life: and in thy light shall we see light. Blessed is the man whom thou choosest, and receivest unto thee: he shall dwell in thy court, and shall be satisfied with the pleasures of thy house, even of thy holy temple. Blessed is the people, O Lord, that can rejoice in thee: they shall walk in the light of thy countenance. Their delight shall be daily in thy name, and in thy righteousness shall they make their boast. For thou art the glory of their strength: and in thy lovingkindness they shall be exalted. As for me, I will behold thy presence in righteousness: and when I awake up after thy likeness, I shall be satisfied with it. Thou shalt shew me the path of life; in thy presence is the fulness of joy, and at thy right hand there is pleasure for evermore* [1].

[1] In his notes on this Sermon (p. 228), Carmichael describes as 'matter of surprise and regret to the Christian reader, that in these two Sermons, the New Testament should have been almost completely ignored.' Is it not then recorded of St. Augustine that when near the point of death, he desired to be recited for him the fifty-first psalm? Is the Church wrong in choosing the Psalms for the staple food of her devotions? The criticism, however respectable the source, appears to me infelicitous and scarcely just.

SERMON XV

UPON THE IGNORANCE OF MAN

When I applied mine heart to know wisdom, and to see the business that is done upon the earth: then I beheld all the work of God, that a man cannot find out the work that is done under the sun: because though a man labour to seek it out, yet he shall not find it; yea farther; though a wise man think to know it, yet shall he not be able to find it.—ECCLES. viii. 16, 17.

§ 1. *The difficulty of learning nature may be the reason of Solomon's dealing mainly with conduct.*

THE writings of Solomon are very much taken up with reflections upon human nature and human life; to which he hath added, in this book, reflections upon the constitution of things. And it is not improbable, that the little satisfaction and the great difficulties he met with in his researches into the general constitution of nature, might be the occasion of his confining himself, so much as he hath done, to life and conduct. However, upon that joint review he expresses great ignorance of the works of God, and the method of his providence in the government of the world; great labour and weariness in the search and observation he had employed himself about; and great disappointment, pain, and even vexation of mind, upon that which he had remarked of the appearances of things, and of what was going forward upon this earth. This whole review and inspection, and the result of it, sorrow, perplexity, a sense of his necessary ignorance, suggests various reflections to his mind. But, notwithstanding all this ignorance and dissatisfaction, there is somewhat upon which he assuredly rests and depends; somewhat, which is the conclusion of the whole matter, and the only concern of man.

§ 2. *Purposed inquiry.*

Following this his method and train of reflection, let us consider,

[I.] The assertion of the text, the ignorance of man; that the wisest and most knowing cannot comprehend the ways and works of God[1] : and then,

[II.] What are the just consequences of this observation and knowledge of our own ignorance, and the reflections which it leads us to.

§ 3. *Of creation, causes, essences, and ends, we are absolutely ignorant.*

[I.] The wisest and most knowing cannot comprehend the works of God, the methods and designs of his providence in the creation and government of the world.

Creation is absolutely and entirely out of our depth, and beyond the extent of our utmost reach. And yet it is as certain that God made the world, as it is certain that effects must have a cause. It is indeed in general no more than effects[2], that the most knowing are acquainted with: for as to causes, they are as entirely in the dark as the most ignorant. What are the laws by which matter acts upon matter, but certain effects; which some, having observed to be frequently repeated, have reduced to general rules? The real nature and essence of beings likewise is what we are altogether ignorant of. All these things are so entirely out of our reach, that we have not the least glimpse of them. And we know little more of ourselves, than we do of the world about us: how we were made, how our being is con-

---

[1] Some of the most important propositions on this subject will be found in the *Analogy*, I. vii. 6, 20, 23.

[2] See Serm. xiv. 15, 16.

tinued and preserved, what the faculties of our minds are, and upon what the power of exercising them depends. *I am fearfully and wonderfully made: marvellous are thy works, and that my soul knoweth right well.* Our own nature, and the objects we are surrounded with, serve to raise our curiosity; but we are quite out of a condition of satisfying it. Every secret which is disclosed, every discovery which is made, every new effect which is brought to view, serves to convince us of numberless more which remain concealed, and which we had before no suspicion of. And what if we were acquainted with the whole creation, in the same way and as thoroughly as we are with any single object in it? What would all this natural knowledge amount to? It must be a low curiosity indeed which such superficial knowledge could satisfy. On the contrary, would it not serve to convince us of our ignorance still; and to raise our desire of knowing the nature of things themselves, the Author, the Cause, and the End of them?

§ 4. *We know some particulars of Providence and life; but the government of the universe is wholly beyond us.*

As to the government of the world: though from consideration of the final causes which come within our knowledge; of characters, personal merit and demerit; of the favour and disapprobation, which respectively are due and belong to the righteous and the wicked, and which therefore must necessarily be in a mind which sees things as they really are; though, I say, from hence we may know somewhat concerning the designs of Providence in the government of the world, enough to enforce upon us religion and the practice of virtue: yet, since the monarchy of the universe is a dominion unlimited in extent, and everlasting in duration; the general system of it must necessarily be quite beyond our comprehension. And, since there appears such a subordination and reference of the several parts to each other, as to constitute it properly one administration or government; we cannot have a thorough knowledge of any part, without knowing the whole. This surely should convince us, that we are.

much less competent judges of the very small part which comes under our notice in this world, than we are apt to imagine. *No heart can think upon these things worthily: and who is able to conceive his way? It is a tempest which no man can see: for the most part of his works are hid. Who can declare the works of his justice? for his covenant is afar off, and the trial of all things is in the end:* i.e. The dealings of God with the children of men are not yet completed, and cannot be judged of by that part which is before us. So that a man cannot say, This is worse than that: for in time they shall be well approved. *Thy faithfulness, O Lord, reacheth unto the clouds: thy righteousness standeth like the strong mountains: thy judgments are like the great deep. He hath made every thing beautiful in his time: also he hath set the world in their heart; so that no man can find out the work that God maketh from the beginning to the end.* And thus St. Paul concludes a long argument upon the various dispensations of Providence: *O the depth of the riches, both of the wisdom and knowledge of God! How unsearchable are his judgments, and his ways past finding out! For who hath known the mind of the Lord?*

§ 5. *Parts cannot be comprehended without the whole.*

Thus the scheme of Providence, the ways and works of God, are too vast, of too large extent for our capacities. There is, as I may speak, such an expanse of power, and wisdom, and goodness, in the formation and government of the world, as is too much for us to take in or comprehend. Power, and wisdom, and goodness are manifest to us in all those works of God, which come within our view: but there are likewise infinite stores of each poured forth throughout the immensity of the creation; no part of which can be thoroughly understood, without taking in its reference and respect to the whole: and this is what we have not faculties for.

§ 6. *Portions may have been advisedly veiled.*

And as the works of God, and his scheme of government, are above our capacities thoroughly to comprehend: so there possibly may be reasons which originally made it fit that many things should be concealed from us, which we have perhaps natural capacities of understanding; many things concerning the designs, methods, and ends of Divine Providence in the government of the world. There is no manner of absurdity in supposing a veil on purpose drawn over some scenes of infinite power, wisdom, and goodness, the sight of which might some way or other strike us too strongly; or that better ends are designed and served by their being concealed, than could be by their being exposed to our knowledge. The Almighty may cast clouds and darkness round about him, for reasons and purposes of which we have not the least glimpse or conception.

§ 7. *Demonstrative proofs may not have been expedient.*

However, it is surely reasonable, and what might have been expected, that creatures in some stage of their being, suppose in the infancy of it, should be placed in a state of discipline and improvement, where their patience and submission is to be tried by afflictions, where temptations are to be resisted, and difficulties gone through in the discharge of their duty. Now if the greatest pleasures and pains of the present life may be overcome and suspended, as they manifestly may, by hope and fear, and other passions and affections; then the evidence of religion, and the sense of the consequences of virtue and vice, might have been such, as entirely in all cases to prevail over those afflictions, difficulties, and temptations; prevail over them so, as to render them absolutely none at all. But the very notion itself, now mentioned, of a state of discipline and improvement, necessarily excludes such sensible evidence and conviction of religion, and of the consequences of virtue and vice.

§ 8. *Strictness in duty with less evidence may produce higher character.*

Religion consists in submission and resignation to the divine will. Our condition in this world is a school of exercise for this temper: and our ignorance, the shallowness of our reason, the temptations, difficulties, afflictions, which we are exposed to, all equally contribute to make it so. The general observation may be carried on; and whoever will attend to the thing will plainly see, that less sensible evidence, with less difficulty in practice, is the same, as more sensible evidence, with greater difficulty in practice. Therefore difficulties in speculation as much come into the notion of a state of discipline, as difficulties in practice: and so the same reason or account is to be given of both. Thus, though it is indeed absurd to talk of the greater merit of assent, upon little or no evidence, than upon demonstration; yet the strict discharge of our duty, with less sensible evidence, does imply in it a better character, than the same diligence in the discharge of it, upon more sensible evidence [1]. This fully accounts for and explains that assertion of our Saviour, *Blessed are they that have not seen, and yet have believed* [a]; have become Christians and obeyed the Gospel, upon less sensible evidence, than that which Thomas, to whom he is speaking, insisted upon.

§ 9. *The provision for us is fully equal to the demands upon us.*

But after all, the same account is to be given, why we were placed in these circumstances of ignorance, as why

---

[a] John xx. 29.

---

[1] It is difficult to comprise in very few words all the material elements of the case. Notice the line to be drawn between this rather summary form of assertion, and the careful one which concludes the sentence. The conditions required for a comparison seem to be as follows:—That the evidence shall be such as—
  (a) To impose labour in the scrutiny and appreciation of the case, which labour, with such an aim in view, will be an elevating discipline;
  (b) To exhibit a reasonable likelihood in the affirmative conclusion, such a likelihood as, under the laws of probable evidence, entails the moral obligation to assent.
This case we are to compare with the case of fuller evidence, entailing less labour, or none. As there will be a diminution of labour under both heads, and as such labour is an exercise with moral profit, a less amount of improving force will be brought to bear upon character, and the result will be proportionably smaller.

nature has not furnished us with wings; namely, that we were designed to be inhabitants of this earth. I am afraid we think too highly of ourselves; of our rank in the creation, and of what is due to us. What sphere of action, what business is assigned to man, that he has not capacities and knowledge fully equal to? It is manifest he has reason, and knowledge, and faculties superior to the business of the present world: faculties which appear superfluous, if we do not take in the respect which they have to somewhat further, and beyond it. If to acquire knowledge were our proper end, we should indeed be but poorly provided: but if somewhat else be our business and duty, we may, notwithstanding our ignorance, be well enough furnished for it; and the observation of our ignorance may be of assistance to us in the discharge of it.

§ 10. *We therefore must not haggle upon kinds of evidence.*

[II.] Let us then consider, what are the consequences of this knowledge and observation of our own ignorance, and the reflection it leads us to.

First, We may learn from it, with what temper of mind a man ought to inquire into the subject of religion; namely, with expectation of finding difficulties, and with a disposition to take up and rest satisfied with any evidence whatever, which is real [1].

He should beforehand expect things mysterious, and such as he will not be able thoroughly to comprehend, or go to the bottom of. To expect a distinct comprehensive view of the whole subject, clear of difficulties and objections, is to forget our nature and condition; neither of which admit of such knowledge, with respect to any science whatever [2].

---

[1] Plainly this does not mean that the evidence need not be sufficient in amount, but that we are not to take objections as to its class or description if we cannot question its reality; which must include its relevancy and its sufficiency.

[2] Carmichael quotes the fine thought of Pascal (*Pensées Morales*, p. 69): 'Les sciences ont deux extrémités qui se touchent. La première est la pure ignorance naturelle, où se trouvent tous les hommes en naissant. L'autre extrémité est celle, où arrivent les grandes âmes, qui, ayant parcouru tout ce que les hommes

And to inquire with this expectation, is not to inquire as a man, but as one of another order of creatures.

Due sense of the general ignorance of man would also beget in us a disposition to take up and rest satisfied with any evidence whatever, which is real. I mention this as the contrary to a disposition, of which there are not wanting instances, to find fault with and reject evidence, because it is not such as was desired.

§ 11. *We must not reject twilight, from even a reasonable desire for broad day.*

If a man were to walk by twilight, must he not follow his eyes as much as if it were broad day and clear sunshine? Or if he were obliged to take a journey by night, would he not *give heed to* any *light shining in the darkness, till the day should break and the day-star arise?* It would not be altogether unnatural for him to reflect how much better it were to have day-light; he might perhaps have great curiosity to see the country round about him; he might lament that the darkness concealed many extended prospects from his eyes, and wish for the sun to draw away the veil: but how ridiculous would it be, to reject with scorn and disdain the guidance and direction which that lesser light might afford him, because it was not the sun itself! If the make and constitution of man, the circumstances he is placed in, or the reason of things affords the least hint or intimation, that virtue is the law he is born under: scepticism itself should lead him to the most strict and inviolable practice of it; that he may not make the dreadful experiment, of leaving the course of life marked out for him by nature, whatever that nature be, and entering paths of his own, of which he can know neither the dangers nor the end. For though no danger be seen, yet darkness, ignorance, and blindness are no manner of security.

---

peuvent savoir, trouvent qu'ils ne savent rien, et se rencontrent dans cette même ignorance d'où ils étaient partis. Mais c'est une ignorance savante qui se connaît. Ceux qui sont sortis de l'ignorance naturelle, et n'ont pu arriver à l'autre, ont quelque teinture de cette science suffisante, et font les entendus. Ceux-là troublent le monde, et jugent plus mal du tout que les autres.'

§ 12. *Our ignorance a proper answer to much that is objected*[1].

Secondly, Our ignorance is the proper answer to many things, which are called objections against religion; particularly, to those which arise from the appearances of evil and irregularity in the constitution of nature and the government of the world. In all other cases it is thought necessary to be thoroughly acquainted with the whole of a scheme, even one of so narrow a compass as those which are formed by men, in order to judge of the goodness or badness of it: and the most slight and superficial view of any human contrivance comes abundantly nearer to a thorough knowledge of it, than that part, which we know of the government of the world, does to the general scheme and system of it; to the whole set of laws by which it is governed. From our ignorance of the constitution of things, and the scheme of Providence in the government of the world; from the reference the several parts have to each other, and to the whole; and from our not being able to see the end and the whole; it follows, that however perfect things are, they must even necessarily appear to us otherwise less perfect than they are [b].

---

[b] NOTE. 1. Suppose some very *complicated piece of work*, some *system* or *constitution*, formed for some *general end*, to which each of the *parts* had a *reference*. The perfection or justness of this work or constitution would consist in the reference and respect, which the several parts have to the general design. This reference of parts to the general design may be infinitely various, both in degree and kind. Thus one part may only contribute and be subservient to another; this to a third; and so on through a long series, the last part of which alone may contribute immediately and directly to the general design. Or a part may have this distant reference to the general design, and may also contribute immediately to it. For instance: If the general design or end, for which the complicated frame of nature was brought into being, is happiness; whatever affords present satisfaction, and likewise tends to carry on the course of things, hath this double respect to the general design. Now suppose a spectator of that work or constitution was in a great

Our ignorance of the whole should affect (differently) our view (a) of the wrong appearances;

---

[1] See *Analogy*, Introd. § 12; I. vii. 6, 20, 23; II. v. 20, 21.

§ 13. *We are not to fret at our ignorance. Knowledge is not our proper happiness.*

Thirdly, Since the constitution of nature, and the methods and designs of Providence in the government of the world, are above our comprehension, we should acquiesce in, and rest satisfied with, our ignorance; turn our thoughts from that which is above and beyond us, and apply ourselves to that which is level to our capacities, and which is our real business and concern. Knowledge is not our proper happiness[1]. Whoever will in the least attend to the thing will see, that it is the gaining, not the having of it, which is the entertainment of the mind[2]. Indeed, if the proper happiness of man consisted in knowledge considered as a possession or treasure, men who are possessed of the measure ignorant of such various reference to the general end, whatever that end be; and that, upon a very slight and partial view which he had of the work, several things appeared to his eye disproportionate and wrong; others, just and beautiful: what would he gather from these appearances? He would immediately conclude there was a probability, if he could see the whole reference of the parts appearing wrong to the general design, that this would destroy the appearance of wrongness and disproportion:

2. But there is no probability, that the reference would destroy the particular right appearances, though that reference might show the things already appearing just, to be so likewise in an higher degree or another manner. There is a probability, that the right appearances were intended: there is no probability, that the wrong appearances were. We cannot suspect irregularity and disorder to be designed. The pillars of a building appear beautiful; but their being likewise its support does not destroy that beauty: there still remains a reason to believe that the architect intended the beautiful appearance, after we have found out the reference, support. It would be reasonable for a man of himself to think thus, upon the first piece of architecture he ever saw.

(b) *Of the right appearances.*

---

[1] See Serm. xiv. § 16.
[2] Meaning the due healthful employment of the mind. Carmichael notices that Aristotle seems not in harmony with this passage of Butler, and suggests a reconciliation. It seems to me that there is a difference, and that while Butler takes the view of knowledge conformable to Christianity, Aristotle, quite naturally in his position, attaches a greater value to the possession of knowledge as such (*Eth. Nic.* X. vii. 3).

largest share would have a very ill time of it; as they would be infinitely more sensible than others of their poverty in this respect. Thus *he who increases knowledge would* eminently *increase sorrow*. Men of deep research and curious inquiry should just be put in mind, not to mistake what they are doing. If their discoveries serve the cause of virtue and religion, in the way of proof, motive to practice, or assistance in it; or if they tend to render life less unhappy, and promote its satisfactions; then they are most usefully employed: but bringing things to light, alone and of itself, is of no manner of use, any otherwise than as an entertainment or diversion. Neither is this at all amiss, if it does not take up the time which should be employed in better work.

§ 14. *Another end is appointed us, in conduct, and duty 'level to our capacities.'*

But it is evident that there is another mark set up for us to aim at; another end appointed us to direct our lives to: an end, which the most knowing may fail of, and the most ignorant arrive at. *The secret things belong unto the Lord our God; but those things which are revealed belong unto us and to our children for ever, that we may do all the words of this law*[1]. Which reflection of Moses, put in general terms, is, that the only knowledge, which is of any avail to us, is that which teaches us our duty, or assists us in the discharge of it. The economy of the universe, the course of nature, almighty power exerted in the creation and government of the world, is out of our reach. What would be the consequence, if we could really get an insight into these things, is very uncertain; whether it would assist us in, or divert us from what we have to do in this present state. If then there be a sphere of knowledge, of contemplation and employment, level to our capacities, and of the utmost importance to us; we ought surely to apply ourselves with all diligence to this our proper business, and esteem every thing else nothing, nothing as to us, in comparison of it.

[1] Deut. xxix. 29.

§ 15. *As declared by Job* xxviii. 28.

Thus Job, discoursing of natural knowledge, how much it is above us, and of wisdom in general, says, *God understandeth the way thereof, and he knoweth the place thereof. And unto man he said, Behold, the fear of the Lord, that is wisdom, and to depart from evil is understanding.* Other orders of creatures may perhaps be let into the secret counsels of heaven; and have the designs and methods of Providence, in the creation and government of the world, communicated to them: but this does not belong to our rank or condition. *The fear of the Lord, and to depart from evil*[1], is the only wisdom which man should aspire after, as his work and business. The same is said, and with the same connection and context, in the conclusion of the Book of Ecclesiastes. Our ignorance, and the little we can know of other things, affords a reason why we should not perplex ourselves about them; but no way invalidates that which is the *conclusion of the whole matter: Fear God, and keep his commandments: for this is the whole concern of man*[2]. So that Socrates was not the first who endeavoured to draw men off from labouring after, and laying stress upon other knowledge, in comparison of that which related to morals[3]. Our province is virtue and religion, life and manners; the science of improving the temper, and making the heart better. This is the field assigned us to cultivate: how much it has lain neglected is indeed astonishing. Virtue is demonstrably the happiness of man: it consists in good actions, pro-

---

[1] Job xxviii. 28.
[2] Eccles. xii. 13.
[3] This is the Socratic view of human life; to look at it as an assemblage of realities and practical details. Grote, *Hist. Greece,* viii. 632.
And Bishop Hampden on Socrates: 'To the same purpose was his disparagement of physical science, and of all merely speculative knowledge, in comparison with that which was useful for human life.... He assailed a branch of knowledge then, at once so barren and so encroaching in its claims on public attention' (*Fathers of Greek Philosophy,* pp. 404, 405).
In *Tusc. Disp.* v. 4, we find the famous words, 'primus philosophiam devocavit a caelo et in urbibus collocavit, et in domos etiam introduxit, et coegit de vita et moribus rebusque bonis et malis quaerere.'

†

ceeding from a good principle, temper, or heart. Overt acts are entirely in our power. What remains is, that we learn to *keep our heart;* to govern and regulate our passions, mind, affections: that so we may be free from the impotencies of fear, envy, malice, covetousness, ambition; that we may be clear of these, considered as vices seated in the heart, considered as constituting a general wrong temper; from which general wrong frame of mind, all the mistaken pursuits, and far the greatest part of the unhappiness of life, proceed. He, who should find out one rule to assist us in this work, would deserve infinitely better of mankind, than all the improvers of other knowledge put together.

§ 16. *The lesson taught is adoration of God,*

Lastly, Let us adore that infinite wisdom and power and goodness, which is above our comprehension. *To whom hath the root of wisdom been revealed? Or who hath known her wise counsels? There is one wise and greatly to be feared; the Lord sitting upon his throne. He created her, and saw her, and numbered her, and poured her out upon all his works.* If it be thought a considerable thing to be acquainted with a few, a very few, of the effects of infinite power and wisdom; the situation, bigness, and revolution of some of the heavenly bodies; what sentiments should our minds be filled with concerning him, who appointed to each its place and measure and sphere of motion, all which are kept with the most uniform constancy! *Who stretched out the heavens*[1], *and telleth the number of the stars, and calleth them all by their names*[2]. *Who laid the foundations of the earth*[3], *who comprehendeth the dust of it in a measure, and weigheth the mountains in scales, and the hills in a balance*[4]. And, when we have recounted all the appearances which come within our view, we must add, *Lo, these are part of his ways; but how little a portion is heard of him*[5]*! Canst thou by searching find out God? Canst thou find out the Almighty unto perfection? It is as high as*

---

[1] Isaiah li. 13.   [2] Ps. cxlvii. 4.   [3] Ps. cii. 25.
[4] Isaiah xl. 12.   [5] Job xxvi. 14.

heaven; what canst thou do? deeper than hell; what canst thou know[1]?

§ 17. *And abatement of self-esteem.*

The conclusion is, that in all lowliness of mind we set lightly by ourselves: that we form our temper to an implicit submission to the Divine Majesty; beget within ourselves an absolute resignation to all the methods of his providence, in his dealings with the children of men: that, in the deepest humility of our souls, we prostrate ourselves before him, and join in that celestial song; *Great and marvellous are thy works, Lord God Almighty! just and true are thy ways, thou King of saints! Who shall not fear thee, O Lord, and glorify thy name*[2]?

---

[1] Job xi. 7, 8.   [2] Rev. xv. 3, 4.

SIX SERMONS
PREACHED UPON PUBLIC OCCASIONS

SERMON I

PREACHED BEFORE THE INCORPORATED SOCIETY FOR THE PROPAGATION OF THE GOSPEL IN FOREIGN PARTS, AT THEIR ANNIVERSARY MEETING IN THE PARISH CHURCH OF ST. MARY-LE-BOW, ON FRIDAY, FEBRUARY 16, 1738-9.

And this gospel of the kingdom shall be preached in all the world, for a witness unto all nations.—MATTHEW xxiv. 14.

---

§ 1. *Of natural or original religion and its decay.*

THE general doctrine of religion, that all things are under the direction of one righteous Governor, having been established by repeated revelations[1] in the first ages of the world, was left with the bulk of mankind, to be honestly preserved pure and entire, or carelessly forgotten, or wilfully corrupted. And though reason, almost intuitively, bare witness to the truth of this moral system of nature, yet it soon appeared, that *they did not like to retain God in their knowledge*[a], as to any purposes of real piety. Natural religion became gradually more and more darkened with superstition, little understood, less regarded in practice; and the face of it scarce discernible at all, in the religious establishments of the most learned, polite nations.

---

[a] Rom. i. 28.

---

[1] The first of which, according to Butler, included what is known as natural religion. See *Analogy*, I. vi. 18; II. ii. 10. Of course he does not mean that the first revelation was confined to natural religion.

§ 2. *Reason incompetent to revive or extend it.*

And how much soever could have been done towards the revival of it by the light of reason, yet this light could not have discovered, what so nearly concerned us, that important part in the scheme of this world, which regards a Mediator; nor how far the settled constitution of its government admitted repentance to be accepted for remission of sins; after the obscure intimations of these things, from tradition, were corrupted or forgotten. One people indeed had clearer notices of them, together with the genuine scheme of natural religion, preserved in the primitive and subsequent revelations committed to their trust; and were designed to be a witness of God, and a providence to the nations around them: but this people also had corrupted themselves and their religion to the highest degree that was consistent with keeping up the form of it.

§ 3. *Its republication and enlargement by the gospel.*

In this state of things, when infinite Wisdom saw proper, the general doctrine of religion was authoritatively republished in its purity[1]; and the particular dispensation of Providence, which this world is under, manifested to all men, even *the dispensation of the grace of God*[h] towards us, as sinful, lost creatures, to be recovered by repentance through a Mediator; who was *to make reconciliation for iniquity, and to bring in everlasting righteousness*[c], and at length establish that new state of things foretold by the prophet Daniel, under the character of *a kingdom*[2], *which the God of heaven would set up, and which should never be destroyed*[d]. This, including a more distinct account of the instituted means, whereby Christ the Mediator would *gather together*

---

[h] Eph. iii. 2.   [c] Dan. ix. 24.   [d] Dan. ii. 44.

[1] See *Analogy*, II. i. 5. The whole matter of these opening sections is more fully set forth in chapters of the Second Part of the *Analogy* (published only two years before).

[2] Compare *Analogy*, II. i. 10.

in one the children of God that were scattered abroad[e], and conduct them to *the place he is gone to prepare for them*[f]; is *the gospel of the kingdom*, which he here foretells, and elsewhere commands, should *be preached in all the world, for a witness unto all nations*. And it *first began to be spoken by the Lord, and was confirmed unto us by them that heard him; God also bearing them witness, both with signs and wonders, and with divers miracles, and gifts of the Holy Ghost, according to his own will*[g]: by which means it was spread very widely among the nations of the world, and became *a witness unto them*.

§ 4. *The new religion left to the care of men, with* (a) *the church, and* (b) *the scripture.*

When thus much was accomplished, as there is a wonderful uniformity in the conduct of Providence, Christianity was left with Christians, to be transmitted down pure and genuine, or to be corrupted and sunk; in like manner as the religion of nature had been before left with mankind in general. There was however this difference, that by an institution of external religion fitted for all men, (consisting in a common form of Christian worship, together with a standing ministry of instruction and discipline), it pleased God to unite Christians in communities or visible churches, and all along to preserve them, over a great part of the world; and thus perpetuate a general publication of the gospel. For these communities, which together make up the catholic visible church, are, first, the repositories of the written oracles of God; and, in every age, have preserved and published them, in every country, where the profession of Christianity has obtained. Hence it has come to pass, and it is a thing very much to be observed in the appointment of Providence, that even such of these communities as, in a long succession of years, have corrupted Christianity the most, have yet continually carried, together with their corruptions, the confutation of them [1]: for they have every

[e] John xi. 52.   [f] John xiv. 2, 3.   [g] Heb. ii. 3, 4.

---

[1] See *Analogy*, I. iv. 9; II. i. 13; vi. 5.

where preserved the pure original standard of it, the scripture, to which recourse might have been had, both by the deceivers and the deceived, in every successive age. Secondly, any particular church, in whatever place established, is like *a city that is set on an hill, which cannot be hid*[h], inviting all who pass by, to enter into it. All persons, to whom any notices of it come, have, in scripture language, the *kingdom of God come nigh unto them*. They are reminded of that religion, which natural conscience attests the truth of: and they may, if they will, be instructed in it more distinctly, and likewise in the gracious means, whereby sinful creatures may obtain eternal life; that chief and final good, which all men, in proportion to their understanding and integrity, even in all ages and countries of the heathen world, were ever in pursuit of. And, lastly, out of these churches have all along gone forth persons, who have preached the gospel in remote places, with greater or less good effect: for the establishment of any profession of Christianity, however corrupt, I call a good effect, whilst accompanied with a continued publication of the scripture, notwithstanding it may for some time lie quite neglected.

§ 5. *Obligation to public worship hence arising.*

From these things, it may be worth observing by the way, appears the weakness of all pleas for neglecting the public service of the church. For though a man prays with as much devotion and less interruption at home, and reads better sermons there, yet that will by no means excuse the neglect of his appointed part in keeping up the profession of Christianity amongst mankind. And this neglect, were it universal, must be the dissolution of the whole visible church, i. e. of all Christian communities; and so must prevent those good purposes, which were intended to be answered by them, and which they have, all along, answered over the world. For we see that by their means the event foretold in the text, which began in the preaching of Christ and the apostles, has been carried on, more or less, ever

[h] Matt. v. 14.

since, and is still carrying on; these being the providential means of its progress. And it is, I suppose, the completion of this event, which St. John had a representation of, under the figure of *an angel flying in the midst of heaven, having the everlasting gospel to preach unto them that dwell on the earth, and to every nation, and kindred, and tongue, and people* [i].

§ 6. *The operation here indicated, not its effect.*

Our Lord adds in the text, that this should be *for a witness unto them:* for an evidence of their duty, and an admonition to perform it. But what would be the effect, or success of the general preaching of the gospel, is not here mentioned. And therefore the prophecy of the text is not parallel to those others in scripture, which seem to foretell the glorious establishment of Christianity in the last days: nor does it appear that they are coincident; otherwise than as the former of these events must be supposed preparatory to the latter. Nay, it is not said here, that *God willeth all men should be saved, and come unto the knowledge of the truth* [k]: though this is the language of scripture elsewhere. The text declares no more, than that it was the appointment of God, in his righteous government over the world, that *the gospel of the kingdom should be preached for a witness unto it.*

§ 7. *The divine kingdom ordained to be a witness.*

The visible constitution and course of nature, the moral law written in our hearts, the positive institutions of religion, and even any memorial of it, are all spoken of in scripture under this, or the like denomination: so are the prophets, apostles, and our Lord himself. They are all *witnesses,* for the most part unregarded witnesses, in behalf of God, to mankind. They inform us of his being and providence, and of the particular dispensation of religion which we are under; and continually remind us of them. And they are equally witnesses of these things, whether we regard them or not. Thus after a declaration, that Ezekiel should be sent with a divine message to the children of

---

[i] Rev. xiv. 6.   [k] 1 Tim. ii. 4.

Israel, it is added, *and they, whether they will hear, or whether they will forbear, (for they are a rebellious house,) yet shall know that there hath been a prophet among them*[1]. And our Lord directs the seventy disciples, upon their departure from any city, which refused to receive them, to declare, *Notwithstanding, be ye sure of this, that the kingdom of God is come nigh unto you*[m]. The thing intended in both these passages is that which is expressed in the text by the word *witness*. And all of them together evidently suggest thus much, that the purposes of Providence are carried on, by the preaching of the gospel to those who reject it, as well as to those who embrace it.

§ 8. *But each person's lot depends upon himself.*

It is indeed true, *God willeth that all men should be saved*: yet, from the unalterable constitution of his government, the salvation of every man cannot but depend upon his behaviour, and therefore cannot but depend upon himself; and is necessarily his own concern, in a sense in which it cannot be another's. All this the scripture declares, in a manner the most forcible and alarming: *Can a man be profitable unto God, as he that is wise may be profitable unto himself? Is it any pleasure to the Almighty, that thou art righteous? or is it gain to Him, that thou makest thy way perfect*[n]? *If thou be wise, thou shalt be wise for thyself: but if thou scornest, thou alone shalt bear it*[o]. *He that heareth, let him hear; and he that forbeareth, let him forbear*[p]. And again, *He that hath ears to hear, let him hear: but if any man be ignorant*, i. e. wilfully, *let him be ignorant*[q]. To the same purpose are those awful words of the angel, in the person of him, to whom *all judgment is committed*[r]: *He that is unjust, let him be unjust still: and he which is filthy, let him be filthy still: and he that is righteous, let him be righteous still: and he that is holy, let him be holy still. And, behold, I come*

---

[1] Ezek. ii. 5, 7.   [m] Luke x. 11.   [n] Job xxii. 2, 3.
[o] Prov. ix. 12.   [p] Ezek. iii. 27.
[q] 1 Cor. xiv. 38.   [r] John v. 22.

quickly; and my reward is with me, to give every man according as his work shall be[s]. The righteous government of the world must be carried on; and, of necessity, men shall remain the subjects of it, by being examples of its mercy or of its justice. *Life and death are set before them, and whether they like shall be given unto them*[t]. They are to make their choice, and abide by it: but which soever their choice be, the gospel is equally a *witness* to them; and the purposes of Providence are answered by this *witness* of the gospel.

§ 9. *It is God's ordinance, that man be instructed by man.*

From the foregoing view of things we should be reminded, that the same reasons which make it our duty to instruct the ignorant in the relation, which the light of nature shows they stand in to God their maker, and in the obligations of obedience, resignation, and love to him, which arise out of that relation; make it our duty likewise to instruct them in all those other relations, which revelation informs us of, and in the obligations of duty, which arise out of them. And the reasons for instructing men in both these are of the very same kind, as for communicating any useful knowledge whatever. God, if he had so pleased, could indeed miraculously have revealed every religious truth which concerns mankind, to every individual man: and so he could have every common truth; and thus have superseded all use of human teaching in either. Yet he has not done this: but has appointed, that men should be instructed by the assistance of their fellow-creatures in both. Further: though all knowledge from reason is as really from God, as revelation is: yet this last is a distinguished favour to us, and naturally strikes us with the greatest awe, and carries in it an assurance, that those things which we are informed of by it are of the utmost importance to us to be informed of.

---

[s] Rev. xxii. 11, 12.   [t] Ecclus. xv. 17.

§ 10. *The gospel, as a trust, entails the obligation to make it known to others.*

Revelation therefore, as it demands to be received with a regard and reverence peculiar to itself; so it lays us under obligations, of a like peculiar sort, to communicate the light of it. Further still: it being an indispensable law of the gospel, that Christians should unite in religious communities, and these being intended for repositories of the written *oracles of God* [u], for standing memorials of religion to unthinking men, and for the propagation of it in the world; Christianity is very particularly to be considered as a trust, deposited with us in behalf of others, in behalf of mankind, as well as for our own instruction. No one has a right to be called a Christian, who doth not do somewhat in his station, towards the discharge of this trust; who doth not, for instance, assist in keeping up the profession of Christianity where he lives.

§ 11. *To our colonies.*

And it is an obligation but little more remote, to assist in doing it in our factories abroad; and in the colonies to which we are related, by their being peopled from our own mother-country, and subjects, indeed very necessary ones, to the same government with ourselves: and nearer yet is the obligation upon such persons in particular, as have the intercourse of an advantageous commerce with them.

§ 12. *Slaves are included in the scheme of redemption: their evil plight.*

Of these our colonies, the slaves ought to be considered as inferior members, and therefore to be treated as members of them; and not merely as cattle or goods, the property of their masters. Nor can the highest property, possible to be acquired in these servants, cancel the obligation to take care of their religious instruction. Despicable as they may appear in our eyes, they are the creatures of God, and

---

[u] *Sup.* § 4.

of the race of mankind, for whom Christ died : and it is inexcusable to keep them in ignorance of the end for which they were made, and the means whereby they may become partakers of the general redemption. On the contrary, if the necessity of the case requires, that they may be treated with the very utmost rigour, that humanity will at all permit, as they certainly are ; and, for our advantage, made as miserable as they well can be in the present world ; this surely heightens our obligation to put them into as advantageous a situation as we are able, with regard to another.

§ 13. *Duty to the Aborigines.*

The like charity we owe to the natives ; owe to them in a much stricter sense than we are apt to consider, were it only from neighbourhood, and our having gotten possessions in their country. For incidental circumstances of this kind appropriate all the general obligations of charity to particular persons ; and make such and such instances of it the duty of one man rather than another. We are most strictly bound to consider these poor unformed creatures, as being in all respects of one family with ourselves, the family of mankind ; and instruct them in our *common salvation*[x] : that they may not pass through this stage of their being like brute beasts ; but be put into a capacity of moral improvements, how low soever they must remain as to others, and so into a capacity of qualifying themselves for an higher state of life hereafter.

§ 14. *Our trade to be consecrated by subserving a great divine plan.*

All our affairs should be carried on in the fear of God, in subserviency to his honour, and the good of mankind. And thus navigation and commerce should be consecrated to the service of religion, by being made the means of propagating it in every country, with which we have any intercourse. And the more widely we endeavour to spread its light and

---

[x] Jude 3.

influence, as the forementioned circumstances, and others of a like kind, open and direct our way, the more faithful shall we be judged in the discharge of that trust [y], which is committed to us as Christians, when our Lord shall require an account of it.

And it may be some encouragement to cheerful perseverance in these endeavours, to observe, not only that they are our duty, but also that they seem the means of carrying on a great scheme of Providence, which shall certainly be accomplished. For *the everlasting gospel shall be preached to every nation*[z]: and *the kingdoms of this world shall become the kingdoms of our Lord, and of his Christ*[a].

§ 15. *Great good attaches to each fresh establishment of Christianity.*

However, we ought not to be discouraged in this good work, though its future success were less clearly foretold; and though its effect now in reforming mankind appeared to be as little as our adversaries pretend. They indeed, and perhaps some others, seem to require more than either experience or scripture give ground to hope for, in the present course of the world. But the bare establishment of Christianity in any place, even the external form and profession of it, is a very important and valuable effect. It is a serious call upon men to attend to the natural and the revealed doctrine of religion. It is a standing publication of the gospel, and renders it a *witness* to them: and by this means the purposes of Providence are carrying on, with regard to remote ages, as well as to the present. *Cast thy bread upon the waters: for thou shalt find it after many days. In the morning sow thy seed, and in the evening withhold not thine hand: for thou knowest not whether shall prosper, either this or that, or whether they both shall be alike good*[b]. We can look but a very little way into the connections and consequences of things: our duty is to spread the *incorruptible seed* as widely as we can, and leave it to *God to give the*

---

[y] Sup. 10.
[a] Rev. xi. 15.
[z] Rev. xiv. 6.
[b] Eccles. xi. 1, 6.

increase[c]. Yet thus much we may be almost assured of, that the gospel, wherever it is planted, will have its genuine effect upon some few; upon more perhaps than are taken notice of in the hurry of the world. There are, at least, a few persons in every country and successive age, scattered up and down, and mixed among the rest of mankind; who, not being corrupted past amendment, but having within them the principles of recovery, will be brought to a moral and religious sense of things, by the establishment of Christianity where they live; and then will be influenced by the peculiar doctrines of it, in proportion to the integrity of their minds, and to the clearness, purity, and evidence, with which it is offered them. Of these our Lord speaks in the parable of the sower, as *understanding the word, and bearing fruit, and bringing forth, some an hundredfold, some sixty, some thirty*[d]. One might add, that these persons, in proportion to their influence, do at present better the state of things: better it even in the civil sense, by giving some check to that avowed profligateness, which is a contradiction to all order and government; and, if not checked, must be the subversion of it.

§ 16. *Apart from miracle, there arises an effective call and admonition.*

These important purposes, which are certainly to be expected from the good work before us, may serve to show, how little weight there is in that objection against it, from the want of those miraculous assistances, with which the first preachers of Christianity proved its truth. The plain state of the case is, that the gospel, though it be not in the same degree a *witness* to all, who have it made known to them; yet in some degree is so to all. Miracles to the spectators of them are intuitive proofs of its truth: but the bare preaching of it is a serious admonition to all who hear it, to attend to the notices which God has given of himself by the light of nature; and, if Christianity be preached

---

[c] 1 Cor. iii. 6.   [d] Matt. xiii. 23.

with its proper evidence, to submit to its peculiar discipline and laws; if not, to inquire honestly after its evidence, in proportion to their capacities. And there are persons of small capacities for inquiry and examination, who yet are wrought upon by it, to *deny ungodliness and worldly lusts, and live soberly, righteously, and godly, in this present world* [e], in expectation of a future judgment by Jesus Christ. Nor can any Christian, who understands his religion, object, that these persons are Christians without evidence: for he cannot be ignorant who has declared, that *if any man will do his will, he shall know of the doctrine, whether it be of God* [f]. And, since the whole end of Christianity is to influence the heart and actions, were an unbeliever to object in that manner, he should be asked, whether he would think it to the purpose to object against persons of like capacities, that they are prudent without evidence, when, as is often the case, they are observed to manage their worldly affairs with discretion.

§ 17. *Here all serious men of all denominations should combine.*

The design before us being therefore in general unexceptionably good, it were much to be wished, that serious men of all denominations would join in it [1]. And let me add, that the foregoing view of things affords distinct reasons why they should. For, first, by so doing, they assist in a work of the most useful importance, that of spreading over the world the scripture itself, as a divine revelation: and it cannot be spread under this character, for a continuance, in any country, unless Christian churches be supported there; but will always more or less, so long as

---

[e] Titus ii. 12.   [f] John vii. 17.

---

[1] Viewing the circumstances of the time and of the Sermon, the meaning here seems to be an appeal to what were then the minor associations of Christians in this country to fall in, and aid the work of the church; rather than the utterance of an abstract opinion that the members of each denomination should at all times assist all the work of every other.

such churches subsist: and therefore their subsistence ought to be provided for. In the next place, they should remember, that if Christianity is to be propagated at all, which they acknowledge it should, it must be in some particular form of profession. And though they think ours liable to objections, yet it is possible they themselves may be mistaken: and whether they are or no, the very nature of society requires some compliance with others. And whilst, together with our particular form of Christianity, the confessed standard of Christian religion, the scripture, is spread; and especially whilst every one is freely allowed to study it, and worship God according to his conscience; the evident tendency is, that genuine Christianity will be understood and prevail. Upon the whole therefore, these persons would do well to consider, how far they can with reason satisfy themselves in neglecting what is certainly right, on account of what is doubtful, whether it be wrong; and when the right is of so much greater consequence one way, than the supposed wrong can be the other.

§ 18. *Irreligion is the chief present danger; superstition one of the roads to it.*

To conclude: Atheistical immorality and profaneness, surely, is not better in itself, nor less contrary to the design of revelation, than superstition. Nor is superstition the distinguishing vice of the present age, either at home or abroad. But if our colonies abroad are left without a public religion, and the means of instruction, what can be expected, but that, from living in a continued forgetfulness of God, they will at length cease to believe in him; and so sink into stupid atheism? And there is too apparent danger of the like horrible depravity at home, without the like excuse for it. Indeed amongst creatures naturally formed for religion, yet so much under the powers of imagination, so apt to deceive themselves, and so liable to be deceived by others, as men are; superstition is an evil, which can never be out of sight. But even against this, true religion is a great security; and the only one. True religion takes up that place in the mind, which superstition would usurp, and so leaves little room 'for it; and likewise lays us under the strongest obligations to oppose it. On the contrary, the danger of superstition cannot but be increased by the prevalence of irreligion: and by its general prevalence, the evil will be unavoidable. For the common people, wanting a religion, will of course take up with almost any superstition, which is thrown in their way: and, in process of time, amidst the infinite vicissitudes of the political world, the leaders of parties will certainly be able to serve themselves of that superstition, whatever it be, which is getting ground; and will not fail to carry it on to the utmost length their occasions require. The general nature of the thing shows this; and history and fact confirm it. But what brings the observation home to ourselves is, that the great superstition of which this nation, in particular, has reason to be afraid, is imminent; and the ways in which we may, very supposably, be overwhelmed by it, obvious. It is therefore wonderful, those people who seem to think there is but one evil in life, that of superstition, should not see, that atheism and profaneness must be the introduction of it. So that in every view of things, and upon all accounts, irreligion is at present our chief danger.

§ 19. *Association is indispensable for the present work. It requires secondary compliances.*

Now the several religious associations among us, in which many good men have of late united, appear to be providentially adapted to this present state of the world. And as all good men are equally concerned in promoting the end of them; to do it more effectually, they ought to unite in promoting it: which yet is scarce practicable upon any new models, and quite impossible upon such as every one would think unexceptionable. They ought therefore to come into those already formed to their hands; and even take advantage of any occasion of union, to add mutual force to each other's endeavours in furthering their common end; however they may differ as to the best means, or any thing else subordinate to it. Indeed there are well-disposed persons, who much want to be admonished, how dangerous a thing it is, to discountenance what is good, because it is not better; and hinder what they approve, by raising prejudices against some under-part of it. Nor can they assist in rectifying what they think capable of amendment, in the manner of carrying on these designs, unless they will join in the designs themselves; which they must acknowledge to be good and necessary ones. For what can be called good and necessary by Christians, if it be not so, to support Christianity where it must otherwise sink, and propagate it where it must otherwise be unknown; to restrain abandoned barefaced vice, by making useful examples, at least of shame, perhaps of repentance; and to take care of the education of such children, as otherwise must be even educated in wickedness, and trained up to destruction? Yet good men separately can do nothing, proportionable to what is wanting, in any of these ways: but their common, united endeavours may do a great deal in all of them.

§ 20. *Reflex action for good on this country.*

And besides the particular purposes, which these several religious associations serve, the more general ones, which they all serve, ought not to be passed over. Every thing of this kind is, in some degree, a safeguard to religion; an obstacle, more or less, in the way of those who want to have it extirpated out of the world. Such societies also contribute more especially towards keeping up the face of Christianity among ourselves; and by their obtaining here, the gospel is rendered more and more a *witness* to us.

§ 21. *How little is done: how much might be.*

And if it were duly attended to, and had its genuine influence upon our minds, there would be no need of persuasions to impart the blessing: nor would the means of doing it be wanting. Indeed the present income of this Society, which depends upon voluntary contributions, with the most frugal management of it, can in no wise sufficiently answer the bare purposes of our charter: but the nation, or even this opulent city itself, has it in its power to do so very much more, that I fear the mention of it may be thought too severe a reproof, since so little is done. But if the gospel had its proper influence upon the Christian world in general, as it is the centre of trade and seat of learning, a very few ages, in all probability, would settle Christianity in every country, without miraculous assistances. For scarce any thing else, I am persuaded, would be wanting to effect this, but laying it before men in its divine simplicity, together with an exemplification of it in the lives of Christian nations. *The unlearned and unbelievers, falling down on their faces, would worship God, and report that God is in us of a truth* [g].

---

[g] 1 Cor. xiv. 24, 25.

SERMON II

PREACHED BEFORE THE RIGHT HON. THE LORD MAYOR, THE COURT OF ALDERMEN, THE SHERIFFS, AND THE GOVERNORS OF THE SEVERAL HOSPITALS OF THE CITY OF LONDON, AT THE PARISH CHURCH OF ST. BRIDGET, ON MONDAY IN EASTER-WEEK, 1740.

The rich and poor meet together: the Lord is the maker of them all.—PROVERBS xxii. 2.

---

§ 1. *Rise of riches;* (a) *in necessaries*[1];

THE constitution of things being such, that the labour of one man, or the united labour of several[2], is sufficient to procure more *necessaries* than he or they stand in need of, which it may be supposed was, in some degree, the case, even in the first ages; this immediately gave room for riches to arise in the world, and for men's acquiring them by honest means; by diligence, frugality, and prudent management. Thus some would very soon acquire greater plenty of *necessaries* than they had occasion for; and others by contrary means, or by cross accidents, would be in want

---

[1] *Origin of riches;* the power of man to produce by labour (on the soil) a surplus over and above the supply of his wants for necessaries.
This surplus would be applied to—
1. Storage.
2. Supply of deficits by failing crops, conflagration, or otherwise.
3. Exchange: e.g. as between hill and valley.

[2] If, as seems probable, the original inequality of mental or moral gifts gave opportunity to the best endowed for grouping others round them, we have here signified the formation of a dependent class, again more clearly indicated in § 2.

of them. And he who should supply their wants would have the property in a proportionable labour of their hands; which he would scarce fail to make use of, instead of his own, or perhaps together with them, to provide future *necessaries* in greater plenty. Riches then were first bestowed upon the world, as they are still continued in it, by the blessing of God upon the industry of men, in the use of their understanding and strength. Riches themselves have always this source; though the possession of them is conveyed to particular persons by different channels. Yet still, *the hand of the diligent maketh rich* [a], and, other circumstances being equal, in proportion to its diligence.

§ 2. (b) *In conveniences* [1];

But to return to the first rich man; whom we left in possession of dependents [2], and plenty of *necessaries* for himself and them. A family would not be long in this state, before *conveniences*, somewhat *ornamental*, and for *entertainment*, would be wanted, looked for, and found out. And, by degrees, these secondary wants, and inventions for the supply of them, the fruits of leisure and ease, came to employ much of men's time and labour. Hence *a new species of riches* came into the world, consisting of things which it might have done well enough without, yet thought desirable, as affording pleasure to the imagination or the senses.

§ 3. *Which soon outran the other: hence* (c) *luxury, or immoderate use* [3].

And these went on increasing, till, at length, the *superfluities* of life took in a vastly larger compass of things than

---

[a] Prov. x. 4.

---

[1] Desire gradually arises for (1) convenience, (2) beauty, (3) social entertainment.

[2] Signified, I presume, in 'the united labour of several,' *sup.* 1.

[3] At length the item of superfluities preponderates. Birth of luxury. The argument for its restraint seems to have presented itself strongly to Butler.

Is it quite clear how, according to Butler, luxury produces

the *necessaries* of it. Thus luxury made its inroad, and all the numerous train of evils its attendants; of which poverty, as bad an one as we may account it, is far from being the worst. Indeed the hands of the generality must be employed: and a very few of them would now be sufficient to provide the world with necessaries: and therefore the rest of them must be employed about what may be called superfluities; which could not be, if these superfluities were not made use of. Yet the desire of such things, insensibly, becomes immoderate, and the use of them, almost of course, degenerates into luxury; which, in every age, has been the dissipation of riches, and, in every sense, the ruin of those who were possessed of them: and therefore cannot be too much guarded against by all opulent cities. And as men sink into luxury, as much from fashion, as direct inclination, the richer sort together may easily restrain this vice, in almost what degree they please: and a few of the chief of them may contribute a great deal towards the restraining it.

§ 4. *Next, money gave increase to* (a) *wealth,* (b) '*the love of riches, the root of all evil.*'

It is to be observed further concerning the progress of riches, that had they continued to consist only in the possession of *the things themselves,* which were necessary, and of *the things themselves,* which were, upon their own account, otherwise desirable; this, in several respects, must have greatly embarrassed trade and commerce; and have set bounds to the increase of riches in all hands, as well as have confined them in the hands of a few. But, in process of time, it was agreed to substitute somewhat more lasting and portable, which should pass every where, in commerce, for real natural riches; as sounds had before, in language, been substituted for thoughts. And this general agreement,

---

poverty? Clearly it produces a sense of poverty, from comparative inferiority of supply. He may mean that luxury, increasing the aggregate of human wants, and making no addition to the means of supplying them, reduces that surplus on which all wealth depends.

(by what means soever it became general,) that *money* should answer all things, together with some other improvements, gave full scope for riches to increase[1] in the hands of particular persons, and likewise to circulate into more hands. Now this, though it was not the first origin of covetousness, yet it gives greater scope, encouragement, and temptation to covetousness than it had before. And there is moreover the appearance, that this artificial kind of riches, money, has begot an artificial kind of passion for them: both which follies well-disposed persons must, by all means, endeavour to keep clear of. For indeed the love of riches is the root of all evil[b]: though riches themselves may be made instrumental in promoting every thing that is good.

§ 5. *Trade has much increased the middle rank: its great merits: and responsibilities.*

The improvement of trade and commerce has made another change, just hinted at, and I think a very happy one, in the state of the world, as it has enlarged the middle rank of people: many of which are, in good measure, free from the vices of the highest and the lowest part of mankind. Now these persons must remember, that whether, in common language, they do or do not pass under the denomination of rich, yet they really are so, with regard to the indigent and necessitous: and that considering the great numbers which make up this middle rank among us, and how much they mix with the poor, they are able to contribute very largely to their relief, and have in all respects a very great influence over them.

§ 6. '*Good sort of people,*' *who need admonition.*

You have heard now the origin and progress of what this great city so much abounds with, riches; as far as I had

---

[b] 1 Tim. vi. 10.

---

[1] Money increases wealth by cheapening the exchange of commodities.

occasion to speak of these things. For this brief account of them has been laid before you for the sake of the good admonitions it afforded. Nor will the admonitions be thought foreign to the charities, which we are endeavouring to promote. For these must necessarily be less, and the occasions for them greater, in proportion as industry should abate, or luxury increase. And the temper of covetousness is, we all know, directly contrary to that of charity, and eats out the very heart of it. Then, lastly, there are good sort of people who really want to be told, that they are included in the admonitions to be given to the rich, though they do see others richer than themselves.

§ 7. *Rich and poor in a standing relation of superiority and dependence.*

The ranks of rich and poor being thus formed, they *meet together;* they continue to make up one society. The mutual want, which they still have of each other, still unites them inseparably. But they *meet* upon a foot of great inequality. For, as Solomon expresses it in brief, and with much force, *the rich ruleth over the poor* [c]. And this their general intercourse, with the superiority on one hand, and dependence on the other, are in no sort accidental, but arise necessarily from a settled providential disposition of things, for their common good. Here then is a real, standing relation between the rich and the poor. And the former must take care to perform the duties belonging to their part of it, for these chiefly the present occasion leads me to speak to, from regard to Him, who placed them in that relation to the poor, from whence those duties arise, and who *is the Maker of them all.*

What these duties are, will easily be seen, and the obligations to them strongly enforced, by a little further reflection upon both these ranks, and the natural situation which they are in with respect to each other.

---

[c] Prov. xxii. 7.

§ 8. *Which gives the rich great means of influence.*

The lower rank of mankind go on, for the most part, in some tract of living, into which they got by direction or example; and to this their understanding and discourse, as well as labour, are greatly confined. Their opinions of persons and things they take upon trust. Their behaviour has very little in it original or of home-growth; very little which may not be traced up to the influence of others, and less which is not capable of being changed by such influence. Then as God has made plentiful provision for all his creatures, the wants of all, even of the poorest, might be supplied, so far as it is fit they should, by a proper distribution of it. This being the condition of the lower part of mankind, consider now what influence, as well as power, their superiors must, from the nature of the case, have over them. For they can instil instruction, and recommend it in a peculiar manner by their example, and enforce it still further with favour and discouragement of various kinds. And experience shows, that they do direct and change the course of the world as they please. Not only the civil welfare, but the morals and religion of their fellow-creatures, greatly depend upon them; much more indeed than they would, if the common people were not greatly wanting to their duty. All this is evidently true of superiors in general; superiors in riches, authority, and understanding, taken together. And need I say how much of this whole superiority goes along with riches? It is no small part of it, which arises out of riches themselves. In all governments, particularly in our own, a good share of civil authority accompanies them. Superior natural understanding may, or may not: but when it does not, yet riches afford great opportunities for improvement, and may command information; which things together are equivalent to natural superiority of understanding.

§ 9. *A great trust hereby imposed.*

But I am sure you will not think I have been reminding you of these advantages of riches in order to beget in you that complacency and trust in them, which you find the scripture every where warning you against. No: the importance of riches, this their power and influence, affords the most serious admonition in the world to those who are possessed of them. For it shows, how very blamable even their carelessness in the use of that power and influence must be: since it must be blamable in a degree proportionate to the importance of what they are thus careless about.

§ 10. *This power needed to save the poor from distress and depravity.*

But it is not only true, that the rich have the power of doing a great deal of good, and must be highly blamable for neglecting to do it: but it is moreover true, that this power is given them by way of trust, in order to their keeping down that vice and misery, with which the lower people would otherwise be quite overrun. For without instruction and good influence they, of course, grow rude and vicious, and reduce themselves to the utmost distresses; often to very terrible ones without deserving much blame. And to these must be added their unavoidable distresses, which yet admit of relief. This their case plainly requires, that some natural provision should be made for it: as the case of children does, who, if left to their own ways, would almost infallibly ruin themselves. Accordingly Providence has made provision for this case of the poor: not only by forming their minds peculiarly apt to be influenced by their superiors, and giving those superiors abilities to direct and relieve them; but also by putting the latter under the care and protection of the former: for this is plainly done, by means of that intercourse of various kinds between them, which, in the natural course of things, is unavoidably necessary.

§ 11. *The primitive domestic organisation gave facility for these duties.*

In the primitive ages of the world, the manner in which *the rich and the poor met together*, was in families. Rich men had the poor for their servants: not only a few for the offices about their persons, and for the care of what we now call domestic affairs; but great numbers also for the keeping of their cattle, the tillage of their fields, for working up their wool into furniture and vestments of necessary use as well as ornament, and for preparing them those many things at home, which now pass through a multitude of unknown poor hands successively, and are by them prepared, at a distance, for the use of the rich. The instruction of these large families, and the oversight of their morals and religion, plainly belonged to the heads of them. And that obvious humanity, which every one feels, must have induced them to be kind to all whom they found under their roof, in sickness and old age. In this state of the world, the relation between the rich and the poor could not but be universally seen and acknowledged. Now indeed it is less in sight, by means of artificial methods of carrying on business, which yet are not blamable.

§ 12. *But the relation and the trust are permanent.*

But the relation still subsists, and the obligations arising out of it; and cannot but remain the same, whilst the rich have the same want of the poor, and make the same use of them, though not so immediately under their eye; and whilst the instruction, and manners, and good or bad state of the poor, really depend in so great a degree upon the rich, as all these things evidently do; partly in their capacity of magistrates, but very much also in their private capacity. In short, he who has distributed men into these different ranks, and at the same time united them into one society, in such sort as men are united, has, by this constitution of things, formally put the poor under the superintendency and patronage of the rich. The rich then are charged, by natural providence, as much as by revealed appointment, with the care of the poor: not to maintain them idle; which, were it possible they could be so maintained, would produce greater mischiefs than those which charity is to prevent; but to take care, that they maintain themselves by their labour, or in case they cannot, then to relieve them; to restrain their vices, and form their minds to virtue and religion. This is a trust, yet it is not a burden, but a privilege, annexed to riches. And if every one discharged his share of the trust faithfully, whatever be his share of it, the world would be quite another place from what it is. But that cannot be, till covetousness, debauchery, and every vice be unknown among the rich. Then, and not before, will the manners of the poor be, in all respects, what they ought to be, and their distresses find the full relief, which they ought to find. And, as far as things of this sort can be calculated, in proportion to the right behaviour of persons whom God has placed in the former of these ranks, will be the right behaviour and good condition of those who are cast into the latter.

§ 13. *The work is to be shared out among us.*

Every one of ability then is to be persuaded to do somewhat towards this, keeping up a sense of virtue and religion among the poor, and relieving their wants; each as much as he can be persuaded to. Since the generality will not part with their vices, it were greatly to be wished, they would bethink themselves, and do what good they are able, so far only as is consistent with them. A vicious rich man cannot pass through life without doing an incredible deal of mischief, were it only by his example and influence; besides neglecting the most important obligations, which arise from his superior fortune. Yet still, the fewer of them he neglects, and the less mischief he does, the less share of the vices and miseries of his inferiors will lie at his door: the less will be his guilt and punishment. But conscientious persons of this rank must revolve again and again in their minds, how great the trust is, which God has annexed to it. They must each of them consider impartially, what is his own particular share of that trust; which is determined by his situation, character, and fortune together: and then set himself to be as useful as he can in those particular ways, which he finds thus marked out for him. This is exactly the precept of St. Peter; *As every man hath received the gift, even so minister the same one to another, as good stewards of the manifold grace of God* [d]. And as rich men, by a right direction of their greater capacity, may entitle themselves to a greater reward; so by a wrong direction of it, or even by great negligence, they may become *partakers of other men's sins* [e], and chargeable with other men's miseries. For if there be at all any measures of proportion, any sort of regularity and order in the administration of things, it is self-evident, that *unto whomsoever much is given, of him shall much be required: and to whom much is committed, of him shall more be demanded* [f].

§ 14. *Each one to give his own account, for following ill example; much more for setting it.*

But still it is to be remembered, that every man's behaviour is his own concern, for every one must give account of his own works; and that the lower people are very greatly to blame in yielding to any ill influence, particularly following the ill example of their superiors; though these are more to blame in setting them such an example. For, as our Lord declares, in the words immediately preceding those just mentioned, *that servant which knew his Lord's will, and prepared not himself, neither did according to his will, shall be beaten with many stripes. But he that knew not, and did commit things worthy of stripes, shall be beaten with few stripes* [g]. Vice is itself of ill-desert, and therefore shall be punished in all; though its ill-desert is greater or less, and so shall be its punishment, in proportion to men's knowledge of God and religion: but it is in the most literal sense true, that *he who knew not his Lord's will, and committed things worthy of stripes, shall be beaten, though with few stripes.* For it being the discernment, that such and such actions are evil, which renders them vicious in him who does them, ignorance of other things, though it may lessen, yet it cannot remit the punishment of such actions in a just administration, because it cannot destroy the guilt of them: much less can corrupt deference and regard to the example of superiors

---

[d] 1 Pet. iv. 10.
[e] 1 Tim. v. 22.
[f] Luke xii. 48.
[g] Ibid. 47, 48.

in matters of plain duty and sin have this effect. Indeed the lowest people know very well, that such ill example affords no reason why they should do ill; but they hope it will be an excuse for them, and thus deceive themselves to their ruin: which is a forcible reason why their superiors should not lay this snare in their way.

All this approves itself to our natural understanding; though it is by means of Christianity chiefly, that it is thus enforced upon our consciences. And Christianity, as it is more than a dispensation of goodness, in the general notion of goodness, even a dispensation of forgiveness, of mercy and favour on God's part, does in a peculiar manner heighten our obligations to charity among ourselves. *In this was manifested the love of God towards us,*—that *he sent his Son to be the propitiation for our sins. Beloved, if God so loved us, we ought also to love one another*[h]. With what unanswerable force is that question of our Lord to be applied to every branch of this duty, *Shouldest not thou also have had compassion on thy fellowservant, even as I had pity on thee*[i]? And can there be a stronger inducement to endeavour the reformation of the world, and bringing it to a sense of virtue and religion, than the assurance given us, *that he which converteth a sinner from the error of his way,* and, in like manner, he also who preventeth a person's being corrupted, by taking care of his education, *shall save a soul from death, and hide a multitude of sins*[k]?

These things lead us to the following observations on the several charities, which are the occasion of these annual solemnities.

§ 15. *The trust requires choice of the best means; which these Societies offer.*

1. What we have to bestow in charity being a trust, we cannot discharge it faithfully, without taking some care to satisfy ourselves in some degree, that we bestow it upon the proper objects of charity. One hears persons complaining, that it is difficult to distinguish who are such; yet often

---

[h] 1 John iv. 9, 10, 11.   [i] Matt. xviii. 33.   [k] James v. 20.

seeming to forget, that this is a reason for using their best endeavours to do it. And others make a custom of giving to idle vagabonds: a kind of charity, very improperly so called, which one really wonders people can allow themselves in; merely to be relieved from importunity, or at best to gratify a false good-nature. For they cannot but know, that it is, at least, very doubtful, whether what they thus give will not immediately be spent in riot and debauchery. Or suppose it be not, yet still they know, they do a great deal of certain mischief, by encouraging this shameful trade of begging in the streets, and all the disorders which accompany it. But the charities towards which I now ask your assistance, as they are always open, so every one may contribute to them with full assurance, that he bestows upon proper objects, and in general that he does vastly more good, than by equal sums given separately to particular persons. For that these charities really have these advantages, has been fully made out, by some who have gone before me in the duty I am discharging, and by the reports annually published at this time.

[*Here the Report was read.*]

Let us thank God for these charities, in behalf of the poor; and also on our own behalf, as they give us such clear opportunities of doing good. Indeed without them, vice and misery, of which there is still so much, would abound so much more in this populous city, as to render it scarce an habitable place.

§ 16. *Their power as memorials, and as influences.*

2. Amongst the peculiar advantages of public charities above private ones, is also to be mentioned, that they are examples of great influence. They serve for perpetual memorials of what I have been observing, of the relation which subsists between the rich and the poor, and the duties which arise out of it. They are standing admonitions to all within sight or hearing of them, to *go and do likewise*[1].

---
[1] Luke x. 37.

Educating poor children in virtue and religion, relieving the sick, and correcting offenders in order to their amendment, are, in themselves, some of the very best of good works. These charities would indeed be the glory of your city, though their influence were confined to it. But important as they are in themselves, their importance still increases, by their being examples to the rest of the nation; which, in process of time, of course copies after the metropolis. It has indeed already imitated every one of these charities; for of late, the most difficult and expensive of them, hospitals for the sick and wounded, have been established; some within your sight, others in remote parts of the kingdom. You will give me leave to mention particularly that [m] in its second trading city; which is conducted with such disinterested fidelity and prudence, as I dare venture to compare with yours. Again, there are particular persons very blamably unactive and careless, yet not without good dispositions, who, by these charities, are reminded of their duty, and *provoked to love and to good works* [n]. And let me add, though one is sorry any should want so slight a reason for contributing to the most excellent designs, yet if any are supposed to do so merely of course, because they see others do it, still they help to support these monuments of charity, which are a continued admonition to the rich, and relief to the poor: and herein all good men *rejoice,*

---

[m] NOTE. As it is of very particular benefit to those, who ought always to be looked upon with particular favour by us, I mean our seamen; so likewise it is of very extensive benefit to the large tracts of country west and north of it. Then the medicinal waters near the city render it a still more proper situation for an infirmary. And so likewise does its neighbourhood to the Bath Hospital. For it may well be supposed, that some poor objects will be sent thither in hopes of relief from the Bath waters, whose case may afterwards be found to require the assistance of physic or surgery: and on the other hand, that some may be sent to our infirmary for help from those arts, whose case may be found to require the Bath waters. So that if I am not greatly partial, the Bristol Infirmary as much deserves encouragement as any charitable foundation in the kingdom. *Case of the Bristol Infirmary.*

[n] Heb. x. 24.

as St. Paul speaks of himself in a like case, *yea, and will rejoice* [o].

§ 17. *Suggestions for raising them to the highest possible perfection: labour, low diet, instruction;*

3. As all human schemes admit of improvement, all public charities, methinks, should be considered as standing open to proposals for it; that the whole plan of them, in all its parts, may be brought to as great perfection as is possible. Now it should seem, that employing some share of the children's time in easy labour, suitable to their age, which is done in some of our charity-schools, might be done in most others of them, with very good effect; as it is in all those of a neighbouring kingdom. Then as the only purposes of punishments less than capital are to reform the offenders themselves, and warn the innocent by their example, every thing which should contribute to make this kind of punishments answer those purposes better than it does, would be a greater improvement. And whether it be not a thing practicable, and what would contribute somewhat towards it, to exclude utterly all sorts of revel-mirth from places where offenders are confined, to separate the young from the old, and force them both, in solitude, with labour and low diet, to make the experiment, how far their natural strength of mind can support them under guilt and shame and poverty; this may deserve consideration. Then again, some religious instruction particularly adapted to their condition would as properly accompany those punishments which are intended to reform, as it does capital ones. God forbid that I should be understood to discourage the provision which is made for it in this latter case: I heartily wish it were better than it is; especially since it may well be supposed, as the state of religion is at present among us, that some condemned malefactors may have never had the doctrine of the gospel enforced upon their consciences. But since it must be acknowledged of greater consequence, in

---

[o] Phil. i. 18.

a religious as well as civil respect, how persons live, than how they die; it cannot but be even more incumbent on us to endeavour, in all ways, to reclaim those offenders who are to return again into the world, than those who are to be removed out of it: and the only effectual means of reclaiming them, is to instil into them a principle of religion. If persons of authority and influence would take things of this and a like kind under their consideration, they might perhaps still improve those charities; which are already, I truly believe, under a better management than any other of so large a compass in the world. But,

§ 18. *Especially as we come nearer to recognising an equality among men.*

4. With regard to the two particular branches of them last mentioned, I would observe, that our laws and whole constitution, civil and ecclesiastical, go more upon supposition of an equality amongst mankind, than the constitution and laws of other countries[1]. Now this plainly requires that more particular regard should be had to the education of the lower people here, than in places, where they are born slaves of power, and to be made slaves of superstition. It is, I suppose, acknowledged, that they have greater liberty here, than they have any where else in the world. But unless care be taken for giving them some inward principle, to prevent their abusing this greater liberty which is their birthright, can we expect it will prove a blessing to them? or will they not in all probability become more dissolute, or more wild and extravagant, whatever wrong turn they happen to take, than people of the same rank in other countries?

---

[1] This sentence suggests a curious contrast to the relation of rich and poor as previously depicted in §§ 10-12. Butler evidently saw a current setting in which would alter the relation of rich and poor: and which has brought us to the point at which that relation has been profoundly modified by the transfer of political power on a very extended scale.

§ 19. *Additional motive for good behaviour in its effect upon inferiors.*

5. Let me again remind you of the additional reason, which persons of fortune have to take particular care of their whole behaviour, that it be in all respects good and exemplary, upon account of the influence which it will have upon the manners of their inferiors. And pray observe how strictly this is connected with the occasion of our present meeting: how much your good behaviour in private life will contribute to promote the good design of all these charities; and how much the contrary would tend to defeat it, and even to produce the evils which they are intended to prevent or to remedy. Whatever care be taken in the education of these poor children at school, there is always danger of their being corrupted, when they come from it. And this danger is greater, in proportion to the greater wickedness of the age they are to pass through. But if, upon their coming abroad into the world, they find the principles of virtue and religion recommended by the example of their superiors, and vice and irreligion really discountenanced, this will confirm them in the good principles in which they have been brought up, and give the best ground to hope they will never depart from them. And the like is to be said of offenders, who may have had a sense of virtue and religion wrought in them, under the discipline of labour and confinement. Again; dissolute and debauched persons of fortune greatly increase the general corruption of manners; and this is what increases want and misery of all kinds.

§ 20. *Even liberal gifts may undo but in part the effect of bad example.*

So that they may contribute largely to any or all of these charities, and yet undo but a very small part of the mischief which they do, by their example, as well as in other ways. But still the mischief which they do, suppose by their example, is an additional reason why they should contribute to them; even in justice to particular persons, in whose ruin they may have an unknown share of guilt; or however in justice to society in general; for which they will deserve commendation, how blamable soever they are for the other. And indeed amidst the dark prospect before us, from that profligateness of manners, and scorn of religion, which so generally abound, this good spirit of charity to the poor discovering itself in so great a degree, upon these occasions, and likewise in the late necessitous time, even amongst persons far from being blameless in other respects; this cannot but afford hopes, that we are not given over by Providence, and also that they themselves will at length consider, and not go on contributing, by the example of their vices, to the introduction of that distress, which they so commendably relieve by their liberality.

§ 21. *By giving as the creatures of God, our charity will become piety.*

To conclude: Let our charity towards men be exalted into piety towards God, from the serious consideration, that we are all his creatures; a consideration which enforces that duty upon our consciences, as we have any regard to him. This kind of adjuration, and a most solemn one it is, one often hears profaned by a very unworthy sort of people, when they ask relief *for God's sake*. But surely the principle itself, which contains in it every thing great, and just, and good, is grievously forgotten among us. To relieve the poor *for God's sake*, is to do it in conformity to the order of nature, and to his will, and his example, who is the Author and Governor of it; and in thankful remembrance, that all we have is from his bounty. It is to do it in his behalf, and as to him. For *he that hath pity upon the poor lendeth unto the Lord* [p]: and our Saviour has declared, that he will take as given to himself, what is given in a well-chosen charity [q]. Lastly, it is to do it under a sense of the account which will be required of what is committed to our trust, when *the rich and poor, who meet* here upon terms of so great inequality, shall *meet* hereafter upon a level, before him who *is the Maker of them all*.

---

[p] Prov. xix. 17.   [q] Matt. xxv. 40.

SERMON III

PREACHED BEFORE THE HOUSE OF LORDS, IN THE ABBEY-CHURCH OF WESTMINSTER, ON FRIDAY, JANUARY 30, 1740-41. BEING THE DAY APPOINTED TO BE OBSERVED AS THE DAY OF THE MARTYRDOM OF KING CHARLES I.

And not using your liberty for a cloke of maliciousness, but as the servants of God.—1 PETER ii. 16.

---

§ 1. *Range of hypocrisy: larger than we suspect.*

AN history so full of important and interesting events as that which this day recalls annually to our thoughts, cannot but afford them very different subjects for their most serious and useful employment. But there seems none which it more naturally leads us to consider than that of hypocrisy, as it sets before us so many examples of it; or which will yield us more practical instruction, as these examples so forcibly admonish us, not only to be upon our guard against the pernicious effects of this vice in others, but also to watch over our own hearts, against every thing of the like kind in ourselves: for hypocrisy, in the moral and religious consideration of things, is of much larger extent than every one may imagine.

§ 2. *Widespread as a species of self-delusion.*

In common language, which is formed upon the common intercourses amongst men, hypocrisy signifies little more than their pretending what they really do not mean, in order to delude one another. But in scripture, which treats chiefly of our behaviour towards God and our own consciences, it signifies not only the endeavour to delude our fellow-creatures, but likewise insincerity towards him, and towards ourselves. And therefore, according to the whole analogy of scripture language, *to use liberty as a cloke of maliciousness*[a], must be understood to mean, not only

---

[a] NOTE. The hypocrisy laid to the charge of the Pharisees and Sadducees, in Matt. xvi. at the beginning, and in Luke xii. 54, is determinately this, that their vicious passions blinded them so as to prevent their discerning the evidence of our Saviour's mission; though no more

1. *Pharisees and Sadducees were hypocrites chiefly towards God and themselves.*

understanding was necessary to discern it, than what they had, and made use of in common matters. Here they are called hypocrites merely upon account of their insincerity towards God and their own consciences, and not at all upon account of any insincerity towards men. This last indeed is included in that general hypocrisy, which, throughout the gospels, is represented as their distinguished character; but the former is as much included. For they were not men, who, without any belief at all of religion, put on the appearance of it only in order to deceive the world: on the contrary, they believed their religion, and were zealous in it. But their religion, which they believed, and were zealous in, was in its nature hypocritical: for it was the form, not the reality; it allowed them in immoral practices; and indeed was itself in some respects immoral, as they indulged their pride and uncharitableness under the notion of zeal for it. See Jer. ix. 6. Psalm lxxviii. 36. Job iii. 19. and Matt. xv. 7-14, and xxiii. 13, 16, 19, 24, 26, where *hypocrite* and *blind* are used promiscuously. Again, the scripture speaks of the *deceitfulness of sin*, and its deceiving those who are guilty of it: Heb. iii. 13. Eph. iv. 22. Rom. vii. 11; of men's acting as if they could *deceive and mock God*: Isa. xxix. 15. Acts v. 3. Gal. vi. 7; of their *blinding their own eyes*: Matt. xiii. 15. Acts xxviii. 27; and *deceiving themselves*, which is quite a different thing from being deceived: 1 Cor. iii. 18. 1 John i. 8. Gal. vi. 3. James i. 22, 26. Many more coincident passages might be mentioned: but I will add only one. In 2 Thess. ii. it is foretold, that by means of some *force*, some *energy of delusion*, men should believe *the lie* which is there treated of: this *force of delusion* is not any thing without them, but somewhat within them, which it is expressly said they should bring upon themselves, by *not receiving the love of the truth, but having pleasure in unrighteousness*. Answering to all this is that very remarkable passage of our Lord, Matt. vi. 22, 23. Luke xi. 34, 35, and that admonition repeated fourteen times in the New Testament, *He that*

endeavouring to impose upon others, by indulging wayward passions, or carrying on indirect designs, under pretences of it; but also excusing and palliating such things to ourselves; serving ourselves of such pretences to quiet our own minds in any thing which is wrong.

§ 3. *Of Liberty* (a) *as escape from the Mosaic law,* (b) *as progress to perfect love,* (c) *as allowed by law and by rules of moral conduct.*

Liberty in the writings of the New Testament, for the most part, signifies, being delivered from the bondage of the ceremonial law; or of sin and the devil, which St. Paul calls *the glorious liberty of the children of God* [b]. This last is a progressive state: and the perfection of it, whether attainable in this world or not, consists in that *perfect love* [c], which St. John speaks of; and which, as it implies an entire coincidence of our wills with the will of God, must be a state of the most absolute freedom, in the most literal and proper sense. But whatever St. Peter distinctly meant by this word, *liberty*, the text gives occasion to consider any kind of it, which is liable to the abuse he here warns us against. However, it appears that he meant to comprehend

---

hath ears to hear, let him hear. And the ground of this whole manner of considering things; for it is not to be spoken of as only a peculiar kind of phraseology, but is a most accurate and strictly just manner of considering characters and moral conduct; the ground of it, I say, is, that when persons will not be influenced by such evidence in religion as they act upon in the daily course of life, or when their notions of religion (and I might add of virtue) are in any sort reconcilable with what is vicious, it is some faulty negligence or prejudice which thus deludes them; in very different ways, perhaps, and very different degrees. But when any one is thus deluded through his own fault, in whatever way or degree it is, he deludes himself. And this is as properly hypocrisy towards himself, as deluding the world is hypocrisy towards the world: and he who is guilty of it acts as if he could deceive and mock God; and therefore is an hypocrite towards him, in as strict and literal a sense as the nature of the subject will admit.

2. *Unequal dealing with evidence leads into hypocrisy towards ourselves.*

[b] Rom. viii. 21.   [c] 1 John iv. 18.

that liberty, were it more or less, which they to whom he was writing enjoyed under civil government: for of civil government he is speaking just before and afterwards: *Submit yourselves to every ordinance of man for the Lord's sake: whether it be to the king, as supreme; or unto governors, as unto them that are sent by him. For so is the will of God, that with well doing,* of which dutiful behaviour towards authority is a very material instance, *ye may put to silence the ignorance of foolish men*[d]: *as free,* perhaps in distinction from the servile state, of which he speaks afterwards, *and not using your liberty for a cloke of maliciousness*[e], of any thing wrong, for so the word signifies; and therefore comprehends petulance, affectation of popularity, with any other like frivolous turn of mind, as well as the more hateful and dangerous passions, such as malice, or ambition; for all of which *liberty* may equally be *used as a cloak.* The apostle adds, *but as the servants of God: as free—but as his servants,* who requires dutiful submission to *every ordinance of man,* to magistracy; and to whom we are accountable for our manner of using the liberty we enjoy under it; as well as for all other parts of our behaviour. *Not using your liberty as a cloak of maliciousness, but as the servants of God.*

§ 4. *Tripartite division.*

Here are three things offered to our consideration:

First, A general supposition, that what is wrong cannot be avowed in its proper colours, but stands in need of some *cloak* to be thrown over it; secondly, A particular one, that there is danger, some singular danger, of liberty's being made use of for this purpose; lastly, An admonition not to make this ill use of our liberty, *but* to use it *as the servants of God.*

§ 5. (1) *Wrong requires a cloak,* (a) *from the world,* (b) *from ourselves.*

[I.] Here is a general supposition, that what is wrong cannot be avowed in its proper colours, but stands in need

---

[d] 1 Pet. ii. 13–15.   [e] Ibid. ii. 16.

of some *cloak* to be thrown over it. God has constituted our nature, and the nature of society, after such a manner, that, generally speaking, men cannot encourage or support themselves in wickedness upon the foot of there being no difference between right and wrong, or by a direct avowal of wrong; but by disguising it, and endeavouring to spread over it some colours of right. And they do this in every capacity and every respect, in which there is a right or a wrong. They do it, not only as social creatures under civil government, but also as moral agents under the government of God; in one case to make a proper figure in the world, and delude their fellow-creatures; in the other to keep peace within themselves, and delude their own consciences. And the delusion in both cases being voluntary, is, in scripture, called by one name, and spoken against in the same manner: though doubtless they are much more explicit with themselves, and more distinctly conscious of what they are about, in one case than in the other.

§ 6. *The moral element in society tempts men to profess.*

The fundamental laws of all governments are virtuous ones, prohibiting treachery, injustice, cruelty: and the law of reputation enforces those civil laws, by rendering these vices every where infamous, and the contrary virtues honourable and of good report. Thus far the constitution of society is visibly moral: and hence it is, that men cannot live in it without taking care to cover those vices when they have them, and make some profession of the opposite virtues, fidelity, justice, kind regard to others when they have them not: but especially is this necessary in order to disguise and colour over indirect purposes, which require the concurrence of several persons.

§ 7. *Often in sheer levity; often to deceive.*

Now all false pretences of this kind are to be called hypocritical, as being contrary to simplicity; though not always designed, properly speaking, to beget a false belief.

For it is to be observed, that they are often made without any formal intention to have them believed, or to have it thought that there is any reality under these pretences. Many examples occur of verbal professions of fidelity, justice, public regards, in cases where there could be no imagination of their being believed. And what other account can be given of these merely verbal professions, but that they were thought the proper language for the public ear; and made in business for the very same kind of reasons as civility is kept up in conversation?

These false professions of virtue, which men have, in all ages, found it necessary to make their appearance with abroad, must have been originally taken up in order to deceive in the proper sense: then they became habitual, and often intended merely by way of form: yet often still, to serve their original purpose of deceiving.

§ 8. *But self-deceit has a large share.*

There is doubtless amongst mankind a great deal of this hypocrisy towards each other: but not so much as may sometimes be supposed. For part which has, at first sight, this appearance, is in reality that other hypocrisy before mentioned; that self-deceit, of which the scripture so remarkably takes notice. There are indeed persons who live *without God in the world*[f]: and some appear so hardened as to keep no measures with themselves. But as very ill men may have a real and strong sense of virtue and religion, in proportion as this is the case with any, they cannot be easy within themselves but by deluding their consciences. And though they should, in great measure, get over their religion, yet this will not do. For as long as they carry about with them any such sense of things, as makes them condemn what is wrong in others, they could not but condemn the same in themselves, and dislike and be disgusted with their own character and conduct, if they would consider them distinctly, and in a full light. But this sometimes they carelessly neglect to do, and sometimes carefully avoid

---

[f] Eph. ii. 12.

doing. And as *the integrity of the upright guides him*[g], guides even a man's judgment; so wickedness may distort it to such a degree, as that he may *call evil good, and good evil; put darkness for light, and light for darkness*[h]; and *think wickedly, that God is such an one as himself*[i]. Even the better sort of men are, in some degree, liable to disguise and palliate their failings to themselves: but perhaps there are few men who go on calmly in a course of very bad things, without somewhat of the kind now described in a very high degree. They try appearances upon themselves as well as upon the world, and with at least as much success; and choose to manage so as to make their own minds easy with their faults, which can scarce be without management, rather than to mend them.

§ 9. *In whichever way, the cloak is almost universally used.*

But whether from men's deluding themselves, or from their intending to delude the world, it is evident scarce any thing wrong in public has ever been accomplished, or even attempted, but under false colours: either by pretending one thing, which was right, to be designed, when it was really another thing, which was wrong; or if that which was wrong was avowed, by endeavouring to give it some appearance of right. For tyranny, and faction so friendly to it, and which is indeed tyranny out of power, and unjust wars, and persecution, by which the earth has been laid waste; all this has all along been carried on with pretences of truth, right, general good. So it is, men cannot find in their heart to join in such things, without such honest words to be the bond of the union, though they know among themselves, that they are only words, and often though they know, that every body else knows it too.

§ 10. *Jan.* 30. *An unheard-of hypocrisy: against the voice of Parliament.*

These observations might be exemplified by numerous instances in the history which led to them: and without

---

[g] Prov. xi. 3.   [h] Isa. v. 20.   [i] Psalm l. 21.

them it is impossible to understand in any sort the general character of the chief actors in it, who were engaged in the black design of subverting the constitution of their country. This they completed with the most enormous act of mere power, in defiance of all laws of God and man, and in express contradiction to the real design and public votes of that assembly, whose commission, they professed, was their only warrant for any thing they did throughout the whole rebellion. Yet with unheard-of hypocrisy towards men, towards God and their own consciences, for without such a complication of it their conduct is inexplicable; even this action, which so little admitted of any cloak, was, we know, contrived and carried into execution, under pretences of authority, religion, liberty, and by profaning the forms of justice in an arraignment and trial, like to what is used in regular legal procedures. No age indeed can show an example of hypocrisy parallel to this. But the history of all ages and all countries will show, what has been really going forward over the face of the earth, to be very different from what has been always pretended; and that virtue has been every where professed much more than it has been any where practised: nor could society, from the very nature of its constitution, subsist without some general public profession of it. Thus the face and appearance which the world has in all times put on, for the ease and ornament of life, and in pursuit of further ends, is the justest satire upon what has in all times been carrying on under it: and ill men are destined, by the condition of their being as social creatures, always to bear about with them, and, in different degrees, to profess, that law of virtue, by which they shall finally be judged and condemned.

§ 11. (2) *Liberty is a very favourite cloak.*

[II.] As fair pretences, of one sort or other, have thus always been made use of by mankind to colour over indirect and wrong designs from the world, and to palliate and excuse them to their own minds; liberty, in common with all other good things, is liable to be made this use of, and is also liable to it in a way more peculiar to itself: which was the second thing to be considered.

In the history which this day refers us to, we find our constitution, in Church and State, destroyed under pretences, not only of religion, but of securing liberty, and carrying it to a greater height. The destruction of the former was with zeal of such a kind, as would not have been warrantable, though it had been employed in the destruction of heathenism. And the confusions, the persecuting spirit, and incredible fanaticism, which grew up upon its ruins, cannot but teach sober-minded men to reverence so mild and reasonable an establishment, now it is restored; for the preservation of Christianity and keeping up a sense of it amongst us, and for the instruction and guide of the ignorant; nay, were it only for guarding religion from such extravagancies: especially as these important purposes are served by it without bearing hard in the least upon any.

§ 12. *A resistance, originally just, became unreasoning.*

And the concurrent course of things, which brought on the ruin of our civil constitution, and what followed upon it, are no less instructive. The opposition, by legal and parliamentary methods, to prerogatives unknown to the constitution, was doubtless formed upon the justest fears in behalf of it. But new distrusts arose: new causes were given for them: these were most unreasonably aggravated. The better part gradually gave way to the more violent: and the better part themselves seem to have insisted upon impracticable securities against that one danger to liberty, of which they had too great cause to be apprehensive; and wonderfully overlooked all other dangers to it, which yet were, and ever will be, many and great. Thus they joined in the current measures, till they were utterly unable to stop the mischiefs, to which, with too much distrust on one side, and too little on the other, they had contributed. Never was a more remarkable example of the Wise Man's observation, that *the beginning of strife is as when one letteth* *out water*ᵏ. For this opposition, thus begun, surely without intent of proceeding to violence; yet, as it went on, like an overflowing stream in its progress, it collected all sort of impurities, and grew more outrageous as it grew more corrupted; till at length it bore down every thing good before it.

§ 13. *The danger to liberty, at the Restoration, was extreme.*

This naturally brought on arbitrary power in one shape, which was odious to every body, and which could not be accommodated to the forms of our constitution; and put us in the utmost danger of having it entailed upon us under another, which might. For at the king's return, such was the just indignation of the public at what it had seen, and fear of feeling again what it had felt, from the popular side; such the depression and compliance, not only of the more guilty, but also of those, who with better meaning had gone on with them; and a great deal too far many of this character had gone; and such the undistinguishing distrust the people had of them all, that the chief security of our liberties seems to have been, their not being attempted at that time.

§ 14. *To overthrow a free constitution is horrible,*

But though persons contributed to all this mischief and danger with different degrees of guilt, none could contribute to them with innocence, who at all knew what they were about. Indeed the destruction of a free constitution of government, though men see or fancy many defects in it, and whatever they design or pretend, ought not to be thought of without horror. For the design is in itself unjust, since it is romantic to suppose it legal: it cannot be prosecuted without the most wicked means; nor accomplished but with the present ruin of liberty, religious as well as civil; for it must be the ruin of its present security.

ᵏ Prov. xvii. 14.

Whereas the restoration of it must depend upon a thousand future contingencies, the integrity, understanding, power of the persons, into whose hands anarchy and confusion should throw things; and who they will be, the history before us may surely serve to show, no human foresight can determine; even though such a terrible crisis were to happen in an age, not distinguished for the want of principle and public spirit, and when nothing particular were to be apprehended from abroad.

§ 15. *Even though in pursuit of an ideal one.*

It would be partiality to say, that no constitution of government can possibly be imagined more perfect than our own. And ingenuous youth may be warmed with the idea of one, against which nothing can be objected. But it is the strongest objection against attempting to put in practice the most perfect theory, that it is impracticable, or too dangerous to be attempted. And whoever will thoroughly consider, in what degree mankind are really influenced by reason, and in what degree by custom, may, I think, be convinced, that the state of human affairs does not even admit of an equivalent for the mischief of setting things afloat; and the danger of parting with those securities of liberty, which arise from regulations of long prescription and ancient usage: especially at a time when the directors are so very numerous, and the obedient so few.

§ 16. *The true plan: reform abuse, supply deficiency.*

Reasonable men therefore will look upon the general plan of our constitution, transmitted down to us by our ancestors, as sacred; and content themselves with calmly doing what their station requires, towards rectifying the particular things which they think amiss, and supplying the particular things which they think deficient in it, so far as is practicable without endangering the whole.

§ 17. *Liberty is apt to degenerate through excess*[1].

But liberty is in many other dangers from itself, besides those which arise from formed designs of destroying it, under hypocritical pretences, or romantic schemes of restoring it upon a more perfect plan. It is particularly liable to become excessive, and to degenerate insensibly into licentiousness; in the same manner as liberality, for example, is apt to degenerate into extravagance. And as men cloak their extravagance to themselves under the notion of liberality, and to the world under the name of it, so licentiousness passes under the name and notion of liberty. Now it is to be observed, that there is, in some respects or other, a very peculiar contrariety between those vices which consist in excess, and the virtues of which they are said to be the excess, and the resemblance, and whose names they affect to bear; the excess of any thing being always to its hurt, and tending to its destruction.

§ 18. *Licentiousness is an infringement on liberty.*

In this manner licentiousness is, in its very nature, a present infringement upon liberty, and dangerous to it for the future. Yet it is treated by many persons with peculiar indulgence under this very notion, as being an excess of liberty. And an excess of liberty it is to the licentious themselves: but what is it to those who suffer by them, and who do not think, that amends is at all made them by having it left in their power to retaliate safely? When by popular insurrections, or defamatory libels, or in any like way, the needy and the turbulent securely injure quiet people in their fortune or good name, so far quiet people are no more free than if a single tyrant used them thus. A particular man may be licentious without being less free: but a community cannot; since the licentiousness of one will unavoidably break in upon the liberty of another. Civil liberty, the liberty of a community, is a severe and a restrained thing; implies in the notion of it, authority,

---

[1] See *inf.* Serm. v. 5.

settled subordinations, subjection, and obedience; and is altogether as much hurt by too little of this kind, as by too much of it. And the love of liberty, when it is indeed the love of liberty, which carries us to withstand tyranny, will as much carry us to reverence authority, and support it; for this most obvious reason, that one is as necessary to the very being of liberty, as the other is destructive of it.

§ 19. *Love of liberty should imply deference to authority.*

And therefore the love of liberty, which does not produce this effect; the love of liberty, which is not a real principle of dutiful behaviour towards authority; is as hypocritical, as the religion which is not productive of a good life. Licentiousness is, in truth, such an excess of liberty as is of the same nature with tyranny. For what is the difference between them, but that one is lawless power exercised under pretence of authority, or by persons invested with it; the other lawless power exercised under pretence of liberty, or without any pretence at all? A people then must always be less free in proportion as they are more licentious; licentiousness being not only different from liberty, but directly contrary to it; a direct breach upon it.

§ 20. *Authority is to be recognised as coming from God.*

It is moreover of a growing nature; and of speedy growth too; and, with the culture which it has amongst us, needs no great length of time to get to such an height as no legal government will be able to restrain or subsist under: which is the condition the historian describes in saying, they could neither bear their vices, nor the remedies of them [1]. I said legal government: for, in the present state of the world, there is no danger of our becoming savages. Had licentiousness finished its work, and destroyed our constitution, power would not be wanting, from one quarter or another, sufficient to subdue us, and keep us in subjection. But government, as distinguished from mere power, free government, necessarily implies reverence

---

[1] Nec vitia nostra, nec remedia pati possumus. Liv. lib. i. c. 1.

in the subjects of it, for authority, or power regulated by laws; and an habit of submission to the subordinations in civil life, throughout its several ranks: nor is a people capable of liberty without somewhat of this kind. But it must be observed, and less surely cannot be observed, this reverence and submission will at best be very precarious, if it be not founded upon a sense of authority being God's ordinance, and the subordinations in life a providential appointment of things.

§ 21. *Pernicious effect of reciprocal denigration by party-leaders.*

Now let it be considered, for surely it is not duly considered, what is really the short amount of those representations, which persons of superior rank give, and encourage to be given of each other, and which are spread over the nation? Is it not somewhat, in itself, and in its circumstances, beyond any thing in any other age or country of the world? And what effect must the continuance of this extravagant licentiousness in them, not to mention other kinds of it, have upon the people in those respects just mentioned? Must it not necessarily tend to wear out of their minds all reverence for authority, and respect for superiors of every sort; and, joined with the irreligious principles we find so industriously propagated, to introduce a total profligateness amongst them; since, let them be as bad as they will, it is scarce possible they can be so bad as they are instructed they may be, or worse than they are told their superiors are? And is there no danger that all this, to mention only one supposable course of it, may raise somewhat like that levelling spirit, upon atheistical principles, which, in the last age, prevailed upon enthusiastic ones? not to speak of the possibility, that different sorts of people may unite in it upon these contrary principles. And may not this spirit, together with a concurrence of ill humours, and of persons who hope to find their account in confusion, soon prevail to such a degree, as will require more of the good old principles of loyalty and of religion to withstand it, than appear to be left amongst us?

§ 22. *Laws general and particular. How liberty presupposes self-command.*

What legal remedies can be provided against these mischiefs, or whether any at all, are considerations the furthest from my thoughts. No government can be free, which is not administered by general stated laws: and these cannot comprehend every case, which wants to be provided against: nor can new ones be made for every particular case, as it arises: and more particular laws, as well as more general ones, admit of infinite evasions: and legal government forbids any but legal methods of redress; which cannot but be liable to the same sort of imperfections: besides the additional one of delay; and whilst redress is delayed, however unavoidably, wrong subsists. Then there are very bad things, which human authority can scarce provide against at all, but by methods dangerous to liberty; nor fully, but by such as would be fatal to it. These things show, that liberty, in the very nature of it, absolutely requires, and even supposes, that people be able to govern themselves in those respects in which they are free; otherwise their wickedness will be in proportion to their liberty, and this greatest of blessings will become a curse.

§ 23. (3) *Main security, the religious character of government.*

[III.] These things show likewise, that there is but one adequate remedy to the forementioned evils, even that which the apostle prescribes in the last words of the text, to consider ourselves *as the servants of God*, who enjoins dutiful submission to civil authority, as his ordinance; and to whom we are accountable for the use we make of the liberty which we enjoy under it. Since men cannot live out of society, nor in it without government, government is plainly a divine appointment; and consequently submission to it, a most evident duty of the law of nature. And we all know in how forcible a manner it is put upon our consciences in scripture. Nor can this obligation be denied formally upon any principles, but such as subvert all other obligations. Yet many amongst us seem not to consider it as any obligation at all. This doubtless is, in a great measure, owing to dissoluteness and corruption of manners: but I think it is partly owing to their having reduced it to nothing in theory.

§ 24. *The rule of obedience has exceptions; not needful to be pressed or specified.*

Whereas this obligation ought to be put upon the same foot with all other general ones, which are not absolute and without exception : and our submission is due in all cases but those, which we really discern to be exceptions to the general rule. And they who are perpetually displaying the exceptions, though they do not indeed contradict the meaning of any particular texts of scripture, which surely intended to make no alteration in men's civil rights; yet they go against the general tenor of scripture. For the scripture, throughout the whole of it, commands submission; supposing men apt enough of themselves to make the exceptions, and not to need being continually reminded of them.

§ 25. *In a free government respect is due, but also freedom of comment.*

Now if we are really under any obligations of duty at all to magistrates, honour and respect, in our behaviour towards them, must doubtless be their due. And they who refuse to pay them this small and easy regard, who *despise dominion, and speak evil of dignities* [m], should seriously ask themselves, what restrains them from any other instance whatever of undutifulness? And if it be principle, why not from this? Indeed free government supposes, that the conduct of affairs may be inquired into, and spoken of with freedom. Yet surely this should be done with decency, for the sake of liberty itself; for its honour and its security. But be it done as it will, it is a very different thing from

---

[m] Jude 8.

libelling, and endeavouring to vilify the persons of such as are in authority. It will be hard to find an instance, in which a serious man could calmly satisfy himself in doing this. It is in no case necessary, and in every case of very pernicious tendency. But the immorality of it increases in proportion to the integrity and superior rank of the persons thus treated.

§ 26. *The special value of our own.*

It is therefore in the highest degree immoral, when it extends to the supreme authority in the person of a prince, from whom our liberties are in no imaginable danger, whatever they may be from ourselves; and whose mild and strictly legal government could not but make any virtuous people happy.

A free government, which the good providence of God has preserved to us through innumerable dangers, is an invaluable blessing. And our ingratitude to him in abusing of it must be great in proportion to the greatness of the blessing, and the providential deliverances by which it has been preserved to us. Yet the crime of abusing this blessing[u] receives further aggravation from hence, that such abuse always is to the reproach, and tends to the ruin of it. The abuse of liberty has directly overturned many free governments, as well as our own, on the popular side; and has, in various ways, contributed to the ruin of many, which have been overturned on the side of authority. Heavy therefore must be their guilt, who shall be found to have given such advantages against it, as well as theirs who have taken them.

§ 27. *Not to forget the judgment to come. Civil government necessarily defective.*

Lastly, The consideration, that we are the servants of God, reminds us, that we are accountable to him for our behaviour in those respects, in which it is out of the reach of all human authority; and is the strongest enforcement of

---

[u] See pp. 279, &c., &c.

sincerity, as *all things are naked and opened unto the eyes of him with whom we have to do* º. Artificial behaviour might perhaps avail much towards quieting our consciences, and making our part good in the short competitions of this world: but what will it avail us considered as under the government of God? Under his government, *there is no darkness, nor shadow of death, where the workers of iniquity may hide themselves* ᵖ. He has indeed instituted civil government over the face of the earth, *for the punishment of evildoers, and for the praise*, the apostle does not say the rewarding, but, *for the praise of them that do well* ᑫ. Yet as the worst answer these ends in some measure, the best can do it very imperfectly [1]. Civil government can by no means take cognizance of *every work*, which is good or evil: many things are done in *secret;* the authors unknown to it, and often the things themselves: then it cannot so much consider actions, under the view of their being morally *good*, or *evil*, as under the view of their being mischievous, or beneficial to society: nor can it in any wise execute *judgment* in rewarding what is *good*, as it can, and ought, and does, in punishing what is *evil*. But *God shall bring every work into judgment, with every secret thing, whether it be good, or whether it be evil* ʳ.

º Heb. iv. 13.   ᵖ Job xxxiv. 22.   ᑫ 1 Pet. ii. 14.
ʳ Eccles. xii. 14.

[1] Comp. *inf.* Serm. v. 4.

SERMON IV

PREACHED IN THE PARISH CHURCH OF CHRIST-CHURCH, LONDON, ON THURSDAY, MAY 9, 1745. BEING THE TIME OF THE YEARLY MEETING OF THE CHILDREN EDUCATED IN THE CHARITY-SCHOOLS IN AND ABOUT THE CITIES OF LONDON AND WESTMINSTER.

Train up a child in the way he should go: and when he is old, he will not depart from it.—PROVERBS xxii. 6.

---

§ 1. *The contraction of early habits cannot safely be left to children alone.*

HUMAN creatures, from the constitution of their nature and the circumstances in which they are placed, cannot but acquire habits during their childhood, by the impressions which are given them, and their own customary actions [1]. And long before they arrive at mature age, these habits form a general settled character. And the observation of the text, that the most early habits are usually the most lasting, is likewise every one's observation. Now whenever children are left to themselves, and to the guides and companions which they choose, or by hazard light upon, we find by experience, that the first impressions they take, and course of action they get into, are very bad; and so consequently must be their habits, and character, and future behaviour. Thus if they are not trained up in the way they *should go*,

---

[1] Comp. Aristotle, *Eth. Nic.* II. i. 8: οὐ μικρὸν οὖν διαφέρει τὸ οὕτως ἢ οὕτως εὐθὺς ἐκ νέων ἐθίζεσθαι, ἀλλὰ πάμπολυ, μᾶλλον δὲ τὸ πᾶν.

they will certainly be trained up in the way they *should not go;* and in all probability will persevere in it, and become miserable themselves, and mischievous to society: which, in event, is worse, upon account of both, than if they had been exposed to perish in their infancy.

§ 2. *Docility and deference mark them for training.*

On the other hand, the ingenuous docility of children before they have been deceived, their distrust of themselves, and natural deference to grown people, whom they find here settled in a world where they themselves are strangers; and to whom they have recourse for advice, as readily as for protection; which deference is still greater towards those who are placed over them: these things give the justest grounds to expect that they may receive such impressions, and be influenced to such a course of behaviour, as will produce lasting good habits; and, together with the dangers before mentioned, are as truly a natural demand upon us to *train them up in the way they should go,* as their bodily wants are a demand to provide them bodily nourishment.

§ 3. *More contracted office of brute parents.*

Brute creatures are appointed to do no more than this last for their offspring, nature forming them by instincts to the particular manner of life appointed them; from which they never deviate. But this is so far from being the case of men, that, on the contrary, considering communities collectively, every successive generation is left, in the ordinary course of Providence, to be formed by the preceding one; and becomes good or bad, though not without its own merit or demerit, as this trust is discharged or violated, chiefly in the management of youth.

§ 4. *The duty distinct from that of admonishing adults.*

We ought, doubtless, to instruct and admonish grown persons; to restrain them from what is evil, and encourage them in what is good, as we are able: but this care of youth, abstracted from all consideration of the parental affection,

I say, this care of youth, which is the general notion of *education*, becomes a distinct subject, and a distinct duty, from the particular danger of their ruin, if left to themselves, and the particular reason we have to expect they will do well, if due care be taken of them. And from hence it follows, that children have as much right to some proper education, as to have their lives preserved; and that when this is not given them by their parents, the care of it devolves upon all persons, it becomes the duty of all, who are capable of contributing to it, and whose help is wanted.

These trite, but most important things, implied indeed in the text, being thus premised as briefly as I could express them, I proceed to consider distinctly the general manner in which the duty of education is there laid before us: which will further show its extent, and further obviate the idle objections which have been made against it. And all this together will naturally lead us to consider the occasion and necessity of schools for the education of poor children, and in what light the objections against them are to be regarded.

§ 5. *Obligation not to inform only, but to mould.*

Solomon might probably intend the text for a particular admonition to educate children in a manner suitable to their respective ranks, and future employments: but certainly he intended it for a general admonition to educate them in virtue and religion, and good conduct of themselves in their temporal concerns. And all this together, in which they are to be educated, he calls *the way they should go;* i.e. he mentions it not as a matter of speculation, but of practice. And conformably to this description of the things in which children are to be educated, he describes education itself: for he calls it *training them up;* which is a very different thing from merely teaching them some truths, necessary to be known or believed. It is endeavouring to form such truths into practical principles in the mind, so as to render them of habitual good influence upon the temper and actions, in all the various occurrences of life. And this is not done by bare instruction; but by that, together with admonishing them frequently as occasion offers; restraining them from what is evil, and exercising them in what is good. Thus the precept of the apostle concerning this matter is, to *bring up children in the nurture and admonition of the Lord*[a]; as it were by way of distinction from acquainting them merely with the principles of Christianity, as you would with any common theory. Though education were nothing more than informing children of some truths of importance to them, relating to religion and common life, yet there would be great reason for it, notwithstanding the frivolous objections concerning the danger of giving them prejudices.

§ 6. *Youth supplies the only available occasion.*

But when we consider that such information itself is really the least part of it; and that it consists in endeavouring to put them into right dispositions of mind, and right habits of living, in every relation and every capacity; this consideration shows such objections to be quite absurd: since it shows them to be objections against doing a thing of the utmost importance at the natural opportunity of our doing it, childhood and youth; and which is indeed, properly speaking, our only one. For when they are grown up to maturity, they are out of our hands, and must be left to themselves. The natural authority on one side ceases, and the deference on the other. God forbid, that it should be impossible for men to recollect themselves, and reform at an advanced age: but it is in no sort in the power of others to gain upon them; to turn them away from what is wrong, and enforce upon them what is right, at that season of their lives, in the manner we might have done in their childhood.

§ 7. *For religion not belief only, but a certain character, is required.*

Doubtless religion requires instruction, for it is founded in knowledge and belief of some truths. And so is common prudence in the management of our temporal affairs. Yet

---

[a] Eph. vi. 4.

neither of them consist in the knowledge or belief even of these fundamental truths; but in our being brought by such knowledge or belief to a correspondent temper and behaviour. Religion, as it stood under the Old Testament, is perpetually styled *the fear of God:* under the New, *faith in Christ*. But as that fear of God does not signify literally being afraid of him, but having a good heart, and leading a good life, in consequence of such fear; so this faith in Christ does not signify literally *believing* in him in the sense that word is used in common language, but becoming his real disciples, in consequence of such belief.

§ 8. *It leads to the chief good: is also the best of temporal and social gifts.*

Our religion being then thus practical, consisting in a frame of mind and course of behaviour, suitable to the dispensation we are under, and which will bring us to our final good; children ought, by education, to be habituated to this course of behaviour, and formed into this frame of mind. And it must ever be remembered, that if no care be taken to do it, they will grow up in a direct contrary behaviour, and be hardened in direct contrary habits. They will more and more corrupt themselves, and spoil their proper nature. They will alienate themselves further from God; and not only neglect, but *trample under foot,* the means which he in his infinite mercy has appointed for our recovery. And upon the whole, the same reasons, which show, that they ought to be instructed and exercised in what will render them useful to society, secure them from the present evils they are in danger of incurring, and procure them that satisfaction which lies within the reach of human prudence; show likewise, that they ought to be instructed and exercised in what is suitable to the highest relations in which we stand, and the most important capacity in which we can be considered; in that temper of mind and course of behaviour, which will secure them from their chief evil, and bring them to their chief good. Besides that religion is the principal security of men's acting a right part in society, and even in respect to their own temporal happiness, all things duly considered.

§ 9. *The risks of spurious training.*

It is true indeed, children may be taught superstition, under the notion of religion ; and it is true also, that, under the notion of prudence, they may be educated in great mistakes as to the nature of real interest and good, respecting the present world. But this is no more a reason for not educating them according to the best of our judgment, than our knowing how very liable we all are to err in other cases, is a reason why we should not, in those other cases, act according to the best of our judgment.

§ 10. *Objection (to schools) of novelty, futile.*

It being then of the greatest importance, that children should be thus educated, the providing schools to give this education to such of them as would not otherwise have it, has the appearance, at least at first sight, of deserving a place amongst the very best of good works. One would be backward, methinks, in entertaining prejudices against it ; and very forward, if one had any, to lay them aside, upon being shown that they were groundless. Let us consider the whole state of the case. For though this will lead us some little compass, yet I choose to do it ; and the rather, because there are people who speak of charity-schools as a new-invented scheme, and therefore to be looked upon with I know not what suspicion. Whereas it will appear, that the scheme of charity-schools, even the part of it which is most looked upon in this light, teaching the children letters and accounts, is no otherwise new, than as the occasion for it is so.

§ 11. *We all need maintenance : children training to boot.*

Formerly not only the education of poor children, but also their maintenance, with that of the other poor, were left to voluntary charities. But great changes of different sorts happening over the nation, and charity becoming more cold, or the poor more numerous, it was found necessary to make some legal provision for them. This might, much more properly than charity-schools, be called a new scheme. For, without question, the education of poor children was all along taken care of by voluntary charities, more or less: but obliging us by law to maintain the poor, was new in the reign of Queen Elizabeth. Yet, because a change of circumstances made it necessary, its novelty was no reason against it. Now in that legal provision for the maintenance of the poor, poor children must doubtless have had a part in common with grown people. But this could never be sufficient for children, because their case always requires more than mere maintenance; it requires that they be educated in some proper manner. Wherever there are poor who want to be maintained by charity, there must be poor children who, besides this, want to be educated by charity. And whenever there began to be need of *legal* provision for the *maintenance* of the poor, there must immediately have been need also of some *particular* legal provision in behalf of poor children for their *education*; this not being included in what we call their maintenance. And many whose parents are able to maintain them, and do so, may yet be utterly neglected as to their education.

§ 12. *Not provided, like the first, by the Act of Elizabeth.*

But possibly it might not at first be attended to, that the case of poor children was thus a case by itself, which required its own particular provision. Certainly it would not appear, to the generality, so urgent an one as the want of food and raiment. And it might be necessary, that a burden so entirely new as that of a poor-tax was at the time I am speaking of, should be as light as possible. Thus the legal provision for the poor was first settled; without any particular consideration of that additional want in the case of children; as it still remains, with scarce any alteration in this respect[1]. In the mean time, as the poor still increased,

---

[1] This anticipation of the future, and recognition of the training of the poorer children as a public care, seems a remarkable example of Butler's sagacious forethought.

or charity still lessened, many poor children were left exposed, not to perish for want of food, but to grow up in society, and learn every thing that is evil and nothing that is good in it; and when they were grown up, greatly at a loss in what honest way to provide for themselves, if they could be supposed inclined to it. And larger numbers, whose case was not as bad as this, yet were very far from having due care taken of their education. And the evil went on increasing, till it was grown to such a degree, as to be quite out of the compass of separate charities to remedy.

§ 13. *Remedy first provided by the S. P. C. K.*

At length some excellent persons, who were united in a Society[b] for carrying on almost every good work, took into consideration the neglected case I have been representing; and first of all, as I understand it, set up charity-schools; or however promoted them, as far as their abilities and influence could extend. Their design was not in any sort to remove poor children out of the rank in which they were born, but, keeping them in it, to give them the assistance which their circumstances plainly called for; by educating them in the principles of religion, as well as civil life;

§ 14. *Maintenance and instruction naturally cohere.*

and likewise making some sort of provision for their maintenance: under which last I include clothing them, giving them such learning, if it is to be called by that name, as may qualify them for some common employment, and placing them out to it, as they grow up. These two general designs coincide in many respects, and cannot be separated. For teaching the children to read, though I have ranked it under the latter, equally belongs to both: and without some advantages of the latter sort, poor people would not send their children to our charity-schools: nor could the poorest

---

[b] Society for Promoting Christian Knowledge.

of all be admitted into any schools, without some charitable provision of clothing. And care is taken, that it be such as cannot but be a restraint upon the children. And if this, or any part of their education, gives them any little vanity, as has been poorly objected, whilst they are children, it is scarce possible but that it will have even a quite contrary effect when they are grown up, and ever after remind them of their rank. Yet still we find it is apprehended, that what they here learn may set them above it.

§ 15. *Suspicion is unjust and impolitic: inaction will lower the position of the poor.*

But why should people be so extremely apprehensive of the danger, that poor persons will make a perverse use of every the least advantage, even the being able to read, whilst they do not appear at all apprehensive of the like danger for themselves or their own children, in respect of riches or power, how much soever; though the danger of perverting these advantages is surely as great, and the perversion itself of much greater and worse consequence? And by what odd reverse of things has it happened, that such as pretend to be distinguished for the love of liberty should be the only persons who plead for keeping down the poor, as one may speak; for keeping them more inferior in this respect, and, which must be the consequence, in other respects, than they were in times past? For till within a century or two all ranks were nearly upon a level as to the learning in question. The art of printing appears to have been providentially reserved till these latter ages, and then providentially brought into use, as what was to be instrumental for the future in carrying on the appointed course of things. The alterations which this art has even already made in the face of the world are not inconsiderable. By means of it, whether immediately or remotely, the methods of carrying on business are, in several respects, improved, *knowledge has been increased*[c], and some sort of literature is become general. And if this be a blessing, we

---

[c] Dan. xii. 4.

ought to let the poor, in their degree, share it with us. The present state of things and course of Providence plainly leads us to do so. And if we do not, it is certain, how little soever it be attended to, that they will be upon a greater disadvantage, on many accounts, especially in populous places, than they were in the dark ages: for they will be more ignorant, comparatively with the people about them, than they were then; and the ordinary affairs of the world are now put in a way which requires that they should have some knowledge of letters, which was not the case then. And therefore, to bring up the poor in their former ignorance, now this knowledge is so much more common and wanted, would be, not to keep them in the same, but to put them into a lower condition of life than what they were in formerly. Nor let people of rank flatter themselves, that ignorance will keep their inferiors more dutiful and in greater subjection to them: for surely there must be danger that it will have a contrary effect under a free government such as ours, and in a dissolute age.

§ 16. *Ignorance will be more led by example, and to this we cannot trust.*

Indeed the principles and manners of the poor, as to virtue and religion, will always be greatly influenced, as they always have been, by the *example* of their superiors, if that would mend the matter. And this influence will, I suppose, be greater, if they are kept more inferior than formerly in all knowledge and improvement. But unless their superiors of the present age, superiors, I mean, of the middle, as well as higher ranks in society, are greater examples of public spirit, of dutiful submission to authority, human and divine, of moderation in diversions, and proper care of their families and domestic affairs; unless, I say, superiors of the present age are greater examples of decency, virtue, and religion, than those of former times; for what reason in the world is it desirable that their example should have this greater influence over the poor? On the contrary, why should not the poor, by being taught to read, be put into a capacity of making some improvement in moral and religious knowledge, and confirming themselves in those good principles, which will be a great security for their following the example of their superiors. if it be good, and some sort of preservative against their following it if it be bad?

§ 17. *Our slenderness of pastoral means strengthens the call for use of books.*

And serious persons will further observe very singular reasons for this amongst us; from the discontinuance of that religious intercourse between pastors and people in private, which remains in protestant churches abroad, as well as in the church of Rome; and from our small public care and provision for keeping up a sense of religion in the lower rank, except by distributing religious books. For in this way they have been assisted; and any well-disposed person may do much good amongst them, and at a very trifling expense, since the worthy Society before mentioned has so greatly lessened the price of such books. But this pious charity is an additional reason why the poor should be taught to read, that they may be in a capacity of receiving the benefit of it. Vain indeed would be the hope, that any thing in this world can be fully secured from abuse. For as it is the general scheme of Divine Providence to bring good out of evil; so the wickedness of men will, if it be possible, bring evil out of good.

§ 18. *Ignorance tends to vice; instruction to virtue, and other utility.*

But upon the whole, incapacity and ignorance must be favourable to error and vice; and knowledge and improvement contribute, in due time, to the destruction of impiety as well as superstition, and to the general prevalence of true religion. But some of these observations may perhaps be thought too remote from the present occasion. It is more obviously to the purpose of it to observe, that reading, writing, and accounts, are useful, and, whatever cause it is owing to, would really now be wanted in the very lowest stations: and that the trustees of our charity-schools are fully convinced of the great fitness of joining to instruction easy labour, of some sort or other, as fast as it is practicable; which they have already been able to do in some of them.

§ 19. *Placing out: not to be neglected.*

Then as to placing out the poor children, as soon as they are arrived at a fit age for it; this must be approved by every one, as it is putting them in a way of industry under domestic government, at a time of life, in some respects, more dangerous than even childhood. And it is a known thing, that care is taken to do it in a manner which does not set them above their rank: though it is not possible always to do it exactly as one would wish. Yet, I hope it may be observed without offence, if any of them happen to be of a very weakly constitution, or of a very distinguished capacity, there can be no impropriety in placing these in employments adapted to their particular cases; though such as would be very improper for the generality.

§ 20. *But training in virtue is the main design.*

But the principal design of this charity is to educate poor children in such a manner, as has a tendency to make them good, and useful, and contented, whatever their particular station be. The care of this is greatly neglected by the poor: nor truly is it more regarded by the rich, considering what might be expected from them. And if it were as practicable to provide charity-schools, which should supply this shameful neglect in the rich, as it is to supply the like, though more excusable, neglect in the poor, I should think certainly, that both ought to be done for the same reasons. And most people, I hope, will think so too, if they attend to the thing I am speaking of; which is the moral and religious part of education; what is equally necessary for all ranks, and grievously wanting in all. Yet in this respect the poor must be greatly upon a disadvantage, from the nature of the case; as will appear to any one who will consider it.

§ 21. *The grave dangers of inaction.*

For if poor children are not sent to school, several years of their childhood, of course, pass away in idleness and loitering. This has a tendency to give them perhaps a feeble listlessness, perhaps an headstrong profligateness of mind; certainly an indisposition to proper application as they grow up, and an aversion afterwards, not only to the restraints of religion, but to those which any particular calling, and even the nature of society, require. Whereas children kept to stated orders, and who many hours of the day are in employment, are by this means habituated both to submit to those who are placed over them, and to govern themselves; and they are also by this means prepared for industry, in any way of life in which they may be placed. And all this holds abstracted from the consideration of their being taught to read; without which, however, it will be impracticable to employ their time: not to repeat the unanswerable reasons for it before mentioned. Now several poor people cannot, others will not be at the expense of sending their children to school. And let me add, that such as can and are willing, yet if it be very inconvenient to them, ought to be eased of it, and the burden of children made as light as may be to their poor parents.

§ 22. *Case of evil parents: aggravated for the poor.*

Consider next the manner in which the children of the poor, who have vicious parents, are brought up, in comparison with other children whose parents are of the same character. The children of dissolute men of fortune may have the happiness of not seeing much of their parents. And this, even though they are educated at home, is often the case, by means of a customary distance between them, which cannot be kept amongst the poor. Nor is it impossible, that a rich man of this character, desiring to have his children better than himself, may provide them such an education as may make them so, without his having any restraint or trouble in the matter. And the education which children of better rank must have, for their improvement in the common accomplishments belonging to it, is of course, as yet, for the most part, attended with some sort of religious education. But the poor, as they cannot provide persons to educate their children; so, from the way in which they live together in poor families, a child must be an eye and ear-witness of the worst part of his parents' talk and behaviour. And it cannot but be expected, that his own will be formed upon it. For as example in general has very great influence upon all persons, especially children, the example of their parents is of authority with them, when there is nothing to balance it on the other side. Now take in the supposition, that these parents are dissolute, profligate people; then, over and above giving their children no sort of good instruction, and a very bad example, there are more crimes than one in which, it may be feared, they will directly instruct and encourage them; besides letting them ramble abroad wherever they will, by which, of course, they learn the very same principles and manners they do at home. And from all these things together, such poor children will have their characters formed to vice, by those whose business it is to restrain them from it. They will be disciplined and trained up to it.

§ 23. *Advises public provision for maintenance.*

This surely is a case which ought to have some public provision made for it. If it cannot have an adequate one, yet such an one as it can: unless it be thought so rare as not to deserve our attention. But in reality, though there should be no more parents of this character amongst the poor, in proportion, than amongst the rich, the case which I have been putting will be far from being uncommon. Now notwithstanding the danger to which the children of such wretched parents cannot but be exposed, from what they see at home; yet by instilling into them the principles of virtue and religion at school, and placing them soon out in sober families, there is ground to hope they may avoid those ill courses, and escape that ruin, into which, without this care, they would almost certainly run. I need not add how much greater ground there is to expect, that those of the children who have religious parents will do well. For such parents, besides setting their children a good example, will likewise repeat and enforce upon them at home the good instructions they receive at school.

§ 24. *Good moral results from charity-schools may be probably affirmed.*

After all, we find the world continues very corrupt. And it would be miraculous indeed, if charity-schools alone should make it otherwise; or if they should make even all who are brought up in them proof against its corruptions. The truth is, every method that can be made use of to prevent or reform the bad manners of the age, will appear to be of less effect, in proportion to the greater occasion there is for it: as cultivation, though the most proper that can be, will produce less fruit, or of a worse sort, in a bad climate than in a good one. And thus the character of the common people, with whom these children are to live, in the ordinary intercourse of business and company when they come out into the world, may more or less defeat the good effects of their education. And so likewise may the character of men of rank, under whose influence they are to live. But whatever danger may be apprehended from either or both of these, it can be no reason why we should not endeavour, by the likeliest methods we can, to better the world, or keep it from growing worse. The good tendency of the method before us is unquestionable. And I think myself obliged to add, that upon a comparison of parishes where charity-schools have been for a considerable time established, with neighbouring ones, in like situations, which have had none, the good effects of them, as I am very credibly informed, are most manifest. Notwithstanding I freely own, that it is extremely difficult to make the necessary comparisons in this case, and form a judgment upon them. And a multitude of circumstances must come in to determine, from appearances only, concerning the positive good which is produced by this charity, and the evil which is prevented by it; which last is full as material as the former, and can scarce be estimated at all. But surely there can be no doubt whether it be useful or not, to educate children in order, virtue, and religion.

§ 25. *Our part is to try; and leave the issue to God.*

However, suppose, which is yet far from being the case, but suppose it should seem, that this undertaking did not answer the expense and trouble of it, in the civil or political way of considering things. What is this to persons who profess to be engaged in it, not only upon mere civil views, but upon moral and Christian ones? We are to do our endeavours to promote virtue and religion amongst men, and leave the success to God: the designs of his providence are answered by these endeavours, *whether they will hear, or whether they will forbear;* i. e. whatever be the success of them: and the least success in such endeavours is a great and valuable effect [d].

§ 26. *The principle is the same as in the case of poor-law relief.*

From these foregoing observations, duly considered, it will appear, that the objections, which have been made against charity-schools, are to be regarded in the same light with those which are made against any other necessary things; for instance, against providing for the sick and the aged poor. Objections in this latter case could be considered no otherwise than merely as warnings of some inconvenience which might accompany such charity, and might, more or less, be guarded against, the charity itself being still kept up; or as proposals for placing it upon some better foot. For though, amidst the disorder and imperfection in all human things, these objections were not obviated, they could not however possibly be understood as reasons for discontinuing such charity; because, thus understood, they would be reasons for leaving necessitous people to perish. Well-disposed persons therefore will take care, that they be not deluded with objections against this before us, any more

---

[d] See the Sermon before the Society for the Propagation of the Gospel.

than against other necessary charities; as though such objections were reasons for suppressing them, or not contributing to their support, unless we can procure an alteration of that to which we object. There can be no possible reasons for leaving poor children in that imminent danger of ruin, in which many of these must be left, were it not for this charity. Therefore objections against it cannot, from the nature of the case, amount to more than reasons for endeavouring, whether with or without success, to put it upon a right and unexceptionable foot, in the particular respects objected against.

§ 27. *The management is commendable for pliancy to public opinion.*

And if this be the intention of the objectors, the managers of it have shown themselves remarkably ready to second them: for they have shown even a docility in receiving admonitions of any thing thought amiss in it, and proposals for rendering it more complete. And, under the influence of this good spirit, the management of it is really improving; particularly in greater endeavours to introduce manufactures into these schools; and in more particular care to place the children out to employments in which they are most wanted, and may be most serviceable, and which are most suitable to their ranks. But if there be any thing in the management of them, which some particular persons think should be altered, and others are of a contrary opinion, these things must be referred to the judgment of the public, and the determination of the public complied with. Such compliance is an essential principle of all charitable associations; for without it they could not subsist at all: and by charitable associations, multitudes are put in mind to do good, who otherwise would not have thought of it; and infinitely more good may be done, than possibly can by the separate endeavours of the same number of charitable persons. Now he who refuses to help forward the good work before us, because it is not conducted exactly in his own way, breaks in upon that general principle of union, which those who are friends to the indigent and distressed part of our fellow-creatures will be very cautious how they do in any case: but more especially will they beware, how they break in upon that necessary principle in a case of so great importance as is the present. For the public is as much interested in the education of poor children, as in the preservation of their lives.

§ 28. *Let each look to his personal duty in the matter.*

This last, I observed, is legally provided for. The former is left amongst other works of charity, neglected by many who care for none of these things, and to be carried on by such only as think it their concern to be doing good. Some of you are able, and in a situation, to assist in it in an eminent degree, by being trustees, and overlooking the management of these schools; or in different ways countenancing and recommending them; as well as by contributing to their maintenance: others can assist only in this latter way. In what manner and degree then it belongs to you, and to me, and to any particular person to help it forward, let us all consider seriously, not for one another, but each of us for himself.

§ 29. *Petition.*

And may the blessing of Almighty God accompany this work of charity, which he has put into the hearts of his servants, in behalf of these poor children; that being now *trained up in the way they should go, when they are old they may not depart from it.* May he, of his mercy, keep them safe amidst the innumerable dangers of this bad world, through which they are to pass, and preserve them unto his heavenly kingdom.

SERMON V

PREACHED BEFORE THE HOUSE OF LORDS, IN THE ABBEY-CHURCH OF WESTMINSTER, ON THURSDAY, JUNE 11, 1747. BEING THE ANNIVERSARY OF HIS MAJESTY'S HAPPY ACCESSION TO THE THRONE.

———◆———

I exhort, that, first of all, supplications, prayers, intercessions, and giving of thanks, be made for all men; for kings, and for all that are in authority; that we may lead a quiet and peaceable life in all godliness and honesty.—1 TIMOTHY ii. 1, 2.

———◆———

§ 1. *The text viewed as against* (a) *insurrection,* (b) *oppression by the state.*

IT is impossible to describe the general end which Providence has appointed us to aim at in our passage through the present world, in more expressive words than these very plain ones of the apostle, *to lead a quiet and peaceable life, in all godliness and honesty: a quiet and peaceable life,* by way of distinction, surely, from eager, tumultuary pursuits in our private capacity, as well as in opposition both to our making insurrections in the state, and to our suffering oppression from it. *To lead a quiet and peaceable life in all godliness and honesty,* is the whole that we have any reason to be concerned for. To this the constitution of our nature carries us; and our external condition is adapted to it.

§ 2. *Civil government founded, with double sanction, against violence and fraud.*

Now in aid to this general appointment of Providence, civil government has been instituted over the world, both by the light of nature and by revelation, to instruct men in the duties of fidelity, justice, and regard to common good, and enforce the practice of these virtues, without which there could have been no peace or quiet amongst mankind; and to preserve, in different ways, a sense of religion as well as virtue, and of God's authority over us. For if we could suppose men to have lived out of government, they must have run wild, and all knowledge of divine things must have been lost from among them. But by means of their uniting under it, they have been preserved in some tolerable security from the fraud and violence of each other; order, a sense of virtue, and the practice of it, has been in some measure kept up; and religion, more or less pure, has been all along spread and propagated. So that I make no scruple to affirm, that civil government has been, in all ages, a standing publication of the law of nature, and an enforcement of it; though never in its perfection, for the most part greatly corrupted, and I suppose always so in some degree.

§ 3. *A figure of the authority divine and universal.*

And considering that civil government is that part of God's government over the world, which he exercises by the instrumentality of men, wherein that which is oppression, injustice, cruelty, as coming from them, is, under his direction, necessary discipline, and just punishment; considering that *all power is of God*[a], all authority is properly of divine appointment; men's very living under magistracy might naturally have led them to the contemplation of authority in its source and origin; the one, supreme, absolute authority of Almighty God; by which he *doeth according to his will in the army of heaven, and among the inhabitants of the earth*[b]: which he now exerts, visibly and invisibly, by different instruments, in different forms of administration, different methods of discipline and punishment; and which he will continue to exert hereafter, not only over mankind when this mortal life shall be ended, but throughout his universal kingdom; till, by having rendered to all according

---

[a] Rom. xiii. 1.   [b] Dan. iv. 35.

to their works, he shall have completely executed that just scheme of government, which he has already begun to execute in this world, by their hands, whom he has appointed, for the present *punishment of evil-doers, and for the praise of them that do well* c.

§ 4. *Good always in degree, sometimes in high degree.*

And though that perfection of justice cannot in any sort take place in this world, even under the very best governments; yet under the worst, men have been enabled to lead much more quiet and peaceable lives, as well as attend to and keep up a sense of religion much more, than they could possibly have done without any government at all. But a free Christian government is adapted to answer these purposes in a higher degree, in proportion to its just liberty, and the purity of its religious establishment. And as we enjoy these advantages, civil and religious, in a very eminent degree, under a good prince, and those he has placed in authority over us, we are eminently obliged to offer up supplications and thanksgivings in their behalf; to pay them all that duty which these prayers imply; and *to lead*, as those advantages enable and have a tendency to dispose us to do, *quiet and peaceable lives in all godliness and honesty.*

§ 5. *The British people, being free, has to guard against licentiousness.*

Of the former of these advantages, our free constitution of civil government, we seem to have a very high value. And if we would keep clear from abuses of it, it could not be overvalued; otherwise than as every thing may, when considered as respecting this world only. We seem, I say, sufficiently sensible of the value of our civil liberty. It is our daily boast, and we are in the highest degree jealous of it. Would to God we were somewhat more judicious in our jealousy of it, so as to guard against its chief enemy, one might say, the only enemy of it, we have at present to

---

c 1 Pet. ii. 14.

fear; I mean licentiousness[1]; which has undermined so many free governments, and without whose treacherous help no free government, perhaps, ever was undermined. This licentiousness indeed is not only dangerous to liberty, but it is actually a present infringement of it in many instances.—But I must not turn this good day into a day of reproach. Dropping then the encroachments which are made upon our liberty, peace, and quiet by licentiousness, we are certainly a freer nation than any other we have an account of; and as free, it seems, as the very nature of government will permit. Every man is equally under the protection of the laws; may have equal justice against the most rich and powerful; and securely enjoy all the common blessings of life, with which the industry of his ancestors, or his own, has furnished him. In some other countries the upper part of the world is free, but in Great Britain the whole body of the people is free.

§ 6. *Recent reform in the northern provinces.*

For we have at length, to the distinguished honour of those who began, and have more particularly laboured in it, emancipated our northern provinces from most of their *legal* remains of slavery[2]: for *voluntary* slavery cannot be abolished, at least not directly, by law. I take leave to speak of this long-desired work as done; since it wants only his concurrence, who, as we have found by many years' experience, considers the good of his people as his own. And I cannot but look upon these acts of the legislature in a further view, as instances of regard to posteriity; and declarations of its readiness to put every subject upon an equal foot of security and freedom, if any of them are not so, in any other respects, which come into its view; and as a precedent and example for doing it.

---

[1] See *sup.* Serm. iii. §§ 15-27.
[2] The allusion is evidently to the Act 20 Geo. II. c. 19. It applied a partial remedy to what Butler most properly calls remains of slavery! It refers to miners, and all labourers employed for fixed periods. It empowers justices to decide disputes, to fix 'a reasonable wage': to distrain upon employers making default, to fine or imprison labourers. No such measure could be thought of in the present day: it is not now on the Statute Book.

§ 7. *Established religion, with toleration, why requisite.*

Liberty, which is the very genius of our civil constitution, and runs through every branch of it, extends its influence to the ecclesiastical part of it. A religious establishment without a toleration of such as think they cannot in conscience conform to it, is itself a general tyranny; because it claims absolute authority over conscience; and would soon beget particular kinds of tyranny of the worst sort, tyranny over the mind, and various superstitions; after the way should be paved for them, as it soon must, by ignorance. On the other hand, a constitution of civil government without any religious establishment is a chimerical project, of which there is no example: and which, leaving the generality without guide and instruction, must leave religion to be sunk and forgotten amongst them; and at the same time give full scope to superstition, and the gloom of enthusiasm; which last, especially, ought surely to be diverted and checked, as far as it can be done without force. Now a reasonable establishment provides instruction for the ignorant, withdraws them, not in the way of force, but of guidance, from running after those kinds of conceits. It doubtless has a tendency likewise to keep up a sense of real religion and real Christianity in a nation: and is moreover necessary for the encouragement of learning; some parts of which the scripture-revelation absolutely requires should be cultivated.

§ 8. *Evils of popery, from which it saves us.*

It is to be remarked further, that the value of any particular religious establishment is not to be estimated merely by what it is in itself, but also by what it is in comparison with those of other nations; a comparison which will sufficiently teach us not to expect perfection in human things. And what is still more material, the value of our own ought to be very much heightened in our esteem, by considering what it is a security from; I mean that great corruption of Christianity, popery, which is ever hard at work to bring us again under its yoke. Whoever will consider the popish claims, to the disposal of the whole earth, as of divine right, to dispense with the most sacred engagements, the claims to supreme absolute authority in religion; in short, the general claims which the canonists express by the words *plenitude of power*—whoever, I say, will consider popery as it is professed at Rome, may see, that it is manifest, open usurpation of all human and divine authority [1].

§ 9. *Found wherever the Roman church prevails.*

But even in those Roman catholic countries where these monstrous claims are not admitted, and the civil power does, in many respects, restrain the papal; yet persecution is professed, as it is absolutely enjoined by what is acknowledged to be their highest authority, a general council, so called, with the pope at the head of it; and is practised in all of them, I think without exception, where it can be done safely. Thus they go on to substitute force instead of argument; and external profession made by force instead of reasonable conviction. And thus corruptions of the grossest sort have been in vogue, for many generations, in many parts of Christendom; and are so still, even where popery obtains in its least absurd form: and their antiquity and wide extent are insisted upon as proofs of their truth; a kind of proof, which at best can be only presumptive, but which loses all its little weight, in proportion as the long and large prevalence of such corruptions have been obtained by force.

---

[1] Considering Butler's general moderation of mind, there is at first sight an appearance, in this very strong denunciation, of his having for once indulged in some departure from it. We find, however, that what he has in view does not seem to be any defined dogmatic system or tenet of the Latin church, but—

(*a*) The papal claim to plenitude of power: which in 1854 and in 1870 showed such a disposition and capacity to break down every opposing barrier.

(*b*) Its doctrine of persecution, and therein the displacement of reason and substitution of force.

(*c*) The exaggerations and abuses which creep in under any system from which guarantees truly conservative have been removed. Perhaps such, pre-eminently, as were brought into public view by Scipio Ricci and the Synod of Pistoia.

This is an imperfect attempt to gather what it is that Butler has here expressed only in the way of a somewhat general indication.

§ 10. *Job xxxi. 26–28 speaks of idolatry when in its infancy.*

Indeed it is said in the Book of Job, that the worship of *the sun and moon was an iniquity to be punished by the judge*[d]. And this, though it is not so much as a precept, much less a general one, is, I think, the only passage of scripture which can with any colour be alleged in favour of persecution of any sort: for what the Jews did, and what they were commanded to do, under their theocracy, are both quite out of the case. But whenever that book was written, the scene of it is laid at a time when idolatry was in its infancy, an acknowledged novelty, essentially destructive of true religion, arising perhaps from mere wantonness of imagination. In these circumstances, this greatest of evils, which afterwards laid waste true religion over the face of the earth, might have been suppressed at once, without danger of mistake or abuse. And one might go on to add, that if those to whom the care of this belonged, instead of serving themselves of prevailing superstitions, had in all ages and countries opposed them in their rise; and adhered faithfully to that primitive religion, which was received *of old, since man was placed upon earth*[e]; there could not possibly have been any such difference of opinion concerning the Almighty Governor of the world, as could have given any pretence for tolerating the idolatries which overspread it. On the contrary, his universal monarchy must have been universally recognised, and the general laws of it more ascertained and known, than the municipal ones of any particular country can be. In such a state of religion, as it could not but have been acknowledged by all mankind, that immorality of every sort was disloyalty to him, *the high and lofty One, that inhabiteth eternity, whose name is Holy*[f]; so it could not but have been manifest, that idolatry, in those determinate instances of it, was plain rebellion against him; and therefore might have been punished as an offence of the highest kind against the Supreme Authority in nature.

---

[d] Job xxxi. 26-28.   [e] Job xx. 4.   [f] Isaiah lvii. 15.

§ 11. *Inapplicable to present facts.*

But this is in no sort applicable to the present state of religion in the world. For if the principle of punishing idolatry were now admitted amongst the several different parties in religion, the weakest in every place would run a great risk of being convicted of it; or, however, heresy and schism would soon be found crimes of the same nature, and equally deserving punishment. Thus the spirit of persecution would range without any stop or control, but what should arise from its want of power. But our religious establishment disclaims all principles of this kind, and desires not to keep persons in its communion, or gain proselytes to it, by any other methods than the Christian ones of argument and conviction.

§ 12. *Recent danger from the Pretender.*

These hints may serve to remind us of the value we ought to set upon our constitution in Church and State, the advantages of which are the proper subjects of our commemoration on this day, as his Majesty has shown himself, not in words, but in the whole course of his reign, the guardian and protector of both. And the blessings of his reign are not only rendered more sensible, but are really heightened, by its securing us from that Pretender to his crown, whom we had almost forgot, till our late danger renewed our apprehensions; who, we know, is a professed enemy to our church; and grown old in resentments and maxims of government directly contrary to our civil constitution; nay his very claim is founded in principles destructive of it. Our deliverance and our security from this danger, with all the other blessings of the king's government, are so many reasons for *supplications, prayers, intercessions, and giving of thanks*, to which we are exhorted; as well as for all other dutiful behaviour towards it; and should also remind us to take care and make due improvement of those blessings, by *leading*, in the enjoyment of them, *quiet and peaceable lives, in all godliness and honesty.*

§ 13. *Loyalty of the church to rulers.*

The Jewish church offered sacrifices even for heathen princes to whom they were in subjection: and the primitive Christian church, the Christian sacrifices of supplications and prayers for the prosperity of the emperor and the state; though they were falsely accused of being enemies to both, because they would not join in their idolatries. In conformity to these examples of the church of God in all ages, prayers for the king and those in authority under him are part of the daily service of our own. And for the day of his inauguration a particular service is appointed, which we are here assembled in the house of God to celebrate. This is the first duty we owe to kings, and those who are in authority under them, that we make prayers and thanksgivings for them. And in it is comprehended, what yet may be considered as another, paying them honour and reverence. Praying for them is itself an instance and expression of this, as it gives them a part in our highest solemnities. It also reminds us of that further honour and reverence which we are to pay them, as occasions offer, throughout the whole course of our behaviour. *Fear God, honour the king*[g], are apostolic precepts; and *despising government, and speaking evil of dignities*[h], apostolic descriptions of such as *are reserved unto the day of judgment to be punished*[i]. And if these *evil speeches* are so highly criminal, it cannot be a thing very innocent to make a custom of entertaining ourselves with them.

§ 14. *Legitimate and illegitimate opposition.*

Further, if we are to pray, *that we may*, that it may be permitted us, to *lead a quiet and peaceable life*, we ought surely to live so, when by means of a mild, equal government, it is permitted us; and be very thankful, first to God, and then to those whom he makes the instruments of so great good to us, and pay them all obedience and duty; though

---

[g] 1 Pet. ii. 17.   [h] 2 Pet. ii. 10.   [i] 2 Pet. ii. 9.

every thing be not conducted according to our judgment, nor every person in employment whom we may think deserving of it. Indeed opposition, in a legal, regular way, to measures which a person thinks wrong, cannot but be allowed in a free government. It is in itself just, and also keeps up the spirit of liberty. But opposition, from indirect motives, to measures which he sees to be necessary, is itself immoral: it keeps up the spirit of licentiousness; is the greatest reproach of liberty, and in many ways most dangerous to it; and has been a principal means of overturning free governments. It is well too if the *legal subjection* to the government we live under, which may accompany such behaviour, be not the reverse of *Christian subjection; subjection for wrath only,* and *not for conscience sake* [k]. And one who wishes well to his country will beware how he inflames the common people against measures, whether right or wrong, which they are not judges of. For no one can foresee how far such disaffection will extend; but every one sees, that it diminishes the reverence which is certainly owing to authority. Our due regards to these things are indeed instances of our loyalty, but they are in reality as much instances of our patriotism too. Happy the people who live under a prince, the justice of whose government renders them coincident.

§ 15. *The equity of our Church and State a rule for personal conduct.*

Lastly, As by the good providence of God we were born under a free government, and are members of a pure reformed church [1], both of which he has wonderfully preserved through infinite dangers; if we do not take

---

[k] Rom. xiii. 5.

---

[1] Butler here adopts, I apprehend, the language of his day. In the early part of my own life (say before 1850), it was customary more than now, in the Bidding Prayer, to pray for the church of Christ, or catholic church, 'and more especially for that pure and apostolical branch of it, to which we belong.'

heed to live like Christians, nor to govern ourselves with decency in those respects in which we are free, we shall be a dishonour to both. Both are most justly to be valued: but they may be valued in the wrong place. It is no more a recommendation of civil than it is of natural liberty[1], that it must put us into a capacity of behaving ill. Let us then value our civil constitution, not because it leaves us the power of acting as mere humour and passion carries us, in those respects, in which governments less free lay men under restraints; but for its equal laws, by which the great are disabled from oppressing those below them. Let us transfer, each of us, the equity of this our civil constitution to our whole personal character; and be sure to be as much afraid of subjection to mere arbitrary will and pleasure in ourselves, as to the arbitrary will of others. For the tyranny of our own lawless passions is the nearest and most dangerous of all tyrannies.

§ 16. *Retrenchments of our outward religion should enhance what is inward.*

Then as to the other part of our constitution; let us value it, not because it leaves us at liberty to have as little religion as we please, without being accountable to human judicatories; but because it affords us the means and assistances to worship God according to his word; because it exhibits to our view, and enforces upon our conscience, genuine Christianity, free from the superstitions with which it is defiled in other countries. These superstitions naturally tend to *abate* its force: our profession of it in its purity is a particular call upon us to yield ourselves up to its *full* influence; *to be pure in heart*[m]; *to be holy in all manner of conversation*[n]. Much of *the form of godliness* is laid aside amongst us: this itself should admonish us to attend more to *the power thereof*[o]. We have discarded many burdensome ceremonies: let us be the more careful to cultivate inward

---

[1] Natural liberty as opposed to necessity, or fate.   [m] Matt. v. 8.
[n] 1 Pet. i. 15.   [o] 2 Tim. iii. 5.

religion. We have thrown off a multitude of superstitious practices, which were called good works: let us the more abound in all moral virtues, these being unquestionably such. Thus our lives will justify and recommend the Reformation; and we shall *adorn the doctrine of God our Saviour in all things* [p].

---

[p] Titus ii. 10.

SERMON VI

PREACHED BEFORE HIS GRACE CHARLES DUKE OF RICHMOND, PRESIDENT, AND THE GOVERNORS OF THE LONDON INFIRMARY, FOR THE RELIEF OF SICK AND DISEASED PERSONS, ESPECIALLY MANUFACTURERS, AND SEAMEN IN MERCHANT-SERVICE, ETC., AT THE PARISH CHURCH OF ST. LAWRENCE-JEWRY, ON THURSDAY, MARCH 31, 1748.

And above all things have fervent charity among yourselves: for charity shall cover the multitude of sins.—1 PETER iv. 8.

---

§ 1. *Behaviour may render us, though sinful in much, proper objects of mercy.*

AS we owe our being, and all our faculties, and the very opportunities of exerting them, to Almighty God, and are plainly his and not our own, we are admonished, even though we should *have done all those things which are commanded us*, to say, We are *unprofitable servants*[a]. And with much deeper humility must we make this acknowledgment, when we consider in how *many things we have all offended*[b]. But still the behaviour of such creatures as men, highly criminal in some respects, may yet in others be such as to render them the proper objects of mercy, and, our Saviour does not decline saying, *thought worthy of it*[c]. And, conformably to our natural sense of things, the scripture is very express,

---

[a] Luke xvii. 10.   [b] James iii. 2.   [c] Luke xx. 35.

that mercy, forgiveness, and, in general, charity to our fellow-creatures, has this efficacy in a very high degree.

§ 2. *Special reason for charity, to make amends.*

Several copious and remote reasons have been alleged, why such pre-eminence is given to this grace or virtue; some of great importance, and none of them perhaps without its weight. But the proper one seems to be very short and obvious, that by fervent charity, with a course of beneficence proceeding from it, a person may make amends[1] for the good he has blamably omitted, and the injuries he has done, so far, as that society would have no demand upon him for such his misbehaviour; nor consequently would justice have any in behalf of society, whatever it might have upon other accounts. Thus by fervent charity he may even merit forgiveness of men: and this seems to afford a very singular reason why it may be graciously granted him by God; a very singular reason, the Christian covenant of pardon always supposed, why divine justice should permit, and divine mercy appoint, that such his charity should be allowed to *cover the multitude of sins.*

§ 3. *Charity is not mere good-humour; which need not imply judgment.*

And this reason leads me to observe, what scripture and the whole nature of the thing shows, that the charity here meant must be such hearty love to our fellow-creatures, as produceth a settled endeavour to promote, according to the best of our judgment, their real lasting good, both present and future; and not that easiness of temper, which with peculiar propriety is expressed by the word *good-humour*, and is a sort of benevolent instinct left to itself, without the direction of our judgment. For this kind of good-humour is so far from making the amends before mentioned, that, though it be agreeable in conversation, it is often most mischievous in every other intercourse of life; and always puts men out of a capacity of doing the good they might, if

---

[1] See *inf.* § 25: 'I can mean only to our fellow-creatures.'

they could withstand importunity, and the sight of distress, when the case requires they should be withstood; many instances of which case daily occur, both in public and private. Nor is it to be supposed, that we can any more promote the lasting good of our fellow-creatures, by acting from mere kind inclinations, without *considering* what are the proper means of promoting it, than that we can attain our own personal good, by a *thoughtless* pursuit of every thing which pleases us. For the love of our neighbour, as much as self-love, the social affections, as much as the private ones, from their very nature, require to be under the direction of our judgment. Yet it is to be remembered, that it does in no sort become such a creature as man to harden himself against the distresses of his neighbour, except where it is really necessary; and that even well-disposed persons may run into great perplexities, and great mistakes too, by being over-solicitous in distinguishing what are the most proper occasions for their charity, or who the greatest objects of it. And therefore, as on the one side we are obliged to take some care not to squander that which, one may say, belongs to the poor, as we shall do, unless we competently satisfy ourselves beforehand, that what we put to our account of charity will answer some good purpose; so on the other side, when we are competently satisfied of this, in any particular instance before us, we ought by no means to neglect such present opportunity of doing good, under the notion of making further inquiries: for of these delays there will be no end.

§ 4. *Excellence of the Charity now under view.*

Having thus briefly laid before you the ground of that singular efficacy, which the text ascribes to charity in general; obviated the objection against its having this efficacy; and distinguished the virtue itself from its counterfeits; let us now proceed to observe the genuineness and excellency of the particular charity, which we are here met together to promote.

Medicine and every other relief, *under the calamity of bodily diseases and casualties,* no less than the daily necessaries of life, are natural provisions, which God has made for our present indigent state; and which he has granted in common to the children of men, whether they be poor or rich: to the rich by inheritance, or acquisition; and by their hands to the disabled poor.

Nor can there be any doubt, but that public infirmaries are the most effectual means of administering such relief; besides that they are attended with incidental advantages of great importance: both which things have been fully shown, and excellently enforced, in the annual sermons upon this and the like occasions.

§ 5. *As to foreigners; and otherwise.*

But indeed public infirmaries are not only the best, they are the only possible means by which the poor, especially in this city, can be provided, in any competent measure, with the several kinds of assistance, which *bodily diseases and casualties* require. Not to mention poor foreigners; it is obvious no other provision can be made for poor strangers out of the country, when they are overtaken by these calamities, as they often must be, whilst they are occasionally attending their affairs in this centre of business. But even the poor who are settled here are in a manner strangers to the people amongst whom they live; and, were it not for this provision, must unavoidably be neglected, in the hurry and concourse around them, and be left unobserved to languish in sickness, and suffer extremely, much more than they could in less populous places; where every one is known to every one; and any great distress presently becomes the common talk; and where also poor families are often under the particular protection of some or other of their rich neighbours, in a very different way from what is commonly the case here. Observations of this kind show, that there is a peculiar occasion, and even a necessity, in such a city as this, for public infirmaries, to which easy admittance may be had; and here in ours no security is required, nor any sort of gratification allowed; and that they ought to be multiplied, or enlarged, proportionably to the increase of our inhabitants: for to this the increase of the poor will always bear proportion; though less in ages of sobriety and diligence, and greater in ages of profusion and debauchery.

§ 6. *Objection to provision for the poor, most futile.*

Now though nothing, to be called an objection in the way of argument, can be alleged against thus providing for poor sick people, in the properest, indeed the only way in which they can be provided for; yet persons of too severe tempers can, even upon this occasion, talk in a manner, which, contrary surely to their intention, has a very malignant influence upon the spirit of charity—talk of the ill-deserts of the poor, the good uses they might make of being let to suffer more than they do, under distresses which they bring upon themselves, or however might, by diligence and frugality, provide against; and the idle uses they may make of knowing beforehand that they shall be relieved in case of those distresses. Indeed there is such a thing as a prejudice against them, arising from their very state of poverty, which ought greatly to be guarded against; a kind of prejudice, to which perhaps most of us, upon some occasions, and in some degree, may inattentively be liable, but which pride and interest may easily work up to a settled hatred of them; the utter reverse of that amiable part of the character of Job, that *he was a father to the poor* [d]. But it is undoubtedly fit, that such of them as are good and industrious should have the satisfaction of knowing beforehand, that they shall be relieved under *diseases and casualties:* and those, it is most obvious, ought to be relieved preferably to others.

§ 7. *Case of the misconducted.*

But these others, who are not of that good character, might possibly have the apprehension of those calamities in so great a degree, as would be very mischievous, and of no service, if they thought they must be left to perish under

---

[d] Job xxix. 16.

them. And though their idleness and extravagance are very inexcusable, and ought by all reasonable methods to be restrained; and they are highly to be blamed for not making some provision against age and supposable disasters, when it is in their power; yet it is not to be desired, that the anxieties of avarice should be added to the natural inconveniences of poverty.

§ 8. *Misdirected indulgences compatible with neglect.*

It is said, that our common fault towards the poor is not harshness, but too great lenity and indulgence. And if allowing them in debauchery, idleness, and open beggary; in drunkenness, profane cursing and swearing in our streets, nay in our houses of correction; if this be lenity, there is doubtless a great deal too much of it. And such lenity towards the poor is very consistent with the most cruel neglects of them, in the extreme misery to which those vices reduce them. Now though this last certainly is not our general fault; yet it cannot be said every one is free from it. For this reason, and that nothing, which has so much as the shadow of an objection against our public charities, may be entirely passed over, you will give me leave to consider a little the supposed case above mentioned, though possibly some may think it unnecessary, that of persons reduced to poverty and distress by their own faults.

Instances of this there certainly are. But it ought to be very distinctly observed, that in judging which are such, we are liable to be mistaken: and more liable to it, in judging to what degree those are faulty, who really are so in some degree.

§ 9. *We expect too much from the poor.*

However, we should always look with mildness upon the behaviour of the poor: and be sure not to expect more from them than can be expected, in a moderate way of considering things. We should be forward, not only to admit and encourage the good deserts of such as do well, but likewise as to those of them who do not, be ever ready to make due allowances for their bad education, or, which is the same, their having had none; for what may be owing to the ill example of their superiors, as well as companions, and for temptations of all kinds. And remember always, that be men's vices what they will, they have not forfeited their claim to relief under necessities, till they have forfeited their lives to justice.

§ 10. *Remedies are not to be withheld from self-sought evils.*

Our heavenly Father is kind to the unthankful and to the evil; and sendeth his rain on the just and on the unjust [e]. And, in imitation of him, our Saviour expressly requires, that our beneficence be promiscuous. But we have moreover the divine example for relieving those distresses which are brought upon persons by their own faults; and this is exactly the case we are considering. Indeed the general dispensation of Christianity is an example of this; for its general design is to save us from our sins, and the punishments which would have been the just consequence of them. But the divine example in the daily course of nature is a more obvious and sensible one. And though the natural miseries which are foreseen to be annexed to a vicious course of life are providentially intended to prevent it, in the same manner as civil penalties are intended to prevent civil crimes; yet those miseries, those natural penalties admit of and receive natural reliefs, no less than any other miseries, which could not have been foreseen or prevented. Charitable providence then, thus manifested in the course of nature, which is the example of our heavenly Father, most evidently leads us to relieve, not only such distresses as were unavoidable, but also such as people by their own faults have brought upon themselves. The case is, that we cannot judge in what degree it was intended they should suffer, by considering what, in the natural course of things, would be the whole bad consequences of their faults, if those consequences were not prevented, when nature has provided means to prevent great part of them. We cannot,

---

[e] Matt. v. 45; Luke vi. 35.

for instance, estimate what degree of present sufferings God has annexed to drunkenness, by considering the diseases which follow from this vice, as they would be if they admitted of no reliefs or remedies; but by considering the remaining misery of those diseases, after the application of such remedies as nature has provided.

§ 11. *The reliefs, like the evils, are providential.*

For as it is certain on the one side, that those diseases are providential corrections of intemperance, it is as certain on the other, that the remedies are providential mitigations of those corrections; and altogether as much providential, when administered by the good hand of charity in the case of our neighbour, as when administered by self-love in our own. Thus the pain, and danger, and other distresses of sickness and poverty remaining, after all the charitable relief which can be procured; and the many uneasy circumstances which cannot but accompany that relief, though distributed with all supposable humanity; these are the natural corrections of idleness and debauchery, supposing these vices brought on those miseries. And very severe corrections they are: and they ought not to be increased by withholding that relief, or by harshness in the distribution of it. Corrections of all kinds, even the most necessary ones, may easily exceed their proper bound: and when they do so, they become mischievous; and mischievous in the measure they exceed it. And the natural corrections which we have been speaking of would be excessive, if the natural mitigations provided for them were not administered.

§ 12. *The religious organisation in infirmaries.*

Then persons who are so scrupulously apprehensive of every thing which can possibly, in the most indirect manner, encourage idleness and vice, (which, by the way, any thing may accidentally do,) ought to turn their thoughts to the moral and religious tendency of infirmaries. The religious manner in which they are carried on has itself a direct tendency to bring the subject of religion into the consideration of those whom they relieve; and, in some degree, to recommend it to their love and practice, as it is productive of so much good to them, as restored ease and health, and a capacity of resuming their several employments. It is to virtue and religion, they may mildly be admonished, that they are indebted for their relief. And this, amongst other admonitions of their spiritual guide, and the quiet and order of their house, out of the way of bad examples, together with a regular course of devotion, which it were greatly to be wished might be daily; these means, it is to be hoped, with the common grace of God, may enforce deeply upon their consciences those serious considerations, to which a state of affliction naturally renders the mind attentive, and that they will return, as from a religious retreat, to their several employments in the world, with lasting impressions of piety in their hearts. By such united advantages, which these poor creatures can in no sort have any other way, very remarkable reformations have been wrought.

§ 13. *Room remains for improvement.*

Persons of the strictest characters therefore would give a more satisfactory proof, not to the world, but to their own consciences, of their desire to suppress vice and idleness, by setting themselves to cultivate the religious part of the institution of infirmaries, which, I think, would admit of great improvements; than by allowing themselves to talk in a manner which tends to discountenance either the institution itself, or any particular branch of it.

§ 14. *Some cavil at these appeals.*

Admitting then the usefulness and necessity of these kinds of charity, which indeed cannot be denied; *yet every thing has its bounds.* And, in the spirit of severity before mentioned, it is imagined, that *people are enough disposed,* such, it seems, is the present turn, *to contribute largely to them.* And some, whether from dislike of the charities themselves, or from mere profligateness, think *these formal recommendations of them at church every year might very well be spared.*

§ 15. *A stated order is desirable: and charity should be associated with devotion.*

But surely it is desirable, that a customary way should be kept open for removing prejudices as they may arise against these institutions; for rectifying any misrepresentations which may, at any time, be made of them; and informing the public of any new emergencies; as well as for repeatedly enforcing the known obligations of charity, and the excellency of this particular kind of it. Then sermons, you know, amongst protestants, always of course accompany these more solemn appearances in the house of God: nor will these latter be kept up without the other. Now public devotions should ever attend and consecrate public charities. And it would be a sad presage of the decay of these charities, if ever they should cease to be professedly carried on in the fear of God, and upon the principles of religion. It may be added, that real charitable persons will approve of these frequent exhortations to charity, even though they should be conscious that they do not themselves stand in need of them, upon account of such as do. And such can possibly have no right to complain of being too often admonished of their duty, till they are pleased to practise it. It is true indeed, we have the satisfaction of seeing a spirit of beneficence prevail, in a very commendable degree, amongst all ranks of people, and in a very distinguished manner in some persons amongst the highest; yet it is evident, too many of all ranks are very deficient in it, who are of great ability, and of whom much might be expected. Though every thing therefore were done in behalf of the poor which is wanted, yet these persons ought repeatedly to be told, how highly blamable they are for letting it be done without them; and done by persons, of whom great numbers must have much less ability than they.

§ 16. *In estimating gifts and needs, givers are as partial as receivers.*

But whoever can really think, that the necessities of the disabled poor are sufficiently provided for already, must be strangely prejudiced. If one were to send you to them themselves to be better informed, you would readily answer, that their demands would be very extravagant; that persons are not to be their own judges in claims of justice, much less in those of charity. You then, I am speaking to the hard people above mentioned, you are to judge, what provision is to be made for the necessitous, so far as it depends upon your contributions. But ought you not to remember that you are interested, that you are parties in the affair as well as they? For is not the giver as really so as the receiver? And as there is danger that the receiver will err one way, is there not danger that the giver may err the other? since it is not matter of arbitrary choice, which has no rule, but matter of real equity, to be considered as in the presence of God, what provision shall be made for the poor? And therefore, though you are yourselves the only judges, what you will do in their behalf, for the case admits no other; yet let me tell you, you will not be impartial, you will not be equitable judges, until you have guarded against the influence which interest is apt to have upon your judgment, and cultivated within you the spirit of charity to balance it. Then you will see the various remaining necessities which call for relief. But that there are many such must be evident at first sight to the most careless observer, were it only from hence, that both this and the other hospitals are often obliged to reject poor objects which offer, even for want of room, or wards to contain them.

§ 17. *Much beneficence exists, and much good is done.* .

Notwithstanding many persons have need of these admonitions, yet there is a good spirit of beneficence, as I observed, pretty generally prevailing. And I must congratulate you upon the great success it has given to the particular good work before us; great, I think, beyond all example for the time it has subsisted. Nor would it be unsuitable to the present occasion to recount the particulars of this success. For the necessary accommodations which have been provided, and the numbers who

have been relieved, in so short a time, cannot but give
high reputation to the London Infirmary. And the reputation of any particular charity, like credit in trade, is so
much real advantage, without the inconveniences to which
that is sometimes liable. It will bring in contributions
for its support; and men of character, as they shall be
wanted, to assist in the management of it; men of skill
in the professions, men of conduct in business, to perpetuate,
improve, and bring it to perfection. So that you, the
contributors to this charity, and more especially those of
you by whose immediate care and economy it is in so high
repute, are encouraged to go on with *your labour of love*[f],
not only by the present good, which you see is here done,
but likewise by the prospect of what will probably be done,
by your means, in future times, when this infirmary shall
become, as I hope it will, no less renowned than the city
in which it is established.

§ 18. *Yet the stint of supply shocks humanity.*

But to see how far it is from being yet complete, for want
of contributions, one need only look upon the settled rules
of the house for *admission of patients*. See there the
limitations which necessity prescribes, as to the persons to
be admitted. Read but that one order, though others
might be mentioned, that *none who are judged to be in an
asthmatic, consumptive, or dying condition be admitted on any
account whatsoever*. Harsh as these words sound, they proceed
out of the mouth of Charity herself. Charity pronounces
it to be better, that poor creatures, who might receive much
ease and relief, should be denied it, if their case does not
admit of recovery, rather than that others, whose case does
admit of it, be left to perish. But it shocks humanity to
hear such an alternative mentioned; and to think, that
there should be a necessity, as there is at present, for such
restrictions, in one of the most beneficent and best managed
schemes in the world. May more numerous or larger contributions, at length, open a door to such as these; that

---

[f] Heb. vi. 10.

what renders their case in the highest degree compassionable, their languishing under incurable diseases, may no longer exclude them from the house of mercy!

§ 19. *Some through neglect want means to be bountiful.*

But besides the persons to whom I have been now more particularly speaking, there are others, who do not cast about for excuses for not contributing to the relief of the necessitous; perhaps are rather disposed to relieve them; who yet are not so careful as they ought to be, to put themselves into a capacity of doing it. For we are as really accountable for not doing the good which we might have in our power to do, if we would manage our affairs with prudence, as we are for not doing the good which is in our power now at present. And hence arise the obligations of economy upon people in the highest, as well as in the lower stations of life, in order to enable themselves to do that good, which, without economy, both of them must be incapable of; even though without it they could answer the strict demands of justice; which yet we find neither of them can. *A good man showeth favour, and lendeth; and,* to enable himself to do so, *he will guide his affairs with discretion*[g]. For want of this, many a one has reduced his family to the necessity of asking relief from those public charities, to which he might have left them in a condition of largely contributing.

§ 20. *How care for our affairs may be charity.*

As economy is the duty of all persons, without exception, frugality and diligence are duties which particularly belong to the middle as well as lower ranks of men; and more particularly still to persons in trade and commerce, whatever their fortunes be. For trade and commerce cannot otherwise be carried on, but is plainly inconsistent with idleness and profusion: though indeed were it only from regard to

---

[g] Psalm cxii. 5.

propriety, and to avoid being absurd, every one should conform his behaviour to what his situation in life requires, without which the order of society must be broken in upon. And considering how inherited riches and a life of leisure are often employed, the generality of mankind have cause to be thankful that their station exempts them from so great temptations; that it engages them in a sober care of their expenses, and in a course of application to business: especially as these virtues, moreover, tend to give them, what is an excellent groundwork for all others, a stayed equality of temper and command of their passions. But when a man is diligent and frugal, in order to have it in his power to do good; when he is more industrious, or more sparing perhaps than his circumstances necessarily require, that he may *have to give to him that needeth* [h]; when he *labours in order to support the weak* [i]; such care of his affairs is itself charity, and the actual beneficence which it enables him to practise is additional charity.

§ 21. *These obligations not adequately recognised.*

You will easily see why I insist thus upon these things, because I would particularly recommend the good work before us to all ranks of people in this great city. And I think I have reason to do so, from the consideration, that it very particularly belongs to them to promote it. The gospel indeed teaches us to look upon every one in distress as our neighbour, yet neighbourhood in the literal sense, and likewise several other circumstances, are providential recommendations of such and such charities, and excitements to them; without which the necessitous would suffer much more than they do at present. For our general disposition to beneficence would not be sufficiently directed, and in other respects would be very ineffectual, if it were not called forth into action by some or other of those providential circumstances, which form particular relations between the rich and the poor, and are of course regarded by every one

---

[h] Ephes. iv. 28.   [i] Acts xx. 35.

in some degree. But though many persons among you, both in the way of contributions, and in other ways no less useful, have done even more than was to be expected, yet I must be allowed to say, that I do not think the relation the inhabitants of this city bear to the persons for whom our infirmary was principally designed, is sufficiently attended to by the generality; which may be owing to its late establishment.

§ 22. *The patients are really our servants.*

It is, you know, designed principally for *diseased manufacturers, seamen in merchant-service, and their wives and children:* and *poor manufacturers* comprehend all who are employed in any labour whatever belonging to trade and commerce. The description of these objects shows their relation, and a very near one it is, to you, my neighbours, the inhabitants of this city. If any of your domestic servants were disabled by sickness, there is none of you but would think himself bound to do somewhat for their relief. Now these seamen and manufacturers are employed in your immediate business. They are servants of merchants, and other principal traders; as much your servants as if they lived under your roof: though by their not doing so, the relation is less in sight. And supposing they do not all depend upon traders of lower rank in exactly the same manner, yet many of them do; and they have all connections with you, which give them a claim to your charity preferably to strangers. They are indeed servants of the public; and so are all industrious poor people as well as they. But that does not hinder the latter from being more immediately yours. And as their being servants to the public is a general recommendation of this charity to all other persons, so their being more immediately yours is, surely, a particular recommendation of it to you. Notwithstanding all this, I will not take upon me to say, that every one of you is blamable who does not contribute to your infirmary, for yours it is in a peculiar sense; but I will say, that those of you who do are highly commendable. I will say more, that you promote a very excellent work, which your particular station is a providential call upon you to promote. And there can be no stronger reason than this for doing any thing, except the one reason, that it would be criminal to omit it.

§ 23. *All bound to contribute; more or less.*

These considerations, methinks, might induce every trader of higher rank in this city to become a subscriber to the infirmary which is named from it; and others of you to contribute somewhat yearly to it, in the way in which smaller contributions are given. This would be a most proper offering out of your increase to him, whose *blessing maketh rich* [k]. Let it be more or less, *Every man according as he purposeth in his heart; not grudgingly, or of necessity: for God loveth a cheerful giver* [l].

The large benefactions of some persons of ability may be necessary in the first establishment of a public charity, and are greatly useful afterwards in maintaining it: but the expenses of this before us, in the extent and degree of perfection to which one would hope it might be brought, cannot be effectually supported, any more than the expenses of civil government, without the contribution of great numbers. You have already the assistance of persons of highest rank and fortune, of which the list of our governors, and the present appearance, are illustrious examples. And their assistance would be far from lessening by a general contribution to it amongst yourselves. On the contrary, the general contribution to it amongst yourselves, which I have been proposing, would give it still higher repute, and more invite such persons to continue their assistance, and accept the honour of being in its direction. For the greatest persons receive honour from taking the direction of a good work, as they likewise give honour to it. And by these concurrent endeavours, our infirmary might at length be brought to answer, in some competent measure, to the occasions of our city.

---

[k] Prov. x. 22.   [l] 2 Cor. ix. 7.

§ 24. *Here lies the best prerogative of riches.*

Blessed are they who employ their riches in promoting so excellent a design. The temporal advantages of them are far from coming up, in enjoyment, to what they promise at a distance. But the distinguished privilege, the prerogative of riches, is, that they increase our power of doing good. This is their proper use. In proportion as men make this use of them, they imitate Almighty God; and cooperate together with him in promoting the happiness of the world; and may expect the most favourable judgment, which their case will admit of, at the last day, upon the general, repeated maxim of the gospel, that we shall then be treated ourselves as we now treat others. They have moreover the prayers of all good men, those of them particularly whom they have befriended; and, by such exercise of charity, they improve within themselves the temper of it, which is the very temper of heaven. Consider next the peculiar force with which this branch of charity, almsgiving, is recommended to us in these words, *He that hath pity upon the poor lendeth unto the Lord* [m] : and in these of our Saviour, *Verily I say unto you, Inasmuch as ye have done it,* relieved the sick and needy, *unto one of the least of these my brethren, ye have done it unto me* [n]. Beware you do not explain away these passages of scripture, under the notion, that they have been made to serve superstitious purposes: but ponder them fairly in your heart; and you will feel them to be of irresistible weight.

§ 25. *We should be stimulated by our sense of sin.*

Lastly, let us remember, in how many instances we have all left undone those things which we ought to have done, and done those things which we ought not to have done. Now whoever has a serious sense of this will most earnestly desire to supply the good, which he was obliged to have done, but has not, and undo the evil which he has done, or neglected to prevent; and when that is impracticable, to make amends, in some other way, for his offences——I can

---

[m] Prov. xix. 17.   [n] Matt. xxv. 40.

mean only to our fellow-creatures. To make amends, in some way or other, to a particular person, against whom we have offended, either by positive injury, or by neglect ; is an express condition of our obtaining forgiveness of God, when it is in our power to make it. And when it is not, surely the next best thing is to make amends to society by fervent charity, in a course of doing good : which riches, as I observed, put very much within our power.

§ 26. *The miserable choice of the dissolute and miserly.*

How unhappy a choice then do those rich men make, who sacrifice all these high prerogatives of their state, to the wretched purposes of dissoluteness and vanity, or to the sordid itch of heaping up, to no purpose at all ; whilst in the mean time they stand charged with the important trust, in which they are thus unfaithful, and of which a strict account remains to be given !

A CHARGE

DELIVERED

TO THE CLERGY

AT THE PRIMARY VISITATION OF THE DIOCESE OF DURHAM, IN THE YEAR MDCCLI.

—※—

§ 1. *General decay of religion; zeal for negation.*

IT is impossible for me, my brethren, upon our first meeting of this kind, to forbear lamenting with you the general decay of religion in this nation; which is now observed by every one, and has been for some time the complaint of all serious persons [1]. The influence of it is more and more wearing out of the minds of men, even of those who do not pretend to enter into speculations upon the subject: but the number of those who do, and who profess themselves unbelievers, increases, and with their numbers their zeal. Zeal, it is natural to ask—for what? Why truly *for* nothing, but *against* every thing that is good and sacred amongst us.

§ 2. *Is predicted, and is the mark of the age.*

Indeed, whatever efforts are made against our religion, no Christian can possibly despair of it. For he, who has

---

[1] Butler here repeats, in 1751, what he had written in 1736. In the Advertisement to the *Analogy* he says that many persons take it for granted that the falsehood of the Christian religion is now 'an agreed point among all people of discernment.'

all power in heaven and earth, has promised, that *he will be with us to the end of the world.* Nor can the present decline of it be any stumbling-block to such as are considerate; since he himself has so strongly expressed what is as remarkably predicted in other passages of scripture, the great defection from his religion which should be in the latter days, by that prophetic question, *When the Son of man cometh, shall he find faith upon the earth?* How near this time is, God only knows; but this kind of scripture signs of it is too apparent. For as different ages have been distinguished by different sorts of particular errors and vices, the deplorable distinction of ours is an avowed scorn of religion in some, and a growing disregard to it in the generality.

§ 3. *Religion binds us to treat negationists with 'meekness of wisdom.'*

As to the professed enemies of religion, I know not how often they may come in your way; but often enough, I fear, in the way of some at least amongst you, to require consideration, what is the proper behaviour towards them. One would, to be sure, avoid great familiarities with these persons; especially if they affect to be licentious and profane in their common talk. Yet if you fall into their company, treat them with the regards which belong to their rank; for so we must people who are vicious in any other respect. We should study what St. James[1], with wonderful elegance and expressiveness, calls *meekness of wisdom*, in our behaviour towards all men; but more especially towards these men; not so much as being what we owe to them, but to ourselves and our religion; that we may *adorn the doctrine of God our Saviour*, in our carriage towards those who labour to vilify it.

§ 4. *Be not too ready to make defence.*

For discourse with them; the caution commonly given, not to attempt answering objections which we have not

---

[1] In ch. iii. 13.

considered, is certainly just. Nor need any one in a particular case be ashamed frankly to acknowledge his ignorance, provided it be not general. And though it were, to talk of what he is not acquainted with, is a dangerous method of endeavouring to conceal it. But a considerate person, however qualified he be to defend his religion, and answer the objections he hears made against it, may sometimes see cause to decline that office. Sceptical and profane men are extremely apt to bring up this subject at meetings of entertainment, and such as are of the freer sort: innocent ones I mean, otherwise I should not suppose you would be present at them.

§ 5. *Frequent and light disputations dangerous.*

Now religion is by far too serious a matter to be the hackney subject upon these occasions. And by preventing its being made so, you will better secure the reverence which is due to it, than by entering into its defence. Every one observes, that men's having examples of vice often before their eyes, familiarizes it to the mind, and has a tendency to take off that just abhorrence of it which the innocent at first felt, even though it should not alter their *judgment* of vice, or make them really *believe* it to be less evil or dangerous. In like manner, the hearing religion often disputed about in light familiar conversation has a tendency to lessen that sacred regard to it, which a good man would endeavour always to keep up, both in himself and others. But this is not all: people are too apt inconsiderately to take for granted, that things are really questionable, because they hear them often disputed. This indeed is so far from being a consequence, that we know demonstrated truths have been disputed, and even matters of fact, the objects of our senses.

§ 6. *What regard would be due to religion, even were it doubtful.*

But were it a consequence, were the evidence of religion no more than doubtful, then it ought not to be concluded false any more than true, nor denied any more than affirmed; for suspense would be the reasonable state of mind with regard to it. And then it ought in all reason, considering its infinite importance, to have nearly the same influence upon practice, as if it were thoroughly believed. For would it not be madness for a man to forsake a safe road, and prefer to it one in which he acknowledges there is an even chance he should lose his life, though there were an even chance likewise of his getting safe through it? Yet there are people absurd enough, to take the supposed doubtfulness of religion for the same thing as a proof of its falsehood, after they have concluded it doubtful from hearing it often called in question. This shows how infinitely unreasonable sceptical men are, with regard to religion, and that they really lay aside their reason upon this subject as much as the most extravagant enthusiasts.

§ 7. *Cavilling always easier than clearing.*

But further, cavilling and objecting upon any subject is much easier than clearing up difficulties: and this last part will always be put upon the defenders of religion. Now a man may be fully convinced of the truth of a matter, and upon the strongest reasons, and yet not be able to answer all the difficulties which may be raised upon it.

§ 8. *The evidences too complex to present, or to draw attention, in cursory conversation.*

Then again, the general evidence of religion is complex and various[1]. It consists of a long series of things, one preparatory to and confirming another, from the very beginning of the world to the present time. And it is easy to see how impossible it must be, in a cursory conversation, to unite all this into one argument, and represent it as it ought; and, could it be done, how utterly indisposed people would be to attend to it—I say in a cursory conversation: whereas unconnected objections are thrown out in a few words, and are easily apprehended,

---

[1] See *Analogy*, II. vii. 30, 48, 59, 62.

without more attention than is usual in common talk. So that, notwithstanding we have the best cause in the world, and though a man were very capable of defending it, yet I know not why he should be forward to undertake it upon so great a disadvantage, and to so little good effect, as it must be done amidst the gaiety and carelessness of common conversation.

§ 9. *Use of protests; of emphatic silence on occasion.*

But then it will be necessary to be very particularly upon your guard, that you may not *seem*, by way of compliance, to join in with any levity of discourse respecting religion. Nor would one let any pretended argument against it pass entirely without notice; nor any gross ribaldry upon it, without expressing our thorough disapprobation. This last may sometimes be done by silence: for silence sometimes is very expressive; as was that of our blessed Saviour before the Sanhedrim and before Pilate. Or it may be done by observing mildly, that religion deserves another sort of treatment, or a more thorough consideration, than such a time, or such circumstances admit. However, as it is absolutely necessary, that we take care, by diligent reading and study, to be always prepared, to be *ready always to give an answer to every man that asketh a reason of the hope that is in us;* so there may be occasions when it will highly become us to do it. And then we must take care to do it in the spirit which the apostle requires, *with meekness and fear*[a]: *meekness* towards those who give occasions for entering into the defence of our religion; and with *fear*, not of them, but of God; with that reverential fear, which the nature of religion requires, and which is so far from being inconsistent with, that it will inspire proper courage towards men.

§ 10. *Pleas for reserve are reasonable.*

Now this reverential fear will lead us to insist strongly upon the infinite greatness of God's scheme of government,

---

[a] 1 Pet. iii. 15.

both in extent and duration, together with the wise connection of its parts, and the impossibility of accounting fully for the several parts, without seeing the whole plan of Providence to which they relate; which is beyond the utmost stretch of our understanding. And to all this must be added the necessary deficiency of human language, when things divine are the subject of it. These observations are a proper full answer to many objections, and very material with regard to all.

§ 11. *Dealing with the people the main matter; sermons should be affirmative, not polemical.*

But your standing business, and which requires constant attention, is with the body of the people; to revive in them the spirit of religion, which is so much declining. And it may seem, that whatever reason there be for caution as to entering into an argumentative defence of religion *in common conversation*, yet that it is necessary to do this *from the pulpit*, in order to guard the people against being corrupted, however in some places. But then surely it should be done in a manner as little controversial as possible. For though such as are capable of seeing the force of objections are capable also of seeing the force of the answers which are given to them; yet the truth is, the people will not competently attend to either. But it is easy to see which they will attend to most. And to hear religion treated of as what many deny, and which has much said against it as well as for it; this cannot but have a tendency to give them ill impressions at any time; and seems particularly improper for all persons at a time of devotion; even for such as are arrived at the most settled state of piety: I say at a time of devotion, when we are assembled to yield ourselves up to the full influence of the divine presence, and to call forth into actual exercise every pious affection of heart. For it is to be repeated, that the heart and course of affections may be disturbed when there is no alteration of judgment. Now the evidence of religion may be laid before men without any air of controversy. The proof of the being of God, from final causes, or the design and wisdom which appears in every part of nature; together with the law of virtue written upon our hearts: the proof of Christianity from miracles, and the accomplishment of prophecies; and the confirmation which the natural and civil history of the world give to the scripture account of things: these evidences of religion might properly be insisted on, in a way to affect and influence the heart, though there were no professed unbelievers in the world; and therefore may be insisted on, without taking much notice that there are such. And even their particular objections may be obviated without a formal mention of them. Besides, as to religion in general, it is a practical thing, and no otherwise a matter of speculation, than common prudence in the management of our worldly affairs is so. And if one were endeavouring to bring a plain man to be more careful with regard to this last, it would be thought a strange method of doing it, to perplex him with stating formally the several objections which men of gaiety or speculation have made against prudence, and the advantages which they pleasantly tell us folly has over it; though one could answer those objections ever so fully.

§ 12. *To make religion a substantive power, form is not sufficient; but is essential.*

Nor does the want of religion in the generality of the common people appear owing to a speculative disbelief or denial of it, but chiefly to thoughtlessness and the common temptations of life. Your chief business therefore is to endeavour to beget a practical sense of it upon their hearts, as what they acknowledge their belief of, and profess they ought to conform themselves to. And this is to be done by keeping up, as we are able, the form and face of religion with decency and reverence, and in such a degree as to bring the thoughts of religion often to their minds; and then endeavouring to make this form more and more subservient to promote the reality and power of it. The form of religion may indeed be where there is little of the thing itself; but the thing itself cannot be preserved amongst mankind without the form. And this form frequently occurring in some instance or other of it will be a frequent admonition to bad men to repent, and to good men to grow better; and also be the [1] means of their doing so.

§ 13. *Effect of observances abroad; Mahometan, and Latin.*

That which men have accounted religion in the several countries of the world, generally speaking, has had a great and conspicuous part in all public appearances, and the face of it been kept up with great reverence throughout all ranks, from the highest to the lowest; not only upon occasional solemnities, but also in the daily course of behaviour. In the heathen world, their superstition was the chief subject of statuary, sculpture, painting, and poetry. It mixed itself with business, civil forms, diversions, domestic entertainments, and every part of common life. The Mahometans are obliged to short devotions five times between morning and evening. In Roman-catholic countries, people cannot pass a day without having religion recalled to their thoughts, by some or other memorial of it; by some ceremony or public religious form occurring in their way: besides their frequent holydays, the short prayers they are daily called to, and the occasional devotions enjoined by confessors. By these means their superstition sinks deep into the minds of the people, and their religion also into the minds of such among them as are serious and well-disposed.

14. *Our reformers reduced these to a minimum; now largely neglected.*

Our reformers, considering that some of these observances were in themselves wrong and superstitious, and others of them made subservient to the purposes of superstition, abolished them, reduced the form of religion to great simplicity, and enjoined no more particular rules, nor left any thing more of what was external in religion, than was in a manner necessary to preserve a sense of religion itself upon the minds of the people. But a great part of this is

---

[1] 'The' seems here no more than equivalent to 'a.'

neglected by the generality amongst us; for instance, the service of the church, not only upon common days, but also upon saints' days: and several other things might be mentioned. Thus they have no customary admonition, no public call to recollect the thoughts of God and religion from one Sunday to another.

§ 15. *How Moses commanded external religion:*

It was far otherwise under the law. *These words,* says Moses to the children of Israel, *which I command thee, shall be in thine heart: and thou shalt teach them diligently unto thy children, and shalt talk of them when thou sittest in thine house, and when thou walkest by the way, and when thou liest down, and when thou risest up*[b]. And as they were commanded this, so it is obvious how much the constitution of that law was adapted to effect it, and keep religion ever in view. And without somewhat of this nature, piety will grow languid even among the better sort of men; and the worst will go on quietly in an abandoned course, with fewer interruptions from within than they would have, were religious reflections forced oftener upon their minds, and consequently with less probability of their amendment.

§ 16. *Which has often been in excess.*

Indeed in most ages of the church, the care of reasonable men has been, as there has been for the most part occasion, to draw the people off from laying too great weight upon external things; upon formal acts of piety. But the state of matters is quite changed now with us. These things are neglected to a degree, which is, and cannot but be attended with a decay of all that is good. It is highly seasonable now to instruct the people in the importance of external religion.

§ 17. *Regard to be paid to fabrics: mainly a lay duty; except the chancels.*

And doubtless under this head must come into consideration a proper regard to the structures which are consecrated

---

[b] Deut. vi. 6, 7.

to the service of God. In the present turn of the age, one may observe a wonderful frugality in every thing which has respect to religion, and extravagance in every thing else. But amidst the appearances of opulence and improvement in all common things, which are now seen in most places, it would be hard to find a reason why these monuments of ancient piety should not be preserved in their original beauty and magnificence. But in the least opulent places they must be preserved in becoming repair; and every thing relating to the divine service be, however, decent and clean; otherwise we shall vilify the face of religion whilst we keep it up. All this is indeed principally the duty of others. Yours is to press strongly upon them what is their duty in this respect, and admonish them of it often, if they are negligent.

But then you must be sure to take care and not neglect that part of the sacred fabric which belongs to you to maintain in repair and decency. Such neglect would be great impiety in you, and of most pernicious example to others. Nor could you, with any success, or any propriety, urge upon them their duty in a regard in which you yourselves should be openly neglectful of it.

§ 18. *Many churches threatened with ruin.*

Bishop Fleetwood has observed [c], that *unless the good public spirit of building, repairing, and adorning churches prevails a great deal more among us, and be more encouraged, an hundred years will bring to the ground an huge number of our churches.* This excellent prelate made this observation forty years ago: and no one, I believe, will imagine, that the good spirit he has recommended prevails more at present than it did then.

§ 19. *Even more regard due to services.*

But if these appendages of the divine service are to be regarded, doubtless the divine service itself is more to be regarded; and the conscientious attendance upon it ought

---

[c] Charge to the Clergy of St. Asaph, 1710.

often to be inculcated upon the people, as a plain precept of the gospel, as the means of grace, and what has peculiar promises annexed to it. But external acts of piety and devotion, and the frequent returns of them, are, moreover, necessary to keep up a sense of religion, which the affairs of the world will otherwise wear out of men's hearts. And the frequent returns, whether of public devotions, or of any thing else, to introduce religion into men's serious thoughts, will have an influence upon them, in proportion as they are susceptible of religion, and not given over to a reprobate mind. For this reason, besides others, the service of the church ought to be celebrated as often as you can have a congregation to attend it.

§ 20. *Weekly service insufficient. Advises prayer:* (a) *family,* (b) *secret,* (c) *morning and evening,* (d) *at set hours,* (e) *grace at meals.*

But since the body of the people, especially in country places, cannot be brought to attend it oftener than one day in a week ; and since this is in no sort enough to keep up in them a due sense of religion ; it were greatly to be wished they could be persuaded to any thing which might, in some measure, supply the want of more frequent public devotions, or serve the like purposes. Family prayers, regularly kept up in every house, would have a great and good effect.

Secret prayer, as expressly as it is commanded by our Saviour, and as evidently as it is implied in the notion of piety, will yet, I fear, be grievously forgotten by the generality, till they can be brought to fix for themselves certain times of the day for it ; since this is not done to their hands, as it was in the Jewish church by custom or authority. Indeed custom, as well as the manifest propriety of the thing, and examples of good men in scripture, justify us in insisting, that none omit their prayers morning or evening, who have not thrown off all regards to piety. But secret prayer comprehends not only devotions before men begin and after they have ended the business of the day, but such also as may be performed while they are employed in it, or even in company. And

truly, if, besides our more set devotions, morning and
evening, all of us would fix upon certain times of the
day, so that the return of the hour should remind us,
to say short prayers, or exercise our thoughts in a way
equivalent to this; perhaps there are few persons in so
high and habitual a state of piety, as not to find the benefit
of it. If it took up no more than a minute or two, or even
less time than that, it would serve the end I am proposing;
it would be a recollection, that we are in the divine presence,
and contribute to our *being in the fear of the Lord all the
day long.*

A duty of the like kind, and serving to the same purpose,
is the particular acknowledgment of God when we are
partaking of his bounty at our meals. The neglect of
this is said to have been scandalous to a proverb in the
heathen world [d]; but it is without shame laid aside at the
tables of the highest and the lowest rank among us.

§ 21. *Religious teaching of children.*

And as parents should be admonished, and it should be
pressed upon their consciences, to teach their children their
prayers and catechism, it being what they are obliged to
upon all accounts; so it is proper to be mentioned here,
as a means by which they will bring the principles of
Christianity often to their own minds, instead of laying
aside all thoughts of it from week's-end to week's-end.

§ 22. *Particular rules needed specially for the careless.*

General exhortations to piety, abstracted from the particular circumstances of it, are of great use to such as are
already got into a religious course of life; but, such as
are not, though they be touched with them, yet when they
go away from church, they scarce know where to begin, or
how to set about what they are exhorted to. And it is
with respect to religion, as in the common affairs of life,

---

[d] Cudworth on the Lord's Supper, p. 8. Casaub. in Athenaeum,
l. i. c. xi. p. 22. Duport. Prael. in Theophrastum, ed. Needham, c.
ix. p. 335, &c.

in which many things of great consequence intended, are yet never done at all, because they may be done at any time, and in any manner; which would not be, were some determinate time and manner voluntarily fixed upon for the doing of them. Particular rules and directions then concerning the times and circumstances of performing acknowledged duties, bring religion nearer to practice; and such as are really proper, and cannot well be mistaken, and are easily observed.—Such particular rules in religion, prudently recommended, would have an influence upon the people.

§ 23. *Promote the form; but infuse holy life into it.*

All this indeed may be called form; as every thing external in religion may be merely so. And therefore whilst we endeavour, in these and other like instances, to keep up the *form of godliness*[e] amongst those who are our care, and over whom we have any influence, we must endeavour also that this form be made more and more subservient to promote the *power* of it[e]. Admonish them to take heed that they mean what they say in their prayers, that their thoughts and intentions go along with their words, that they really in their hearts exert and exercise before God the affections they express with their mouth. Teach them, not that external religion is nothing, for this is not true in any sense; it being scarce possible, but that it will lay some sort of restraint upon a man's morals; and it is moreover of good effect with respect to the world about him. But teach them that regard to one duty will in no sort atone for the neglect of any other. Endeavour to raise in their hearts such a sense of God as shall be an habitual, ready principle of reverence, love, gratitude, hope, trust, resignation, and obedience. Exhort them to make use of every circumstance, which brings the subject of religion at all before them; to turn their hearts habitually to him; to recollect seriously the thoughts of his presence *in whom they live and move and have their being*, and by a short act of their

---

[e] 2 Tim. iii. 5.

mind devote themselves to his service.—If, for instance, persons would accustom themselves to be thus admonished by the very sight of a church, could it be called superstition? Enforce upon them the necessity of making religion their principal concern, as what is the express condition of the gospel covenant, and what the very nature of the thing requires. Explain to them the terms of that covenant of mercy, founded in the incarnation, sacrifice, and intercession of Christ, together with the promised assistance of the Holy Ghost, not to supersede our own endeavours, but to render them effectual.

§ 24. *Improve all occasions: the great festivals; incidental solemnities; private intercourse; crises of life.*

The greater festivals of the church, being instituted for commemorating the several parts of the gospel history, of course lead you to explain these its several doctrines, and show the Christian practice which arises out of them. And the more occasional solemnities of religion, as well as these festivals, will often afford you the fairest opportunities of enforcing all these things in familiar conversation. Indeed all *affectation* of talking piously is quite nauseous: and though there be nothing of this, yet men will easily be disgusted at the too great frequency or length of these occasional admonitions. But a word of God and religion dropped sometimes in conversation, gently, and without any thing severe or forbidding in the manner of it, this is not unacceptable. It leaves an impression, is repeated again by the hearers, and often remembered by plain well-disposed persons longer than one would think. Particular circumstances too, which render men more apt to receive instruction, should be laid hold of to talk seriously to their consciences. For instance, after a man's recovery from a dangerous sickness, how proper is it to advise him to recollect and ever bear in mind, what were his hopes or fears, his wishes and resolutions, when under the apprehension of death; in order to bring him to repentance, or confirm him in a course of piety, according as his life and character has been. So likewise the terrible accidents which often happen from riot and debauchery, and indeed almost every vice, are occasions providentially thrown in your way, to discourse against these vices in common conversation, as well as from the pulpit, upon any such accidents happening in your parish, or in a neighbouring one. Occasions and circumstances of a like kind to some or other of these occur often, and ought, if I may so speak, to be catched at, as opportunities of conveying instruction, both public and private, with great force and advantage.

§ 25. *In public instructions, few appropriate personally.*

Public instruction is absolutely necessary, and can in no sort be dispensed with. But as it is common to all who are present, many persons strangely neglect to appropriate what they hear to themselves, to their own heart and life. Now the only remedy for this in our power is a particular personal application. And a personal application makes a very different impression from a common, general one. It were therefore greatly to be wished, that every man should have the principles of Christianity, and his own particular duty enforced upon his conscience, in a manner suited to his capacity, in private.

§ 26. *Stated occasions: confirmation; first communion.*

And besides the occasional opportunities of doing this, some of which have been intimated, there are stated opportunities of doing it. Such, for instance, is confirmation: and the usual age for confirmation is that time of life, from which youth must become more and more their own masters, when they are often leaving their father's house, going out into the wide world and all its numerous temptations; against which they particularly want to be fortified, by having strong and lively impressions of religion made upon their minds. Now the 61st canon expressly requires, that every minister that hath care of souls shall use his best endeavour to prepare and make able as many as he can to be confirmed; which cannot be done as it ought without such personal application to each candidate in particular as I am recommending. Another opportunity for doing this is, when any one of your parishioners signifies his name, as intending for the first time to be partaker of the communion. The rubric requires, that all persons, whenever they intend to receive, shall signify their names beforehand to the minister; which, if it be not insisted upon in all cases, ought absolutely to be insisted upon for the first time. Now this even lays it in your way to discourse with them in private upon the nature and benefits of this sacrament, and enforce upon them the importance and necessity of religion. However I do not mean to put this upon the same foot with catechising youth, and preparing them for confirmation; these being indispensable obligations, and expressly commanded by our canons. This private intercourse with your parishioners preparatory to their first communion, let it, if you please, be considered as a voluntary service to religion on your part, and a voluntary instance of docility on theirs. I will only add as to this practice, that it is regularly kept up by some persons, and particularly by one, whose exemplary behaviour in every part of the pastoral office is enforced upon you by his station of authority and influence in (this part [f] especially) of the diocese.

§ 27. *Allowances to be made: should not be excessive.*

I am very sensible, my brethren, that some of these things in places where they are greatly wanted are impracticable; from the largeness of parishes, suppose. And where there is no impediment of this sort, yet the performance of them will depend upon others, as well as upon you. People cannot be admonished or instructed in private, unless they will permit it. And little will you be able to do in forming the minds of children to a sense of religion, if their parents will not assist you in it; and yet much less, if they will frustrate your endeavours, by their bad example, and giving encouragement to their children to be dissolute. The like is to be said also of your influence

---

[f] The archdeaconry of Northumberland.

in reforming the common people in general, in proportion as their superiors act in like manner to such parents; and whilst they, the lower people I mean, must have such numerous temptations to drunkenness and riot every where placed in their way. And it is cruel usage we often meet with, in being censured for not doing what we cannot do, without, what we cannot have, the concurrence of our censurers. Doubtless very much reproach which now lights upon the clergy, would be found to fall elsewhere, if due allowances were made for things of this kind. But then we, my brethren, must take care and not make more than due allowances for them. If others deal uncharitably with us, we must deal impartially with ourselves, as in a matter of conscience, in determining what good is in our power to do: and not let indolence keep us from setting about what really is in our power; nor any heat of temper create obstacles in the prosecution of it, or render insuperable such as we find, when perhaps gentleness and patience would prevent or overcome them.

§ 28. *Self-devotion obligatory on the clergy,*

Indeed all this diligence to which I have been exhorting you and myself, for God forbid I should not consider myself as included in all the general admonitions you receive from me; all this diligence in these things does indeed suppose, that we *give ourselves wholly to them.* It supposes, not only that we have a real sense of religion upon our own minds, but also, that to promote the practice of it in others is habitually uppermost in our thought and intention, as the business of our lives. And this, my brethren, is the business of our lives, in every sense, and upon every account. It is the general business of all Christians as they have opportunity: it is our particular business. It is so, as we have devoted ourselves to it by the most solemn engagements; as, according to our *Lord's appointment* we *live of the gospel*[g]; and as the preservation and advancement of religion, in such and such districts, are, in some respects, our appropriated trust.

---

[g] 1 Cor. ix. 14.

§ 29. *And self-rewarding.*

By being faithful in the discharge of this our trust, by thus *taking heed to the ministry we have received in the Lord, that we fulfil it*[h], we shall do our part towards reviving a practical sense of religion amongst the people committed to our care. And this will be the securest barrier against the efforts of infidelity; a great source of which plainly is, the endeavour to get rid of religious restraints. But whatever be our success with regard to others, we shall have the approbation of our consciences, and may rest assured, that, as to ourselves at least, *our labour is not in vain in the Lord*[i].

---

[h] Col. iv. 17.   [i] 1 Cor. xv. 58.

APPENDIX

CONTENTS

	PAGE
I. Documents extracted from 'Some Remains (hitherto unpublished) of Joseph Butler, LL.D., sometime Lord Bishop of Durham,' with a Prefatory Note—	
A. B. C. Fragmentary Pieces	355
D. Letter to a Person unknown	358
E. F. Letters to Dr. Clarke	358
G. Prayers of Bishop Butler	361
II. Two Letters from Bishop Butler to the Duke of Newcastle	364
III. A Conversation between Bishop Butler and the Rev. John Wesley; and Letter from Rev. George Whitefield to Bishop Butler	366
IV. A Letter to a Lady concerning Church Property	369
V. A Sermon which has been ascribed to Bishop Butler, with a Prefatory Note	371

APPENDIX

I.

[IN 1853, Bishop (then Mr.) Steere published in London (Rivingtons), chiefly from MSS. in the British Museum, some remains of Bishop Butler never before given to the world. From this brief pamphlet (now extremely rare), kindly lent to me by the Bishop of Oxford, I have extracted all such papers as, apart from any biographical interest, seemed likely to throw any light upon his Works.

I have, however, printed in this Appendix two Letters from Bishop Butler to the Duke of Newcastle, which the authorities of the Museum were good enough to tender to me. They have not been hitherto published. They exhibit, in a marked manner, more than one of the ethical qualities which are so transparently manifested in his Works.]

(A.)

[British Museum, Additional MS. 9815, f. 31; Pamphlet, pp. 7, 8.]

God cannot approve of any thing but what is in itself Right, Fit, Just. We should worship and endeavour to obey him with this Consciousness and Recollection. To endeavour to please a man merely, is a different thing, from endeavouring to please him as a wise and good man, i. e. endeavouring to please him in the particular way of behaving towards him, as we think the Relations we stand in to him, and the Intercourse we have with him require. Almighty God is to be sure infinitely removed from all those human weaknesses which we express by the words captious, apt to take offence, &c. But an unthinking world does not consider what may be absolutely due to Him from all Creatures capable of considering themselves as His Creatures. Recollect the Idea, inadequate as it is, which we have of God, and the Idea of ourselves, and Carelessness with Regard to Him, whether we are to worship Him at all; whether we worship Him in a right manner or conceited Confidence that we do so, will seem to imply unspeakable Presumption: neither do we know what necessary, unalterable Connection there may be, between moral

Right and Happiness, moral Wrong and Misery. Sincerity is doubtless the thing, and not whether we hit the right manner, &c. But a sense of the Imperfection of our Worship, Apprehension that it may, and a Degree of Fear that it is, in some Respects erroneous, may perhaps be a Temper of mind not unbecoming such poor creatures as we are, in our addresses to God. In proportion as we are assured that we are honest and sincere, we may not [?] be satisfied that God cannot be offended with us. But Indifference whether what we do be materially or in the nature of the thing abstracted from our way of considering it, Good and Right,—such Indifference is utterly inconsistent with sincerity. No Person who has just notions of God can be afraid of his Displeasure any further than as he is afraid of his own character, whether it be what it ought. But so far as a man has Reason to fear his own Character so far there must be reason to fear God's Displeasure, or Disapprobation, not from any Doubt of his Perfection and Goodness, but merely from the Belief [in] it. Is it possible that People can be Scepticks in *opinion*, and yet without any Doubtfulness or Sollicitude about their *Actions* and *Behaviour*?

(B.)

[British Museum, Additional MS. 9815, f. 26; Pamphlet, pp. 9, 10.]

What a wonderful Incongruity it is for a man to see the Doubtfulness in which things are involved, and yet be impatient out of Action or vehement in it. Say a man is a Sceptick, and add, what was said of *Brutus quicquid vult valde vult*, and you say, there is the greatest Contrariety between his understanding and his Temper that can be express'd in words.

In general a man ought not to do other Peoples Duty for them: for their Duty was appointed them for their Exercise, and besides, who And some men [*sic*] will do it in case of his Death. ~~Nor has a man any~~ Right to raise in others such a Dependance upon him as that they must be miserable in case of his Death, tho' whilst he lives he answers that Dependance.

Hobbes's Definition of Benevolence, that 'tis the Love of Power is *base* and false. But there is *more* of Truth in it than appears at first sight: the real Benevolence of men being, I think for the most Part, not indeed the single Love of Power, but the Love of Power to be exercised in the way of doing good, which is a different thing from Love to the Good or Happiness of others by whomsoever effected, which last I would call single or simple Benevolence.

How little there is of this in the world may appear by observing how many Persons can bear with great Tranquillity that a Friend or Child should live in misery, who yet cannot bear the Thought of their Death.

Good men surely are not treated in this world as they deserve, yet 'tis seldom, very seldom their Goodness which makes them disliked, even in cases where it may seem to be so. But 'tis some Behaviour or other, which however excusable, perhaps infinitely overbalanced by their virtues, yet is offensive, possibly wrong: however such, it may be, as would pass very well in a man of the world.

(C.)

[British Museum, Additional MS. 9815, f. 29; Pamphlet, pp. 10, 11.]

Shall I not be faithful to God? If He puts a Part upon me to do, shall I neglect or refuse it? A Part to suffer, and shall I say I would not if I could help it? Can words more illsorted, more shocking be put together? And is not the thing express'd by them more so, tho' not express'd in words? What then shall I prefer to the sovereign Good, supream Excellence, absolute Perfection? To whom shall
     Directions
I apply for advice in opposition to infinite wisdom? to whom for Protection against Almighty Power?

Sunday Evening, *June* 13, 1742.

Hunger and thirst after Righteousness till filled with it by being made partaker of the Divine nature.

Ad te levo oculos meos, qui habitas in coelis. Sicut oculi servorum *intenti sunt* ad manum dominorum suorum, sicut oculi ancillae ad manum dominae suae, ita oculi nostri ad Deum nostrum, donec miscreantur nostri.

As I ~~would subject~~[1] all my Passions and affections to my Reason such as it is, so in consideration of the Fallibility and infinite Deficiencies of this my Reason I would subject it to God, that he may guide and succour it.

Our Wants as Creatures, our Demerits as Sinners. That I may have a due sense of the Hand of God in every thing, and then put myself into his Hand to lead me through whatever Ways he shall think fit, either to add to my Burden or lighten it, or wholly discharge me of it.

Be more afraid of myself than of the world.

To discern the Hand of God in every thing and have a due sense of it.

Instead of deluding oneself in imagining one should behave well in such circumstances other than those in which one is placed, to take care and be faithful and behave well in those one is placed in,

---

[1] Two other words written over, but erased and now illegible.

that God would please to make my way plain before my face and deliver me from offendiculum of scruplousness or if not assist me to act the right Part under it.

(D.)

Letter, from a copy formerly belonging to Dr. Birch, and now in the Library of the British Museum.

[British Museum, Additional MS. 4370; Pamphlet, pp. 12, 13.]

Rev. D^r

Twas but last night I received your letter from Gloucester, having left that place three weeks since. It revived in my mind some very melancholy thoughts I had upon my being obliged to quit those studies that had a direct tendency to divinity; that being what I should choose for the business of my life, it being I think of all other studies the most suitable to a reasonable nature. I say my being obliged, for there is every encouragement (whether one regards interest or usefulness) nowadays for any to enter that profession, who has not got a way of commanding his assent to received opinions without examination.

I had some thoughts, Sir, of paying you my acknowledgments in person for that surprising air of candour and affability with which you have treated me in the Letters that have passed between us. But really I could not put on so bold a face as to intrude into a gentleman's company with no other excuse but that of having received an obligation from him. I have not the least prospect of ever being in a capacity of giving any more than a verbal declaration of my gratitude: so I hope you'll accept that, and believe it's with the utmost sincerity I subscribe myself, Sir,

Your most obliged, most obedient humble servant,

J. BUTLER.

HEMLIN'S COFFEEHOUSE,
   Tuesday morning.

(E.)

Letter to Dr. Clarke and Reply.

[Pamphlet, pp. 13–17.]

The original of this Letter, with the answer, which is roughly written on the blank leaf, is I believe now in the library of Oriel College, Oxford. I am indebted for my copy to the kindness of the Rev. J. H. Newman, D.D., formerly of that College.

Rev. Sir,

I had long resisted an Inclination to desire your Thoughts upon the difficulty mentioned in my last, till I considered that the trouble in answering it would be only carrying on the general purpose of your Life, and that I might claim the same right to your Instructions with others; notwithstanding which I should not have mentioned it to you had I not thought (which is natural when one fancies one sees a thing clearly) that I could easily express it with clearness to others. However I should by no means have given you a second trouble upon the subject had I not had your particular leave. I thought proper just to mention these things that you might not suspect me to take advantage from your civility to trouble you with any thing, but only such objections as seem to me of Weight, and which I cannot get rid of any other way. A disposition in our natures to be influenced by right motives is as absolutely necessary to render us moral Agents as a Capacity to discern right motives is. These two are I think quite *distinct* perceptions, the *former* proceeding from a desire inseparable from a Conscious Being of its own happiness, the *latter* being only our Understanding, or Faculty of seeing Truth. Since a *disposition* to be influenced by right motives is a *sine quâ non* to Virtuous Actions, an Indifferency to right motives must *incapacitate* us for Virtuous Actions, or render us in that particular not moral agents. I do indeed think that no Rational Creature is *strictly speaking Indifferent* to Right Motives, but yet there seems to be somewhat which to all intents of the present question is the same, viz. *a stronger disposition to be influenced by contrary or wrong motives*, and this I take to be always the case when any vice is committed. But since it may be said, as you hint, that this stronger disposition to be influenced by Vicious Motives may have been contracted by repeated Acts of Wickedness, we will pitch upon the *first Vicious Action* any one is guilty of. No man would have committed this first Vicious Action if he had not had a *stronger* (at least as strong) *disposition* in him to be influenced by the *motives of the Vicious Action*, than by the *motives of the contrary Virtuous Action*; from whence I infallibly conclude that since every man has committed some first Vice, every man had, *antecedent* to the commission of it a *stronger disposition* to be influenced by the *Vicious* than the *Virtuous* motive. My difficulty upon this is, that a *stronger natural disposition* to be influenced by the Vicious than the Virtuous Motive (which every one has antecedent to his first Vice) seems, to all purposes of the present question, to put the Man in the same condition as though he was *indifferent to the Virtuous Motive*; and since an *indifferency to the Virtuous Motive* would have *incapacitated* a Man from being a *moral Agent* or *contracting guilt*, is not a *stronger disposition* to be influenced by the *Vicious* Motive as great an *Incapacity*? Suppose I have two diversions offered me, *both* of which I could not enjoy, I like both of them, but yet have a *stronger* inclination to one than to the other, I am not indeed strictly *indifferent* to either, because I should be glad to *enjoy both;* but am I not exactly *in the same case, to all intents and purposes of acting* as though I was *absolutely indifferent* to that diversion which I have the *least* inclination to? You suppose Man to be endued naturally with a *disposition to be influenced by Virtuous Motives* and that *this Disposition is a sine quâ non to Virtuous Actions,* both which I fully believe; but then you *omit* to consider the natural Inclination to be influenced by Vicious Motives, which, *whenever a Vice is committed,* is at least *equally strong* with the other, and in the first Vice *is not affected by Habits* but is as *natural,* and as much *out of a man's power* as the other.

I am much obliged to your offer of writing to Mr. Laughton, which I shall very thankfully accept of, but am not certain when I shall go to Cambridge; However I believe it will be about the middle of the next month.

I am, Rev. Sir,
Your most obliged humble servant,
J. BUTLER.

ORIEL, *Oct. the 6th.*

The Answer.

Your objection seems indeed very dexterous, and yet I really think that there is at bottom nothing in it. But of this you are to judge, not from my assertion, but from the reason I shall endeavour to give to it.

I think, then, that a *disposition to be influenced by right motives* being what we call *rationality,* there cannot be on the contrary (properly speaking) any such thing naturally in rational creatures as a *disposition to be influenced by wrong motives.* This can be nothing but mere *perverseness of will;* and whether even that can be said to amount to a disposition to be influenced by wrong motives, *formally,* and as such, may (I think) well be doubted. Men have by nature strong inclinations to certain objects. None of these inclinations are vicious, but vice consists in pursuing the inclination towards any object in certain circumstances, notwithstanding *reason,* or the natural disposition to be influenced by right motives, declares to the man's conscience at the same time (or would do, if he attended to it) that the object ought not to be pursued in those circumstances. Nevertheless, where the man commits the crime, the *natural disposition* was only towards the *object,* not formally towards the doing it upon wrong motives; and generally the very essence of the crime consists in the liberty of the will forcibly overruling the *actual disposition towards being influenced by right motives,* and not at all (as you suppose) in the man's having any *natural disposition to be influenced by wrong motives,* as such.

APPENDIX

(F.)

Letter to Dr. Clarke.

[British Museum, Additional MS. 12,101, f. 13; pp. 17, 18 of Pamphlet.]

Revd Sir,

I had the Honour of your kind Letter yesterday, and must own that I do now see a *Difference* between the nature of *that Disposition which we have to be influenced by virtuous motives, and that contrary Disposition* (or whatever else it may *properly* be called) which is the occasion of our committing *Sin*, and hope in time to get a thorough Insight into this subject by means of those Helps you have been pleased to afford me. I find it necessary to consider such very abstruse Questions at different times, and in different Dispositions; and have found particular use of this method upon the Abstract subject of Necessity, for tho' I did not see the force of your Argument, for the *Unity of the Divine Nature* when I had done writing to you upon that subject yet by frequent considering what you have offered upon it, I am now *fully satisfied* that it is conclusive. I will only just add that I suppose somewhat in my last letter was not clearly expressed, for I did not at all *design* to say that *the Essence of any Crime consisted in the man's having a natural Disposition to be influenced by wrong motives.*

[*Note.*—The rest of the letter relates to his keeping terms at *Cambridge*, and has been scored through.]

(*Signed*) J. Butler.

Oriel Coll. *Oct.* 10, 1717.

Endorsed : To the Rev. Dr. Clarke,
    Rector of St. James's,
      Westminster.

(G.)

PRAYERS.

From a copy in Bishop Butler's handwriting, now in the Library at the British Museum.

[British Museum, Additional MS. 9,815; pp. 20-23 of Pamphlet.]

O Almighty God, Maker and Preserver of the world, Governor and Judge of all creatures, whom Thou hast endued with understanding so as to render them accountable for their actions and capable of being judged for them; we prostrate ourselves as in Thy presence, and worship Thee the Sovereign Lord of all, in Whom we live and move and have our being. The greatness and perfection of Thy Nature is infinitely beyond all possible comprehension, but in proportion to our capacities we would endeavour to have a true conception of Thy Divine Majesty and to live under a just sense and apprehension of it: that we may fear Thee and hope in Thee as we entirely depend on Thee; that we may love Thee as supremely good, and have our wills conformed to Thy will in all righteousness and truth; that we may be thankful to Thee for every thing we enjoy, as the gift of Thine hand, and be patient under every affliction as what Thou sendest or permittest.

We desire to be duly sensible of what we have done amiss, and we solemnly resolve before Thee that for the time to come we will endeavour to obey all Thy commands as they are made known to us.

We are Thy Creatures by Nature; we give up ourselves to be Thy servants voluntarily and by choice, and present ourselves body and soul, a living sacrifice to Thee.

But, O Almighty God, as Thou hast manifested Thyself to the world by Jesus Christ; as Thou hast given Him to be a Propitiation for the sins of it, and the Mediator between God and Man; we lay hold with all humility and thankfulness on so inestimable a Benefit, and come unto Thee according to Thine appointment in His Name, and in the form and manner which He has taught us.

Our Father, &c.

Morning Prayer.

Almighty God, by whose protection we were preserved the night passed, and are here before Thee this morning in health and safety; we dedicate this day, and all the days we live to Thy service; resolving, that we will abstain from all evil, that we will take heed to the thing that is right in all our actions, and endeavour to do our duty in that state of life in which Thy Providence has placed us. We would remind ourselves that we are always, wherever we may go, in Thy presence. We would be always in Thy fear; and we beg the continuance of Thy merciful protection, and that Thou would'st guide and keep us in all our ways, through Jesus Christ our Lord.

Evening Prayer.

Almighty God, whose continued providence ordereth all things both in Heaven and Earth; Who never slumberest nor sleepest; but hast divided the light from the darkness, and made the day for employment and the night for rest to Thy creatures the inhabitants of the earth: we acknowledge with all thankfulness Thy merciful preservation of us this day, by which we are brought in safety to the evening of it. We implore Thy forgiveness of all the offences which we have been guilty of in it, whether in thought, word, or deed; and desire to have a due sense of Thy goodness in keeping us out of the way of those temptations by which we might have fallen into greater sins, and in preserving us from those misfortunes and sad accidents, common to every day, and which must have befallen many others. We humbly commit ourselves to the same good providence this night, that we may sleep in quiet under Thy protection and wake, if it be Thy will, in the morning in renewed life and strength. And we beg assistance of Thy grace to live in such a manner, that when the few days and nights which Thou shalt allot us in this world be passed away we may die in peace and finally obtain the resurrection unto eternal life through Jesus Christ our Lord.

Almighty God whose tender mercies are over all Thy works, Who feedest the fowls of the air and the beasts of the field and hast given unto us all things that pertain unto life and godliness; we desire to have our souls possessed with a due sense of Thy blessings, and to show forth our thankfulness by being kind and compassionate to those who are in distress, and by all those good works which Thou hast appointed us to walk in. And we humbly hope we shall at last experience all Thy goodness to us consummate in that future state, which Thou hast prepared for them that love and fear Thee, through Jesus Christ our Lord.

II.

TWO LETTERS TO THE DUKE OF NEWCASTLE.

The Bishop of Bristol to the Duke of Newcastle.

[British Museum, Additional MS. 32,722, f. 56.]

BRISTOL, 5 *Aug.*, 1750.

MY LORD,

I have this afternoon the Honour of your Grace's letter informing me of my Nomination to the Bishoprick of Durham, which I am sensible is the greatest Instance of Favour I could receive from the King. As I read on your letter, my Lord, my answer to it in my own Thoughts was, to return your Grace my humble Thanks for all your Favours particularly for your kind concurrence and assistances upon this occasion and the obliging satisfaction you take in the success of them. But when I came to the postscript and found a Command accompanying that nomination it gave me greater Disturbance of mind than I think I ever felt. Your Grace will please to remember that when you mentioned this to me near three-quarters of a year agoe, I made not a word of answer, but went on talking of other things, and upon your repeating the mention of it at the same time, just as I was going out of your Dressing Room, I told your Grace it did not admit of an Answer. This my Silence, and this my Reply were owing to my being in so great a surprize at such a thing being asked of me *beforehand* that I durst not trust myself to talk upon the subject. But upon settling within myself what I ought to say, I proposed to wait upon your Grace and let you know that I could not take any Church Promotion upon the condition of any such Promise or Intimation as your Grace seemed to expect.

But before I had time for this I met the Archbishop who began as from you to talk to me of the affair, upon which I desired him to let your Grace know what I had purposed, as I now said, to tell you myself. My words, so far as I can remember were, that my Principles would not permit me to accept of any Promotion upon the condition of making any Promise or raising any Expectation *beforehand* of giving away Preferment. After all this, my Lord, I had not the most distant suspicion but that if his Majesty would nominate me to Durham, your Grace would have permitted the Nomination to come free.

My Lord, the Bishops as well as the inferior Clergy take the Oaths against Simony and as I should think an express Promise of Preferment to a Patron *beforehand* an express Breach of that Oath, and would deny Institution upon it, so I should think a tacit Promise a tacit Breach of it. I am afraid your Grace may think I have already said too much, but as this affair that I am to give Dr. Chapman the first Prebend of Durham, is common Talk at Cambridge, and consequently will be so, if it be not already, wherever I am known, I think myself bound, whatever be the Consequence of my Simplicity and Openness to add that it will be impossible for me to do it consistently with my Character and Honour, since if I should, it would be understood (tho' your Grace and I know the contrary) to be done in consequence of some previous Promise, either express or tacit. I am, my Lord, in great Discomposure of mind upon this affair, and very unfit to write to your Grace. Yet I think it absolutely necessary to return your Grace an *immediate* answer by the King's Messenger, and I must also write to His Majesty.

So I hope your Grace will put a candid construction upon any improper Expressions which may have escaped me. For I can have no Desire (and my present situation is surely a Proof of it) to say any thing or express myself in any manner disagreeable to your Grace, further than what my Principles may have obliged me to.

I am, with the greatest Respect
Your Grace's most obedient, devoted humble Servant
Jo. Bristol.

Your Grace recollects that if a Prebend of D. held by Com^m becomes vacant by my Promotion it of course devolves to the Crown.

The Bishop of Durham to the Duke of Newcastle.

[British Museum, Additional MS. 32,725.]

Hampstead, *Dec. 1st,* 1751.

My Lord,

I shall pay all the Regard to your Grace's Recommendation that, I am persuaded, you yourself will think reasonable. But as I am altogether unacquainted with the character of the Person recommended I must desire a little time to inquire into it; especially as I am inclined to think he is a stranger to your Grace.

I must likewise beg leave to add that Eglinham being a Vicarage I cannot give leave of absence to any one whom I myself shall present to it.

I am, with the greatest Respect,
my Lord,
Your Grace's most obliged, most obedient
and most humble servant.
Jo. Duresme.

III.

Conversation of the Rev. John Wesley with the Bishop of Bristol in 1739.

[Extracted from Vol. xiii of the Works of John Wesley (Fourteen-Vol. Edition, 1872), p. 499.]

Bishop. Why, Sir, our faith itself is a good work; it is a virtuous temper of mind.

Mr. Wesley. My Lord, whatever faith is, our Church asserts, we are justified by faith alone. But how it can be called a good work, I see not: It is the gift of God; and a gift that presupposes nothing in us, but sin and misery.

B. How, Sir? Then you make God a tyrannical Being, if he justifies some without any goodness in them preceding, and does not justify all. If these are not justified on account of some moral goodness in them, why are not those justified too?

W. Because, my Lord, they 'resist his Spirit'; because 'they will not come to Him that they may have life'; because they suffer Him not to 'work in them both to will and to do.' They cannot be saved, because they will not believe.

B. Sir, what do you mean by faith?

W. My Lord, by justifying faith I mean a conviction wrought in a man by the Holy Ghost, that Christ hath loved him and given himself for him; and that, through Christ, his sins are forgiven.

B. I believe some good men have this, but not all. But how do you prove this to be the justifying faith taught by our Church?

W. My Lord, from her Homily on Salvation where she describes it thus: 'A sure trust and confidence which a man hath in God, that through the merits of Christ his sins are forgiven and he reconciled to the favour of God.'

B. Why, Sir, this is quite another thing.

W. My Lord, I conceive it to be the very same.

B. Mr. Wesley, I will deal plainly with you. I once thought you and Mr. Whitefield well-meaning men; But I cannot think so now; for I have heard more of you; matters of fact, Sir. And Mr. Whitefield says in his Journal, 'There are promises still to be fulfilled in me,' Sir, the pretending to extraordinary revelations and gifts of the Holy Ghost is a horrid thing, a very horrid thing!

W. My Lord, for what Mr. Whitefield says, Mr. Whitefield, and not I, is accountable. I pretend to no extraordinary revelations or gifts of the Holy Ghost; none but what every Christian may receive, and ought to expect and pray for. But I do not wonder your Lordship has heard facts asserted, which, if true, would prove the contrary; nor do I wonder, that your Lordship, believing them true, should alter the opinion you once had of me. A quarter of an hour I spent with your Lordship before, and about an hour now; and perhaps you have never conversed one other hour with any who spake in my favour.

But how many with those who spake on the other side! So that your Lordship could not but think as you do— But pray, my Lord, what are those facts you have heard?

B. I hear you administer the sacrament in your societies.

W. My Lord, I never did yet; and I believe never shall.

B. I hear too, that many people fall into fits in your societies, and that you pray over them.

W. I do so, my Lord, when any show, by strong cries and tears, that their soul is in deep anguish. I frequently pray to God to deliver them from it, and our prayer is often heard in that hour.

B. Very extraordinary indeed! Well, Sir, since you ask my advice, I will give it you very freely. You have no business here. You are not commissioned to preach in this diocese. Therefore I advise you to go hence.

W. My Lord, my business on earth is, to do what good I can. Wherever therefore I think I can do most good, there must I stay, so long as I think so. At present I think I can do most good here; therefore, here I stay.

As to my preaching here, a dispensation of the Gospel is committed to me; and woe is me, if I preach not the Gospel, wherever I am in the habitable world. Your Lordship knows, being ordained a Priest, by the commission I then received, I am a Priest of the Church universal; and being ordained as Fellow of a College, I was not limited to any particular cure, but have an indeterminate commission to preach the word of God, in any part of the Church of England. I do not therefore conceive that, in preaching here by this commission, I break any human law. When I am convinced I do, then it will be time to ask, Shall I obey God or man?

But if I should be convinced in the meanwhile, that I could advance the glory of God, and the salvation of souls, in any other place, more than in Bristol; in that hour, by God's help, I will go hence; which till then I may not do.

[Though the uprightness of Wesley's intention in recording this conversation cannot for a moment be questioned, I cannot but doubt whether the observations of Bishop Butler are given as fully as he uttered them. It is extremely difficult for one of the parties to a conversation to recollect in full the words of the other.—W. E. G.]

Whitefield to Bishop Butler.

[Tyerman's *Life of Whitefield*, Vol. i. p. 182.]

BRISTOL, *February* 24*th*, 1739.

MY LORD,

I humbly thank your lordship for the favour of your lordship's letter. It gave abundant satisfaction to me and many others, who have not failed to pray in a particular manner for your lordship's temporal and eternal welfare. To-day I showed your lordship's letter to the chancellor, who (notwithstanding he promised not to prohibit my preaching for the Orphan House if your lordship was only neutral in the affair) has influenced most of the clergy to deny me their pulpits either on that or any other occasion. Last week he was pleased to charge me with false doctrine. To-day he has forgotten that he said so.

He also threatened to excommunicate me for preaching in your lordship's diocese. I offered to take a license, but was denied.

If your lordship should ask, What evil have I done? I answer None, save that I visit the Religious Societies, preach to the prisoners in Newgate, and to the poor colliers in Kingswood, who I am told are little better than heathens.

I am charged with being a Dissenter; though many are brought to the Church by my preaching not one taken from it. The chancellor is pleased to tell me my conduct is contrary to the canons; but I told him that the canons, which he produced, were not intended against such meetings as mine are, where His Majesty is constantly prayed for, and every one is free to see what is done. I am sorry to give your lordship this trouble; but I thought it proper to mention these particulars, that I might know wherein my conduct is exceptionable.

I heartily thank your lordship for your intended benefaction. I think the design is truly good, and will meet with success, because so much opposed.

God knows my heart. I desire only to promote His glory. If I am spoken evil of for His sake, I rejoice in it. My Master was long since spoken evil of before me.

But I intrude on your lordship's patience.

I am with all possible thanks, my lord, your lordship's
dutiful son and servant,

GEORGE WHITEFIELD.

IV.

LETTER TO A LADY.

London, Dec. 22, 1747.

Madam,

Your letter of the 14th current, which did not come to hand till the 18th, cannot, indeed, require any sort of apology. I know not how to refuse my judgment, such as it is, in a case of conscience, to any person that asks it: but I think myself strictly bound to give it to good persons of my own diocese. For I mention only this demand that you have upon me, because, upon such an occasion as the present, I do not choose to speak of your rank, Madam, nor of the great civilities I have received from you.

The corruption and disorder of human affairs is such as has perplexed the rule of right, and made it hard in some cases to say how one ought to act. But I apprehend there is no such difficulty in the case you put. Property in general is, and must be, regulated by the laws of the community. This, in general, is, I say, allowed on all hands. If, therefore, there be any sort of property exempt from these regulations, or any exception to the general method of regulating it, such exception must appear, either from the light of nature, or from revelation. But neither of these do, I think, show any such exception : and, therefore, we may with a good conscience retain any possessions, Church Lands, or Tithes, which the laws of the State we live under give us a property in. And there seems less ground for scruple here in England, than in some other countries; because our ecclesiastical laws agree with our civil ones in this matter. Under the Mosaic dispensation, indeed, God himself assigned to the Priests and Levites tithes, and other possessions; and in those possessions they had a divine right: a property, quite superior to all human laws, ecclesiastical as well as civil. But every donation to the Christian Church is a human donation, and no more; and, therefore, cannot give a divine right, but such a right only as must be subject, in common with all other property, to the regulation of human laws. I would not carry you, Madam, into abstruse speculations; but think it might be clearly shown that no one can have a right of perpetuity in any lands, except it be given by God, as the land of Canaan was to Abraham. There is no other means by which such a kind of property or right can be acquired; and plain absurdities would follow from the supposition of it. The persons, then, who gave these lands to the Church, had themselves no right of perpetuity in them; consequently, could convey no such right to the Church. But all scruples concerning the lawfulness of laymen's possessing these lands go upon supposition that the Church has such a right of perpetuity in them; and therefore all those scruples must be groundless, as going upon a false supposition.

As you do not mention, Madam, in what particular light you consider this matter, I chose to put it in different ones. And having said thus much concerning the strict justice of the case, I think myself obliged to add that, great disorders having been committed at the Reformation, and a multitude of parochial cures left scandalously poor, and become yet poorer by accidental circumstances, I think a man's possession of one of these impoverished cures is, not indeed an obligation in justice, but a providential admonition, to do somewhat, according to his abilities, towards settling some competent maintenance upon it, in one way or another; in like manner as a person in distress, being my neighbour, dependent, or even acquaintance, is a providential admonition to me in particular to assist him, over and above the general obligation to charity, which would call upon me to assist such a person, in common with all others who were informed of his case. But I think I ought to say, since I can say it with great truth, that I mention this, not, Madam, as thinking that you want to be reminded of it, but as the subject itself I write upon requires it should be mentioned.

You need not, Madam, have given yourself the trouble of desiring secrecy, since the thing itself so plainly demands it.

I am with the truest esteem, Madam,
Your most obedient, most faithful, and most humble servant,
Jo. BRISTOL.

I have considered Tithes and Church lands as the same, because I see no sort of proof that tithes, under the Gospel, are of divine right; and, if they are not, they must come under the same consideration with lands.

V.

A SERMON SUPPOSED TO BE WRITTEN BY BISHOP BUTLER.

Prefatory Note to Sermon.

THE following sermon was published for the first time by Bartlett in the volume (1839) which contains his Life of Bishop Butler. Its probable genuineness has been recognised in some subsequent works. While Bartlett will not venture to pronounce an opinion (p. 280), and refers the matter to his readers, he cites a statement from Nichols's *Anecdotes* that some of Butler's MS. Sermons are still in being (p. 279). He tells us that he examined the papers 'in the possession of the bishop's family,' but found nothing calling for notice except this sermon. With regard to it he offers the following remarks :—

1. The handwriting 'strongly resembles the early autograph of the bishop.'

2. It carries a date somewhat indistinct but apparently that of 1739, when he was still Rector of Stanhope.

3. It bears written upon it the abbreviated name of Stanhope.

4. The bishop's Greek Testament has a note on the word παλιγγενεσίας in Titus iii. 5, 'The change and renovation of the soul or affections for the better, spiritually accomplished by Christ in our hearts.' This note is in close accord with the sermon, which indeed may be viewed as an expansion of it. I add that both are in accord with the clear though succinct language of the *Analogy* (Part II. i. 24).

The combined effect of these heads of testimony is, as it seems to me, considerable. It does not, however, exclude the necessity of considering the evidence furnished by the discourse itself. To my mind, it raises presumptions entirely satisfactory, and suggests no single ground for doubt. It seems to be such a discourse as we might expect from Butler when lowering the severe demands of his strain of thought to the level, or more nearly to the level, of his rural parishioners. It has all the bishop's solidity, all his measure. It does not contain a waste word. To counterfeit the style of Butler, or produce its parallel, would require a rare hand.

An extraordinary interest attaches to this discourse, if genuine.

For it is the only specimen we possess of his pastoral manner. On the special occasions, or before the learned auditories, with which his known sermons had to do, the pastoral tone and colour were hardly within his option. In this point of view, the discourse ought of itself pretty nearly to suffice for putting to flight the host of criticisms which have been passed upon Butler as having failed adequately to represent the evangelical character of Christian doctrine.

SERMON.

The wind bloweth where it listeth, and thou canst not tell whence it cometh nor whither it goeth; so is every one that is born of the Spirit. St. John iii. 8.

When we read of Nicodemus visiting Jesus, and acknowledging the conviction wrought upon some of the beholders, that they concluded from thence His mission to be divine, it is plain something more than mere curiosity led him to this conference. He was desirous of instruction, and our blessed Saviour deigned to gratify him by entering on a discourse concerning the kingdom of God. Whether Nicodemus had attained those qualifications requisite to prepare men for, and admit them into this kingdom, we know not; or, whether Christ of His own accord fell upon this point as of the greatest importance, was not material for St. John to acquaint us. That which is of the greatest consequence is, that He makes a man's being born again, the indispensable condition of seeing that kingdom. And this deserves the greater attention, because a master of Israel mistook it; as if God had intended the impossibility of going through the course of a natural birth a second time. From such misconstruction our Lord delivers Himself, and explains the nature of regeneration. That water and the Spirit, the washing of baptism outwardly, and the inward sanctification of the Holy Ghost, are the principles by which it is effected; that, though it could be compassed in that gross manner Nicodemus misapprehended, yet that would be of no efficacy at all in this case. For since in all productions the thing born receives the nature and resemblance of that, whence its being was derived, flesh could only produce flesh; but the new creature which God requires, consists in the mind, and therefore, to bring forth a new spirit, it is necessary that the vital principle should be a spirit. And, however he might find some difficulty in assenting to this, because neither the cause nor the manner of its operation, falls under the notice of human sense, yet that is no objection against the reality of the fact. A very familiar instance whereof, he alleges in the words of the text, 'The wind bloweth,' &c., &c.

The words plainly consist of two parts, a Similitude, and the Application. It will be proper therefore to divide my discourse into these two heads. First, from the Similitude, I shall draw some general conclusions, which may direct us in our contemplation of divine truths, and especially that of regeneration, which is the subject of our Saviour's argument with Nicodemus. Secondly, from the Application, I shall consider, how far the properties of the wind here mentioned, will give us any just ground to judge of the Holy Spirit's workings upon the souls of men.

First, a man may have sufficient reason to assure himself that a thing really is, without being able to give an account how it came to be. For the cause of a thing is indeed one and a very satisfactory way of coming to the distinct knowledge of its nature. But this is but one way of many; and some things which we cannot come at this way may be so certain to us, that it would be extreme obstinacy to deny them. For as things have causes, so have they effects, and properties, and other characters by which they may be distinguished. And it is sufficient if any of these give evidence of their existing. For we are every way as sure, that what hath no being of its own cannot have properties, and effects, as we are that what hath these could never have been without a cause. And therefore, when we are able to assign any such properties or effects, that is a demonstration of the reality of the thing. Thus, if there be certain marks by which being born of the Spirit is evidently discerned, and distinguished from another that is not so born, we may from those marks conclude, that such a man is regenerate, though we could not positively determine from whence this principle of new life took its rise; or if we know, as we may know, that it could be owing to no other cause but the operations of the Holy Ghost, we may then, where such marks appear, be confident, that the sanctifying operations of the Holy Ghost have passed upon that person, though neither we who were bystanders, nor perhaps the man himself, was conscious of the manner in which they were begun and carried on in his mind.

I shall secondly consider, from the application in the text, how far the properties of the wind, mentioned in this similitude, will give us any just ground to judge of the Holy Spirit's workings upon the minds of men.

The Application is contained in the last clause of the verse, 'So is every one that is born of the Spirit.' That is, the work of Regeneration carries great resemblance to what is observed of the wind: for, as there we gather its blowing from its sound and other effects, though we do not see the blast, nor its rise and passage, nor are acquainted with the cause that sets it on ; so may a child of God know he is such, by the effects and characters of that relation ; though he do not see the Spirit that renews him, though the operations, by which he is renewed, be such as fall not under the observation of his outward senses, nor is perhaps his own mind conscious to many things by which that change is wrought in him.

And first, from that expression, 'The wind bloweth where it listeth,' we may, I think, fairly infer the freedom of God's grace. That He giveth it liberally, and of His own accord, and that it is what no merit of ours can oblige Him to give. In this argument St. Paul has laboured much to show, that the very nature of grace is contrary to that of works. That Abraham, the father and the pattern of the faithful, received the call and promise of God, while he was yet among Idolaters, and could have no works to boast of: that when Jews and Gentiles were both concluded under sin, God chose the Gentiles, as He did Jacob before Esau, freely, while yet in the womb; not that the one of these had any wrong done him, or was used worse than he deserved, but the other found great favour, and was used better than he deserved. Thus it is in the work of Regeneration. God gives us His preventing graces freely. He imparts the light of His gospel, and it is a marvellous blessing to be born and educated in those happy regions which are enlightened with the pure lustre of it. When we believe this gospel, it is His grace that disposes our minds to do so; when that faith exerts itself in works of obedience, this also is owing to the assistance of His grace. When we improve to higher excellencies, and approach nearer to the perfections of a spiritual and divine life, this is again from the more abundant communications of the same Spirit. 'Tis true, indeed, Christ has promised an increase of talents to those, who make a good use of the talents they already have; He hath assured us that our Father will not fail to 'grant the Holy Spirit to them that ask Him.' But still it is by the aid and influence of that very Spirit, that we ask the talents we have not, and that we improve those we have. So that this does but enhance God's mercy and bounty so much the more, which first enables us to act, and then rewards us for acting. For that is, in effect, to crown and complete His own work rather than our desert; since what we do acquires a title to His promise, and yet it is what we could not do, if He did not impart to us the power of doing it. Now it is to be remembered that if good actions, where they are conspicuous, declare that they are wrought by the Spirit, and that God hath renewed that man, and did and does, still act and dwell in him ;—then it is no less certain, that, where the contrary vices and dispositions are predominant, those men are not regenerate, nor does the Spirit of God work in them. 'Let no man deceive you,' says the Apostle; 'whoever doth not righteousness is not of God, neither he that loveth not his brother.' Men may delude themselves and their ignorant followers with boasting pretences; they may have the impiety to sanctify their blackest crimes, by fathering them upon divine impulse and inspiration. But, while we see them turbulent and factious, proud and disobedient, censorious and bitter, unjust and uncharitable; can we think that God is the Author of, or dwells with, those froward dispositions? It were a contradiction to all religion to suppose so; and, however they may be exalted by their own vain imaginations, yet alas! they know not themselves nor what spirit they are of.

I proceed now to a second reflection concerning the manner of the Spirit's working upon our minds,—which is, that as we can give no account of the rise, the increase, the quieting of the wind; where it began, where it will stop, or how long it will last: so, the operations of the Spirit are often very remote from our understandings. He may move us without our having any distinct perception of the thing; nor can we always say, then the impulse began, thus long it continued, and now it ceases to move me. And this cannot seem very strange to any, that shall consider by what steps he hath come off from a wicked life, or proceeded in a good one. For in all this, he will find nothing of violence, or external compulsion, but such motives all along as were entirely agreeable to his faculties, and the methods by which He proceeds in other cases. For did not this change begin with a conviction of sin, and the evil of it, and in consequence of this, an hatred and detestation of it, grounded upon such arguments as these; that it is contrary to reason, displeasing to God, destructive to soul and body, in rendering both obnoxious to the divine wrath and vengeance, and to that eternity of misery, which the present fleeting pleasures of wickedness are a very poor exchange for? Again, will not his advance in virtue be found to owe itself to the contemplation of the beauty, the reasonableness. the advantages of holiness, the alluring rewards it proposes, the happiness it secures in this life, and the next? How, then, did these arguments prevail at last? Was it not by frequent meditation, by insinuating themselves into the mind by degrees, by the common methods of reading, of hearing, and weighing God's words? by conquering the prejudices of our corrupt hearts, by discussing and displaying the evidence of truth, by faithful and honest application, by exciting good desires, strengthening those desires with holy resolutions, and making good those resolutions by diligent endeavours, and steadfast perseverance? But still the finger of God is in all this. It is He who brings these considerations into our hearts first; He that fastens them upon us when they are there; He that adds new life and vigour to our desires and intentions, and gives efficacy and success, to our otherwise weak and imperfect attempts. He convinces our judgments, kindles good inclinations, persuades, allures, threatens, deters, terrifies, reproaches, comforts, commends; and performs all other offices necessary to piety.

But these He performs *in* us, and *with* us, and *by* us. From Him, as we acknowledge in our daily prayers, 'all holy desires, all good counsels, and all just works, do proceed.' But they proceed from Him in such a manner, as still to be our desires, our counsels, and our works. What has been said deserves well to be considered, in order to make men very careful not to resist any of the good motions, nor to withstand the warnings of conscience; to be careful that they do not quench, grieve, resist, or do despite to the Spirit of God, since it is a great and heinous sin. If, as hath been said, it act upon us by the outward ministry of the word, by the inward dictates and reasonings of our minds,—if the *effects* only of His working be visible, but the manner of it imperceptible: then every admonition from the pulpit, every wholesome law, every advice from a friend, or a parent, every good book, every pious example, every motion and intention to do well, every conviction, every check of conscience, is a blowing of this wind, a call, or impulse from above; and as often as any man refuses to comply with these things, so often he resists God, and quenches His Holy Spirit.

Lastly, this shows us what course we should take, in order to grow in grace. We should diligently use the word and sacraments and other means of grace vouchsafed us, in order to improve in virtue; and then we need not doubt of God's assistance. He will forward and strengthen our good intentions, and will not fail to finish what He, Himself hath begun, but will perform and continue it until the day of Christ Jesus, and reward us with a crown of glory.

INDEX TO VOLUME II

References to the Preface	. . . . .	Pref.
,,	,,	Fifteen Sermons . .	S. i., S. ii., &c.
,,	,,	Six Sermons . . .	SS. i., SS. ii., &c.
,,	,,	Charge	Char.
,,	,,	Appendix	App.

Aborigines, their title to communication of the gospel, SS. i. 13.
Action. See **Agent**.
Affairs, pecuniary: self-deceit produces reluctance to examine, S. x. 14.
Affections and Passions, other than benevolence and self-love, yet which operate for their ends, S. i. 6.
 illustrations hereof, S. i. 6 n.
 the operation sometimes unconscious: is the work of God, S. i. 6.
 principles which tend to good, not being benevolence nor self-love, S. i. 12.
 that they may warp judgment is no just plea against pity, S. v. 4.
 have their proper place in our nature, *ibid.*
 not a defect, but a supply to its imperfections, S. v. 5, 6.
 life would be bettered by their having more free scope, S. v. 7.
 all conduct requires stimulus or restraint from them, S. v. 10.
 men wanting in, have to reckon with their action in others, S. v. 11.
 want of affection is like want of appetite, S. v. 12.
 the obstinacy of such as are bad, *ibid.*
 we should encourage those favourable to our fellow-men, S. vi. 9.
 of a mixed nature, but useful for our present state, S. ix. 1.
 particular, rest upon objects, not on the pleasure they give, S. xi. 3.
 sharply distinguished from self-love, S. xi. 5.
 affection need not, because altruistic, abate enjoyment, S. xi. 12.
 every genuine affection rests upon its object as an end, S. xiii. 4.
 regard to an ulterior aim is perhaps for this life rather than the future life, S. xiii. 5.
 affection for good is itself good, S. xiii. 6.
 new developments of affection possible in a higher state of being, S. xiii. 17.
 when raised to their highest, will still fall short, S. xiv. 9.
Agents: as such we have our nature in our own power; hence responsibility, Pref. 13.
 action to be tested by correspondence with the nature of the agent, S. ii. 14, S. iii. 13.
 moral: we become such through the supremacy of conscience, S. ii. 11.

Anger is not sin, though near to it, S. viii. 5.
    sudden, instinctive, and without injury received, S. viii. 6, 7.

Appetites to be in entire subjection to conscience, and in just proportion to one another, S. iii. 2 *n.*
    required by the constitution of our nature, S. iii. 6.

Associations, religious, the appropriate antidote to the irreligion of the day, SS. i. 19.
    charitable, among the best of good works, SS. ii. 16.
    to be raised to the highest perfection, SS. ii. 17; labour, low diet, instruction, as means hereto, *ibid.*
    especially as we approximate to the idea of an equality among men, SS. ii. 18.

Atheism the final goal of irreligion and depravity, SS. i. 18.
    will itself lead to superstition: a special kind of it imminent, *ibid.*

Attention rarely due to persons, but always to subjects in proportion to what their nature requires, Pref. 3.

Authority, distinguished from power, S. ii. 19.
    civil, proceeds from God, SS. iii. 20.
    disparaged by the licence of denigration in party leaders, SS. iii. 21.
    of conscience, supreme; is the complement of human nature, Pref. 18.
    overrides all conduct, Pref. 19.

Balaam, his proceedings in Moab, S. vii. 2.
    strains for an object he knows to be unlawful, S. vii. 5, 6.
    obtains permission: the conflict in his mind, S. vii. 6.
    gives shameful counsel to seduce the Israelites, S. vii. 7.
    contradiction and inconsistency in his character, S. vii. 8.
    case not uncommon now, S. vii. 9.
    wickedness lacking support from reason, he resorts to subterfuge, S. vii. 10.
    his mood betwixt hope and despair, S. vii. 11.
    combined sound belief with ill conduct, and sought to compound with God, S. vii. 12, 13.
    considering our duty often means explaining it away, S. vii. 14.
    true remedy for self-deceit lies in becoming 'little children,' S. vii. 15.
    to secure 'the death of the righteous,' let us deal plainly with ourselves, S. vii. 16.

Beauty (with order, harmony, proportion), as an idea, has less weight for us than happiness and misery, S. xi. 21.
    these ideas as real as that of truth, *ibid.*
    are productive of natural legitimate delight, S. xiv. 14.

Begging, in the streets, a shameful trade; indiscriminate alms-giving wrong, SS. ii. 15.

Benevolence, has no special antagonism to self-love, Pref. 32, S. xi. 11, 16.
    its relation to society resembles that of self-love to the individual, S. i. 4.
    shown not to be love of power, S. i. 4 *n.* 1-4.
    its insufficient development, S. i. 5.
    coincides largely with self-love, *ibid.*
    or public-spirit, greatly needs the aid of the affections, S. v. 10.
    compared with ambition and covetousness, S. xi. 12, 13.
    gives enjoyment even beyond other particular affections, S. xi. 20.
    considered as including all virtues, S. xii. 19; with due reserves, *ibid.* 19, 22.
    is the source of the common virtues, sustaining Rom. xiii. 9, S. xii. 22.
    its relation to piety arises through God's perfect goodness, S. xii. 23.
    Hobbes's definition of, App. I. n.
    loves power with a view to good, *ibid.*

Body: compare with the double duty belonging to each member of a literal body, the duty of man to himself and to society, S. i. 3.

Body (*continued*).
    contrary supposition absurd, S. i. 10.
    even as to external form men are not wholly agreed, S. ii. 2.
Bristol Infirmary commended, SS. ii. 16 *n*.
Brutes have instincts to obey, but have not conscience, Pref. 15, S. ii. 5.
    follow their nature which has no discords, Pref. 17.
    rushing into a snare, contrasted with a man doing the like, S. ii. 13.
    have no law of right written within them, S. iii. 3.
    resentment in, S. viii. 6.
    have several advantages over us, S. xiv. 4.
    their parental office more contracted than ours, SS. iv. 3.

Capacity, apart from good sense, does not save men from gross error, S. v. 16.
Causes. See **Final Causes.**
Character, parts in, more varied than features in a face, S. xii. 6.
    of the great varieties in the balance of faculties, S. xii. 7; consequent misjudgment, *ibid*.
Charge to the Clergy of Durham.
    religion decays, zeal for negation increases, Char. 1.
    has been predicted, and is the note of the age, Char. 2.
    avoid the profane; treat negation with the 'meekness of wisdom,' Char. 3.
    against arguing without consideration; hasty disputation dangerous, Char. 5; cavilling easier than proof, *ibid*. 7.
    great regard due to religion, even if evidences be doubtful, Char. 6.
    they cannot be duly presented or weighed in cursory conversation, Char. 8.
    of protests to be made; silence sometimes advisable, Char. 9.
    strong reasons for reserve in treatment, Char. 10.
    main matter, instruction of the people; should be affirmative, not polemical, Char. 11.
    for effective religion, form is insufficient but essential, Char. 12.
    observances abroad; Mahometan and Latin, Char. 13.
    reduced by our reformers to a minimum: now largely neglected, Char. 14.
    Moses commanded external religion, Char. 15.
    has often been in excess, Char. 16.
    care for churches, and chancels, Char. 17; many threatened with ruin, *ibid*. 18.
    even more regard due to services, Char. 19.
    weekly services insufficient: supplemental expedients, Char. 20.
    care for the religious teaching of children, Char. 21.
    particular rules needful, most of all for the careless, Char. 22.
    holy life to be infused into the form, Char. 23.
    for turning all occasions to account, Char. 24.
    lack of personal appropriation in public instruction, Char. 25.
    Confirmation and first Communion, Char. 26.
    due allowances always to be made, Char. 27.
    the clergy bound to entire self-devotion, which is self-rewarding, Char. 28, 29.
Charles I: his execution an unheard-of hypocrisy, SS. iii. 10; against the voice of Parliament, *ibid*.
    under pretence of liberty and of extending it, SS. iii. 11.
    the resistance offered to him originally just, SS. iii. 12.
    became ungovernable and lawless, *ibid*.
Church: why the primitive sense of membership was so direct and lively, S. i. 1.
    missionary work of the, SS. i. 4.
    its public worship is of the essence of Christianity, SS. i. 5.
    the measure of success has not been guaranteed, SS. i. 6.

Church (*continued*).
    is, like nature, and human nature, a witness to mankind, SS. i. 7.
    for each man to accept or refuse, SS. i. 8.
    man to be instructed by man, so God ordains, SS. i. 9.
    we hold the gospel in trust to propagate it, SS. i. 10; especially in our Colonies, *ibid.* 11; and to the slaves, *ibid.* 12; and Aborigines, *ibid.* 13.
    our trade subserves the work of missions, SS. i. 14.
    each new planting out of the church a great good, SS. i. 15; at least by its effect upon a few, *ibid.*
    the gospel preached, without miracle, a serious admonition to men, SS. i. 16.
    all denominations should join in the work, SS. i. 17.
    establishment of, in England, mild and reasonable, SS. iii. 11.
    a state without an establishment of religion a chimerical project, SS. v. 7.
    an establishment, with toleration, requisite, *ibid.*
    necessary for encouragement of learning, *ibid.*
    saves us from the evils of popery, SS. v. 8, 9.
    the moderation in our church and state a model for personal conduct, SS. v. 15.
    letter on church property, App. IV.

Civil government, at best very imperfect, SS. iii. 27.
    insurrection and oppression both condemned, SS. v. 1.
    founded, against violence and fraud, under double religious sanction, SS. v. 2.
    a figure of the universal divine authority, SS. v. 3.
    always a good, sometimes in high degree, SS. v. 4.
    we, being free, have to guard against licentiousness, SS. v. 5.
    recent reform in the northern provinces, SS. v. 6.
    mischief of persecution, SS. v. 9; Job xxxi. 26-28 now inapplicable, *ibid.* 10, 11.
    our recent danger from the Pretender, SS. v. 12.
    the loyalty of church-rulers, SS. v. 13.
    opposition to, (*a*) legitimate and (*b*) illegitimate, SS. v. 14.
    the equity of our church and state a model for conduct, SS. v. 15.
    retrenchments effected in outward religion should enhance inward, SS. v. 16.
    See also **Liberty, Obedience.**

Civil punishments, aim at preventing future mischief, Pref. 24.
Clarke, Dr., letter to, and reply, App. I. E; second letter, *ibid.* F.
Colonies, their special claim on us for imparting the gospel, SS. i. 11.
Compassion is not a form of self-regard, as Hobbes teaches, S. v. 1 *n.*
    is more common than joy-sharing, S. v. 2, 7, 14.
    utility of this arrangement, S. v. 3.
    gives a balance of satisfaction over pain, S. v. 7, 8.
    callousness implies a great loss, S. v. 9.
    the example of Christ, S. v. 14.
    its double office to prevent misery and relieve it, S. vi. 3.
    pleads within us for giving consideration to cases, S. vi. 5.
    may be got rid of more easily than hunger, S. vi. 6.
    how distinguished from mercy, S. vi. 7.
    prefers relief to prevention as more fruitful, S. vi. 8.
    capable of excess; but the prevailing excess is indifference, S. vi. 10.
    begets a sober and discerning view of life, S. vi. 12.
    also a docility of mind and heart, S. vi. 13.
    and a sense of being wayfarers in this world, S. vi. 14.

Conscience, or **reflection**: chief relation among parts in man is determined by the supremacy of conscience, Pref. 12.
    its presence places us in contrast with brutes, Pref. 15.

Conscience (*continued*).
  claims universal authority, Pref. 18, 19, S. ii. 19, S. iii. 1.
  a reflecting principle, judging of actions morally, S. i. 7, 8.
  restrains from evil, fortifies for good, both public and private, S. i. 8, 9.
  is thought to work specially for public good, S. i. 9; thus testifies to the social end of our being, *ibid.*
  essential to the rule of following nature, S. ii. 2.
  decides disputes on the true meaning of nature, S. ii. 10.
  makes us moral agents; is self-attested, S. ii. 11.
  what it disapproves is unnatural, S. ii. 12.
  has authority as against mere strength of any feeling or principle, S. ii. 17, 18.
  is to have entire command over appetites, S. iii. 2 *n.*
  carries an obligation independent of reward or punishment, S. iii. 6.
  and reasonable self-love, the superior principles in our nature, S. iii. 13.
Conversation, to be recreative, should be mutual, S. iv. 11.
  be slow to handle the character and concerns of others, S. iv. 16.
  in handling, be most scrupulous, S. iv. 17.
  mere truth does not suffice to justify mention, S. iv. 18, 19.
Corruptions of religion, SS. i. 4; with these, the confutations have been transmitted, *ibid.*
  Popery, SS. v. 8.
  which have crept into the Latin church under the shelter of persecution, SS. v. 9.

David gave scope to compassion and good will, S. x. 9.
  an extreme case of self-deceit; the mode inscrutable, S. x. 11.
  perhaps the highest possible instance, S. x. 19.
Death: relation of a good life to a good end, S. vii. 1.
Degree: only when held in degree do worldly objects satisfy, S. i. 15.
Determinate, the: is not to be looked for in the primary forms of moral propositions, Pref. 3.
Determination (under resentment) not to be convinced, S. vi. 15.
Discourses: the collection here in great part accidental, Pref. 39.
Disengagement absolutely necessary to enjoyment, S. xi. 7.
Disinterested: an epithet applicable to the self-ruining acts of bad men, Pref. 34.
Disposition, every, limited by degree, and errs if in excess, Serm. v. 8.
Divinity, grief to part from his studies in, App. I. D.
Doubtfulness should check impatience and vehemence, App. I. B.
Duty, we have a duty both to ourselves and to others, S. v. 1.
  consideration of: often means explaining it away, S. vii. 14.
  perfectly coincides with interest, S. iii. 13.
  enhanced by the love manifested in the Incarnation, S. xi. 23.
  evasions and excuses easily found if desired, S. xii. 5.
  strictness in, with stinted evidence, may train higher character, S. xv. 8.
  not to do other people's, App. I. B.

Education of children, a special object for religious associations, SS. i. 19.
  the formation of early habits not to be left to children alone, SS. iv. 1.
  docility and deference mark them for training, SS. iv. 2.
  a larger office than in the case of brutes, SS. iv. 3.
  it differs from that of admonition to adults, SS. iv. 4.
  means to mould and not only to inform, SS. iv. 5.
  youth the only available occasion, SS. iv. 6.
  religion requires of us character as well as belief, SS. iv. 7.
  this is the best of all present gifts, and the road to our chief good, SS. iv. 8.
  the risks of spurious training are great, SS. iv. 9.

Education (*continued*).
  the objection to schools futile, SS. iv. 10.
  all ages need maintenance, provided by our law : children training also, not provided, SS. iv. 11, 12.
  first attempt at remedy by the S. P. C. K., SS. iv. 13.
  maintenance naturally coheres with instruction, SS. iv. 14, 23, 26 ; placing out, *ibid.* 19.
  suspicion and inaction dangerous : a new necessity for knowledge, SS. iv. 15 ; of inaction, *ibid.* 21.
  ignorance heightens the risks from bad example, SS. iv. 16; tends to vice, training to good, *ibid.* 18.
  our poverty in pastoral means heightens the need for books, SS. iv. 17.
  training in virtue is the main design, *ibid.* ; shamefully neglected, especially by the rich, *ibid.*
  evil parentage, aggravation in humble life, SS. iv. 22.
  results from schools seem satisfactory, SS. iv. 24 ; management improves : industrial training, *ibid.* 27.
  the duty enforced, SS. iv. 25, 27, Char. 21.
Enjoyment, enhancement of, a lesser object than avoidance of misery, S. vi. 11.
Epicureans : place the *summum bonum* in the absence of pain, Pref. 31.
  teach to cultivate self-love as against passion, Pref. 36.
Equality : an equality of mankind beginning to be recognised, SS. ii. 18.
Equivalents : leisure, information, civil authority, are the social equivalents of superior understanding, SS. ii. 8.
Example of Christ in forgiveness of injury, S. ix. 19.
  Christ an example of perfect goodness in our own nature, S. xi. 23.
Extravagance of the period, except in gifts for religion, Char. 17.
Extremes, interaction of, in religion, S. xiii. 1.
Eye given us to see with : comp. shame, S. ii. 1, 3.

Family prayer recommended, Char. 20.
Fear : goodness, not malice, the proper object of just fear, Pref. 25.
Festivals, the greater : to be specially used for inculcating religion, Char. 24 ; also the Occasional services, *ibid.*
Final causes, exhibited in the adaptation of man's nature to his environment as well as in external nature, S. vi. 1.
  final causes of compassion, S. vi. 3.
Following nature, virtue consists in, Pref. 7, 8, S. ii. 6, 9, 12, 14, and iii. 1.
  when rightly understood, a true rule of virtue, Pref. 14.
Forgiveness of injuries, why an obligation, Pref. 28, S. ix. 8, 9.
  the virtue most insisted on : most becomes a faulty creature ; most in danger of being violated from virtuous motives, Pref. 28.
  is not to be cancelled by guilt, S. ix. 11.
  nor by natural self-regard, S. ix. 13.
  injured man should feel as would the good man not injured, *ibid.*
  if he is reasonable, this should be practicable, S. ix. 14.
  anger and hatred make it hard to obtain a true point of view, S. ix. 15, 16.
  things to be looked at as they really are, S. ix. 17.
  there is no such thing as pure ill-will, S. ix. 18.
  implacability horrible in a sinful creature, S. ix. 20.
  the placable have direct encouragement from our Lord, S. ix. 21.
  the right temper is set forth in 1 Cor. xiii, S. xii. 13.
Frugality of the age, only in gifts for religion, Char. 17.
Future life : heightens the disparity between earthly aims and values, S. vi. 10.
  some of our affections may only have full scope in it, S. xiii. 3.
  new forms of thought may then be presented to us, S. xiv. 13.
  new manifestations of God and his counsels and qualities, S. xiv. 15–17.

George II: his government mild and strictly legal: the respect due to it, SS. iii. 25, 26.
God: we have nearer intercourse with him than with any creature, Pref. 38.
as an object of affection apart from reward and punishment, *ibid.*
is displaced, if strength of mental impulses is to imply right, S. ii. 21.
as regards the affections, his nature no parallel to ours, S. v. 5.
love of, means all affections due to him and resting in him as their end, S. xiii. 2, 3.
of these, some especially suited to the present life, S. xiii. 3.
a being trained to the highest human goodness must inspire love, S. xiii. 8.
if having special care for us, then all the more, S. xiii. 9.
if our Ruler and Guide, we shall obey and contemplate him, S. xiii. 10.
the infinity of his attributes should raise our affections to their highest point, S. xiii. 10.
his presence not less intimate because insensible, S. xiii. 12.
apply to the Creator the rule in force for the creature, S. xiii. 13.
the only adequate object of our affection: honour, shame, love of esteem, to be wholly referred to him, S. xiii. 14.
this is not abandonment of our interest, S. xiii. 15.
we are specially stirred by divine benefits when done to ourselves, S. xiii. 16.
new developments of affection possible in a higher state of being, S. xiii. 17.
our affections at their highest strain towards him, will still fall short, S. xiv. 9.
is alone adequate to give us all that our nature wants, S. xiv. 12.
possible new forms of manifestation in a future life, S. xiv. 15.
a vision of essence, and not merely as now of effect, S. xiv. 16.
and of goodness, the chief end of man, S. xiv. 17.
from the effect of human presences, conceive the divine, S. xiv. 18.
the Bible seems to promise a kind of vision here unknown, S. xiv. 19.
with this the Psalms in many places correspond, S. xiv. 20.
can only approve the right, fit, and just, App. I. A.
Good done to fellow-men, the more the better, S. xii. 9.
Goodness (see **Virtue**) is the proper object of just fear, Pref. 25.
Good-will may beget enhanced strictness in judgment, S. x. 8 *n*.
Gospel, the, left in the charge of men furnished with the scripture and the church, SS. i. 4.
Christians united in communities (not so in natural religion), *ibid.*
corruptions of, *ibid.*
each church is a city set on an hill, *ibid.*
would soon be planted universally, were Christians in earnest, SS. i. 20.
Grace at meals recommended, Char. 20.

Habits of evil will certainly be formed, unless stopped by good ones, SS. iv. 8.
Happiness, substantive, less eligible as an object of pursuit than the avoidance of evil, S. vi. 11.
lies in the enjoyment of objects suited to our nature, S. xi. 6.
in the gratification of particular passions, *ibid.*
in the enjoyment of objects 'by nature adapted to our several faculties,' S. xi. 13.
is not in immediate connection with self-love, S. xi. 16.
and misery, ideas weightier for us than order, beauty, harmony, proportion, S. xi. 21.
conduciveness to, seems not to be the sole standard of moral judgments, S. xii. 22 *n*.
Hobbes confounds particular affections with self-love, Pref. 29.
wrongly teaches that benevolence is love of power, S. i. 4 *n*.

Hobbes (*continued*).
  his false account of compassion confuted, S. v. 1 *n.*
  his definition of benevolence, App. I. *n.*
Hypocrisy has a much wider range than we suppose, SS. iii. 1.
  especially as a power of self-delusion, SS. iii. 2 and *n.*
  what is wrong is felt to require a cloak, SS. iii. 4.
  both from the world and from ourselves, SS. iii. 5.
  social conditions tempt men to profession, SS. iii. 6.
  often in levity rather than deliberate fraud, SS. iii. 7.
  self-deceit largely contributing, SS. iii. 8.
  use of this cloak almost universal, SS. iii. 9.

Ideas, in morals, are never *per se* determinate : but become so by a process, Pref. 3.
Ignorance, the, of mankind : we know nothing of creation, causes, essences, and ends, S. xv. 3.
  some particulars of Providence and life are known to us ; not the scheme, S. xv. 4.
  parts cannot be truly known, without knowing the whole, S. xv. 5.
  portions may have been designedly veiled, S. xv. 6.
  demonstrative proof perhaps inconsistent with the discipline of life, S. xv. 7.
  strictness in duty with less evidence may produce higher form of character, S. xv. 8.
  the provision made for us fully meets the demand upon us, S. xv. 9.
  we are not to haggle upon the kind of evidence given us, S. xv. 10.
  nor reject twilight from wishing for broad day, S. xv. 11.
  it is often the proper answer to objections, S. xv. 12.
  should affect our views both of right appearances and wrong ones, S. xv. 12 *n.*
  why we are not to fret at, S. xv. 13.
  the lessons taught : adoration of God, S. xv. 16 ; and abatement of self-esteem, *ibid.* 17.
Imagination, works of, are bound to be easy : certain other works cannot, Pref. 3.
Implacability dreadful when combined with sinfulness, S. ix. 20.
Indifference not compatible with sincerity, App. I. A.
Injury, not harm, is the proper object of resentment, Pref. 27.
  not to be more highly resented because against ourselves, S. ix. 12.
  such injury nearly sure to be over-estimated, S. ix. 15.
  to avoid such over-estimation is not humility, but common sense, S. ix. 17.
  never springs from pure ill-will, S. ix. 18.
  injurer is to be pitied : he injures himself most, S. ix. 19.
Injustice, contrary to our whole nature : contrary in a higher sense than pain, Pref. 14, S. iii. 2.
  never loved for its own sake, S. i. 11.
Insensibility to suffering frightfully prevalent, S. vi. 10.
Intercourse with men cannot mostly be brought under determinate rules, S. x. 10.
Interest : 'interested' or 'disinterested' do not fix the moral value of actions, Pref. 34.
  perfectly coincides with duty, S. iii. 13.

Jews put in charge of a religion highly corrupted, SS. i. 2.
Judgments, such as usually formed, do not deserve the name, Pref. 1.
  biassed by passion, S. x. 8.
  even so as to include the case of others, *ibid.*

Knowledge : but few are at all curious to know, Pref. 1.
  redundance of futile claims to universal, Pref. 2.

Knowledge (*continued*).
    is not the chief good of man, S. xiv. 17; xv. 13.
    chief value is in the acquisition, not the possession of, S. xv. 13.
    another end is appointed us in conduct and duty, S. xv. 14; see Job xxviii. 28, *ibid.* 15.

Law, inward, has authority, Pref. 24.
    failure to perceive it will not exempt from consequences, *ibid.*
Laws, general and stated, essential to a free government, SS. iii. 22.
Liberty: its threefold meaning in the New Testament, SS. iii. 3.
    a favourite cloak for the hypocrite to use, SS. iii. 4, 11.
    was in extreme danger at the Restoration, SS. iii. 13.
    using it to overthrow a free constitution is horrible, SS. iii. 14.
    even if in pursuit of an ideal one, SS. iii. 15.
    the wise course is to reform abuse, and supply deficiency, SS. iii. 16.
    apt to degenerate through its own excess, SS. iii. 17.
    licentiousness of a community *ipso facto* infringes it, SS. iii. 18.
    to love liberty includes revering authority, SS. iii. 19.
    requires and presupposes self-command, SS. iii. 22.
    its main security lies in the religious character of government, SS. iii. 23.
    respect is due to government, but comment should be free, SS. iii. 25.
    may itself overthrow government, or contribute to its overthrow by authority, SS. iii. 26.
    civil government necessarily very defective, SS. iii. 27.
Loquacity makes a man insignificant, S. iv. 13.
    proper occasions for silence, S. iv. 14, 19.
Love of God. See **Affections**: also **God**.
    includes all affections rightly due to God and resting in him as their end, S. xiii. 2, 3.
    of these, some more especially appropriate to the present life, S. xiii. 3.
    in its perfection scarce attainable, yet we may get beyond servile fear, and attain to resignation, S. xiv. 2.
    all earthly objects leave a void in us, S. xiv. 11.
    which only God himself, and in himself, can adequately supply, S. xiv. 12.
Love, to enemies, enjoined, S. ix. 3.
    defined, S. ix. 9.
    And see **Forgiveness**.
Luxury, the mother of poverty: greatly the result of fashion; the dissipation of riches, and the ruin of the possessors, SS. ii. 3.

Malevolence is contrary to human nature, and like self-hatred, S. i. 11.
Man. See **Nature (human)**.
Meditations, fragmentary, App. I. c.
Member: has a double duty to itself and to the body, so man to himself and to others, S. i. 3.
    these ends perfectly coincide, *ibid.*
Middle class, largely exempted from the vices of the high and the low; its great opportunities, SS. ii. 5.
Mind: its action more quick and transient than that of sense, S. x. 13.
Miracles have now totally ceased, S. i. 1.
    are intuitive proofs for spectators, SS. i. 16.
Misery, we are more largely concerned with, than with joy: hence the need of compassion, S. vi. 2.
    prevention of, a higher trust than promotion of happiness, *ibid.*
    our state not one of unmixed, S. vi. 4.
Mitigation and relief for sorrow in life, there is a law of, S. vi. 4.
Money came to be substituted for barter of goods, SS. ii. 3.
    augmented (*a*) wealth, (*b*) covetousness, *ibid.*

Morals, ideas in, never determinate *per se*, Pref. 3.
    treatable διχῶς: as to (*a*) abstract fitness, (*b*) the nature of man; these methods serve one another, Pref. 7.
    respective advantages of the methods, Pref. 7.
    morality and religion appeal to plain common sense, S. v. 15.
Motives, discernment of right, distinct from disposition to act on them, App. I. E, F.

Nathan, with David, S. x. 1.
Nature (human): following nature does not mean to follow each or any part of it, Pref. 9.
    a whole, whereof the parts have reciprocal relations, Pref. 10.
    its adaptation to virtue, Pref. 13.
    distinguished by 'reflection or conscience' from the brutes, Pref. 15.
    is a mixed constitution, as to good and evil instincts, Pref. 16.
    includes conscience, its legitimate sovereign, Pref. 18, 19.
    low standard of action followed by men not the worst, Pref. 19.
    our inward approval of good is our nearest and clearest obligation, Pref. 22.
    recognises a claim of religion anterior to the gospel, S. i. 2.
    essentially social, shown by conscience, and by many signs, S. i. 9, 10.
    malevolence is alien to it, S. i. 11.
    may fail in affection to others or to ourselves, S. i. 13.
    violated by wrong no less in regard to self than in regard to others, S. i. 16.
    natural adaptations show the Maker's purpose, S. ii. 1.
    only a guide when followed (*a*) normally, (*b*) in the eye of conscience, S. ii. 2.
    does not admit the title of the strongest impulse to prevail, S. ii. 4.
    the term is construed in several ways, S. ii. 5, 7, 8; in Rom. ii. 14 different from Eph. ii. 3, *ibid*. 8, 9.
    following nature is not 'acting as we please,' S. ii. 5; is following the law of right written in it, *ibid*. 9.
    dispute on the true meaning is decided by conscience, S. ii. 10.
    an act is known to be unnatural by comparison with the agent, S. ii. 14.
    a group of attributes under one which is supreme, S. iii. 1.
    the law written within, not hard for fair minds to discern, S. iii. 3, 4.
    superstition sometimes constitutes a difficulty, S. iii. 5.
    is framed for a certain course of action, S. iii. 13.
    action conformable to, is natural; and *vice versâ*, *ibid*.
    the voice of God within us, S. vi. 8.
    frivolous to inquire why we are not otherwise placed and constituted, S. viii. 1.
    but useful to scan its relation to its environment, S. viii. 2.
    ought to be held sacred, S. viii. 19.
Nature (outward), difficulty of the study of; probably led Solomon to study man, S. xv. 1.
    man's adaptation to, supplies matter for the argument of final causes, S. vi. 1.
Neighbour, our, means 'that part of our country which comes under our immediate notice,' S. xii. 2.
    is to be loved, not as God, but as self, S. xii. 3.
    with the same sensibility on his behalf, as on our own, S. xii. 4.
    'as thyself': to secure its being habitual, and in cases indeterminate, S. xii. 5.
    in proportion as we love self; to be taken as a whole, S. xii. 6.
    will be determined by the balance between benevolence and other principles, S. xii. 8.

Neighbour (*continued*).
> virtue lies in their due proportion; to be fixed by each man for himself. S. xii. 9.
> the further we carry benevolence, the nearer the perfect law, *ibid.*
> *as* may mean *equally with*: but each man must be mainly busied on himself, S. xii. 10.
> there is a limit in natural possibilities, S. xii. 12; which overspreads the entire life, *ibid.* 14.
> the good man a social blessing to his neighbours, S. xii. 15.
> such a temper restrains party-spirit, S. xii. 16.
> and strife generally, S. xii. 17.
> duty to, summed up in promoting his happiness, S. xii. 20.
> hence a fresh spur to personal virtue, S. xii. 21.

Newcastle, Duke of, two letters to, App. II.

Obedience, civil, has exceptions which do not need to be specified, SS. iii. 24.
Obscurity in some discourses admitted; was it avoidable? Pref. 4.
> a different thing from confusion and perplexity, *ibid.*
> sometimes due to readers of inadequate information, Pref. 5.
> admitted to be in sermons a defect, Pref. 6.

Pain in the natural world comes out as an instance of God's goodness, S. viii. 19.
Particular affections: without these self-love would have no aim except the avoidance of pain, Pref. 31.
> terminate on their objects; not to be resolved into self-love, S. xi. 3, 4.
> all, virtue included, are equally disinterested or the reverse, S. xi. 10.
> conduce to enjoyment, S. xi. 20.

Parts of a whole have mutual relations needing to be understood, Pref. 10-12.
Party, leaders of, do much evil by reciprocal denigration, SS. iii. 21.
> spirit of, condemned, S. xii. 16.

Passions. See **Affections.**
> no passion given us by God evil *per se*, S. viii. 4.
> pervert the judgment, S. x. 8.

Perception will exist in a future state, if not by sensitive organs, S. xiv. 13.
Perfection of goodness consists in love to the entire universe, S. xii. 2; this is God's perfection, *ibid.*
Persecution enjoined and practised in the Latin church. SS. v. 9.
Pleasure, men of: the reason of their opinion about the affections, S. v. 13.
> the losses they suffer, *ibid.*
> so called with too great indulgence, S. x. 13.

Pleasure-seekers, their hard-heartedness, Pref. 36.
Poor. See **Rich.**
Popery a great corruption of Christianity, SS. v. 8.
> plenitude of power claimed for the pope, *ibid.*
> effectiveness of visible signs abroad, for religion as well as superstition, Char. 13.

Poverty, a result of luxury: not the worst of its evils, SS. ii. 3.
Prayer, as termination of sermon, S. xii. 24; SS. iv. 25.
> weekly, public, insufficient, Char. 20.
> family, recommended, *ibid.*
> secret, ditto, *ibid.*
> morning and evening, ditto, *ibid.*
> at set hours, ditto, *ibid.*
> grace at meals, ditto, *ibid.*
> three prayers of author's, App. I. α.

Propensions to evil in us, have no sanction from the judge, like those to good, S. ii. 4.
    some suited to the present life, not to a perfect state, S. ix. 1.
Property, its idea; the possible origin of supposing that benevolence clashed with self-love, S. xi. 19.
    as a general rule, depends on law, App. IV.
Psalms, their language presents the highest anticipations of the vision of God, S. xiv. 20.
Public good, sense of, especially dependent upon conscience, S. i. 9.
    men little disposed to follow, S. xi. 12.
    pursuit of, does not traverse private good, S. xi. 16.
Public spirit, as synonymous with the love of our neighbour, S. xii. 1; with charity, benevolence, and good-will, *ibid.* 2.
Punishment, capital, how justified, S. viii. 11.

Readers: has often wished them left to draw conclusions for themselves, Pref. 1.
    who expect every thing to be made easy to them, Pref. 3.
Reading, as commonly conducted, is mostly dawdling, Pref. 2.
Reflection. See **Conscience**.
Relations: to know a whole, we must know the reciprocal relations of the parts, Pref. 10, 12.
Religion alone prevents men from the pursuit of disappointing objects, S. i. 15.
    and morality, appeal to plain common sense, S. v. 15.
    does not disown self-love, but appeals to it, S. xi. 21.
    natural, established by revelation, SS. i. 1; its decay, *ibid.*
    reason was incompetent to revive or extend it, SS. i. 2.
    republished and enlarged by the gospel, SS. i. 3.
Renunciation of things good but unsuitable, S. xiv. 3.
Republication of natural religion by the gospel, SS. i 3.
Resentment is of two kinds, (*a*) sudden = anger, (*b*) deliberate, S. viii. 5.
    anger is not sin, though near to it, *ibid.*
    (*a*) is often instinctive, and without injury received, S. viii. 6.
    often is the only defence against destruction, S. viii. 7.
    (*b*) settled anger, or resentment proper, is aimed at evil and injury, not harm, S. viii. 8, 11.
    heightened when against ourselves, S. viii. 9.
    is against injury done, rather than planned, S. viii. 10.
    (*a*) and (*b*), in themselves distinct, may coincide, S viii. 11.
    abusive forms of, various, S. viii. 13–15.
    it is needed (*a*) to balance pity, (*b*) to assist just severity, S. viii. 16.
    inferior to pure reason, yet a good influence, S. viii. 17.
    an inward witness for virtue, and against wickedness, S. viii. 18, 19.
    excess in it forbidden, S. ix. 2.
    revenge forbidden, love of enemies enjoined, S. ix. 3.
    bound to intend the production of outweighing good, S. ix. 6.
    drawbacks attendant upon it, S. ix. 7.
    can only be exercised innocently when it subserves its higher end, S. ix. 8.
    not incompatible with loving our enemies, S. ix. 10.
Resignation, the whole of piety, S. xiv. 3.
    rids us of cares and supernumerary troubles, S. xiv. 5.
    perfect, is the absorption of our will in God's will: a state reasonable and natural, S. xiv. 6.
    this is truly to walk with God, and is devotion put in act, S. xiv. 7, 8.
    how to be exalted when God is seen face to face, S. xiv. 10.
Responsibility: as agents we have power over our own natures; hence become responsible, Pref. 13.
Restoration an epoch of extreme danger to liberty, SS. iii. 13.
Retaliation (and see **Revenge**), the law of, is unsatisfactory, S. viii. 3.

INDEX

Revenge forbidden, despite of custom, S. ix. 3.
    engenders counter-revenge, S. ix. 4.
    difficulty of limitation, tendency to excess, S. ix. 5.
    incompatible with love to enemies, S. ix. 10.
Rich, great need of admonition ; good sort of people, SS. ii. 6.
    and poor, have standing relation of superiority and dependence, SS. ii. 7.
    the rich have great influence and power, *ibid.*
    and if not superior understanding, the equivalents of it, SS. ii. 8.
    have a trust to keep down vice and misery otherwise inevitable, SS. ii. 10.
    the poor under their care, and reception of their influence, *ibid.*
    primitive domestic order well adapted to their duty, SS. ii. 11.
    but the relation and the trust are permanent, SS. ii. 12 ; a privilege, *ibid.*
    improved conduct of the rich needful for the poor, *ibid.*
    the work to be carried on in association, SS. ii. 13.
    each must give account for following ill example, yet more for setting it, SS. ii. 14.
    our duty to choose the best instruments ; such as charitable Societies, SS. ii. 15.
    which remind us of duty, and carry influence, SS. ii. 16.
    their duties further enforced by the certain good effect on their inferiors, SS. ii. 19.
    the dissolute rich, even if liberal givers, undo but a trifle of the mischief done by their example, SS. ii. 19, 20.
    by giving as the creatures of God, we elevate charity into piety, SS. ii. 21.
Riches, their first stage was in surplus of necessaries, SS. ii. 1.
    second stage : conveniences, including ornament, SS. ii. 2.
    third stage : preponderance of superfluities ; luxury, or immoderate use, SS. ii. 3.
    poverty not the worst of the resulting evils, *ibid.*
    fourth stage : money replacing barter of goods, SS. ii. 4.
    riches of London, SS. ii. 6.
    entail leisure ; information ; much civil authority, SS. ii. 8.
    their great power in England, *ibid.*
    a great trust, SS. ii. 9.
Righteous, meaning of, in Micah vi, S. vii. 3.

Satisfaction, temper of, from compassion ; its elements, S. v. 8.
Saviour, the : his love, exhibited in the Incarnation, enhances duty, S. xi. 23.
    his unexampled gentleness, S. iv. 18.
Self : our duties to, as well as to society, S. i. 3.
    each man is a special trust to himself, S. xii. 11.
    as to self and our neighbour there is a limit in natural possibilities, S. xii. 12.
Self-deceit closely associated with deceiving others, Pref. 26.
    the existing self-partiality one of the strangest sights, S. x. 2.
    hence the 'know thyself,' S. x. 3.
    usual temper : (*a*) absence of mistrust, (*b*) assumption that all is right, (*c*) disregard of precepts as to ourselves, S. x. 4.
    and an exclusive self-interest, S. x. 5.
    inquiry means self-justification, S. x. 6.
    self-ignorance sometimes confined to the peccant part, S. x. 7.
    perversion of the judgment through the passions, S. x. 8.
    the large proportion of wrong-doing due to it, S. x. 9.
    aided by the frequent difficulty of defining vice, S. x. 10.
    is in itself extreme guilt, the blinding of the inward eye, S. x. 12.
    often or always attended with an implicit suspicion, S. x. 13.
    comparison with those who shun looking into their money affairs, S. x. 14.
    each owns self-deceit to be in all save himself, S. x. 15.
    ought to take for granted that he has it abundantly, S. x. 16.

Self-deceit (*continued*).
> as a test, what would your enemy first charge upon you ? S. x. 17.
> our Lord's rule includes a double substitution, S. x. 18.
> vulgar hardy sin less perilous than this poison at the root, S. x. 19.
> a strong element in hypocrisy, SS. iii. 2, and *n*.
> unequal dealing with evidence, an efficient form of, SS. iii. 2 *n*.

Self-display, seldom successful, S. x. 8 *n*.
Self-inspection may be excessive, and grow morbid, S. x. 8 *n*.
Self-interest, an enhanced regard to, a note of the age, S. xi. 1.
Selfishness, cool or settled, to be distinguished from passionate or sensual, Pref. 29.
> 'selfish' often wholly excludes regard to the good of others, S. xi. 9.
> that is, if the phrase cannot be dropped, *ibid*.

Self-flattery } cause a very great part of existing wickedness, Pref. 26.
Self-partiality }

Self-love: why, even without regard to a future state, it should renounce vice, Pref. 23.
> confused with particular affections, and thus held adverse to benevolence, Pref. 29, S. i. 6 *n*., S. xi. 3, 5, 8.
> may blend with these, or may be overborne by them, Pref. 30.
> has no special antagonism to benevolence, Pref. 32, S. xi. 2, 8, 9, 11 ; clashes more with other propensions, S. xi. 17.
> they are distinguished, not opposed, Pref. 33.
> in due degree, as good as any other affection, Pref. 34.
> considered as pursuit of temporal good, does not fulfil the religious or moral idea, *ibid*.
> does not require reduction in quantity, Pref. 35.
> needs to be more enlightened and considerate, Pref. 36.
> we offend as much against self-love as against society, S. i. 14.
> reflective, superior in authority to the passions, S. ii. 15, 16.
> when it falsifies judgments, S. x. 8.
> mostly coincides with virtue, even when addressed only to temporal interests, S. iii. 12 ; the two to be set in harmony, S. xi. 22.
> reasonable, associated with conscience, S. iii. 13.
> cool, one part of our nature : particular affections another, S. xi. 4, 5.
> is a regard to ourselves ; our interest, happiness, private good, S. xi. 5.
> does not constitute our good, but puts us on obtaining it, S. xi. 6.
> contracted, self-love may work against our happiness, S. xi. 7.
> ought to teach the limitation of self-regard, *ibid*.
> (perverted), may be missing greater pleasures than those which absorb it, S. xi. 15.
> to covet wealth for an ulterior end is a phase of, S. xi. 17.
> how the idea of its opposition to benevolence may have grown up, S. xi. 19.

Self-regard and suspicion of others are generated by experience of life, S. xii. 13.
Senses: our strongest impressions are derived through them, S. xiv. 2.
> will be dispensed with in a future state, S. xiv. 13.

Sermons, obscurity in, allowed to be a defect, Pref. 6.
> sermon ascribed to Butler, App. V.

Shaftesbury, Lord, places our interest in virtue and *vice versâ*, Pref. 20.
> but leaves the sceptic, if not convinced of this, without remedy, *ibid*.
> sets up the obligation of interest, which at best is doubtful and secondary, Pref. 21.
> wrongly teaches that malice only, not goodness, is the proper object of fear, Pref. 25.

Shame, as manifestly as the eye, given for a purpose, S. ii. 3.
Sick, care of the : behaviour may make us, though sinful in much, proper objects of mercy, SS. vi. 1.

Sick (*continued*).
> charity enables us to make amends, SS. vi. 2.
> is not mere good humour, which need not imply discretion, SS. vi. 3.
> relief of bodily disease and casualty by infirmaries, SS. vi. 4; for foreigners as well as others, *ibid.* 5.
> futility of objections, and prejudices, against relief of the poor, SS. vi. 6.
> case of misconduct, SS. vi. 7; self-sought evils, *ibid.* 10.
> misdirected indulgence is compatible with neglect, SS. vi. 8.
> we expect too much from the poor, SS. vi. 9.
> evils consequent on vice are providential, but so are the mitigations, SS. vi. 11.
> infirmaries have a provision for religion, SS. vi. 12; highly seasonable, *ibid.*; highly improvable, *ibid.* 13.
> cavils against such appeals for alms, SS. vi. 14; but rule is desirable, and charity should be associated with devotion, *ibid.* 15.
> in comparing gifts and needs, we are parties, as much as the receivers, SS. vi. 16.
> though much benevolence exists, and good is done, yet the stint of means shocks humanity, SS. vi. 17, 18.
> some through neglect lack means for bounty, so thrift may be charity, SS. vi. 19, 20.
> these duties are inadequately recognised, SS. vi. 21.
> yet these persons are really our servants, SS. vi. 22.
> all are bound to contribute in their degree, SS. vi. 23.
> it is the best prerogative of riches, SS. vi. 24.
> consciousness of sin should be a stimulus, SS. vi. 25.
> the miserable choice of the miser and the dissolute, SS. vi. 26.

Slavery, remains of, in the northern provinces, before the Act 20 Geo. II. c. 19, SS. v. 6.

Slaves, in the Colonies, 'made as miserable as they well can be,' SS. i. 12.
> their title to the gospel, *ibid.*

Society: man has duties to, S. i. 3, 9, 10.
> we offend as much against self-love as against society, S. i. 14.
> a cavil: why not dismiss the labour of regard to society? S. iii. 7.
> answer: enjoyment is not to be had from mere self-regard, S. iii. 8.
> virtues that regard others often yield more delight than opposite vices, S. iii. 9, 10.

Speculations are beyond the reach of the generality, S. v. 15.

Strength of powers or instincts in us, no true criterion of actions, Pref. 18, S. ii. 15, S. iii. 13.
> prevailing against conscience, is mere usurpation, S. ii. 17, 18.
> consequences of accepting it as a criterion, as respects God, S. ii. 20, 21.
> as respects our neighbour, S. ii. 22.

Study, of divinity, the most suited to a reasonable nature, App. I. D.

Superstition, an exception or partial exception to easy discernment of the right, S. iii. 5.
> an extravagance like enthusiasm, S. v. 16.
> will not serve instead of innocence, S. vii. 16.
> true religion the only security against it, SS. i. 18.
> the great superstition imminent over this nation, *ibid.*
> religion, as well as superstition, promoted by visible signs abroad, Char. 13.
> the tricks it plays to soothe evil consciences, S. vii. 15.

Time, operation of, in mitigating sorrow, S. vi. 4.

Tongue, government of, essential to real religion, S. iv. 1.
> talkativeness is the evil aimed at in James i. 26, S. iv. 3.
> which leads on to other evils, S. iv. 4.

Tongue (*continued*).
    is like a torrent, or a fire, S. iv. 4; or a sword held by a madman, *ibid.* 7.
    means talking for talking's sake, S. iv. 5; and thirst for attention, *ibid.* 6, 19.
    fatal to equity of speech, S. iv. 7.
    given for pleasure as well as necessary use, S. iv. 8.
    full of peril, but this may be avoided, S. iv. 9, 10.

Torture, or death, less contrary to nature than vice, Pref. 8, 9, 14, S. iii. 2.

Trade, over-sea, to be consecrated by aiding the work of missions, SS. i. 14.
    has much increased the middle class, SS. ii. 5.

Trifles: beware of treating things serious as if indifferent, S. iv. 15.

Truth: of the few curious to know at all, but few care to know truth, Pref. 1.

Unity of God, author is satisfied with Clarke's argument on, App. I. F.

Vice held by some ancients to be more contrary to our nature than tortures or death, Pref. 8.
    but this requires further explication, Pref. 9.
    its contrariety to nature, Pref. 14.
    offers small satisfaction, Pref. 23.
    never loved for its own sake, S. i. 11.
    often outdone by virtue in the satisfaction reaped, S. iii. 10.
    and carries other pains, S. iii. 11.
    as the object both of pity and of indignation, S. vi. 9.
    must be our misery, S. vii. 16.
    disturbance inherent in; commonly founded in extravagance of self-regard, S. x. 8.

Virtue: following nature indiscriminately not a rule of virtue, Pref. 9.
    every affection has its proper end; that to virtue pursues it for itself, Pref. 37.
    virtues often outdo vice in satisfaction yielded, S. iii. 10.
    may be called interested or the reverse, S. xi. 10.
    the good man finds his account in goodness, S. xi. 14.
    these pretensions have been tested by experience, S. xi. 15.
    required to be set in harmony with self-love, S. xi. 22.
    the common virtues flow from benevolence, S. xii. 22.
    goodness may grow to be the determining element of character, S. xiii. 7.
    goodness, not knowledge, the supreme end of man, S. xiv. 16.
    our obligation to follow, even if not convinced that it is our interest, Pref. 20, 21.
    remains even if all else be in doubt, Pref. 22.
    and if the sanction be disbelieved, Pref. 24.

Watch, not known by knowing its parts without their relations to one another, Pref. 11.

Wealth: to covet this for an end is a phase of self-love, S. xi. 17.

Wesley, Rev. John, author's conversation with, App. III.

Whitefield, letter from, App. III.

Wickedness, the only proper object of abhorrence, S. viii. 19.

Wollaston, referred to with honour, Pref. 9.

THE END.

www.ingramcontent.com/pod-product-compliance
Lightning Source LLC
Chambersburg PA
CBHW030425300426
44112CB00009B/863